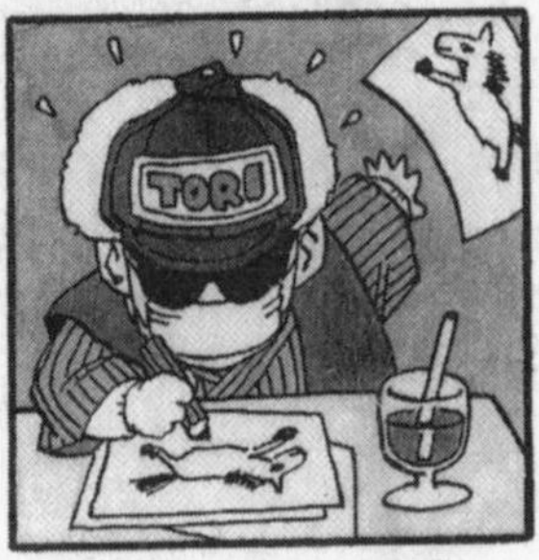
TORI

鳥山 明

If I want something I have a habit of drawing it until I get whatever it is or I lose interest in it. When I was a kid I really wanted a horse, so every day I would draw horses. Eventually I gave up on getting a horse, and I just drew monkeys every day. After that I drew bicycles. I just kept drawing the things I wanted. As a result, even though I misbehaved, at least I could draw well. That habit eventually developed into my job and I still continue to draw today.

–Akira Toriyama, 1990

Artist/writer Akira Toriyama burst onto the manga scene in 1980 with the wildly popular **Dr. Slump**, a science fiction comedy about the adventures of a mad scientist and his android "daughter." In 1984 he created his hit series **Dragon Ball**, which ran until 1995 in Shueisha's best-selling magazine **Weekly Shonen Jump**, and was translated into foreign languages around the world. Since **Dragon Ball**, he has worked on a variety of short series, including **Cowa!**, **Kajika**, **SandLand**, and **Neko Majin**, as well as a children's book, **Toccio the Angel**. He is also known for his design work on video games, particularly the **Dragon Warrior** RPG series. He lives with his family in Japan.

DRAGON BALL Z VOL. 4
The SHONEN JUMP Manga Edition

This volume is number 20 in a series of 42.

STORY AND ART BY
AKIRA TORIYAMA

ENGLISH ADAPTATION BY
GERARD JONES

Translation/Lillian Olsen
Touch-Up Art & Lettering/Wayne Truman
Cover Design/Izumi Evers & Dan Ziegler
Graphics & Design/Sean Lee
Original Editor/Trish Ledoux
Graphic Novel Editor/Jason Thompson

Editor in Chief, Books/Alvin Lu
Editor in Chief, Magazines/Marc Weidenbaum
VP of Publishing Licensing/Rika Inouye
VP of Sales/Gonzalo Ferreyra
Sr. VP of Marketing/Liza Coppola
Publisher/Hyoe Narita

Printed in Canada

In the original Japanese edition, DRAGON BALL and DRAGON
BALL Z are known collectively as the 42-volume series DRAGON
BALL. The English DRAGON BALL Z was originally volumes 17-42
of the Japanese DRAGON BALL.

Published by VIZ Media, LLC
P.O. Box 77010 • San Francisco, CA 94107

SHONEN JUMP Manga Edition
10 9 8 7 6 5
First printing, March 2003
Fifth printing, March 2008

PARENTAL ADVISORY
DRAGON BALL is rated A for All Ages. It
contains fantasy violence. It is recommended
for all ages.
ratings.viz.com

THE WORLD'S
MOST POPULAR MANGA

www.viz.com

www.shonenjump.com

SHONEN JUMP MANGA

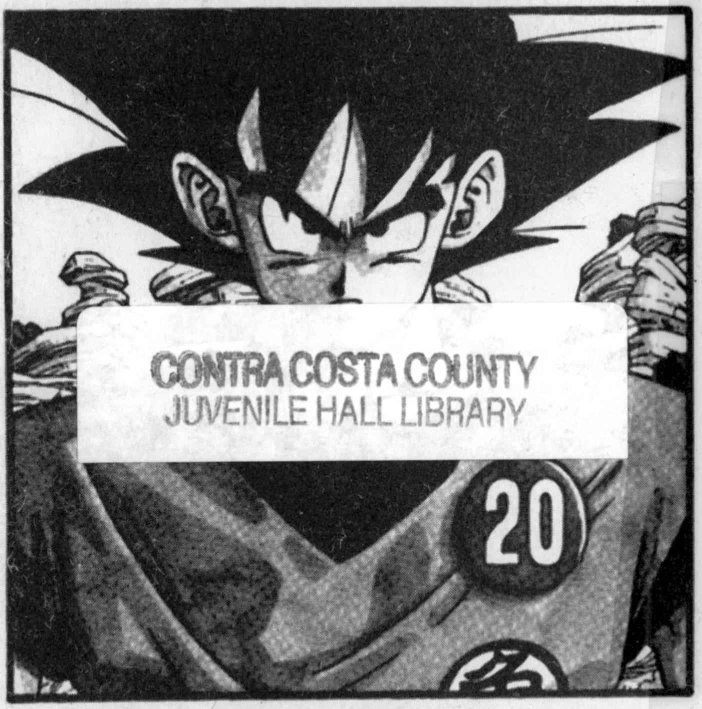
20

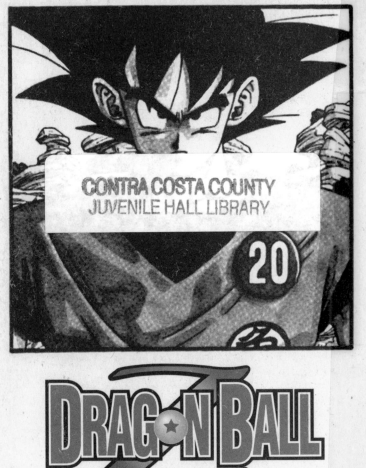

DRAGON BALL Z

Vol. 4

DB: 20 of 42

STORY AND ART BY
AKIRA TORIYAMA

THE MAIN CHARACTERS

Bulma
Goku's oldest friend, Bulma is a scientific genius. She met Goku while on a quest for the seven magical Dragon Balls which, when gathered together, can grant any wish.

Son Goku
The greatest martial artist on Earth, he owes his strength to the fact that he's one of the alien Saiyans. How far can he go with the secrets of Kaiô-sama's training?

Kaiô-sama
Also known as the "Lord of Worlds", he is one of the deities of the Dragon Ball universe. He lives in the Other World at the end of the Serpent Road.

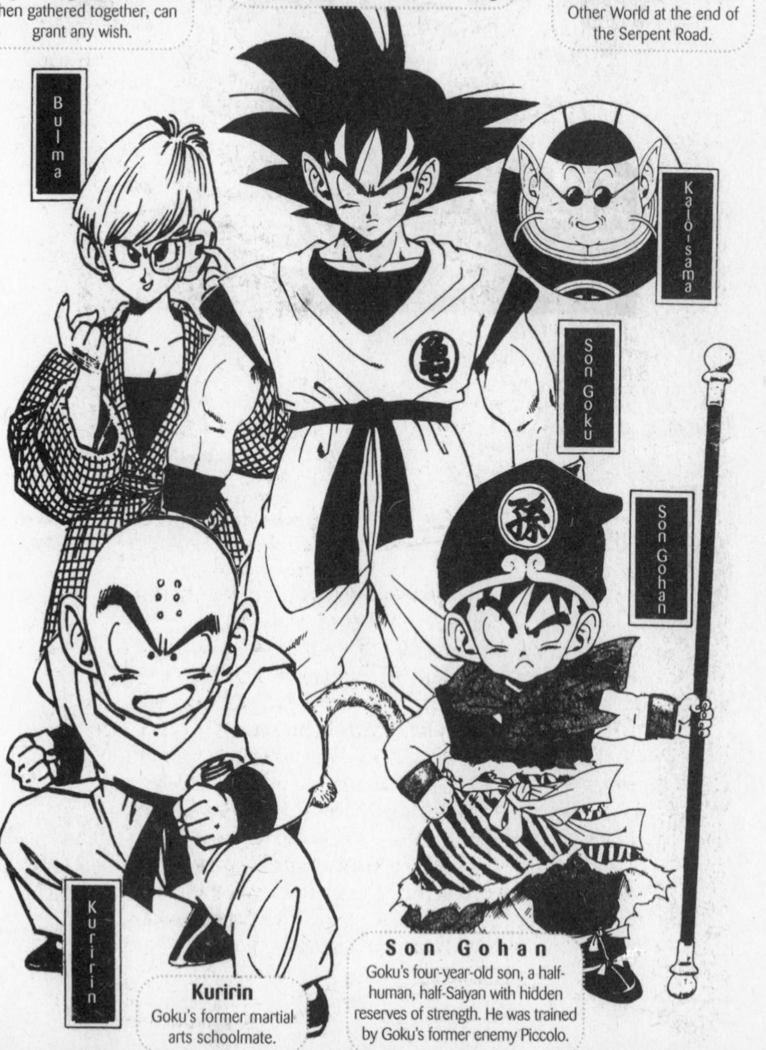
Bulma
Son Goku
Kaiô-sama
Son Gohan
Kuririn

Kuririn
Goku's former martial arts schoolmate.

Son Gohan
Goku's four-year-old son, a half-human, half-Saiyan with hidden reserves of strength. He was trained by Goku's former enemy Piccolo.

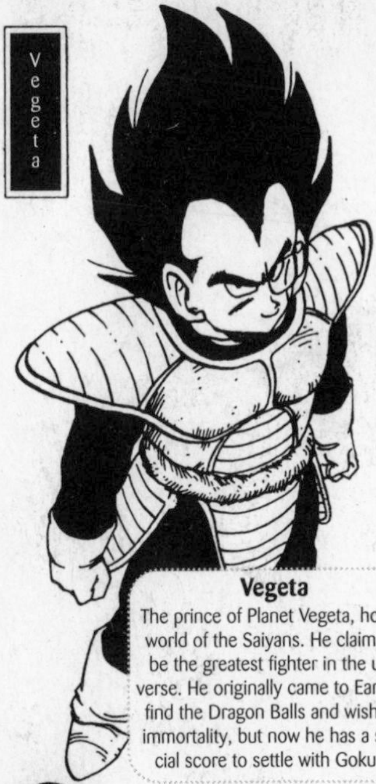
Vegeta

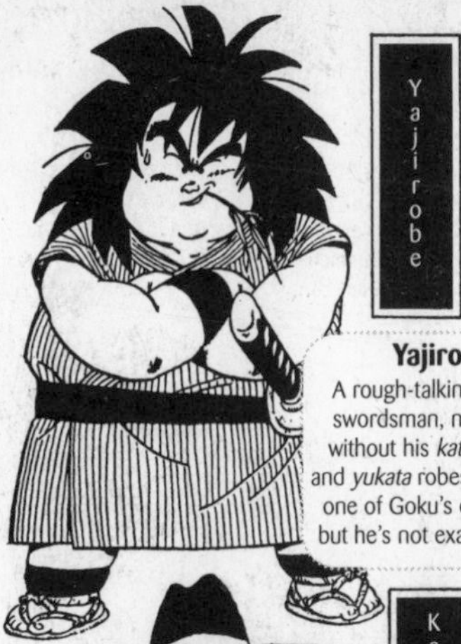
Yajirobe

Yajirobe

A rough-talking, solitary swordsman, never seen without his *katana* sword and *yukata* robes. Yajirobe is one of Goku's old friends, but he's not exactly heroic.

Vegeta

The prince of Planet Vegeta, homeworld of the Saiyans. He claims to be the greatest fighter in the universe. He originally came to Earth to find the Dragon Balls and wish for immortality, but now he has a special score to settle with Goku...

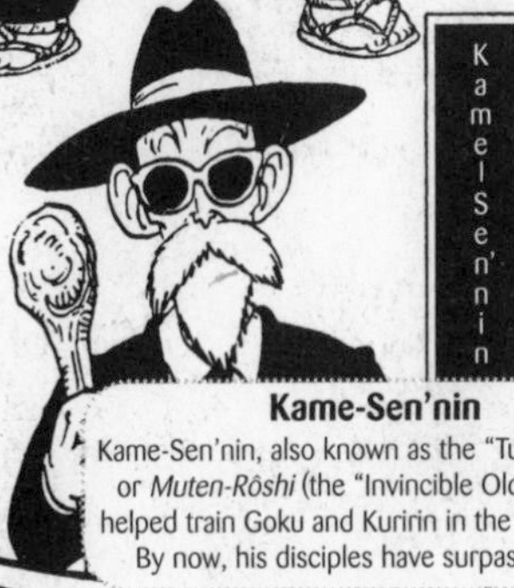
Kame-Sen'nin

Kame-Sen'nin

Kame-Sen'nin, also known as the "Turtle Hermit" or *Muten-Rôshi* (the "Invincible Old Master"), helped train Goku and Kuririn in the martial arts. By now, his disciples have surpassed him.

Son Goku was Earth's greatest hero, until he died fighting his own brother Raditz, a member of the warlike alien race called the Saiyans. Goku's friends intended to use the seven magical Dragon Balls to bring Goku back to life...but, knowing that two even stronger Saiyans would arrive on Earth in one year, Goku chose to remain in the afterlife where he could train under the great martial arts teacher Kaiô-sama. But the Saiyans arrived a day early, and by the time Goku returned to Earth, his friends Yamcha, Tenshinhan, Chaozu and Piccolo had already been killed by the invaders. Goku defeated Nappa, one of the Saiyans, but now he must use his new techniques against Nappa's commander Vegeta...a warrior so deadly and ruthless he killed Nappa for daring to lose!

DRAGON BALL Z 4

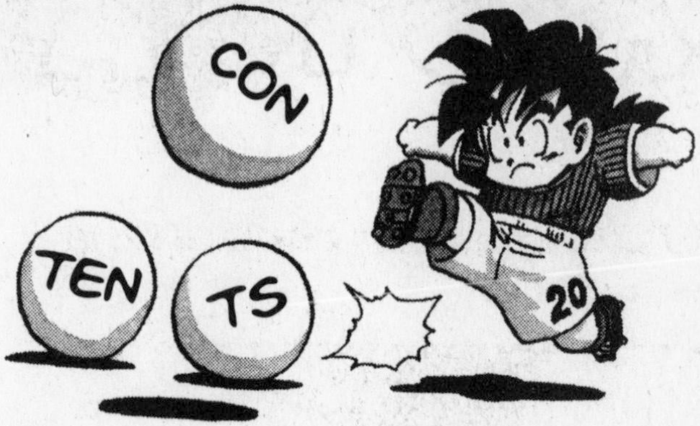
CON
TEN
TS
20

ドラゴンボール

DRAGON BALL

DBZ:35 • The Decisive Battle at Last!!

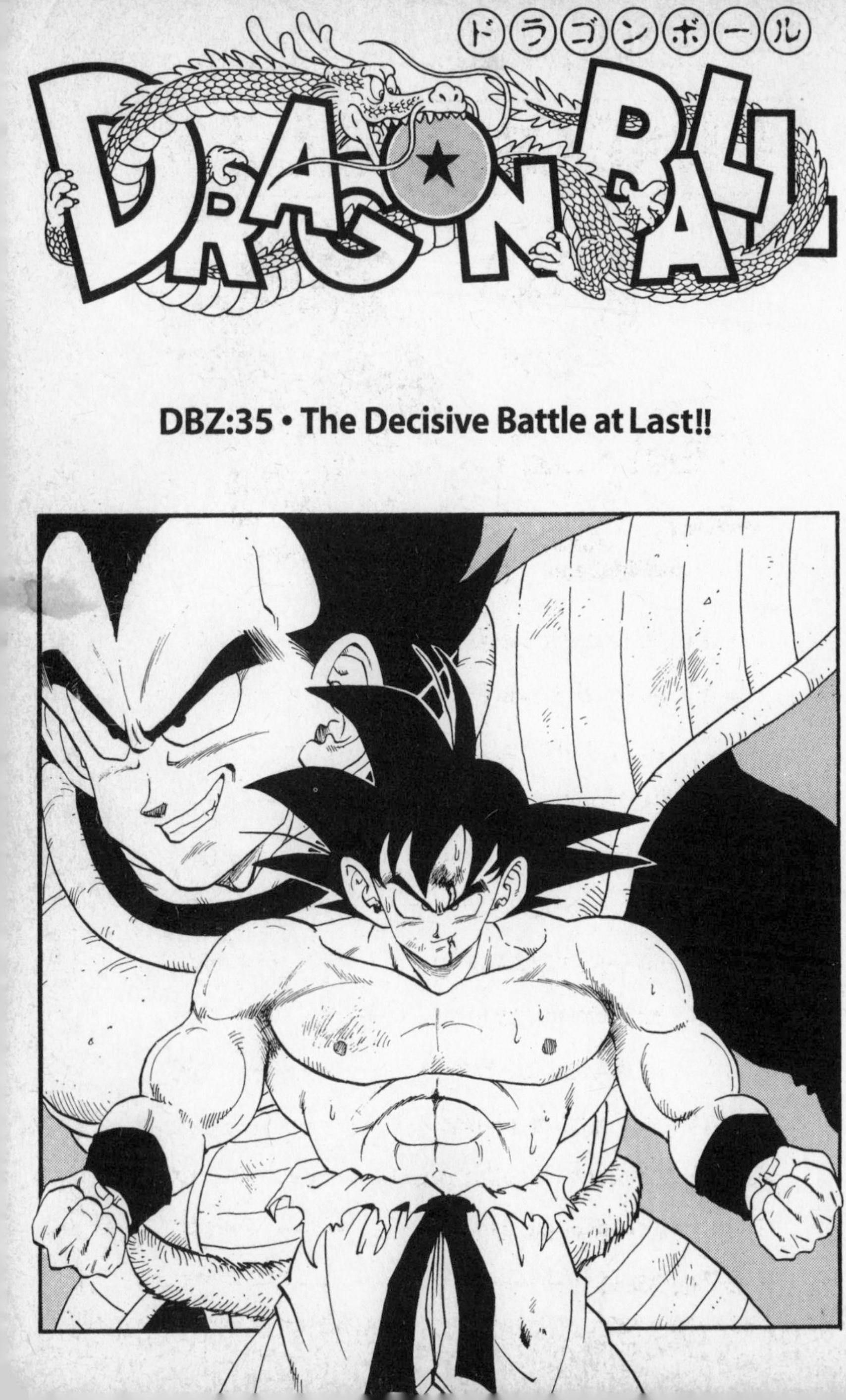

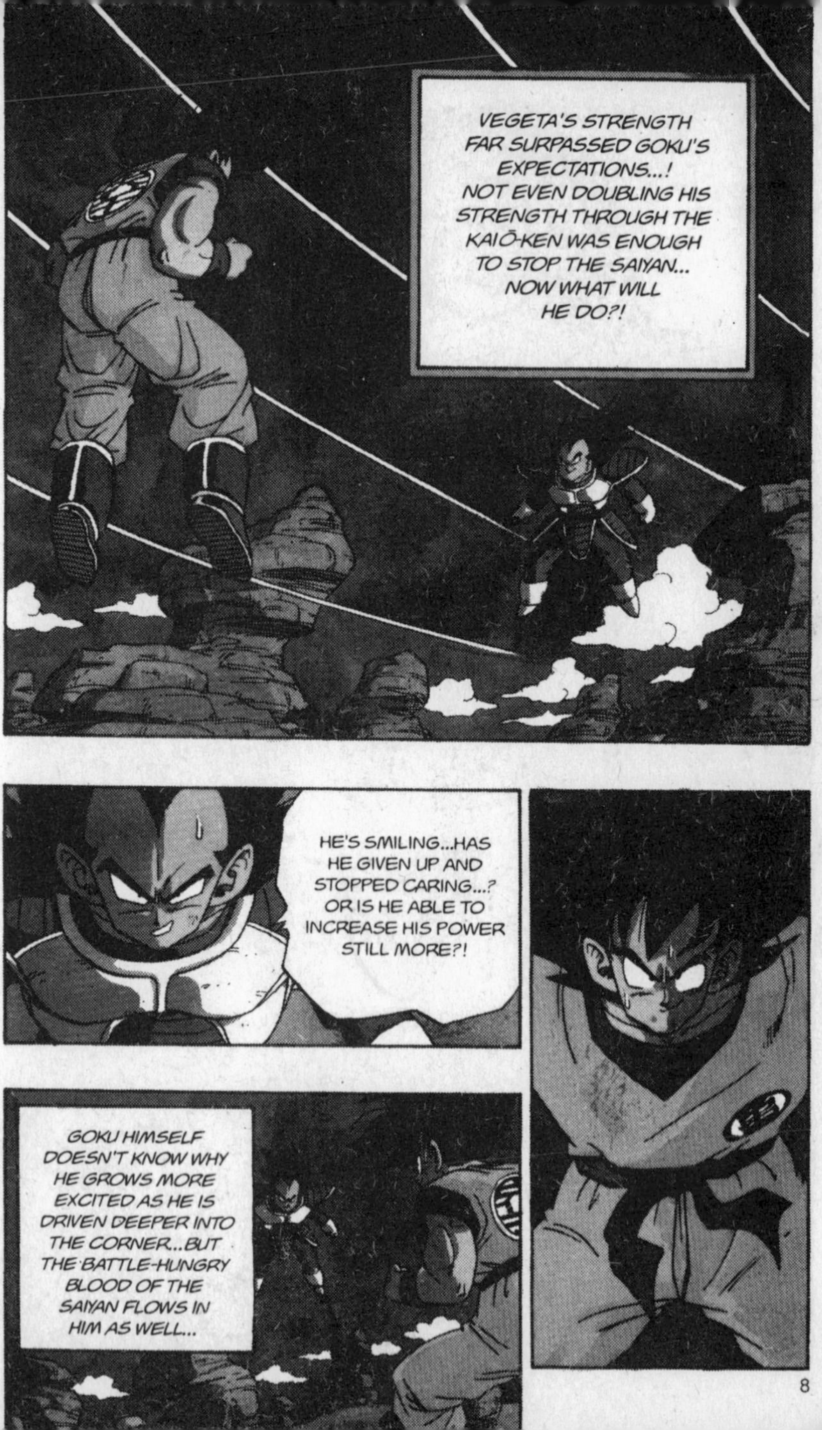
VEGETA'S STRENGTH FAR SURPASSED GOKU'S EXPECTATIONS...! NOT EVEN DOUBLING HIS STRENGTH THROUGH THE KAIŌ-KEN WAS ENOUGH TO STOP THE SAIYAN... NOW WHAT WILL HE DO?!
HE'S SMILING...HAS HE GIVEN UP AND STOPPED CARING...? OR IS HE ABLE TO INCREASE HIS POWER STILL MORE?!
GOKU HIMSELF DOESN'T KNOW WHY HE GROWS MORE EXCITED AS HE IS DRIVEN DEEPER INTO THE CORNER...BUT THE BATTLE-HUNGRY BLOOD OF THE SAIYAN FLOWS IN HIM AS WELL...

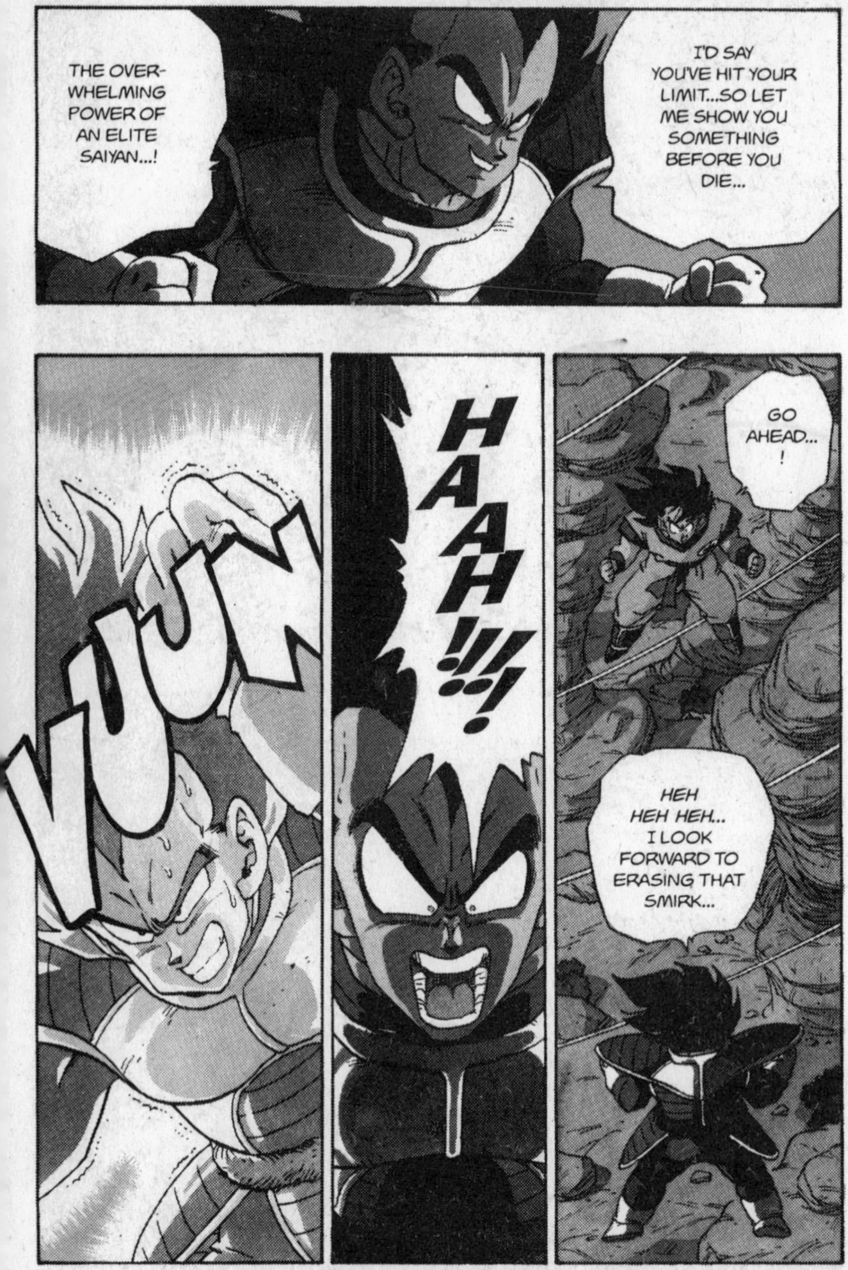
I'D SAY YOU'VE HIT YOUR LIMIT...SO LET ME SHOW YOU SOMETHING BEFORE YOU DIE...
THE OVER-WHELMING POWER OF AN ELITE SAIYAN...!
GO AHEAD... !
HEH HEH HEH... I LOOK FORWARD TO ERASING THAT SMIRK...
HAAAH!!!!
VZUN

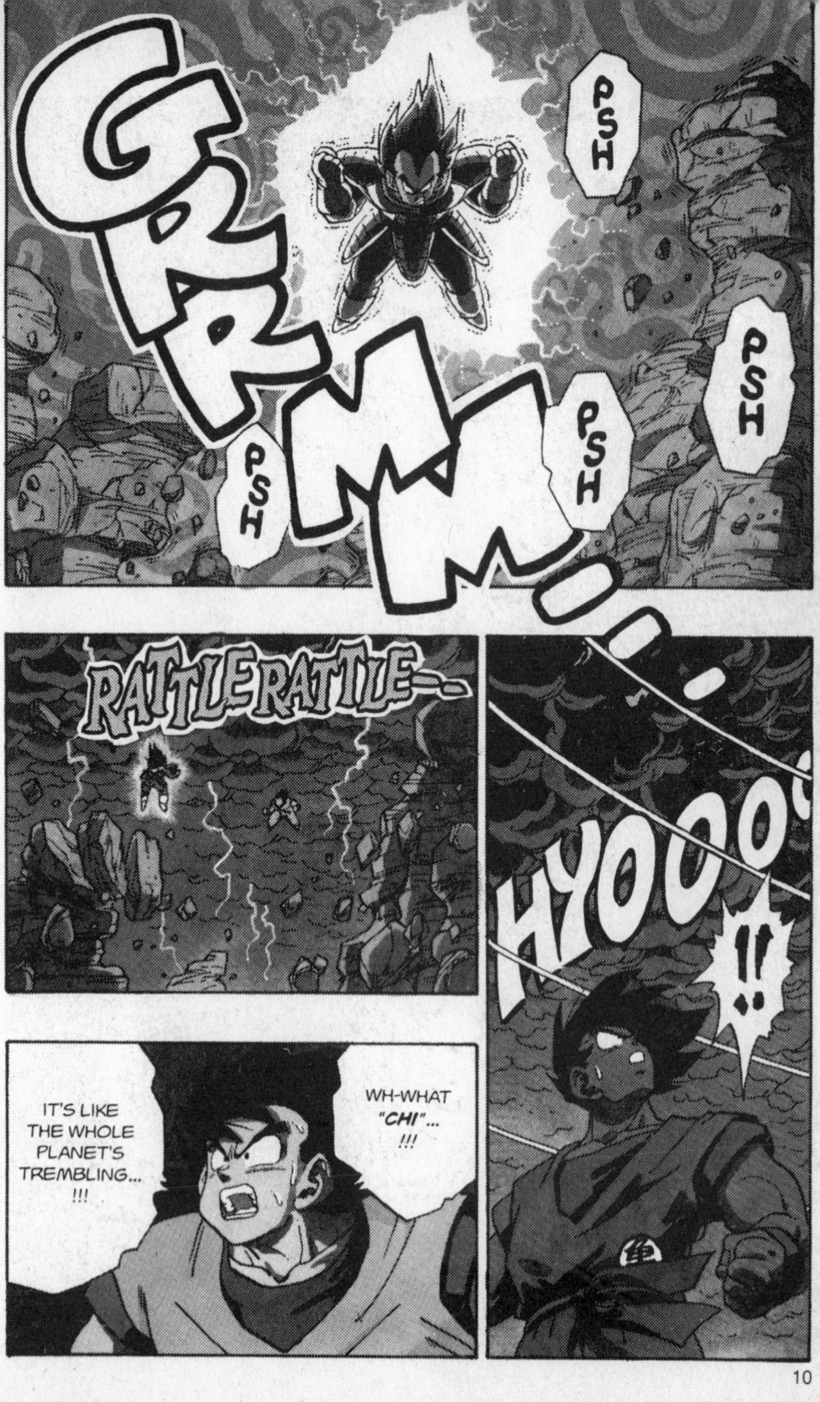
GRMM...
PSH
PSH
PSH
PSH
HYOOOO
!!
RATTLE RATTLE---
WH-WHAT "CHI"... !!!
IT'S LIKE THE WHOLE PLANET'S TREMBLING... !!!

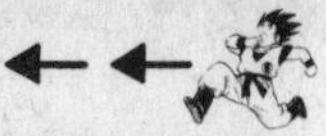

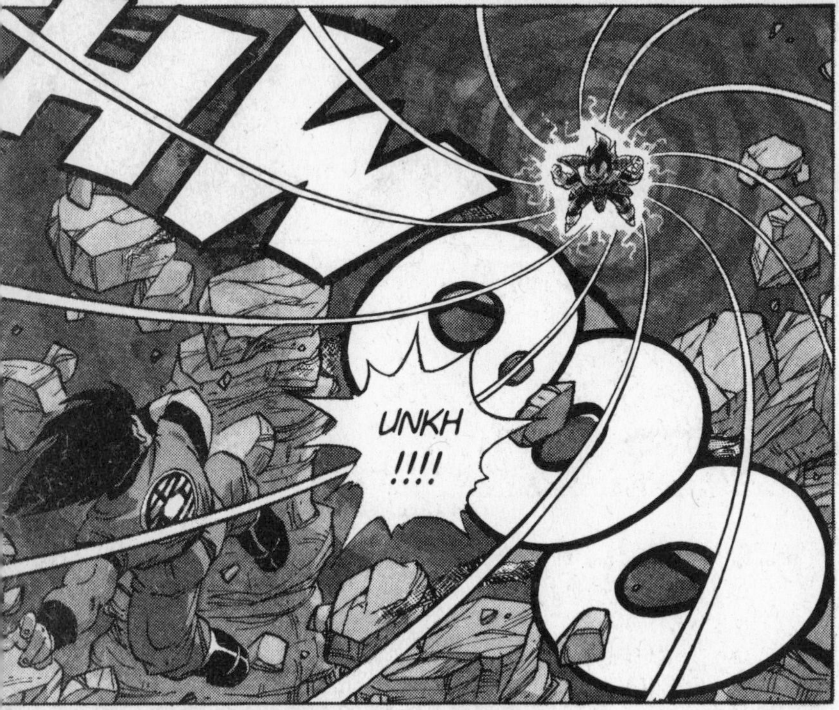
UNKH
!!!!

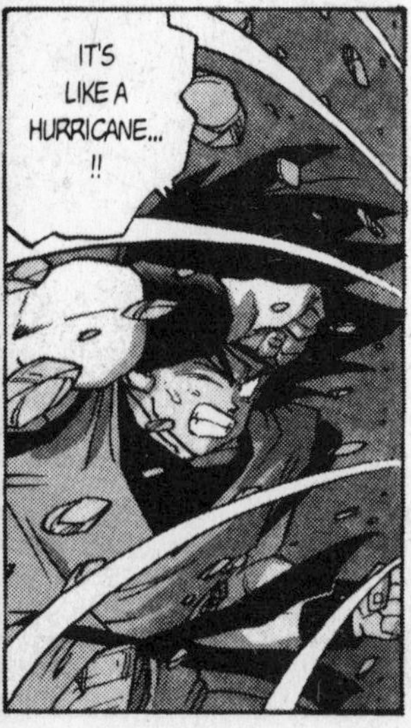
IT'S LIKE A HURRICANE...
!!

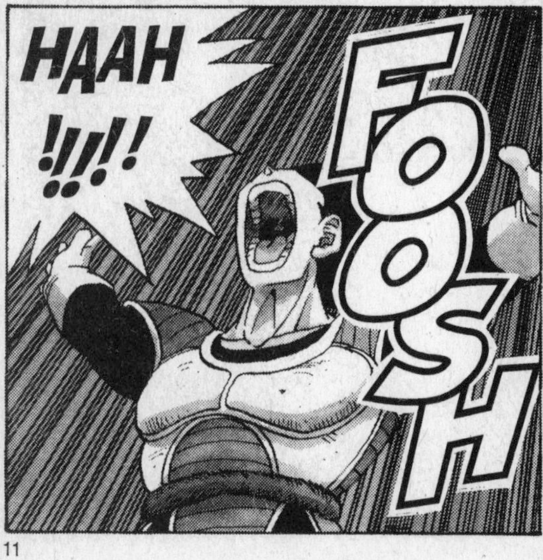
HAAH
!!!!!
FOOOSH

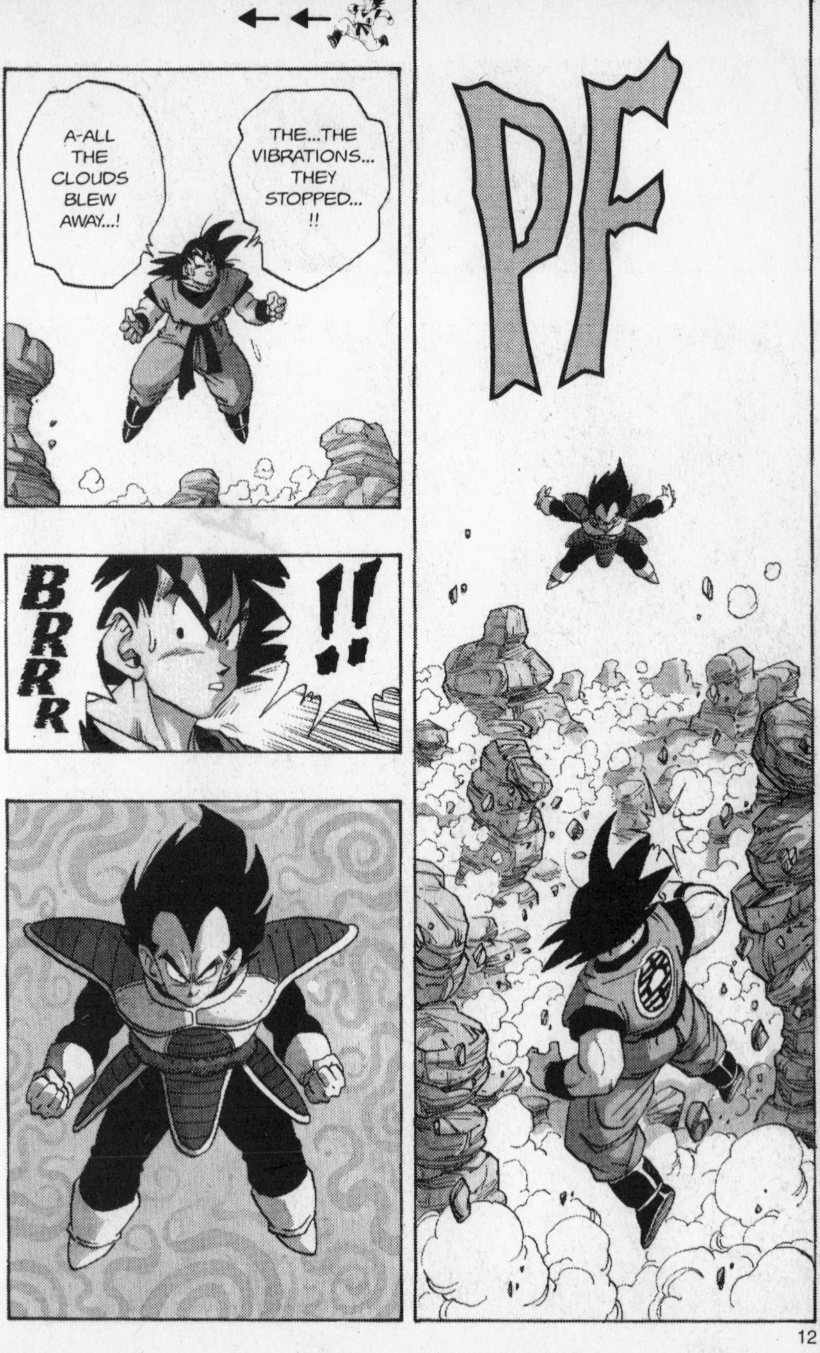
PF
THE...THE VIBRATIONS... THEY STOPPED... !!
A-ALL THE CLOUDS BLEW AWAY...!
!!
BRRRR

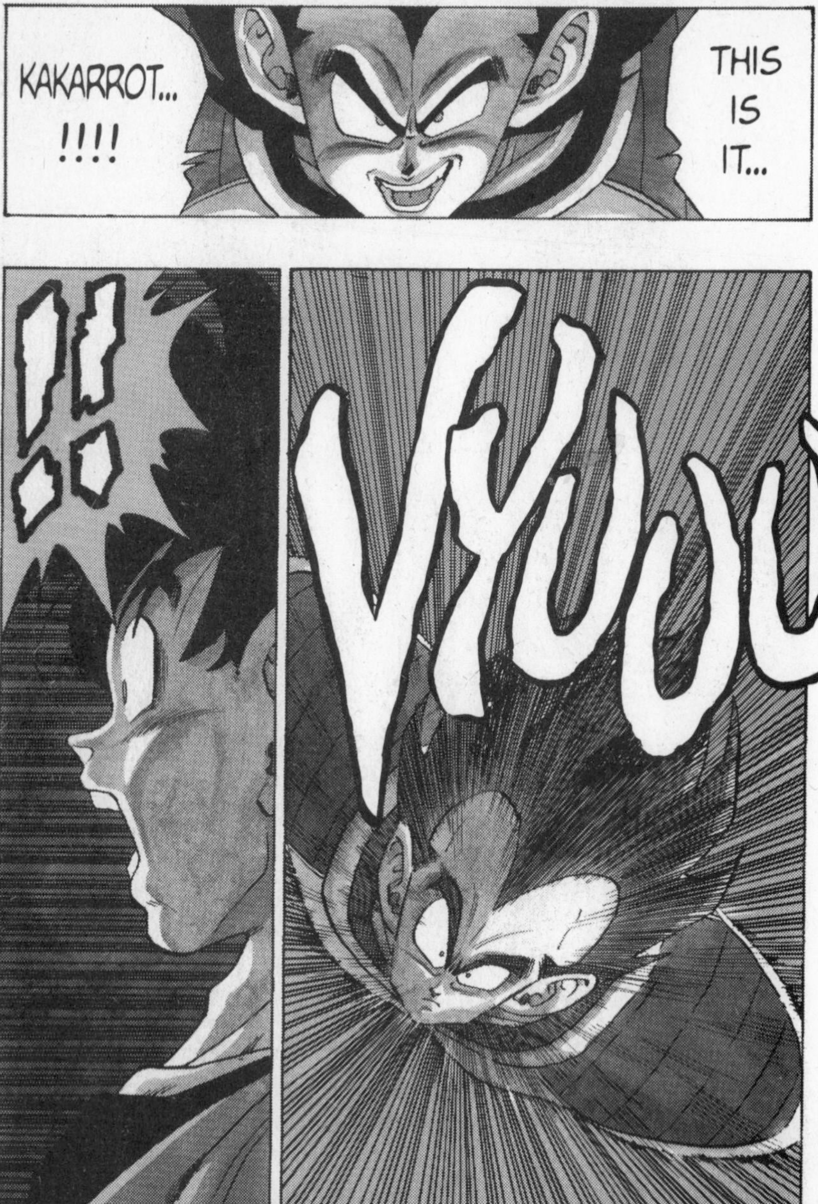
THIS IS IT...
KAKARROT... !!!!
VYUU
!!

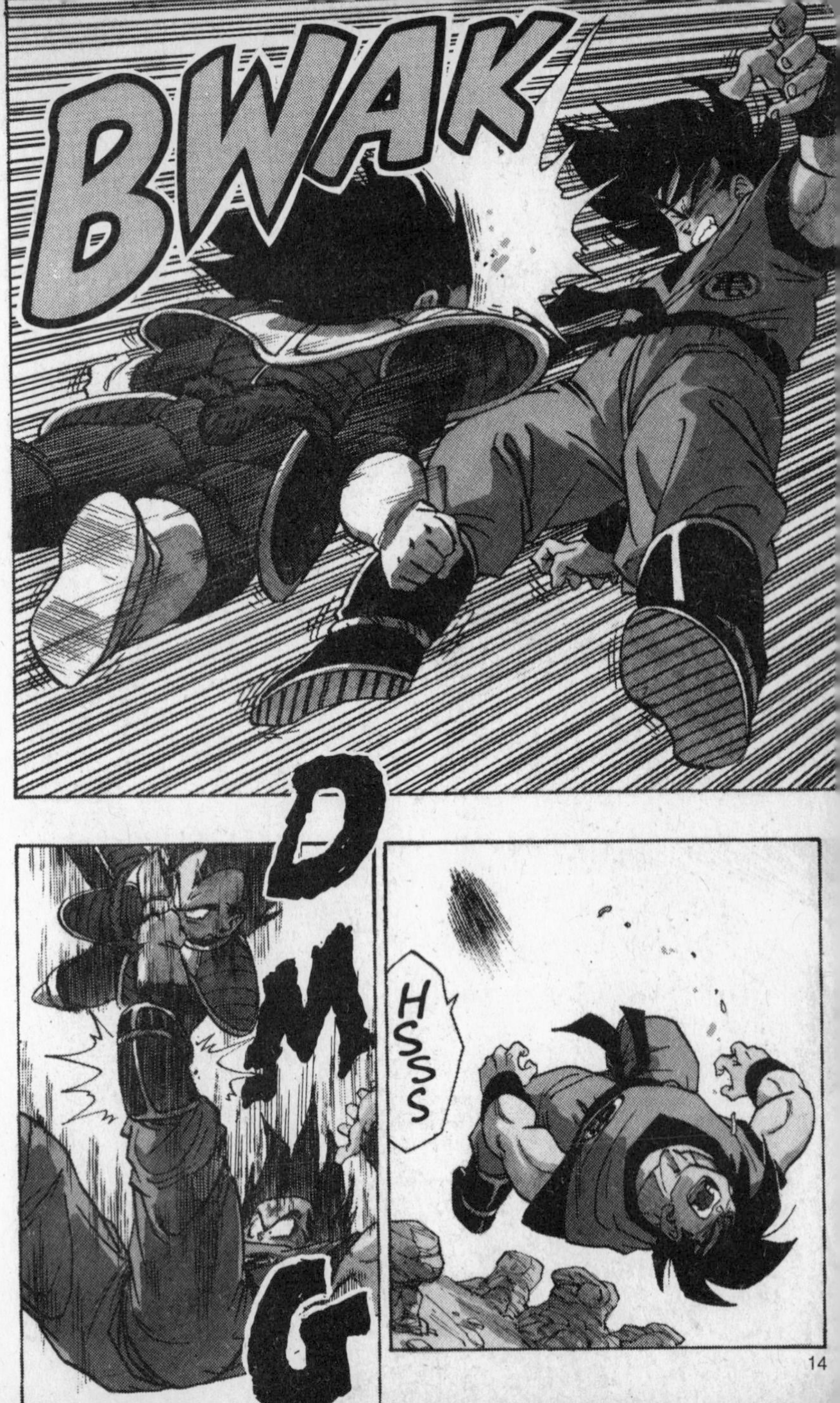
BWAK
HSSS
DMG

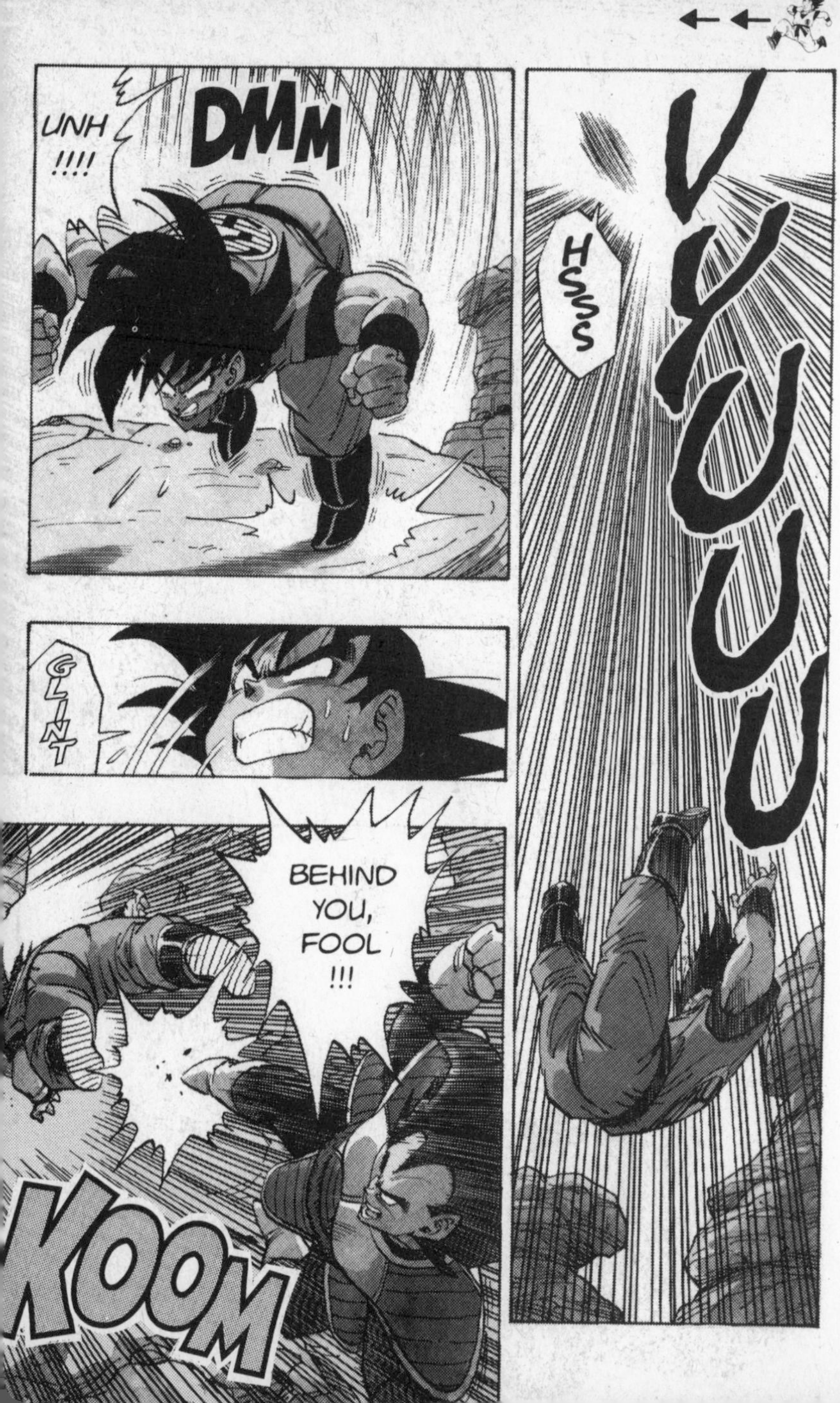
VHUUUU
HSSSS
UNH !!!!
DMM
GLINT
BEHIND YOU, FOOL !!!
KOOM

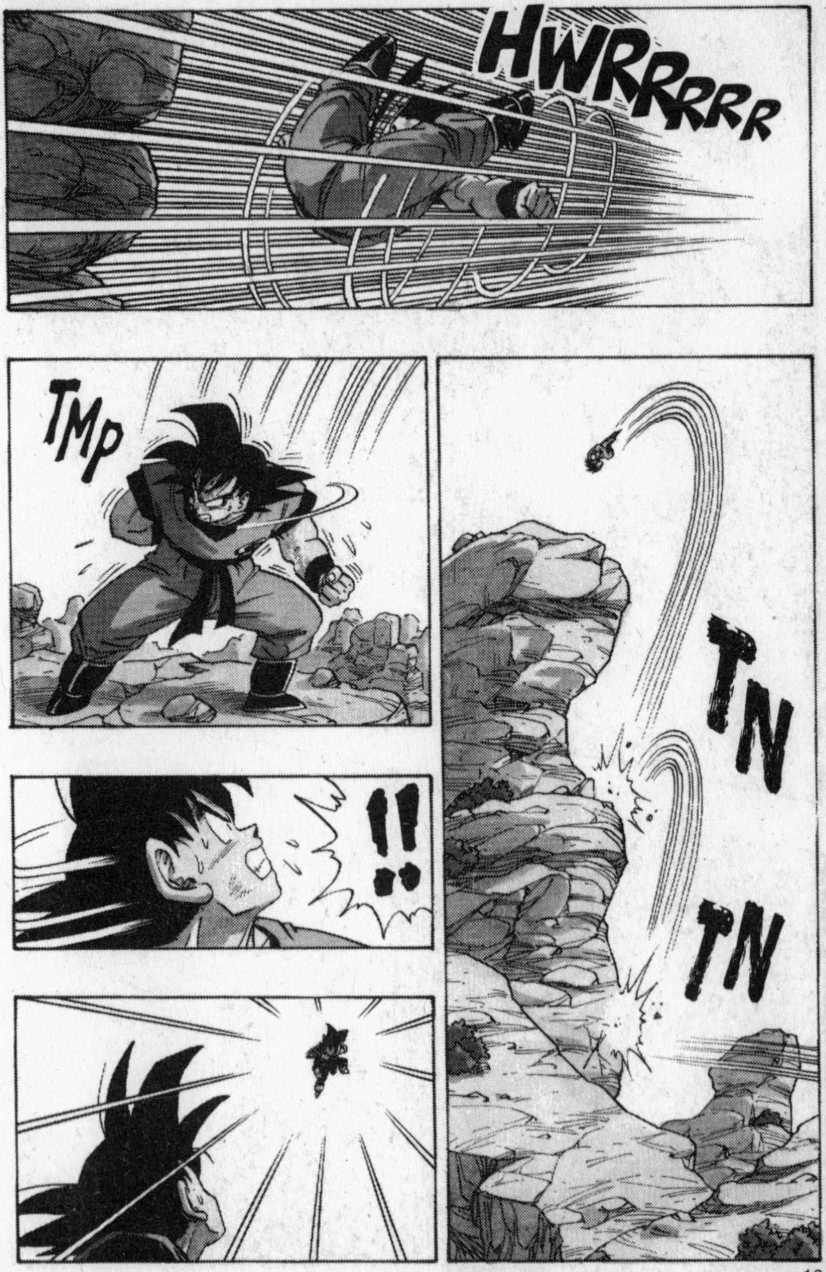
HWRRRRRR
TN
TN
TMP
!!

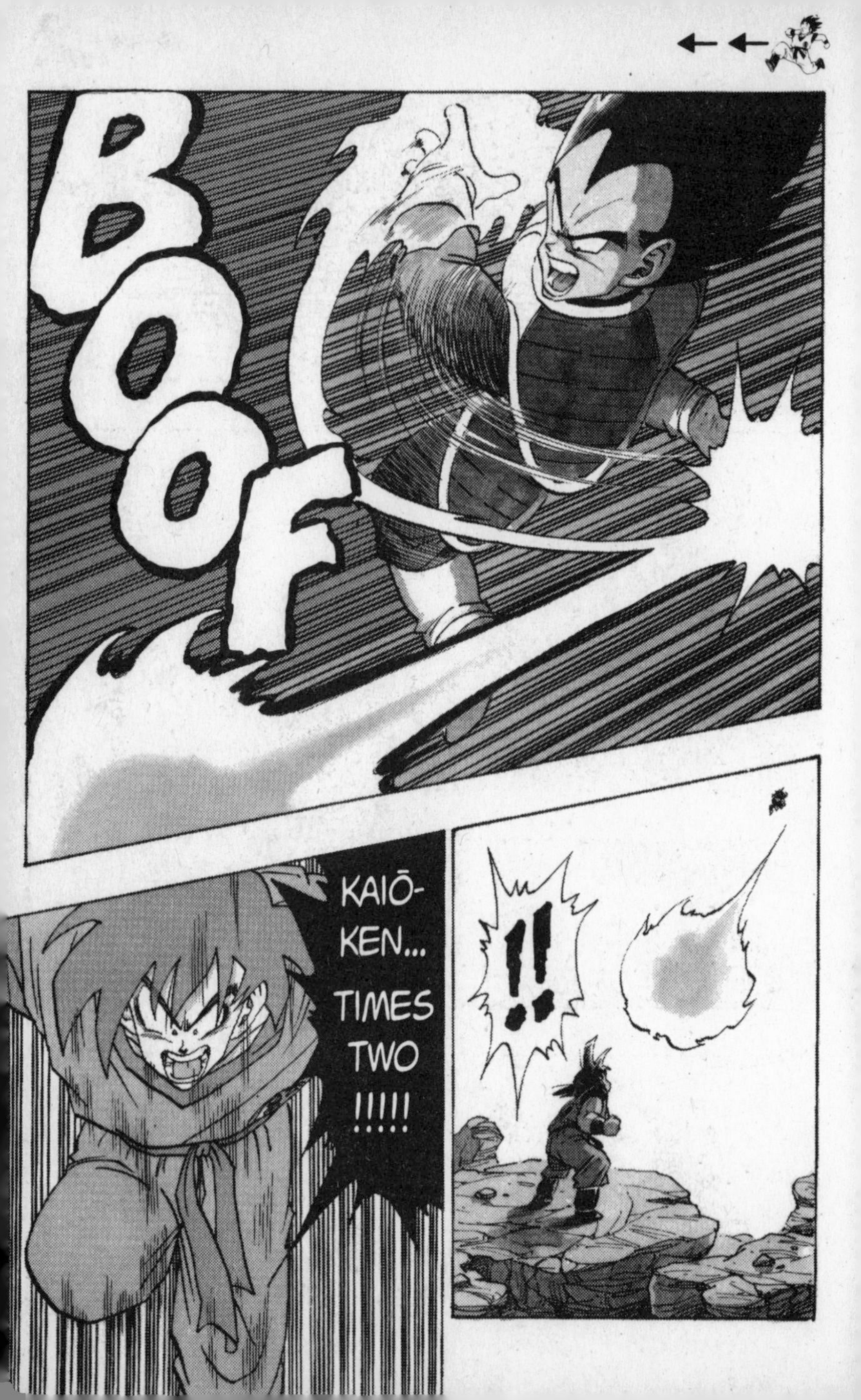
BOOF
!!
KAIŌ-
KEN...
TIMES
TWO
!!!!!

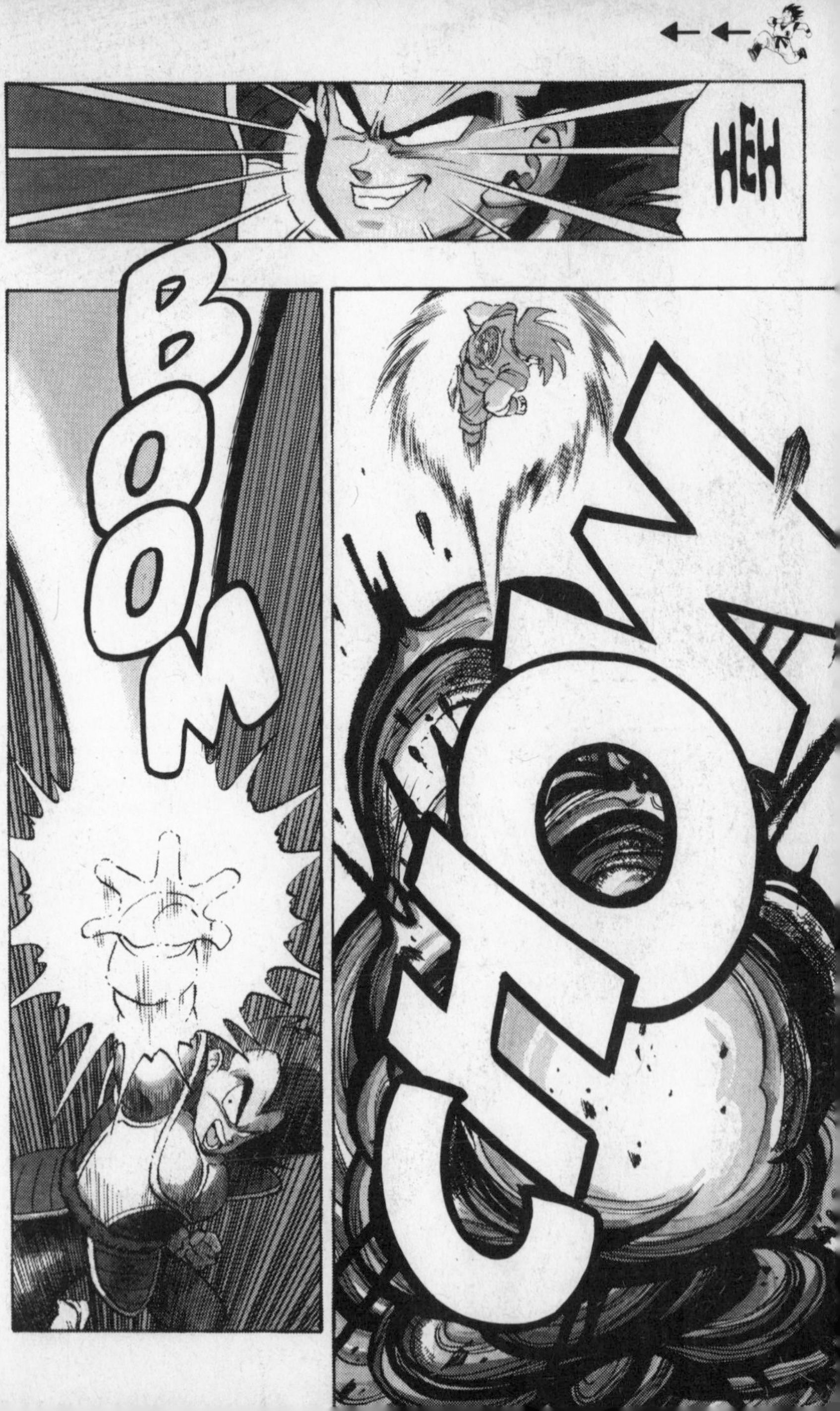
HEH
BOOM

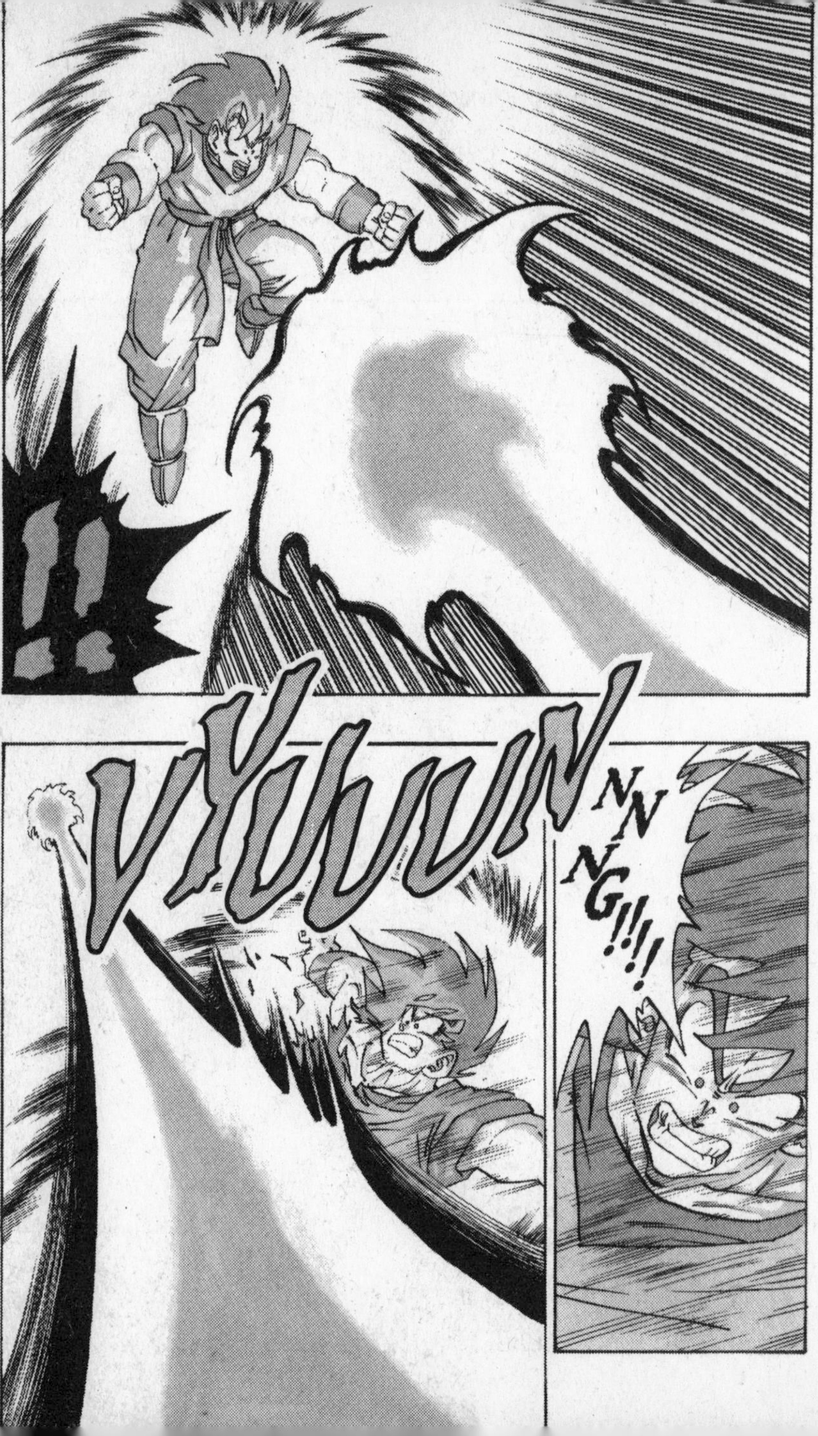
!!
NNNG!!!!
VYUUUN

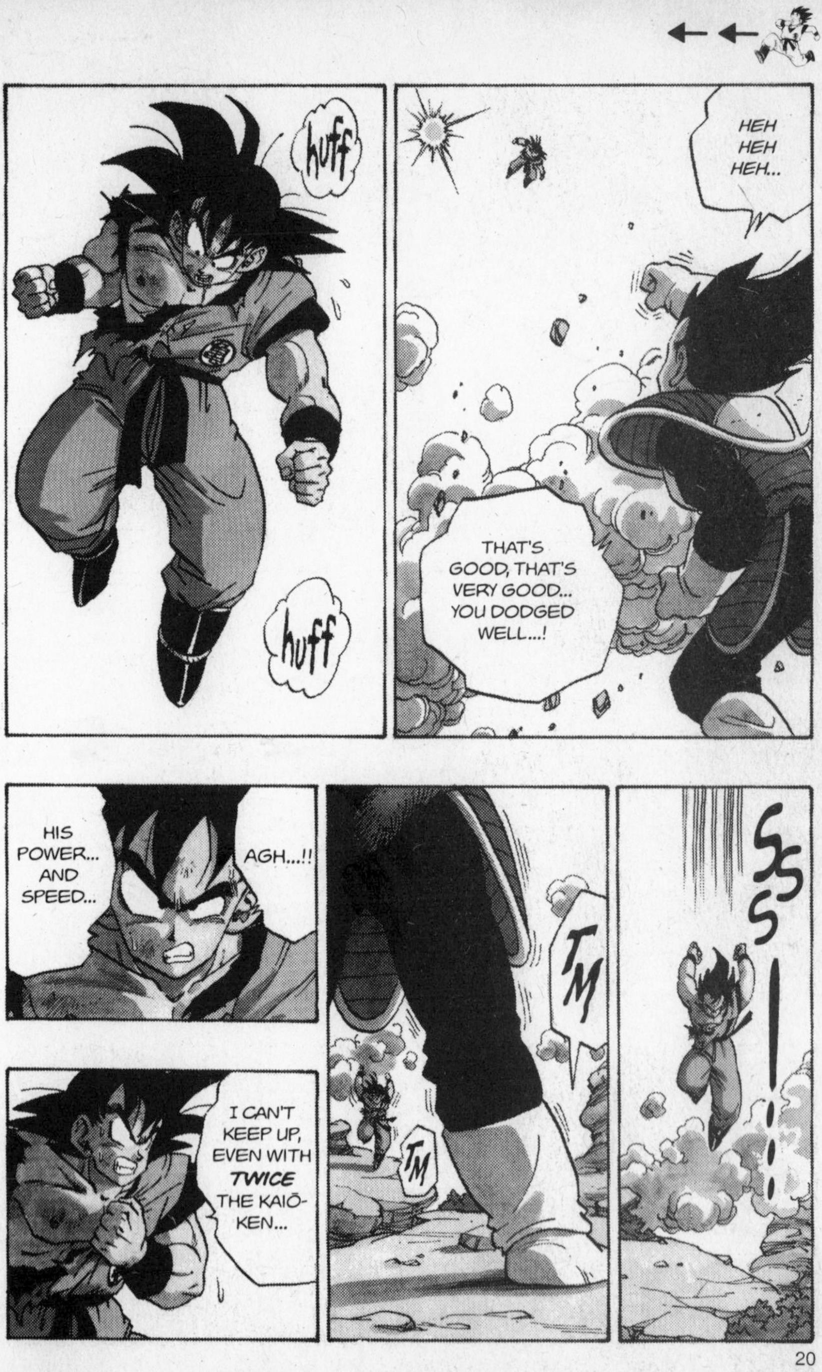
HEH HEH HEH...
THAT'S GOOD, THAT'S VERY GOOD... YOU DODGED WELL...!
huff
huff
SSS
TM
TM
AGH...!!
HIS POWER... AND SPEED...
I CAN'T KEEP UP, EVEN WITH *TWICE* THE KAIŌ-KEN...

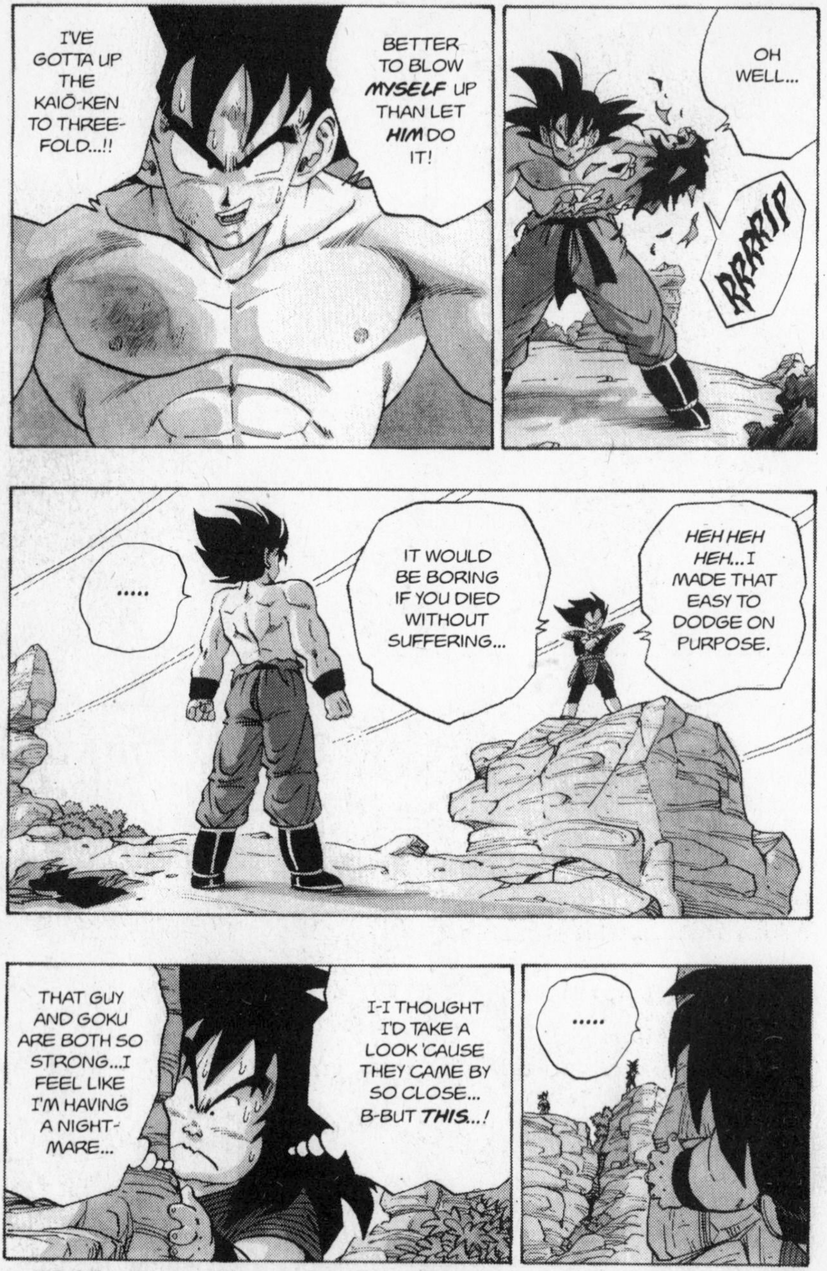
OH WELL...
RRRRIP
BETTER TO BLOW MYSELF UP THAN LET HIM DO IT!
I'VE GOTTA UP THE KAIŌ-KEN TO THREEFOLD...!!
HEH HEH HEH...I MADE THAT EASY TO DODGE ON PURPOSE.
IT WOULD BE BORING IF YOU DIED WITHOUT SUFFERING...
.....
.....
I-I THOUGHT I'D TAKE A LOOK 'CAUSE THEY CAME BY SO CLOSE... B-BUT THIS...!
THAT GUY AND GOKU ARE BOTH SO STRONG...I FEEL LIKE I'M HAVING A NIGHTMARE...

NEXT: Three Times the Danger...!

DBZ:36 • Too Much Power?

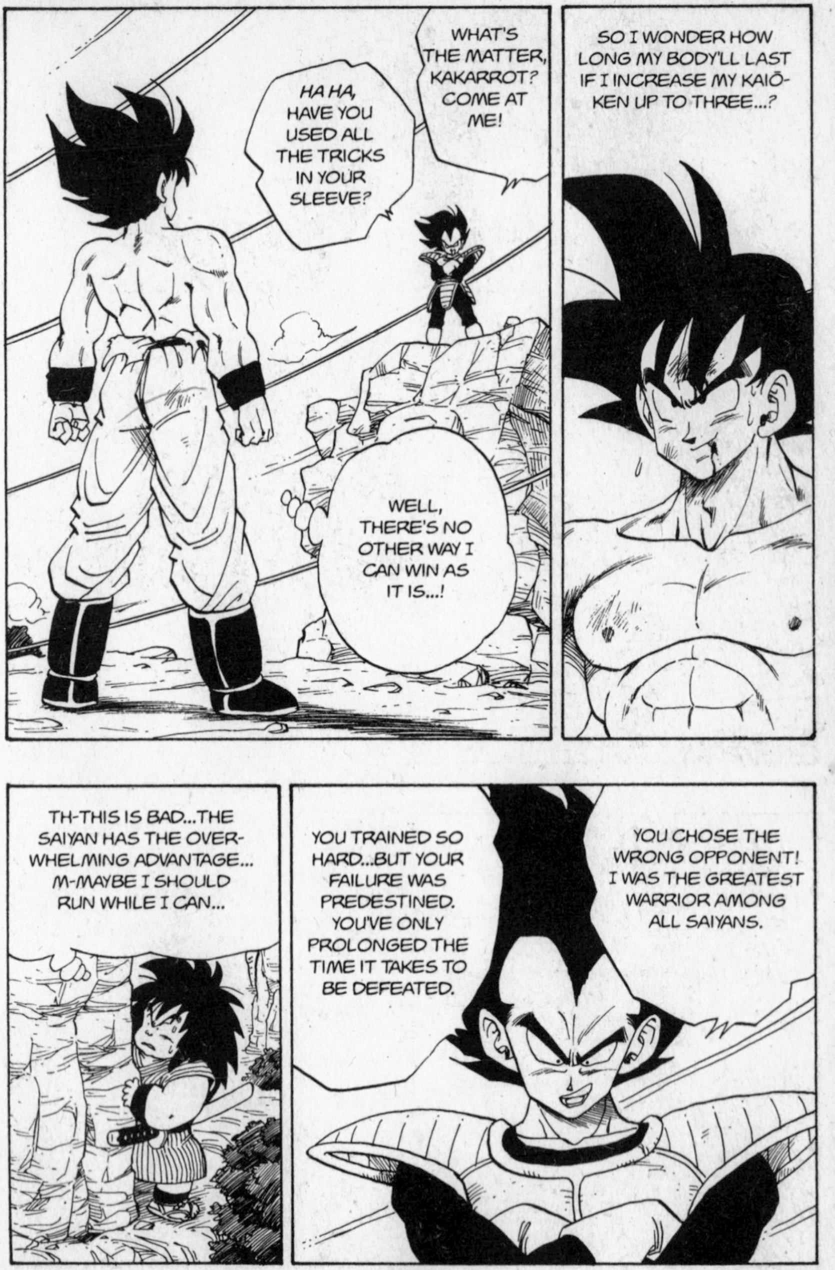
SO I WONDER HOW LONG MY BODY'LL LAST IF I INCREASE MY KAIŌ-KEN UP TO THREE...?
WHAT'S THE MATTER, KAKARROT? COME AT ME!
HA HA, HAVE YOU USED ALL THE TRICKS IN YOUR SLEEVE?
WELL, THERE'S NO OTHER WAY I CAN WIN AS IT IS...!
YOU CHOSE THE WRONG OPPONENT! I WAS THE GREATEST WARRIOR AMONG ALL SAIYANS.
YOU TRAINED SO HARD...BUT YOUR FAILURE WAS PREDESTINED. YOU'VE ONLY PROLONGED THE TIME IT TAKES TO BE DEFEATED.
TH-THIS IS BAD...THE SAIYAN HAS THE OVER-WHELMING ADVANTAGE... M-MAYBE I SHOULD RUN WHILE I CAN...

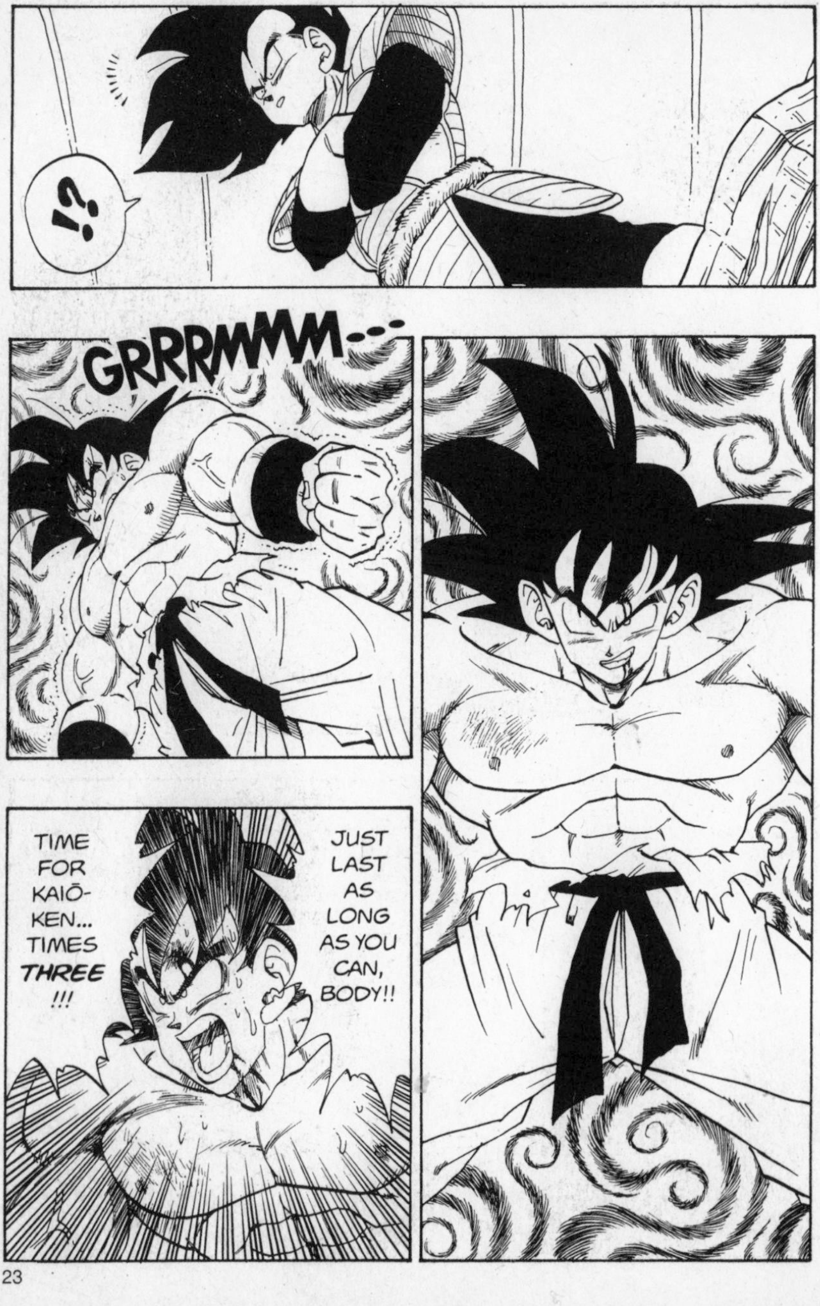
!?
GRRRMMM...
JUST LAST AS LONG AS YOU CAN, BODY!!
TIME FOR KAIŌ-KEN... TIMES *THREE* !!!

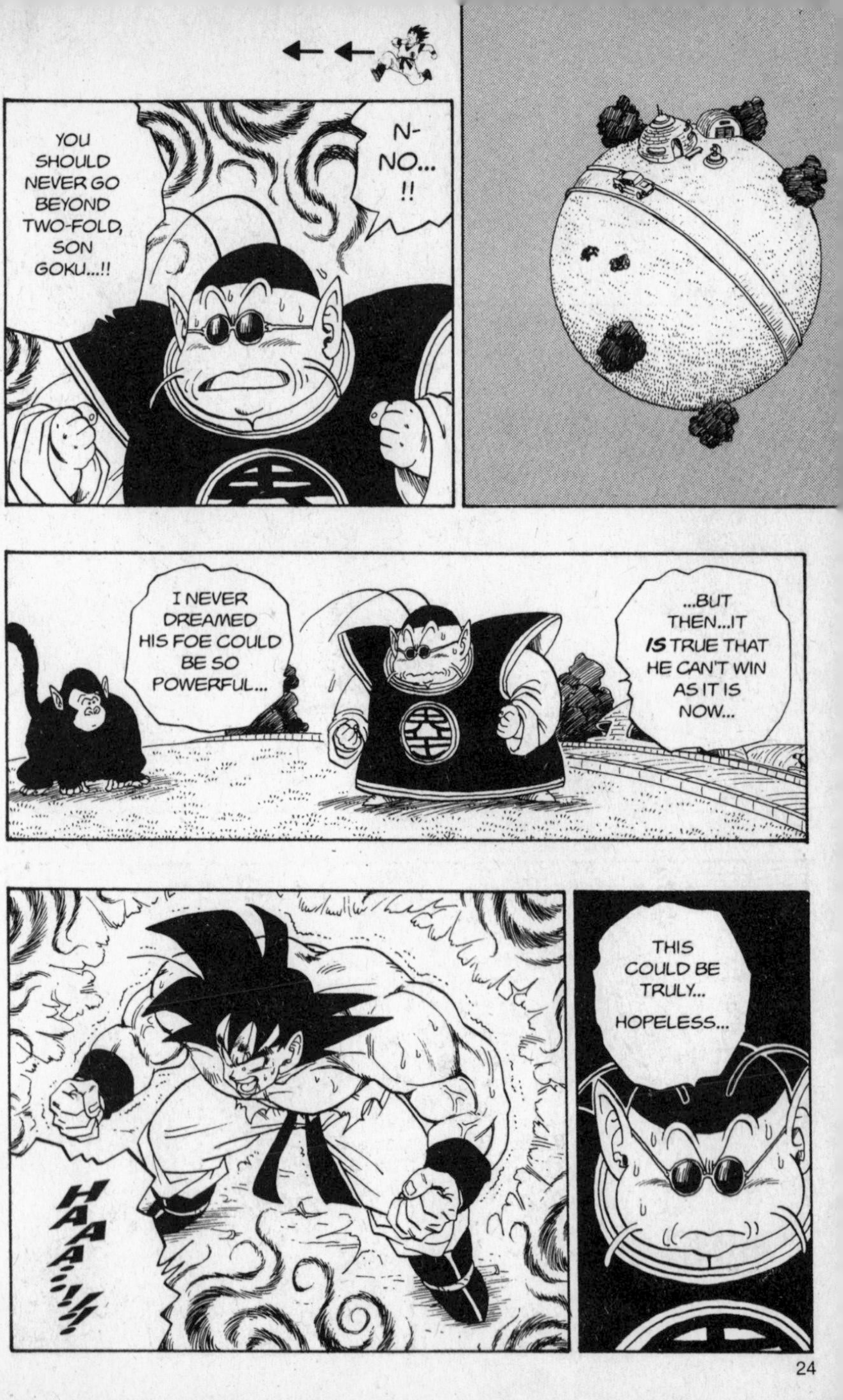
N-NO...!!
YOU SHOULD NEVER GO BEYOND TWO-FOLD, SON GOKU...!!
...BUT THEN...IT *IS* TRUE THAT HE CAN'T WIN AS IT IS NOW...
I NEVER DREAMED HIS FOE COULD BE SO POWERFUL...
THIS COULD BE TRULY... HOPELESS...
HAAA...!!!

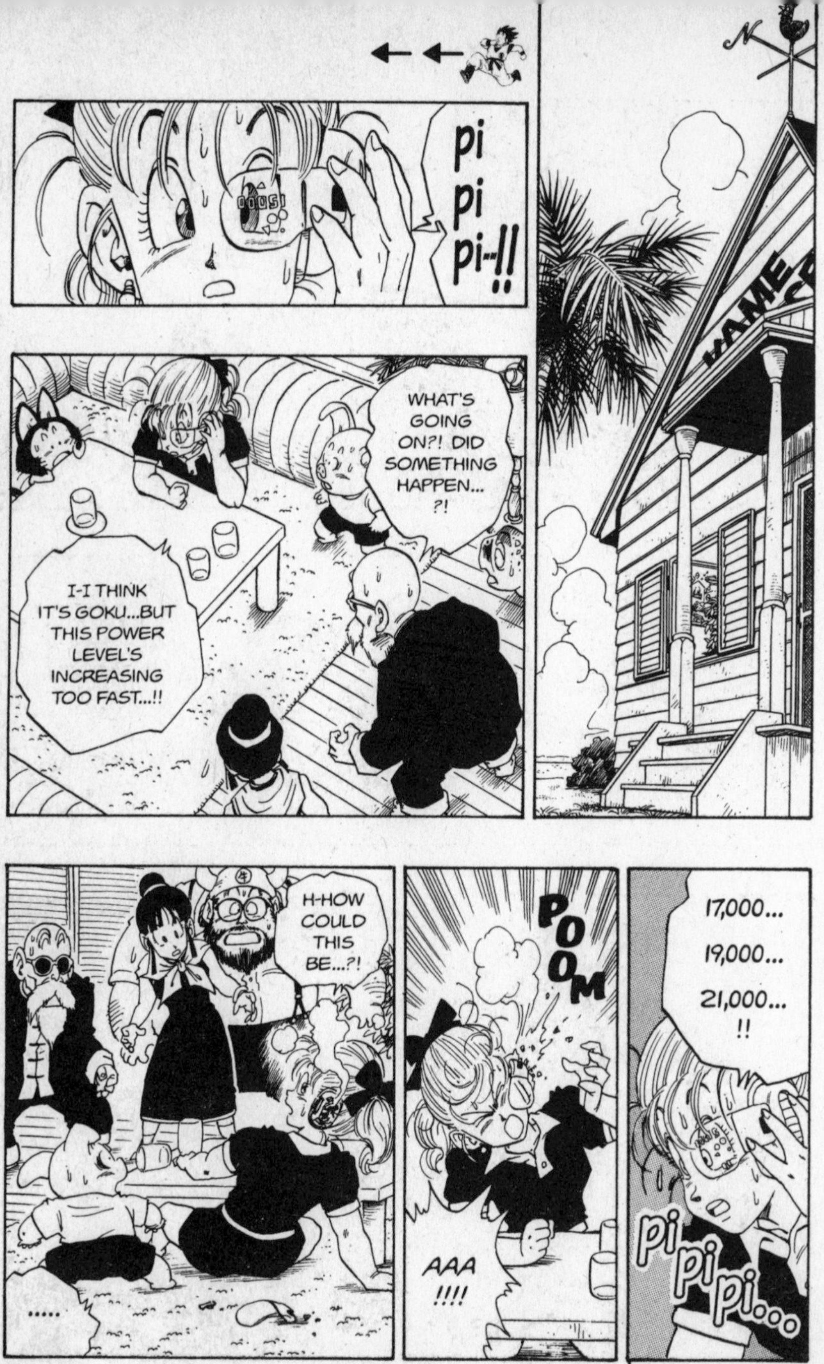
pi
pi
pi--!!
WHAT'S GOING ON?! DID SOMETHING HAPPEN...?!
I-I THINK IT'S GOKU...BUT THIS POWER LEVEL'S INCREASING TOO FAST...!!
17,000...
19,000...
21,000...
!!
pi pi pi...
POOM
AAA!!!!
H-HOW COULD THIS BE...?!
.....

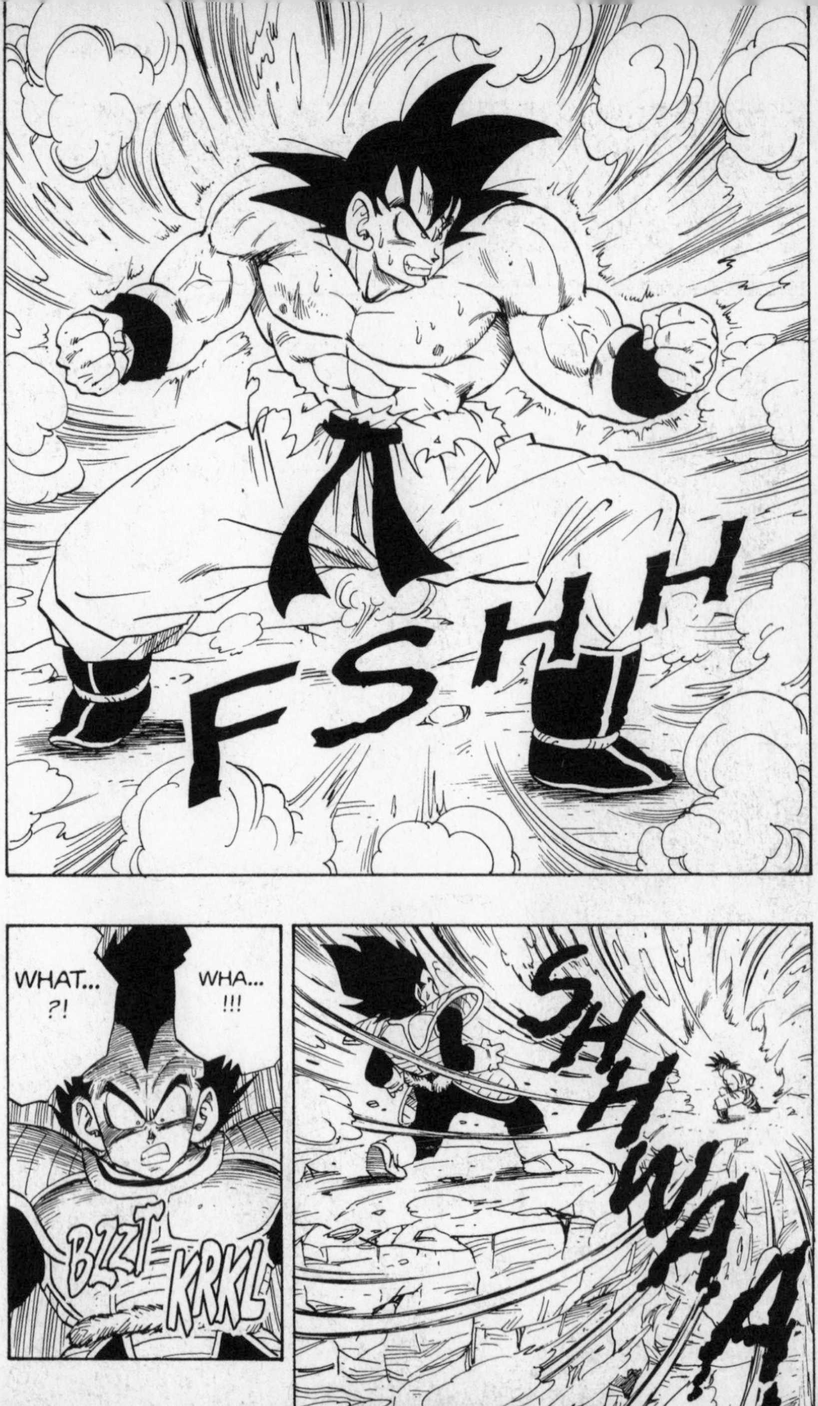
FSHH
SHWAA
WHA... !!!
WHAT... ?!
BZZT
KRKL

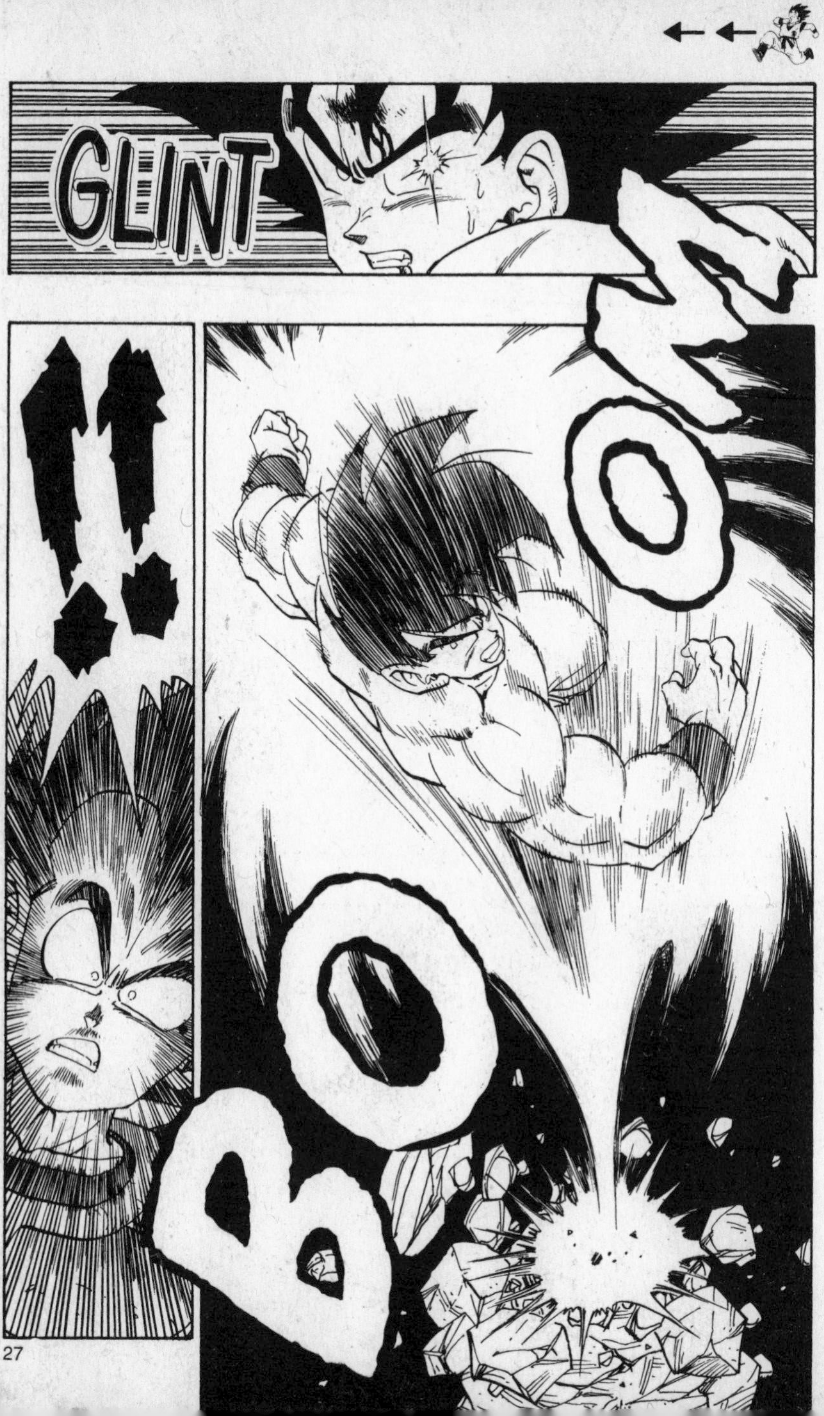
GLINT
BOOM
!!

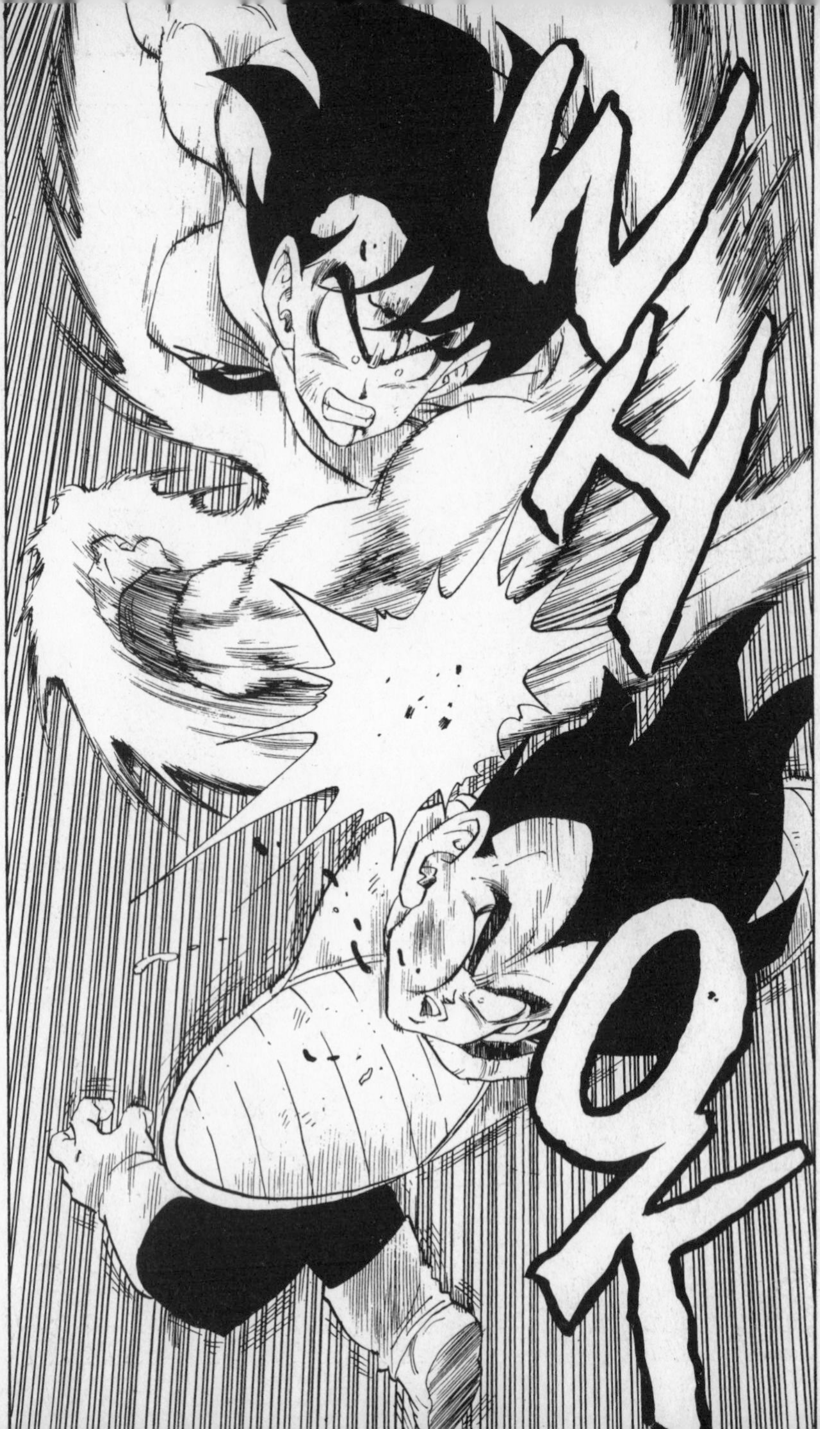

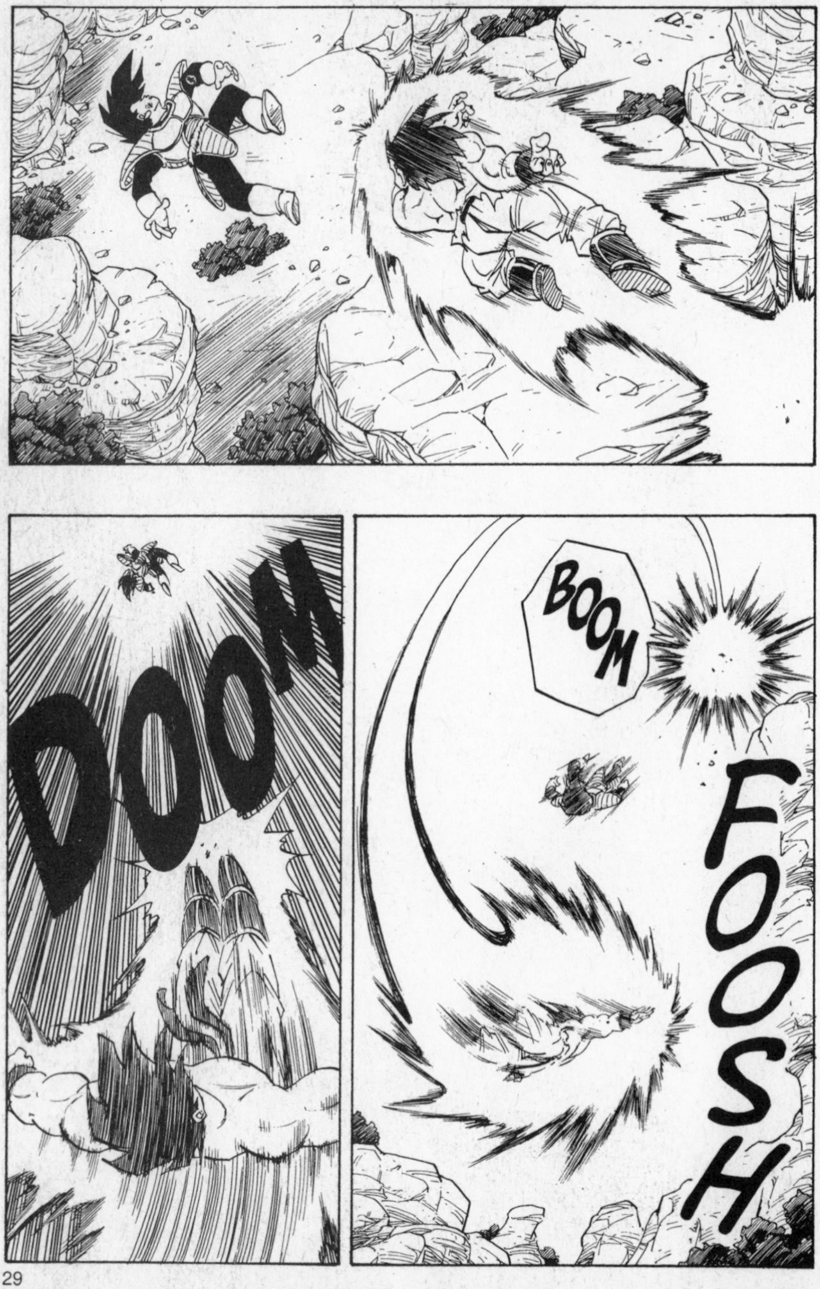
BOOM
FOOSH
DOOM

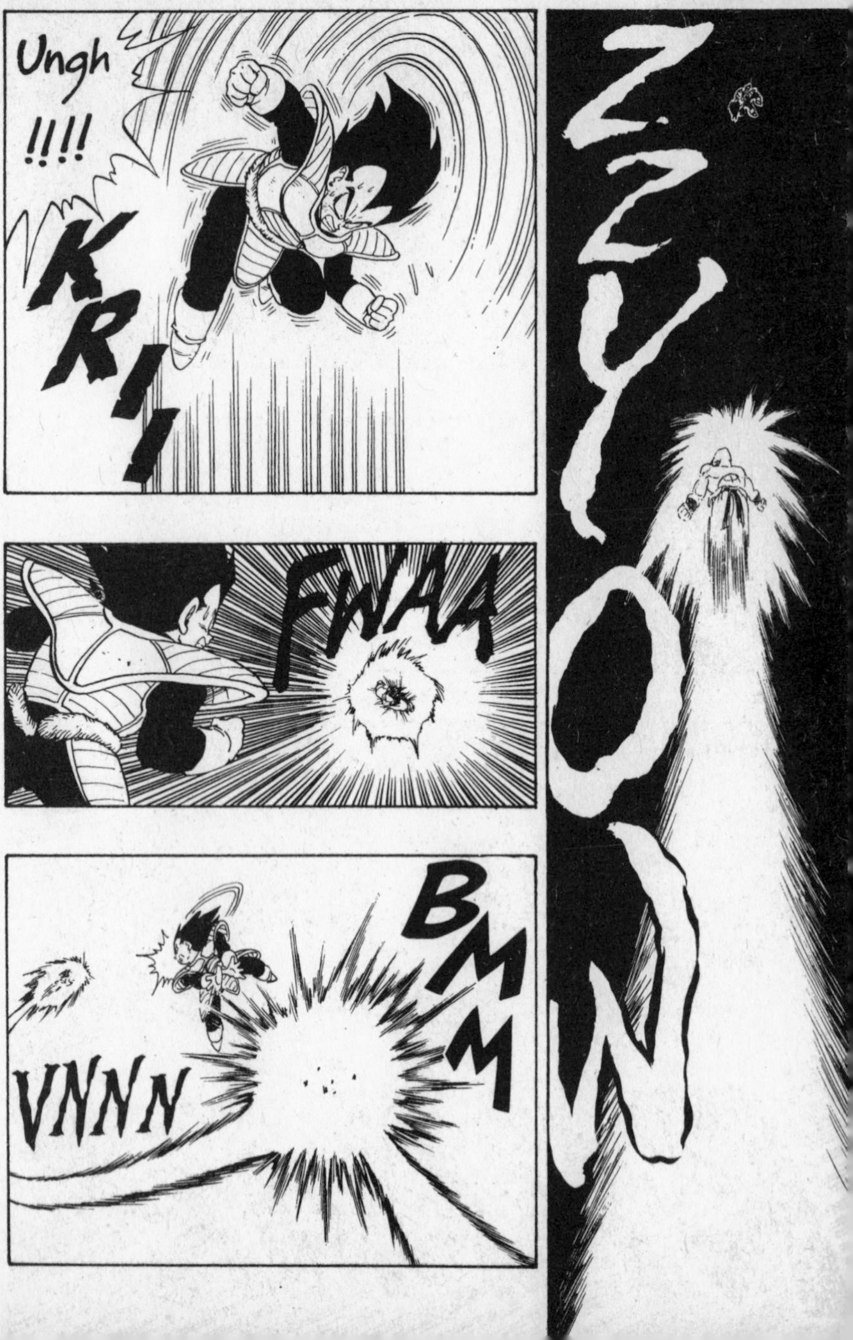
ZZUON
Ungh !!!!
KRII
FWAA
BMMM
VNNN

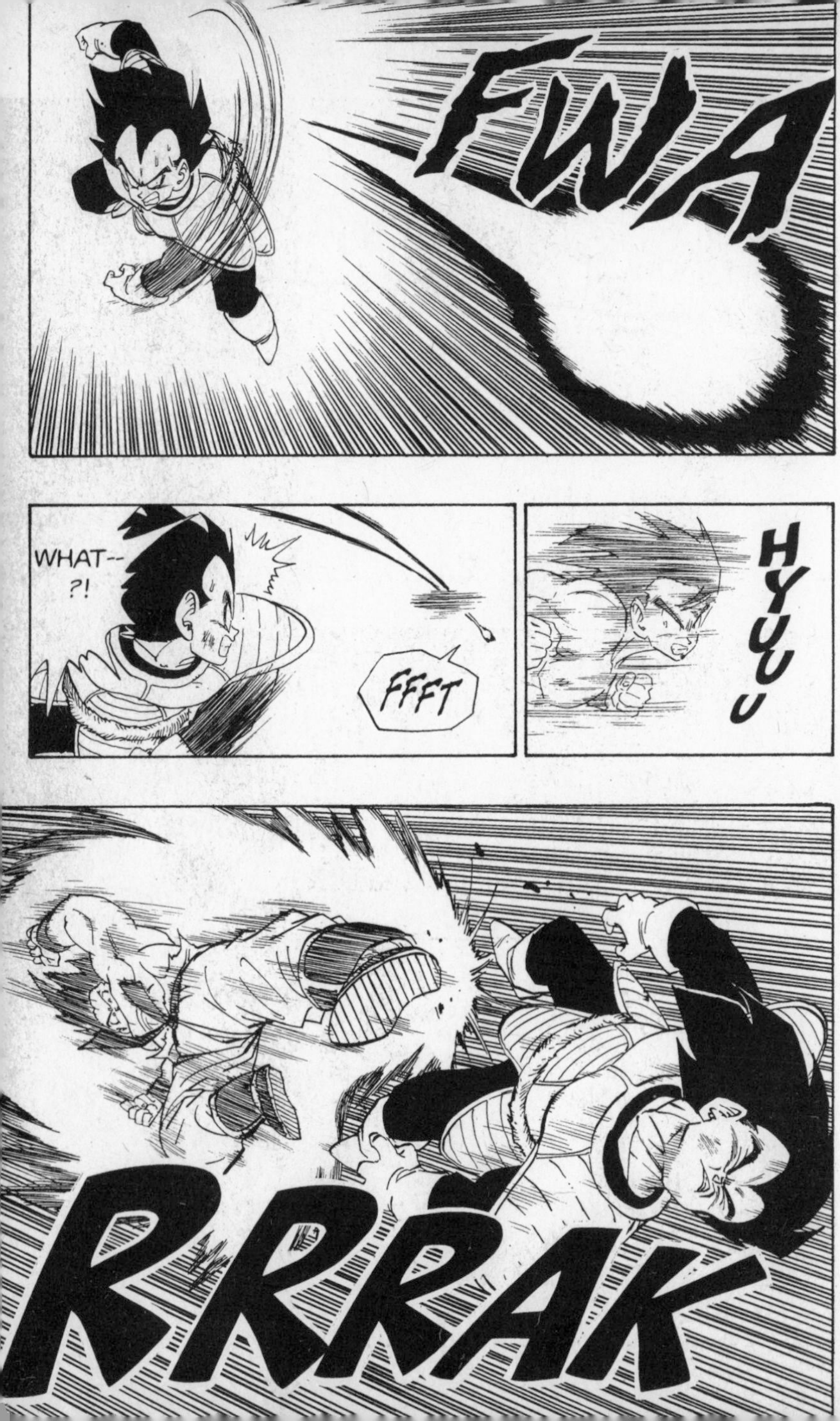
FWA
HYUUU
WHAT--?!
FFFT
RRRAK

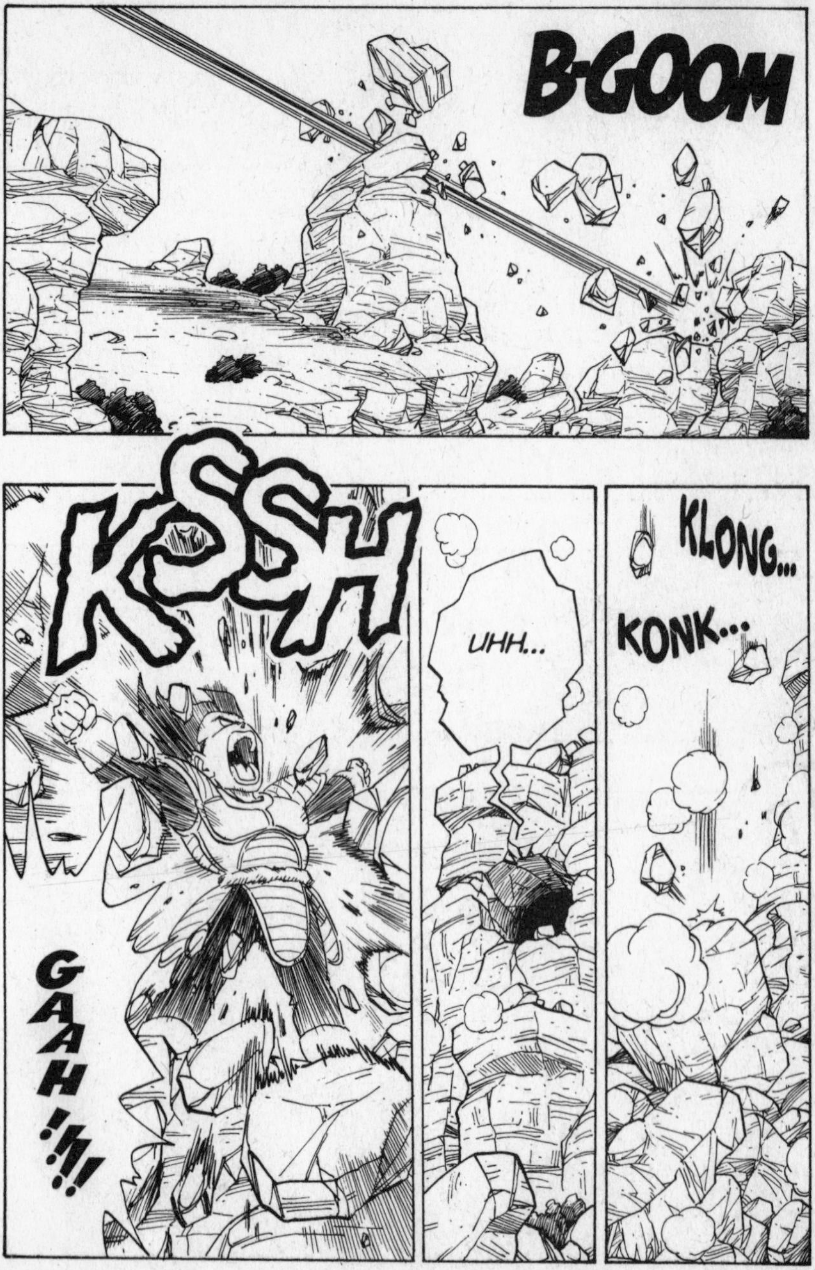
B-GOOM
KLONG...
KONK...
UHH...
KSSH
GAAH!!!

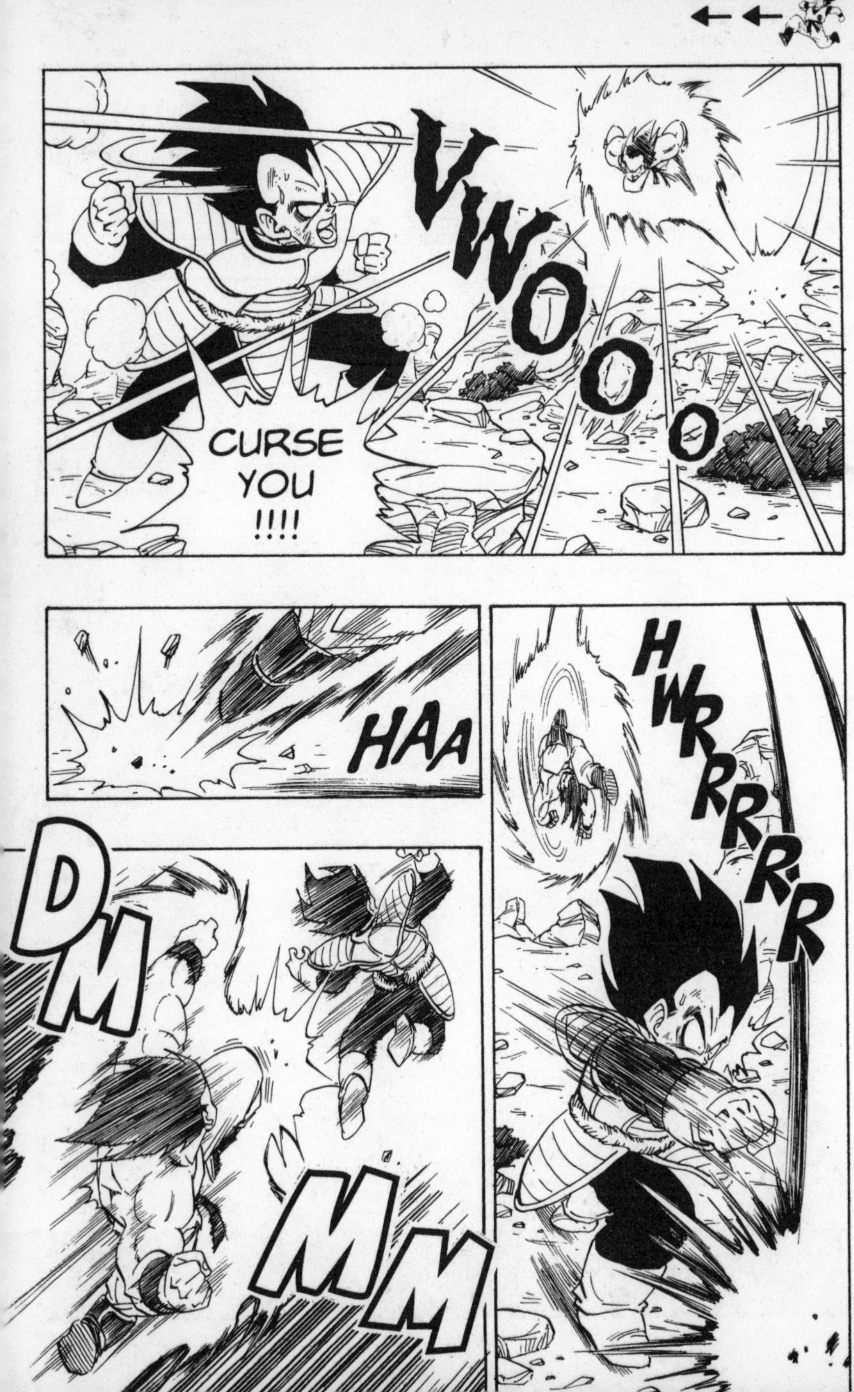
CURSE YOU !!!!
VWOOOO
HWRRRRR
HAA
DMMM

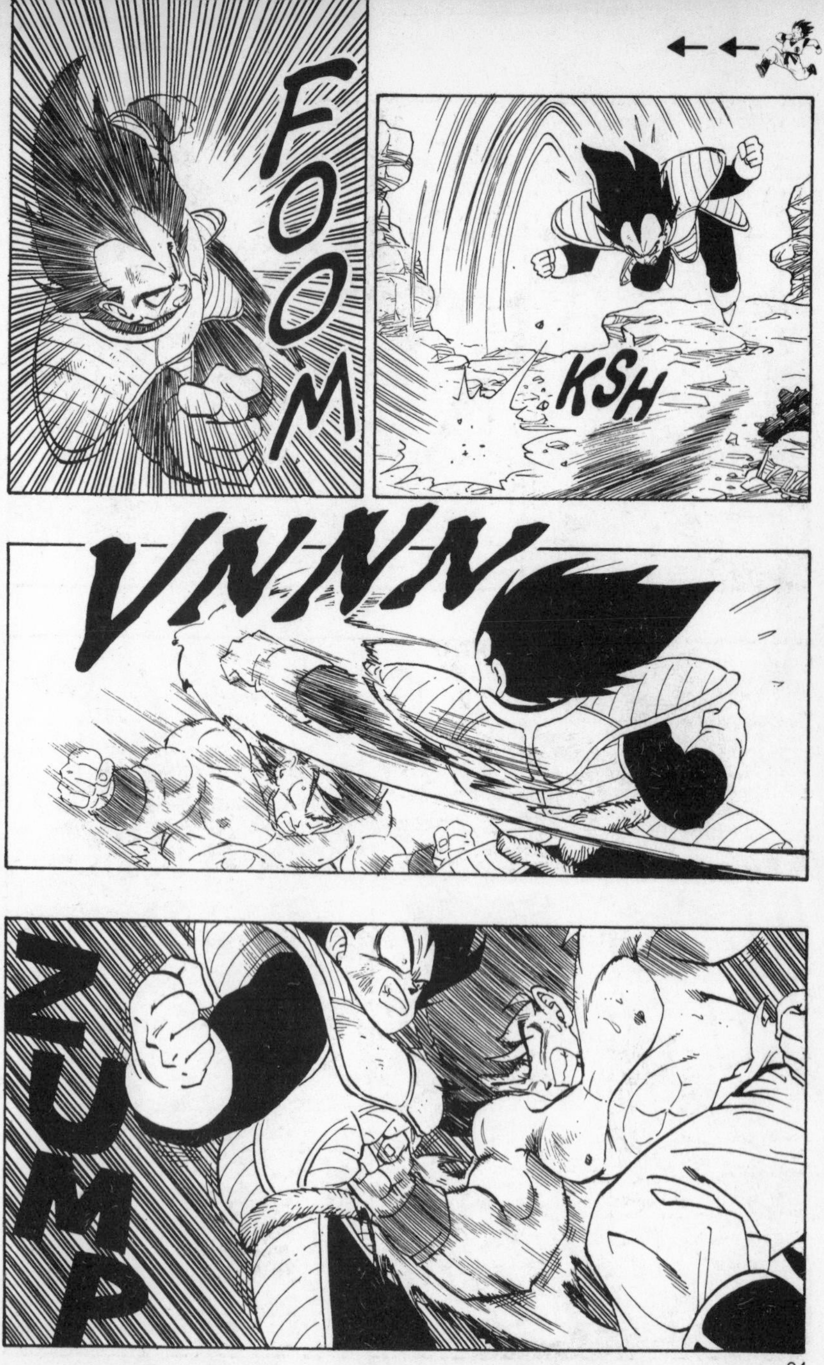
KSH
FOOM
VNNN
NUMP

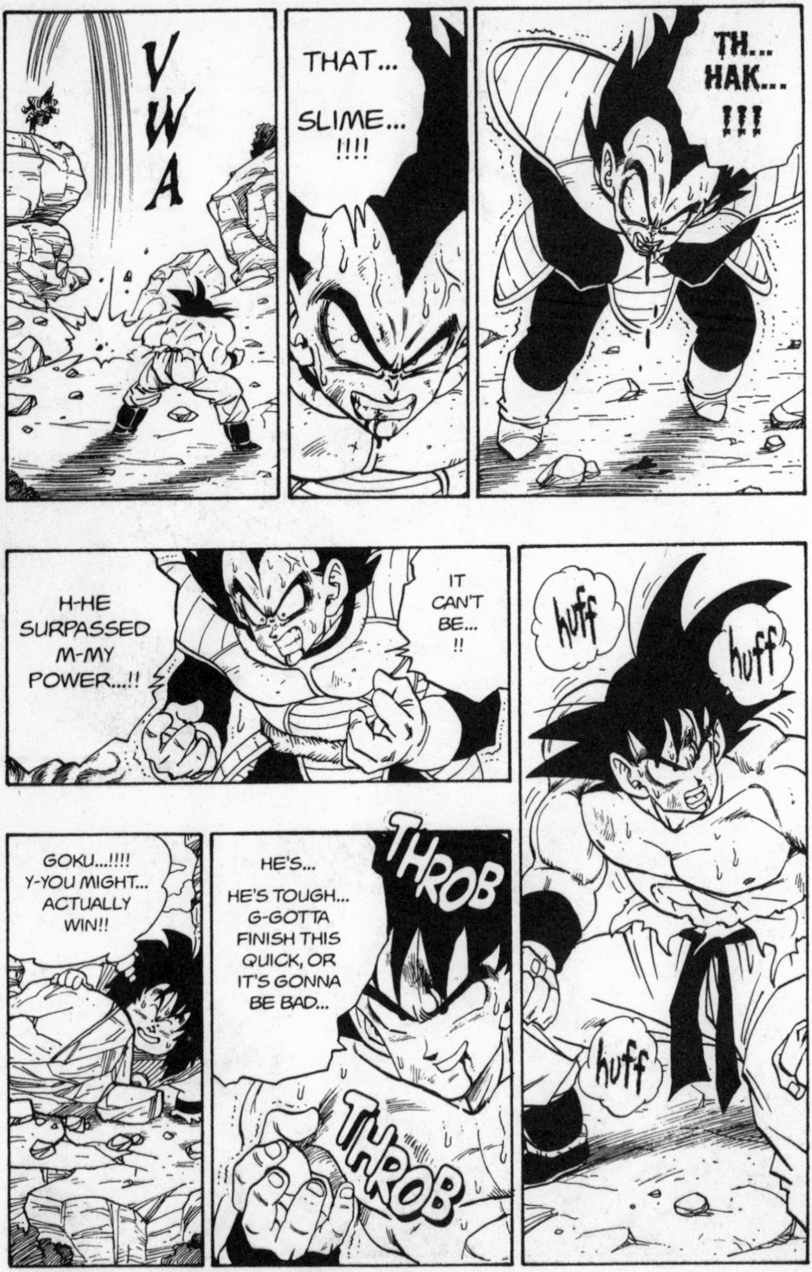
TH... HAK... !!!
THAT...
SLIME... !!!!
VWA
huff
huff
huff
IT CAN'T BE... !!
H-HE SURPASSED M-MY POWER...!!
THROB
HE'S...
HE'S TOUGH... G-GOTTA FINISH THIS QUICK, OR IT'S GONNA BE BAD...
THROB
GOKU...!!!! Y-YOU MIGHT... ACTUALLY WIN!!

NEXT: A Battle in the Red Zone!

DBZ:37 • Battle in the Red Zone!!

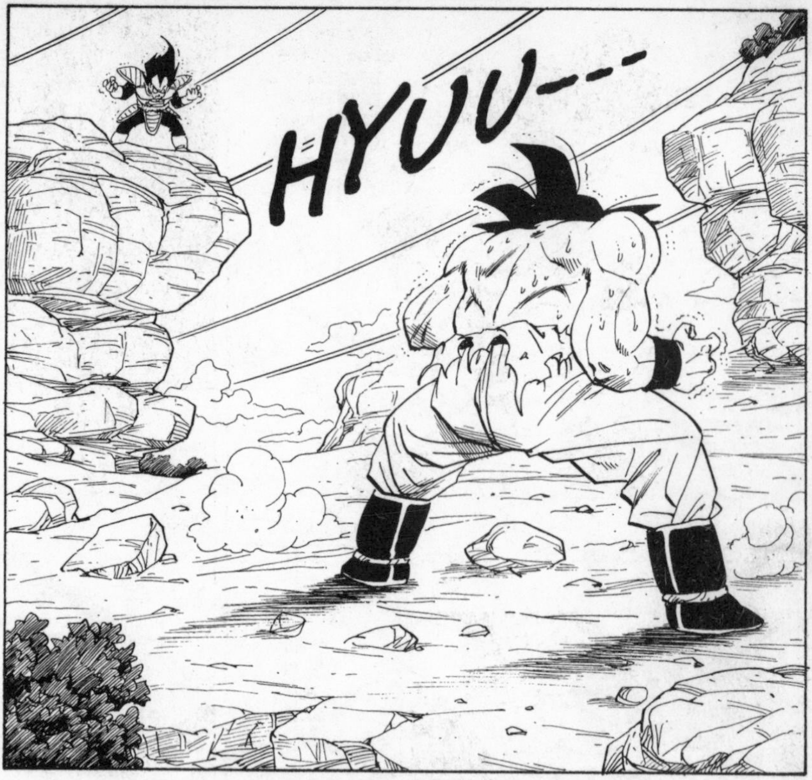
HYUU---

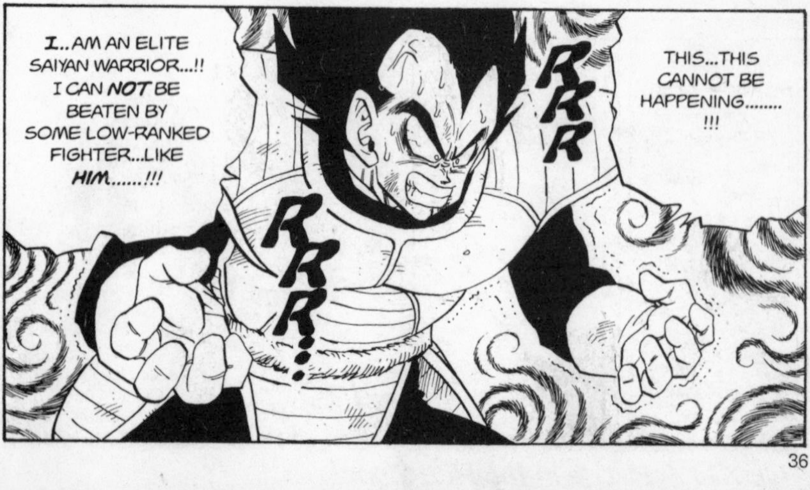
THIS...THIS CANNOT BE HAPPENING........!!!
RRR
RRR!!
I..AM AN ELITE SAIYAN WARRIOR...!! I CAN **NOT** BE BEATEN BY SOME LOW-RANKED FIGHTER...LIKE ***HIM***.......!!!

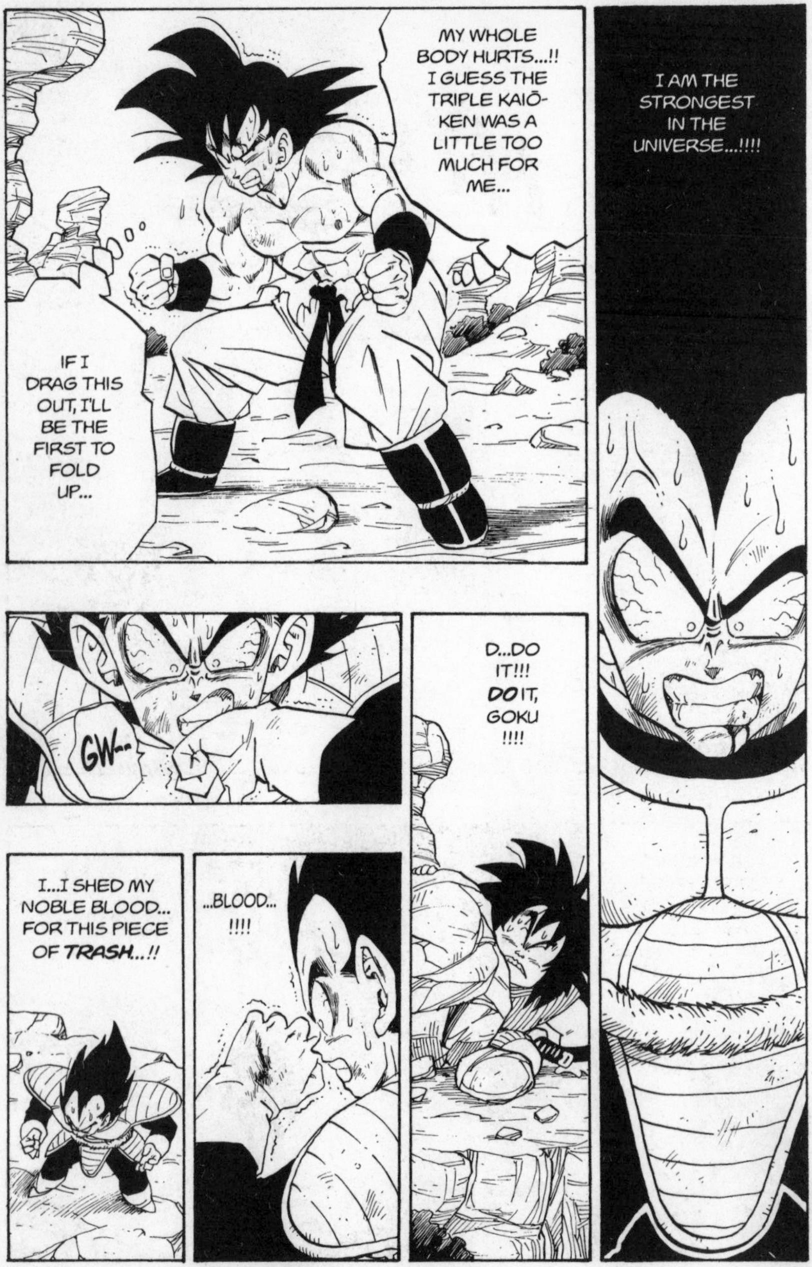
I AM THE STRONGEST IN THE UNIVERSE...!!!!
MY WHOLE BODY HURTS...!! I GUESS THE TRIPLE KAIŌ-KEN WAS A LITTLE TOO MUCH FOR ME...
IF I DRAG THIS OUT, I'LL BE THE FIRST TO FOLD UP...
D...DO IT!!! DO IT, GOKU !!!!
GW--
...BLOOD... !!!!
I...I SHED MY NOBLE BLOOD... FOR THIS PIECE OF TRASH...!!

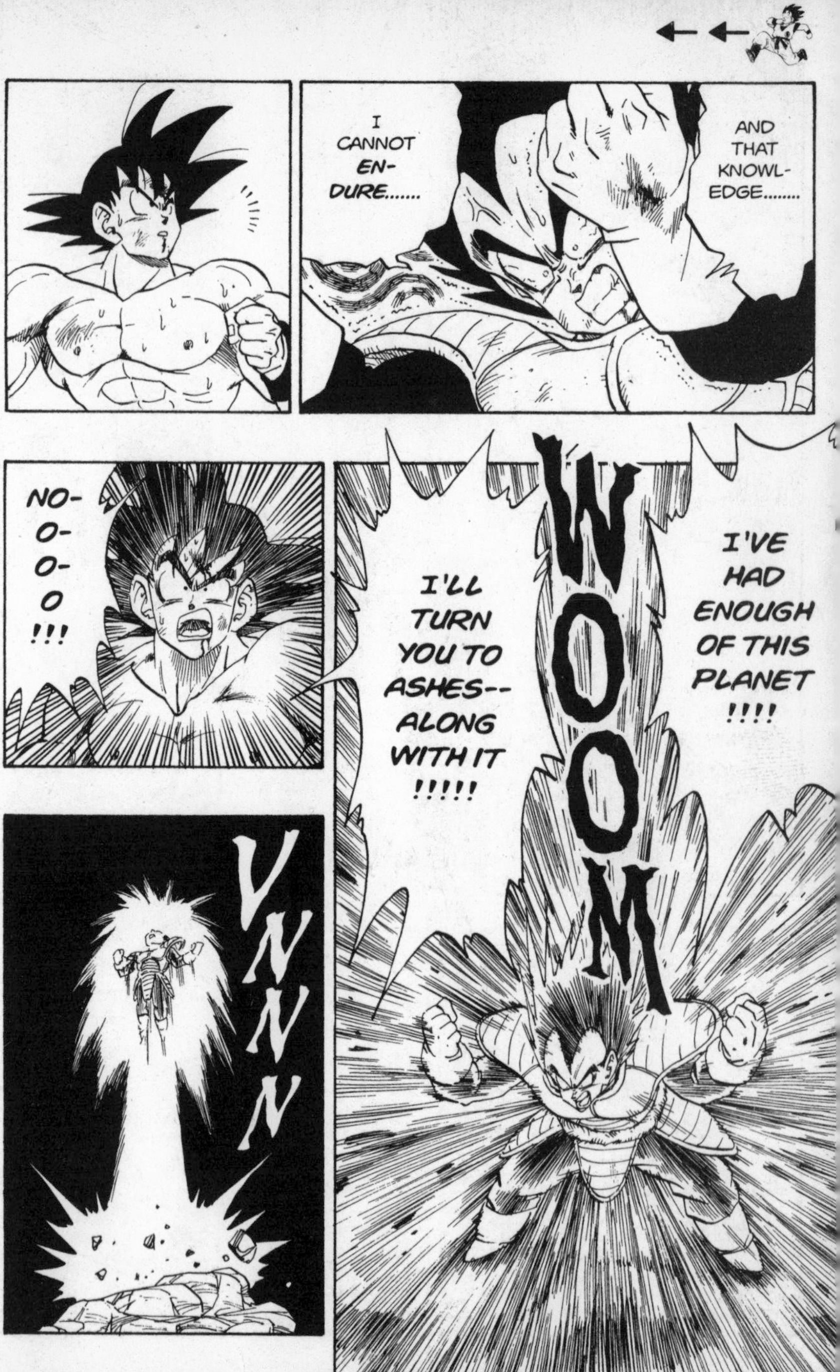
AND THAT KNOWLEDGE........
I CANNOT ENDURE.......
I'VE HAD ENOUGH OF THIS PLANET!!!!
WOOM
I'LL TURN YOU TO ASHES--ALONG WITH IT!!!!!
NO-O-O-O!!!
VNNN

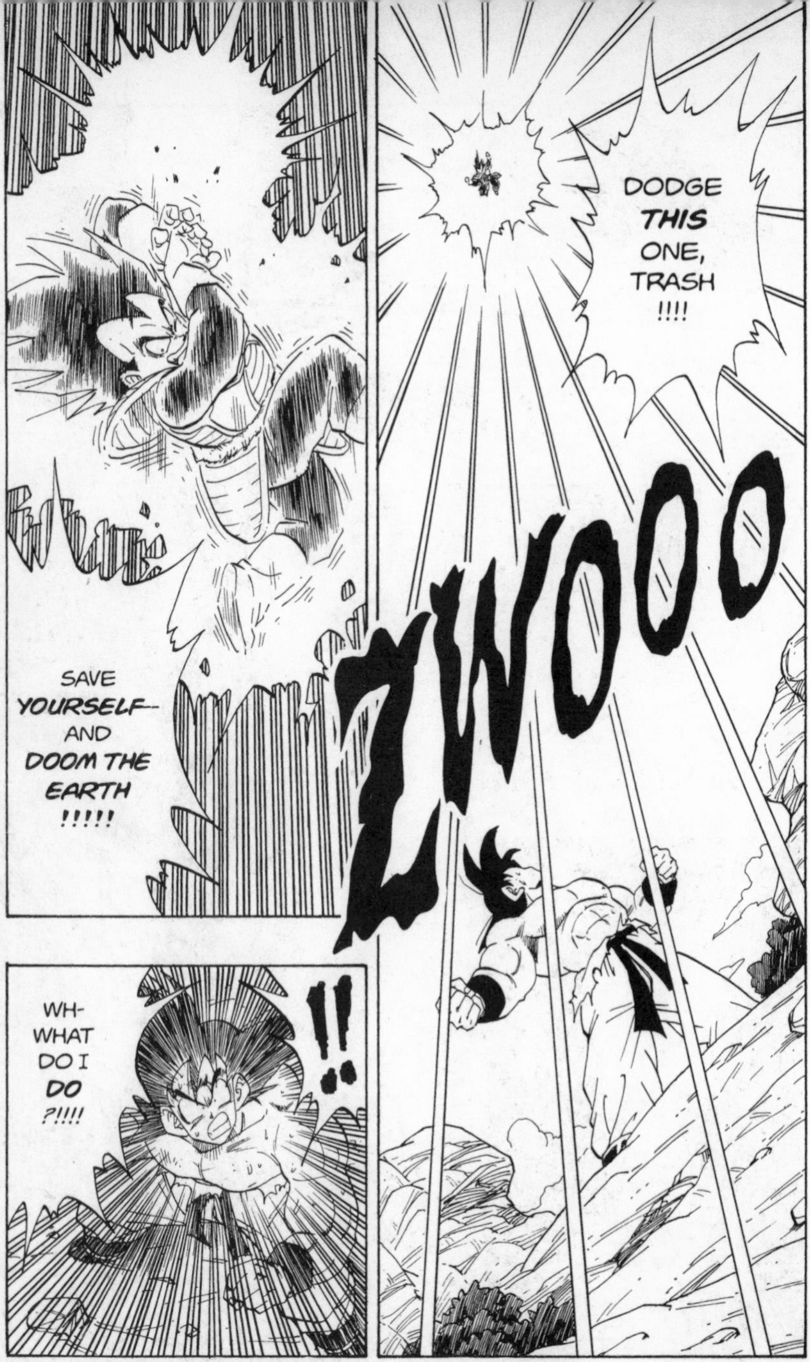
DODGE **THIS** ONE, TRASH !!!!
ZWOOO
SAVE **YOURSELF**-- AND **DOOM THE EARTH** !!!!!
WH- WHAT DO I **DO** ?!!!!
!!

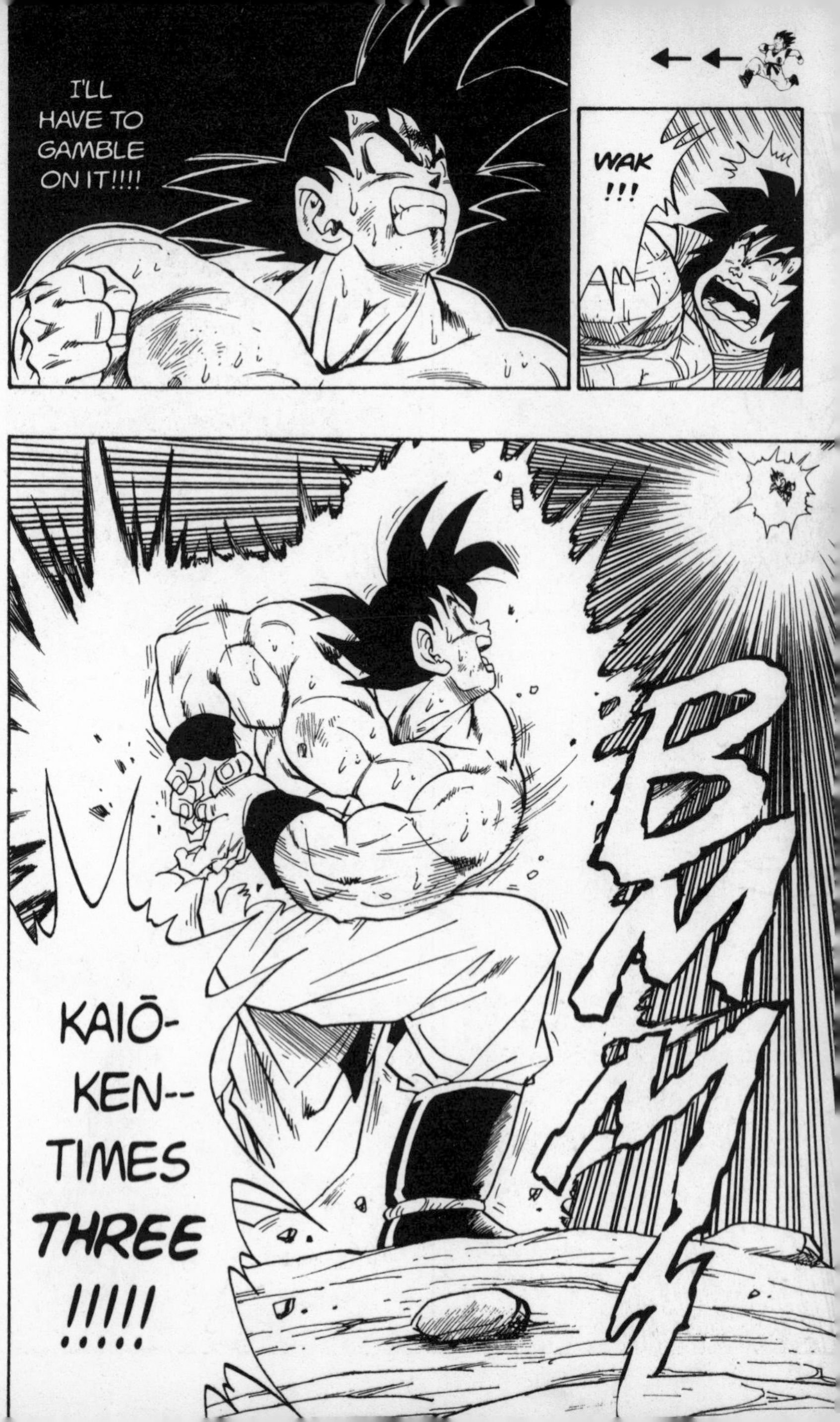
WAK !!!
I'LL HAVE TO GAMBLE ON IT!!!!
KAIŌ-KEN--TIMES THREE!!!!!

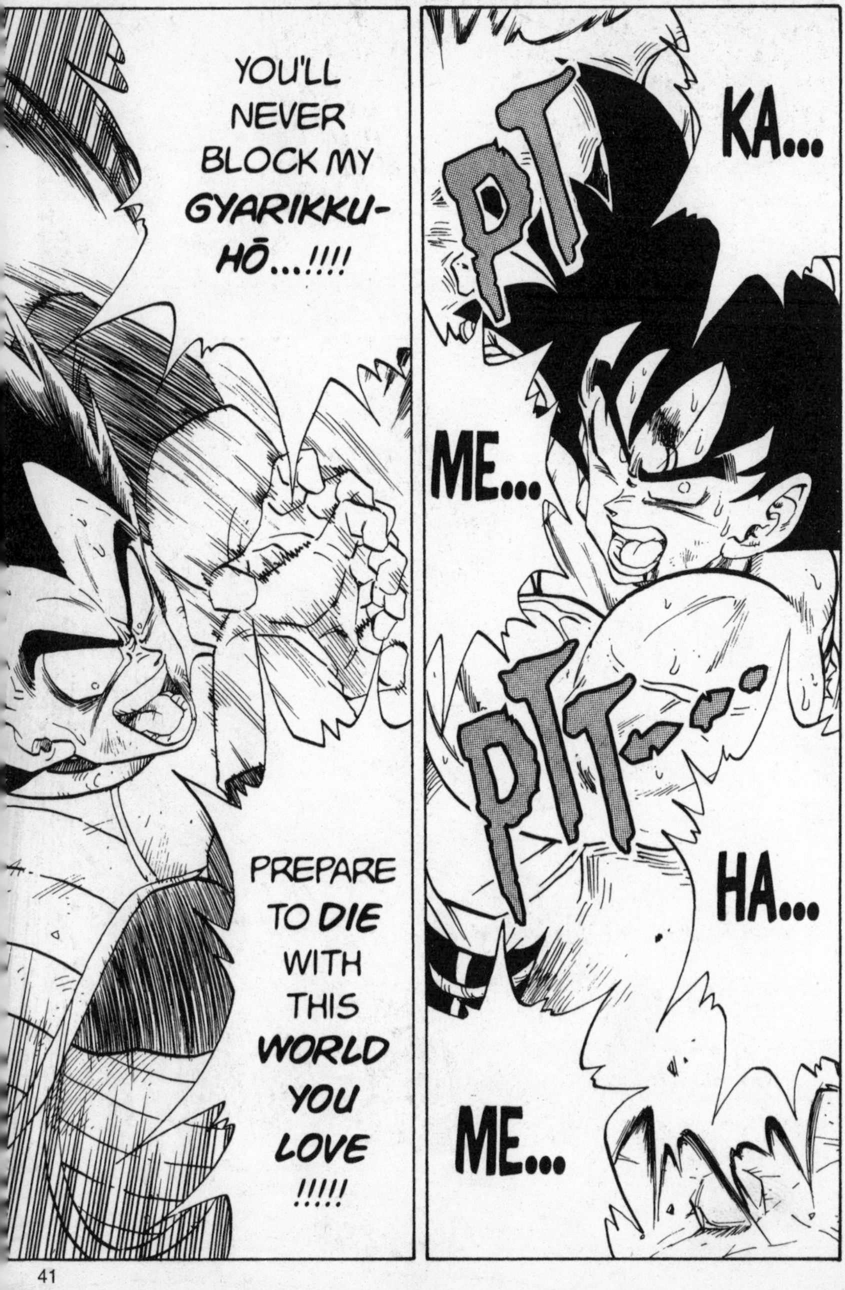
KA...
PIT
ME...
PIT...
HA...
ME...
YOU'LL NEVER BLOCK MY GYARIKKU-HŌ...!!!!
PREPARE TO DIE WITH THIS WORLD YOU LOVE !!!!!

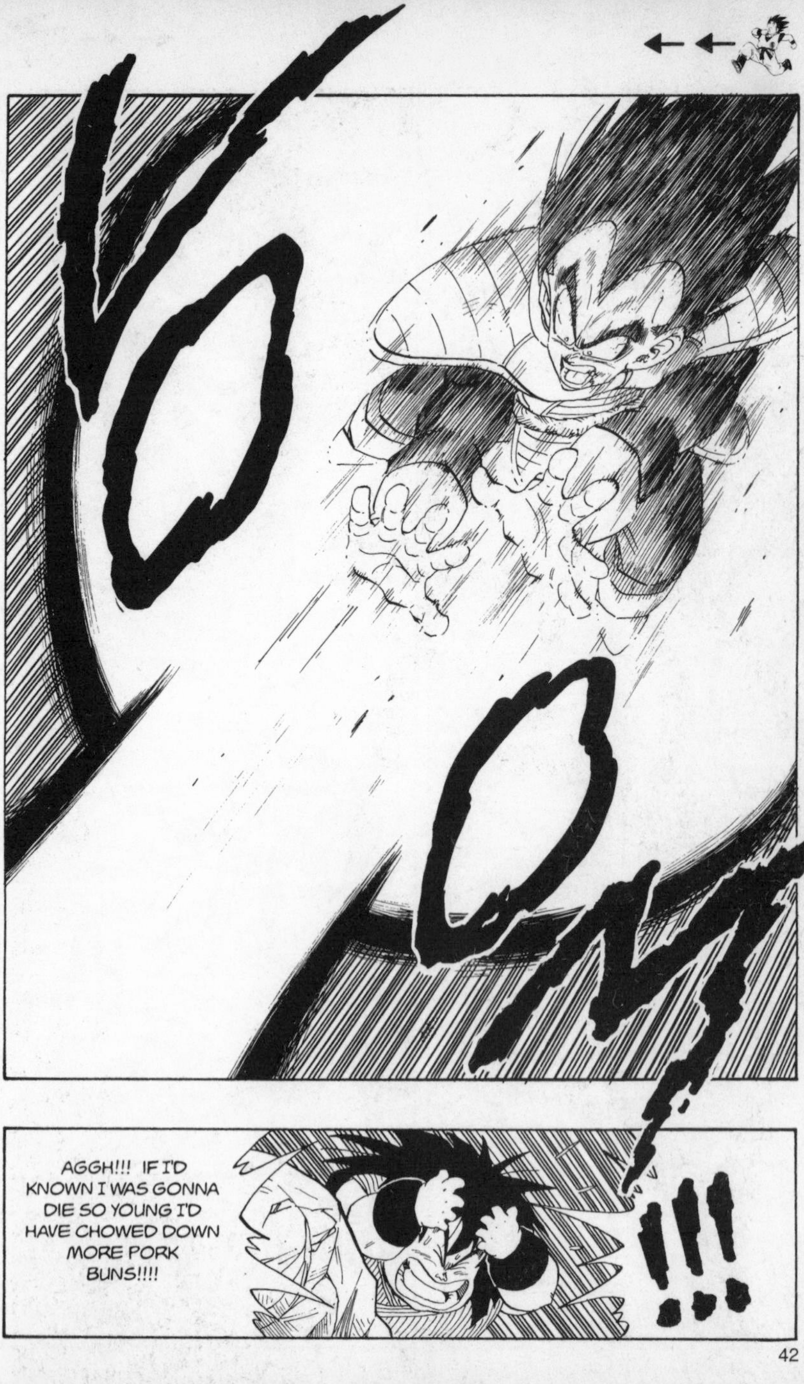
AGGH!!! IF I'D KNOWN I WAS GONNA DIE SO YOUNG I'D HAVE CHOWED DOWN MORE PORK BUNS!!!!
!!!

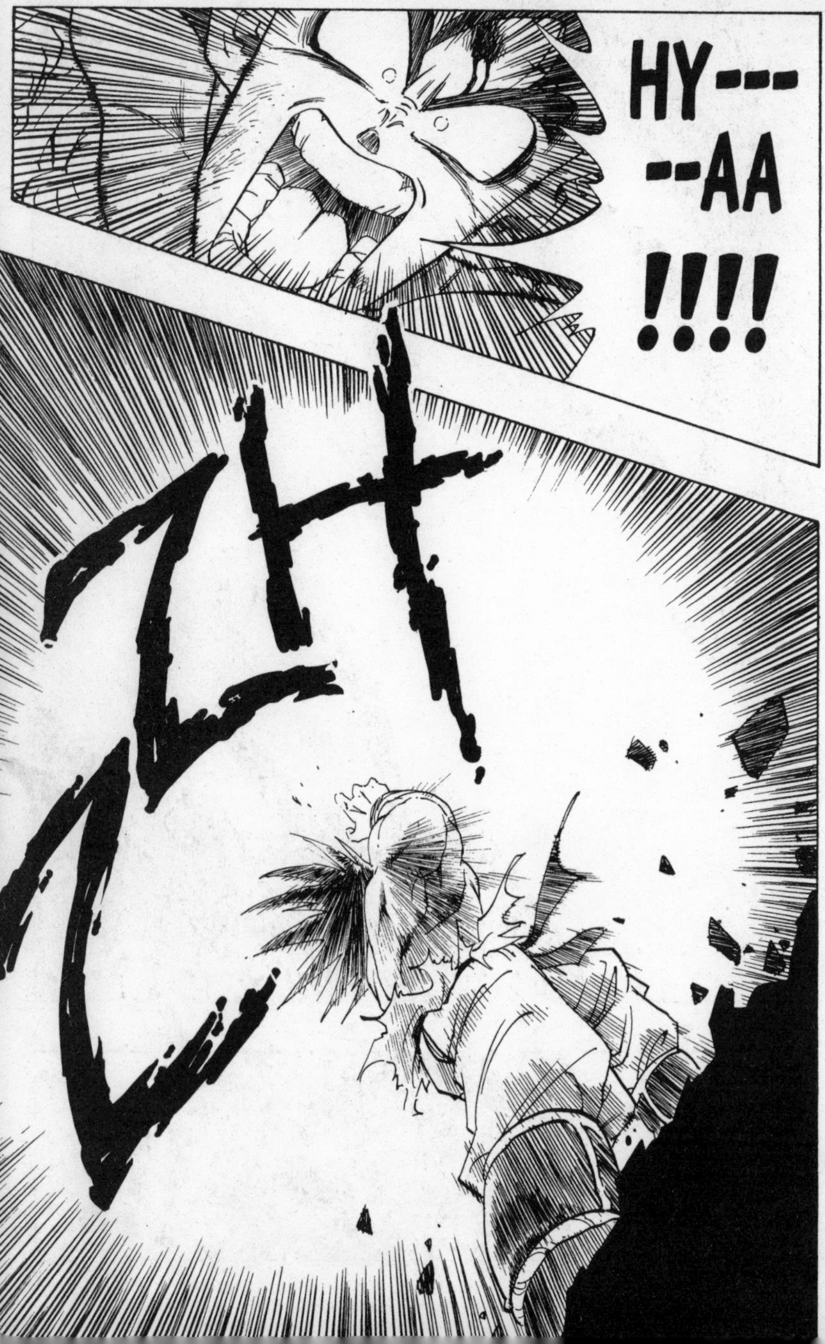
HY-----AA!!!!

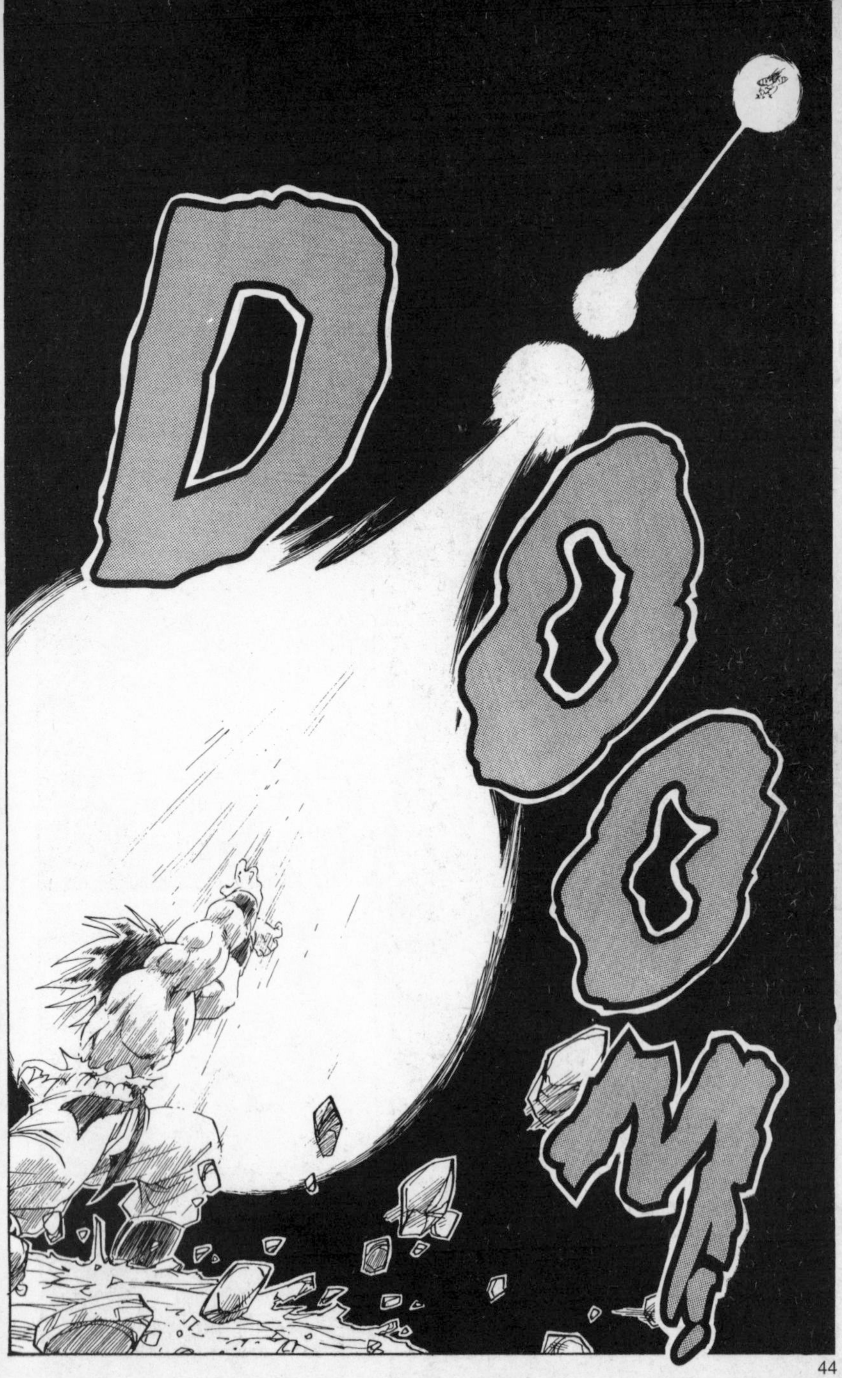
DOOM

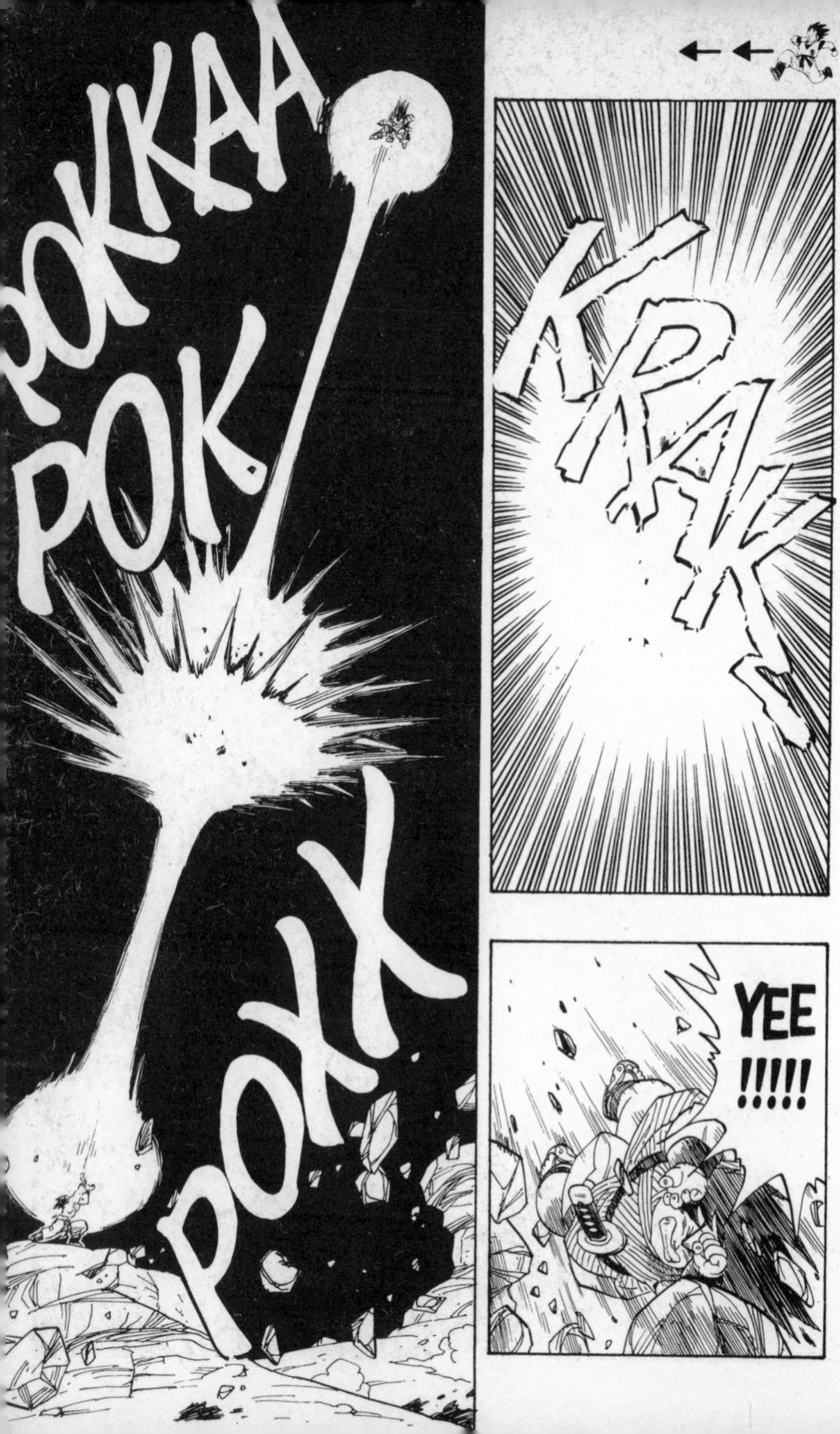
KRAK
YEE !!!!!
POKKAA
POK
POK

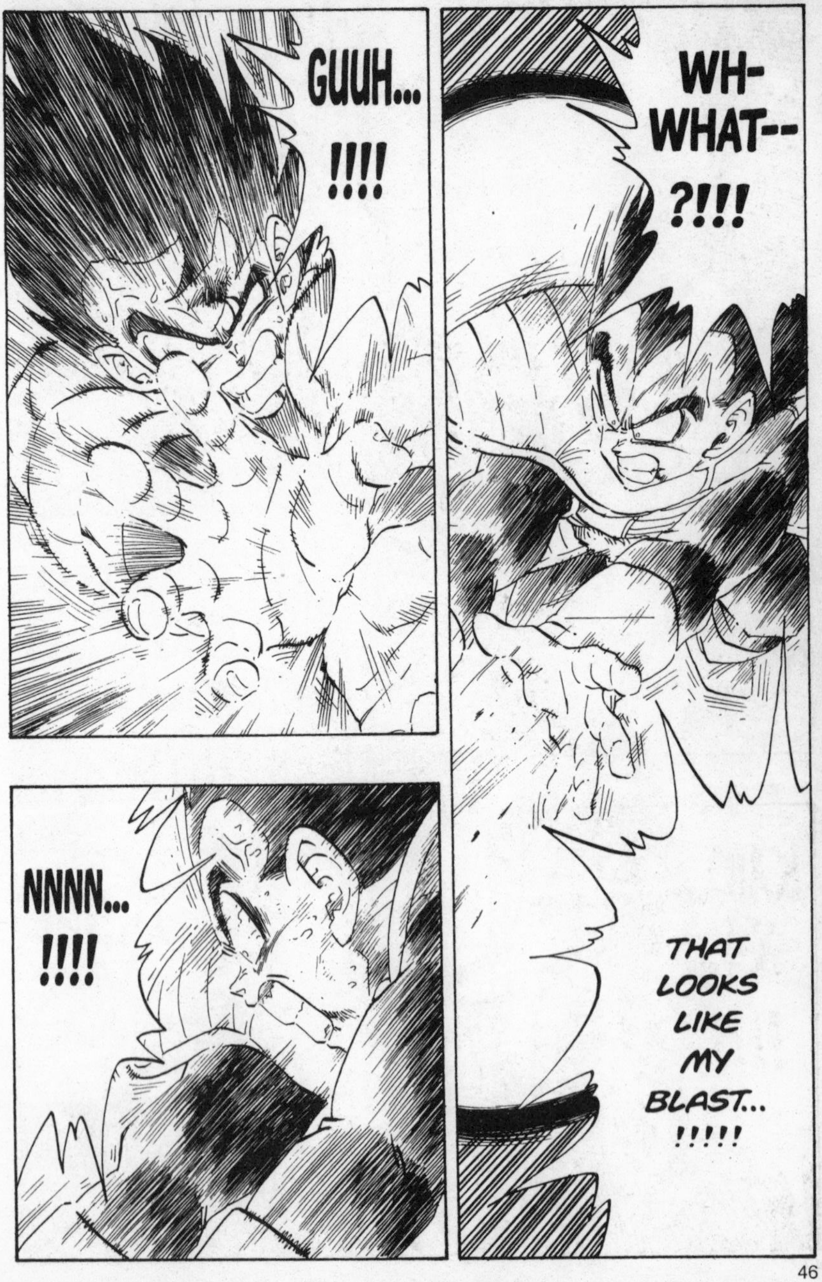
WH-WHAT--?!!!
THAT LOOKS LIKE MY BLAST...!!!!!
GUUH...!!!!
NNNN...!!!!

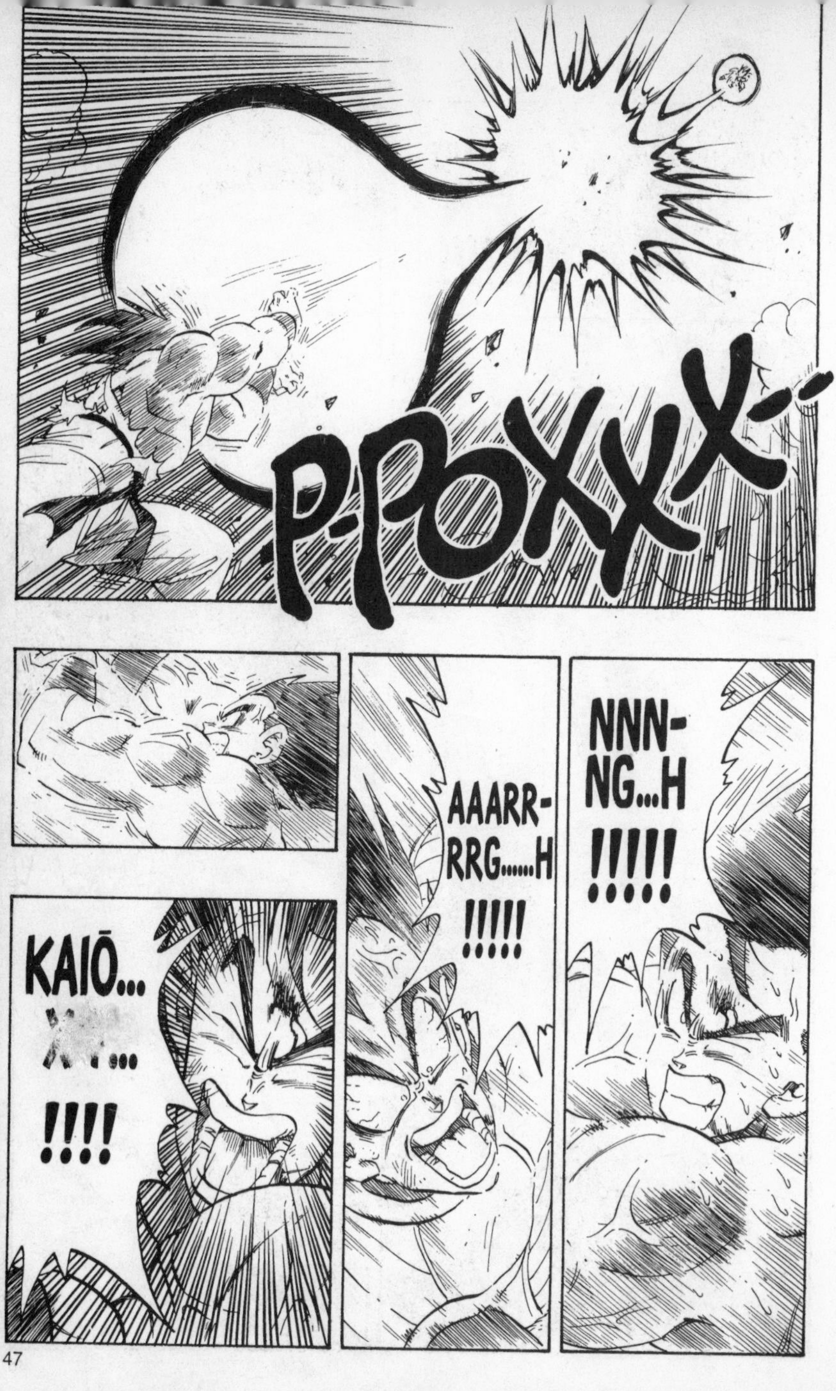
P-POXXX
NNN-NG...H !!!!!
AAARR-RRG......H !!!!!
KAIŌ...
!!!!

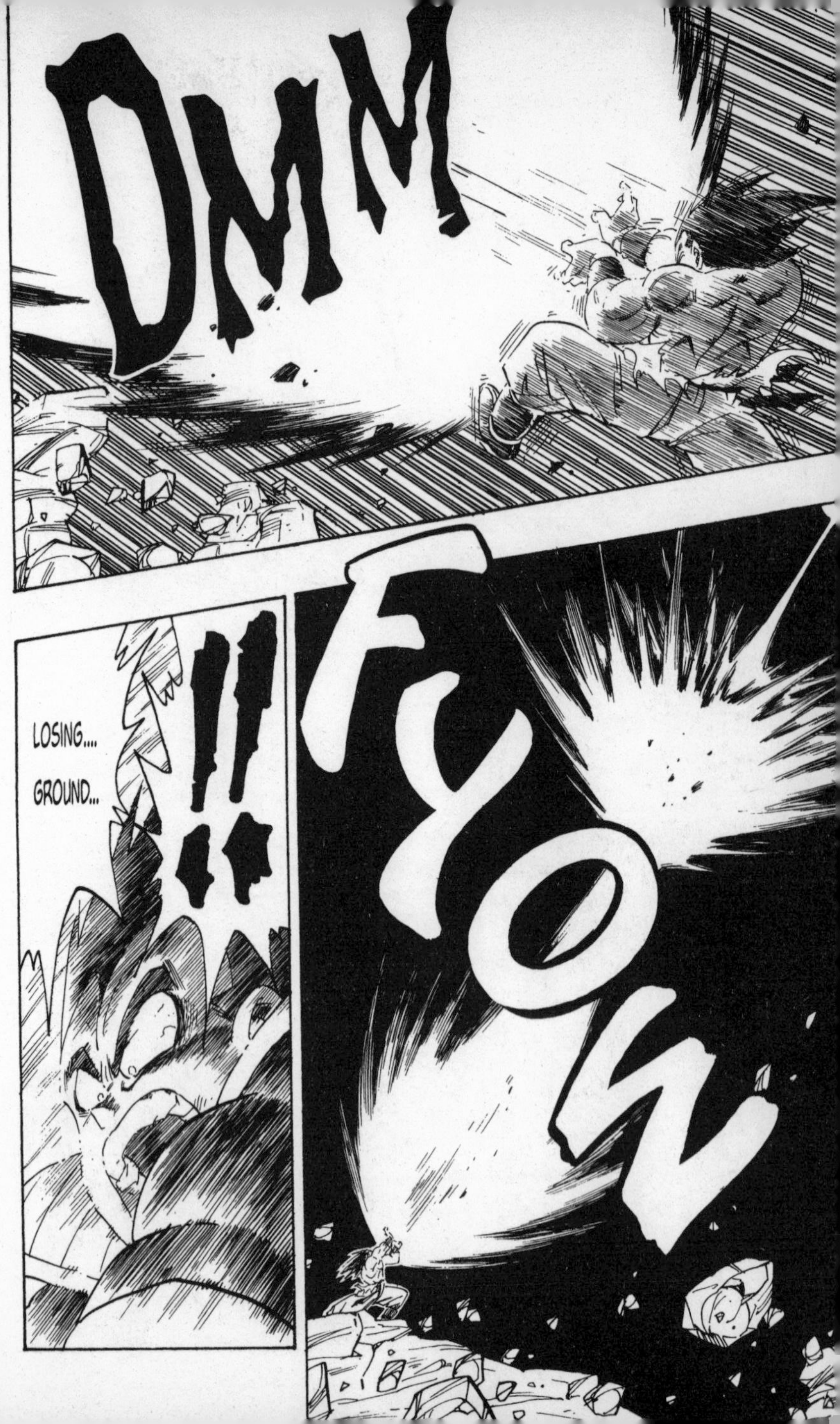
DMM
FZOW
!!
LOSING....
GROUND...

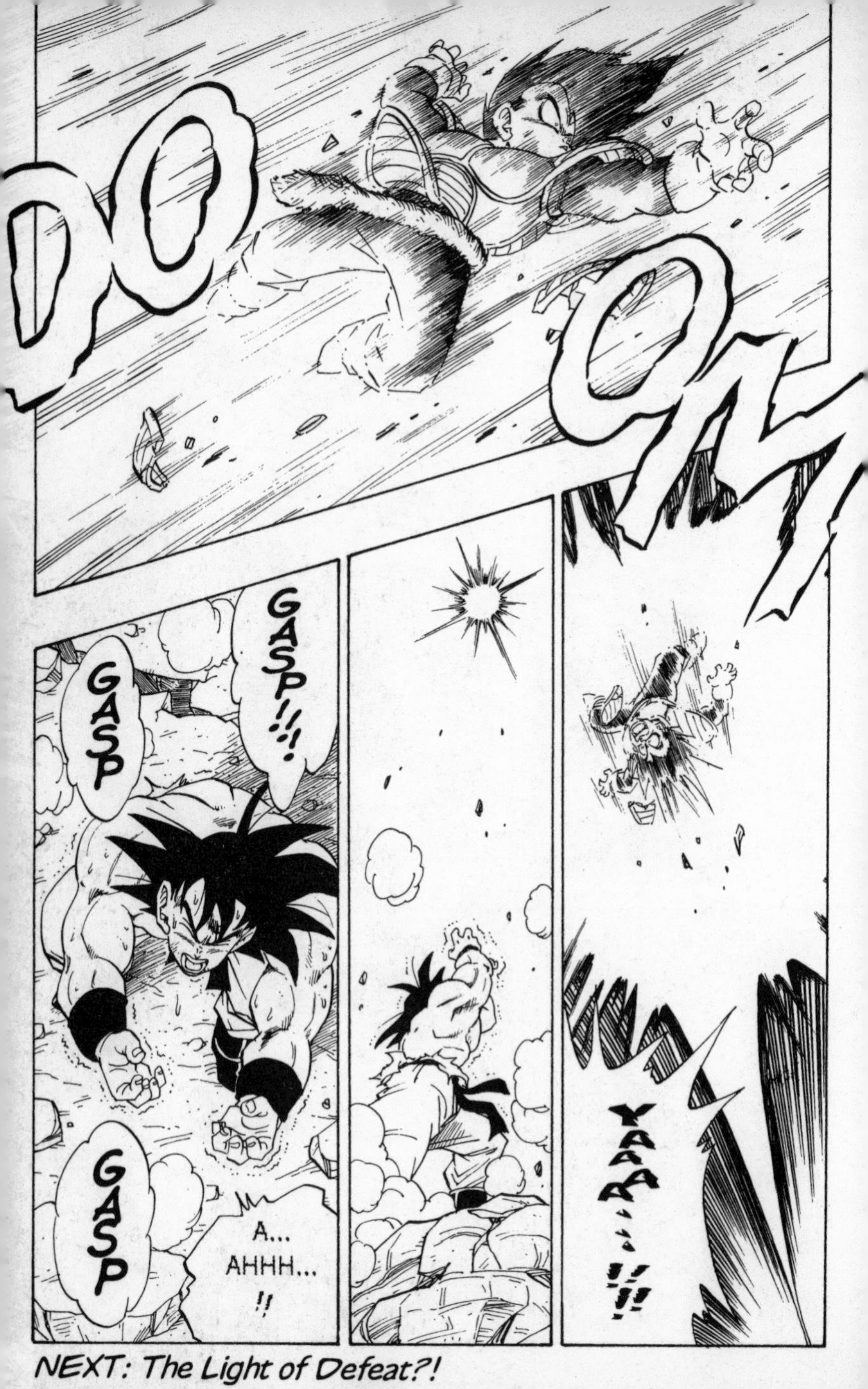
DOO
OM!
YAAA...!!
GASP!!!
GASP
A... AHHH...!!
GASP

NEXT: The Light of Defeat?!

DBZ:38 • The Moon

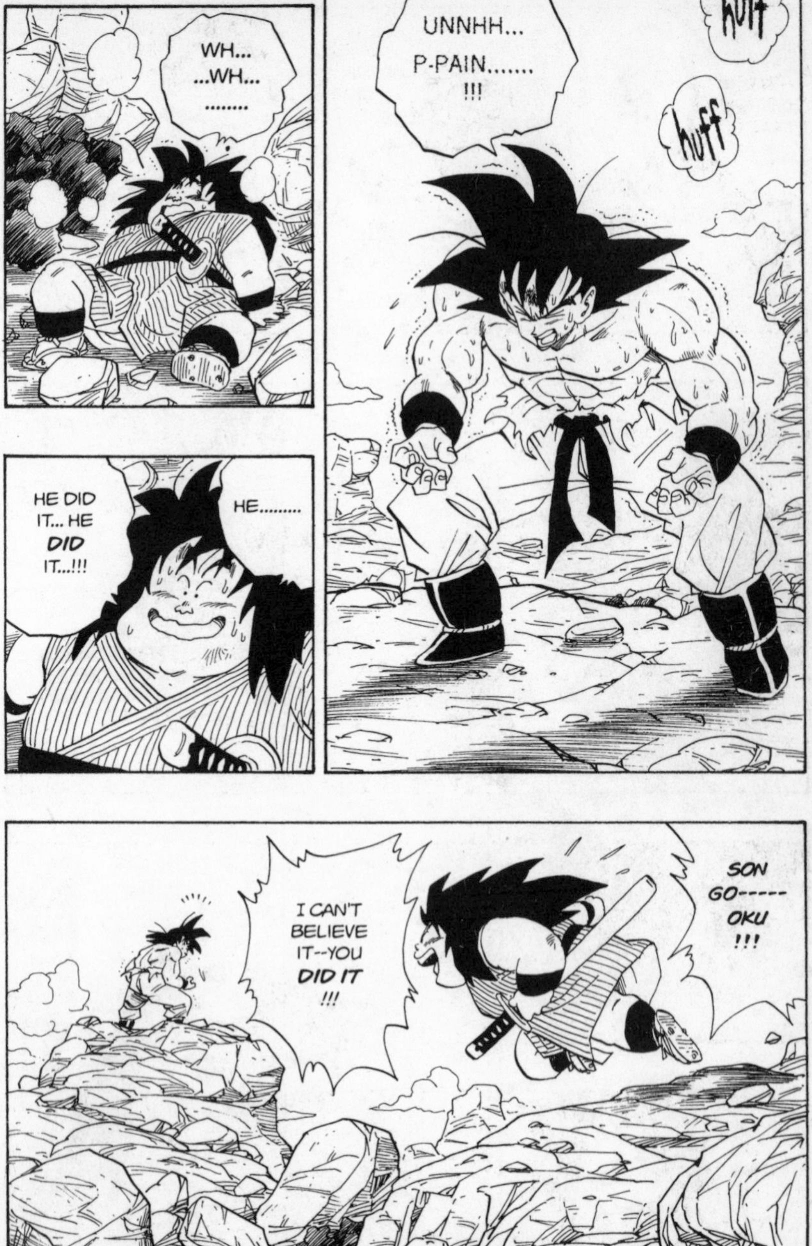
huff
huff
UNNHH... P-PAIN....... !!!
WH... ...WH... ....
HE.........
HE DID IT... HE *DID* IT...!!!
SON GO-----OKU !!!
I CAN'T BELIEVE IT--YOU *DID IT* !!!

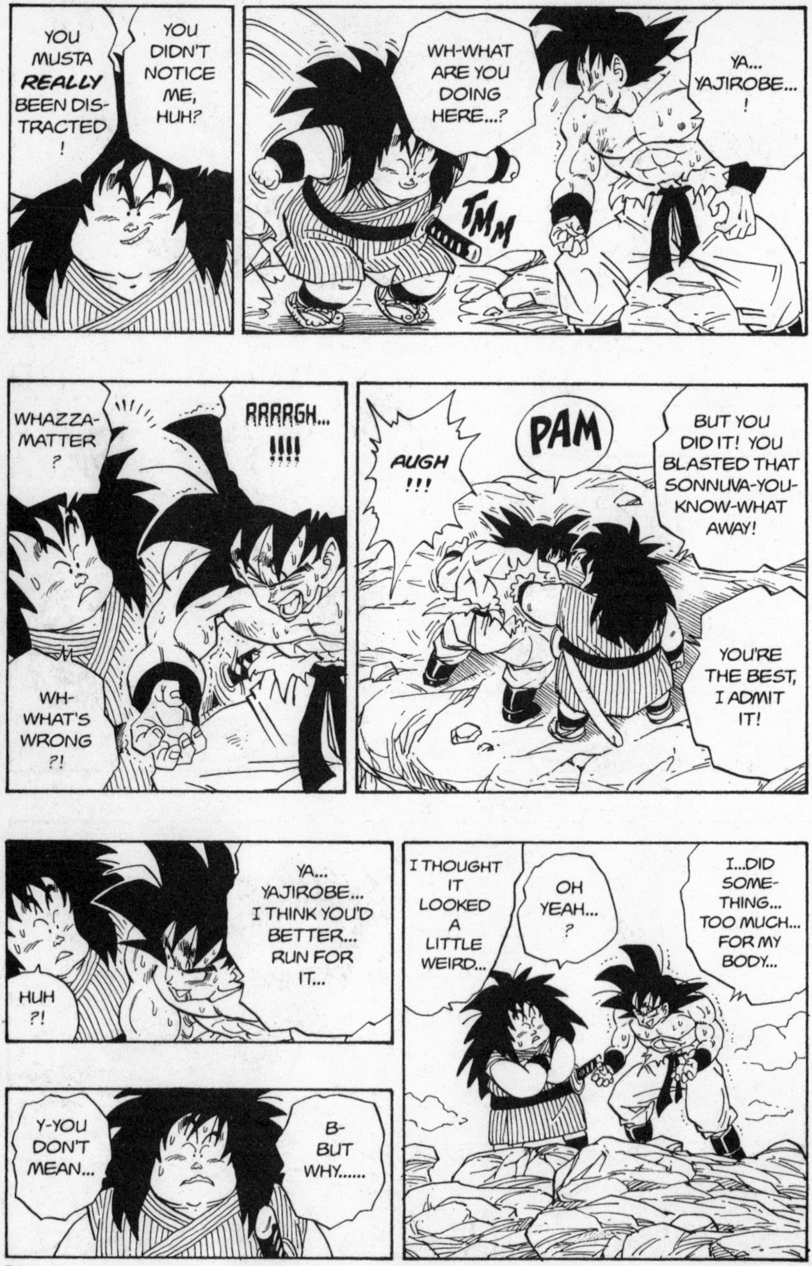
YA... YAJIROBE...!
WH-WHAT ARE YOU DOING HERE...?
TMM
YOU DIDN'T NOTICE ME, HUH?
YOU MUSTA **REALLY** BEEN DISTRACTED!
BUT YOU DID IT! YOU BLASTED THAT SONNUVA-YOU-KNOW-WHAT AWAY!
PAM
AUGH!!!
YOU'RE THE BEST, I ADMIT IT!
RRRRGH...!!!!
WHAZZA-MATTER?
WH-WHAT'S WRONG?!
I...DID SOMETHING... TOO MUCH... FOR MY BODY...
OH YEAH...?
I THOUGHT IT LOOKED A LITTLE WEIRD...
YA... YAJIROBE... I THINK YOU'D BETTER... RUN FOR IT...
HUH?!
B-BUT WHY......
Y-YOU DON'T MEAN...

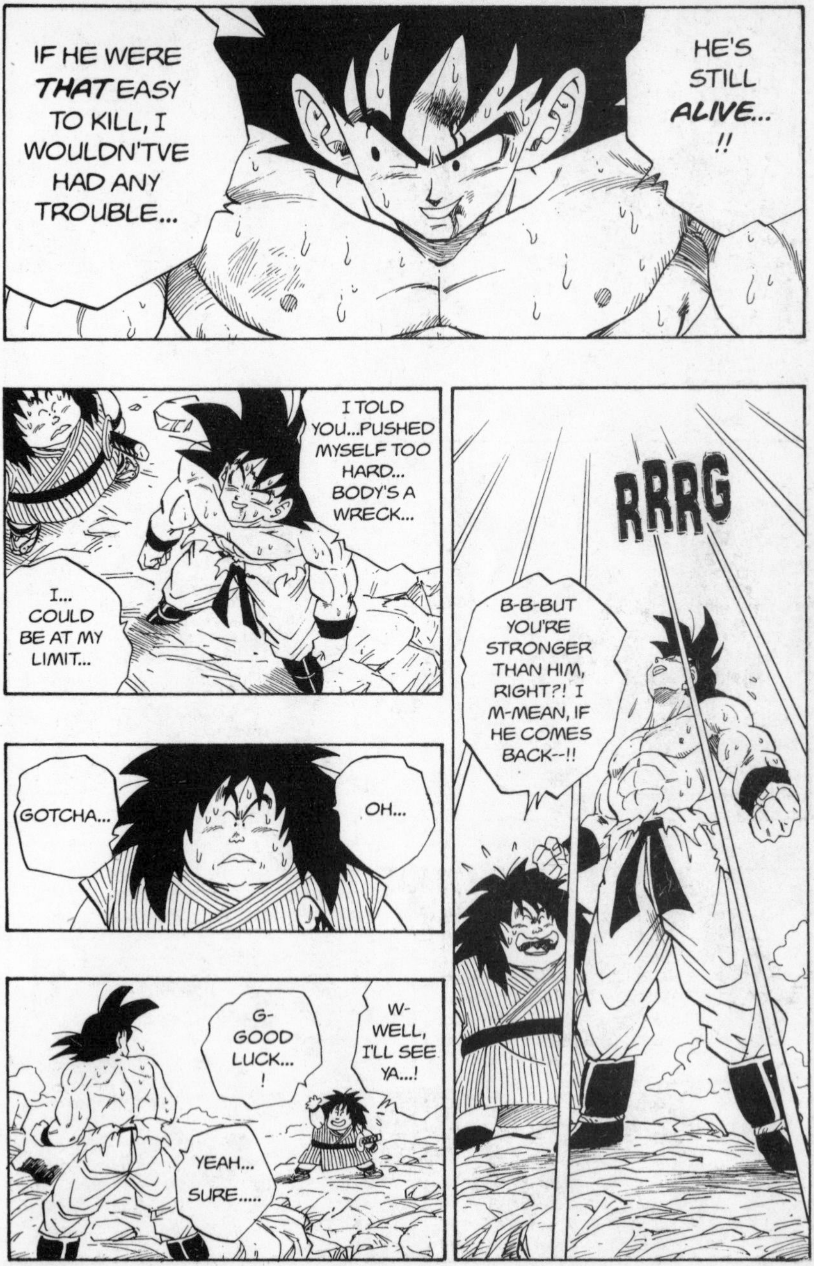
HE'S STILL ALIVE... !!
IF HE WERE THAT EASY TO KILL, I WOULDN'TVE HAD ANY TROUBLE...
RRRG
B-B-BUT YOU'RE STRONGER THAN HIM, RIGHT?! I M-MEAN, IF HE COMES BACK--!!
I TOLD YOU...PUSHED MYSELF TOO HARD... BODY'S A WRECK...
I... COULD BE AT MY LIMIT...
OH...
GOTCHA...
W-WELL, I'LL SEE YA...!
G-GOOD LUCK...!
YEAH... SURE.....

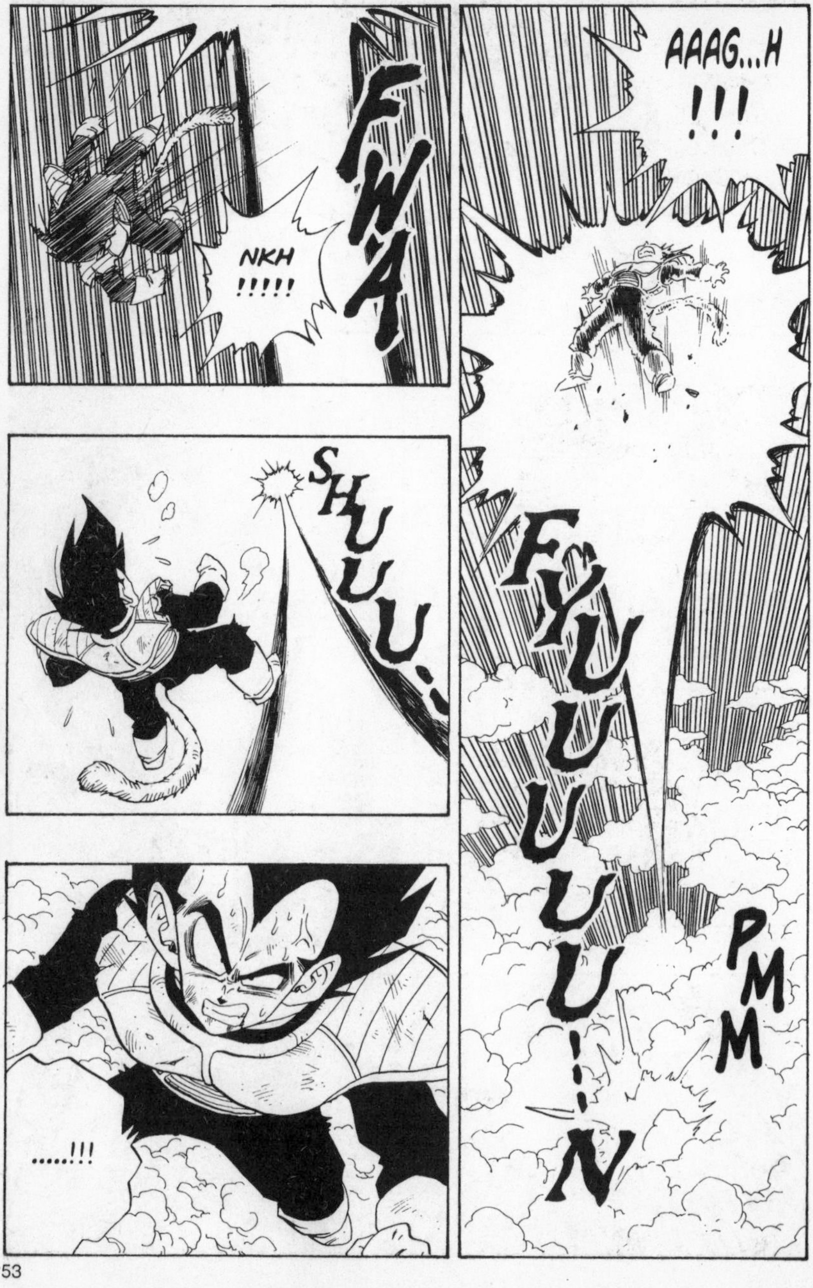

AAAG...H !!!
FYUUUUUU...N
PMM
FWA
NKH !!!!!
SHUUU...
.....!!!

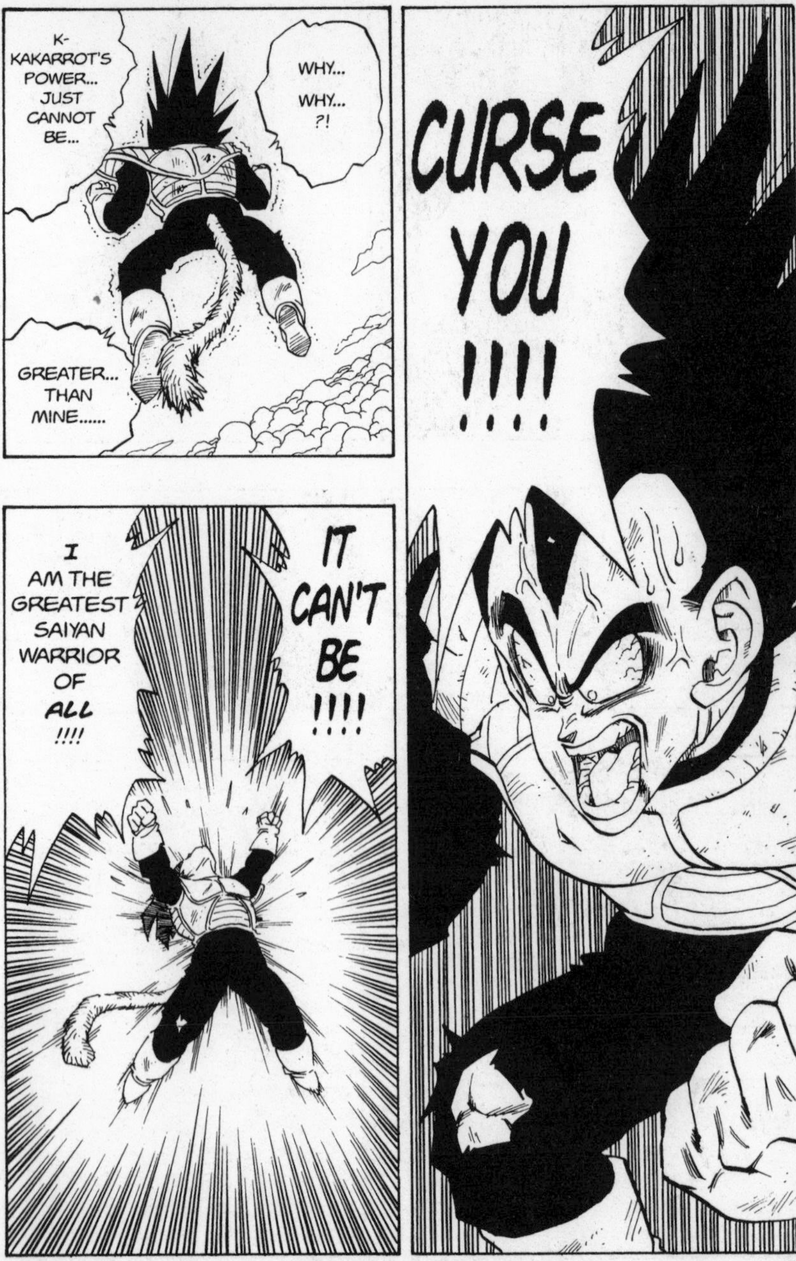
CURSE YOU !!!!
WHY... WHY... ?!
K-KAKARROT'S POWER... JUST CANNOT BE...
GREATER... THAN MINE......
IT CAN'T BE !!!!
I AM THE GREATEST SAIYAN WARRIOR OF ALL !!!!

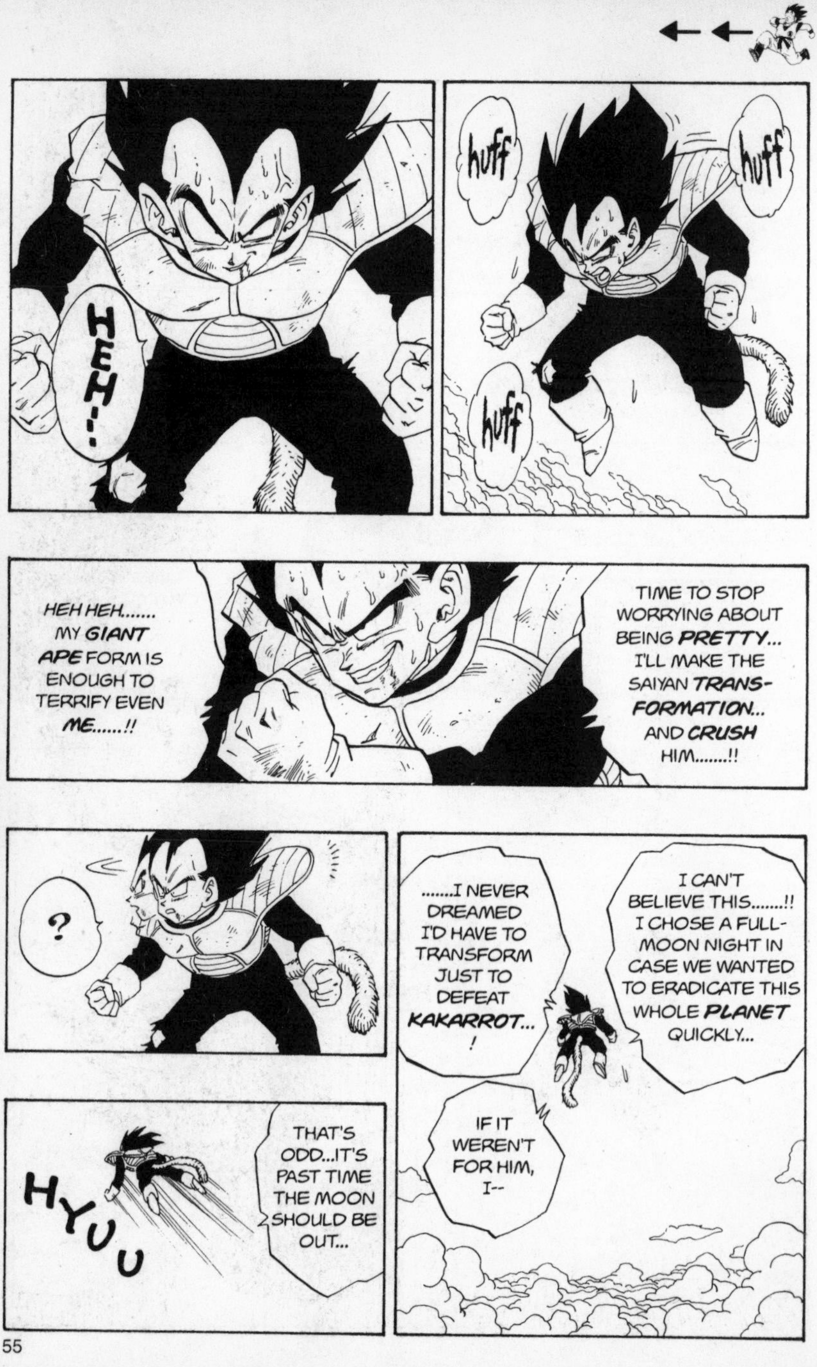
huff
huff
huff
HEH!!
TIME TO STOP WORRYING ABOUT BEING PRETTY... I'LL MAKE THE SAIYAN TRANS-FORMATION... AND CRUSH HIM.......!!
HEH HEH...... MY GIANT APE FORM IS ENOUGH TO TERRIFY EVEN ME......!!
I CAN'T BELIEVE THIS.......!! I CHOSE A FULL-MOON NIGHT IN CASE WE WANTED TO ERADICATE THIS WHOLE PLANET QUICKLY...
.......I NEVER DREAMED I'D HAVE TO TRANSFORM JUST TO DEFEAT KAKARROT... !
IF IT WEREN'T FOR HIM, I--
?
THAT'S ODD...IT'S PAST TIME THE MOON SHOULD BE OUT...
HYUU

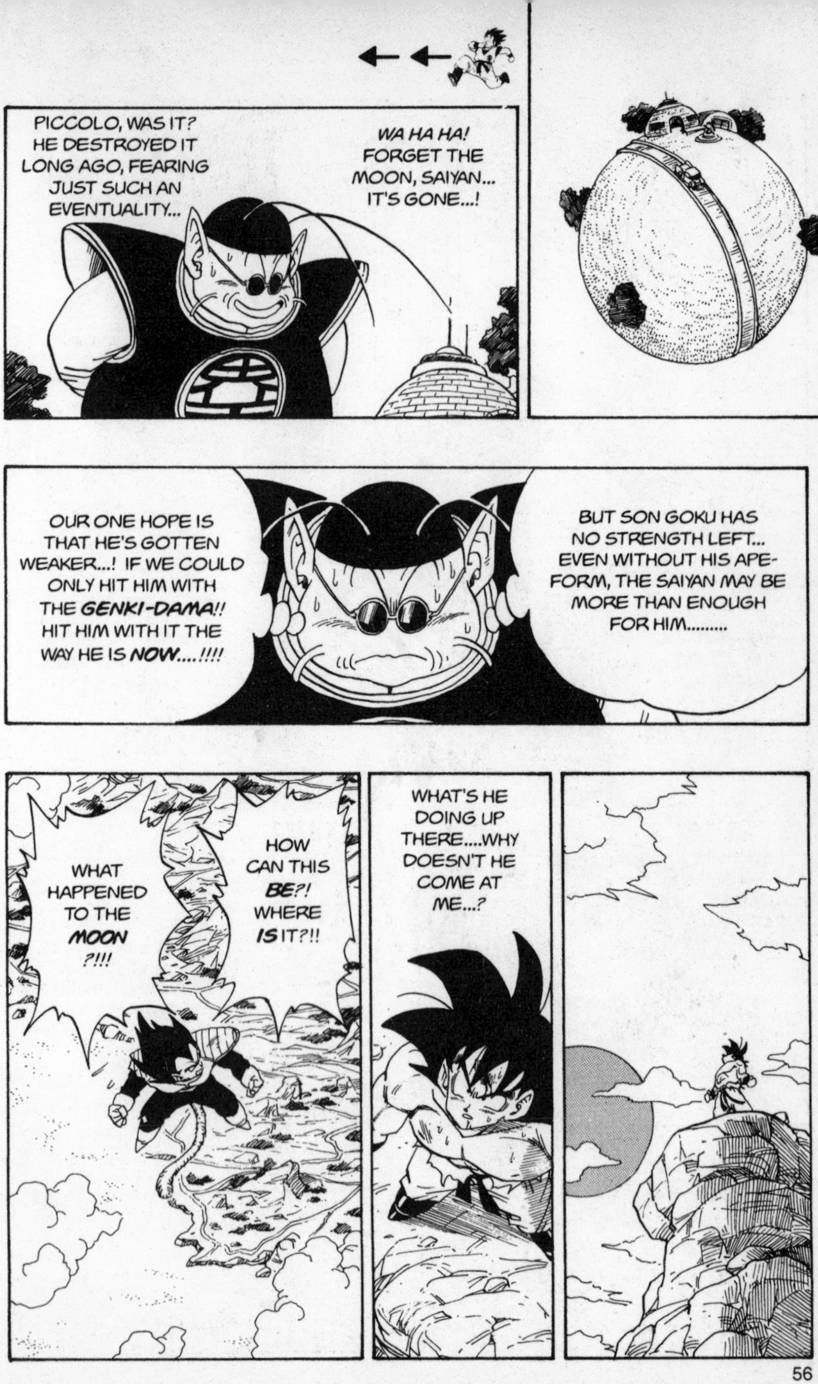

WA HA HA! FORGET THE MOON, SAIYAN... IT'S GONE...!
PICCOLO, WAS IT? HE DESTROYED IT LONG AGO, FEARING JUST SUCH AN EVENTUALITY...
BUT SON GOKU HAS NO STRENGTH LEFT... EVEN WITHOUT HIS APE-FORM, THE SAIYAN MAY BE MORE THAN ENOUGH FOR HIM.........
OUR ONE HOPE IS THAT HE'S GOTTEN WEAKER...! IF WE COULD ONLY HIT HIM WITH THE GENKI-DAMA!! HIT HIM WITH IT THE WAY HE IS NOW....!!!!
WHAT'S HE DOING UP THERE....WHY DOESN'T HE COME AT ME...?
HOW CAN THIS BE?! WHERE IS IT?!!
WHAT HAPPENED TO THE MOON ?!!!

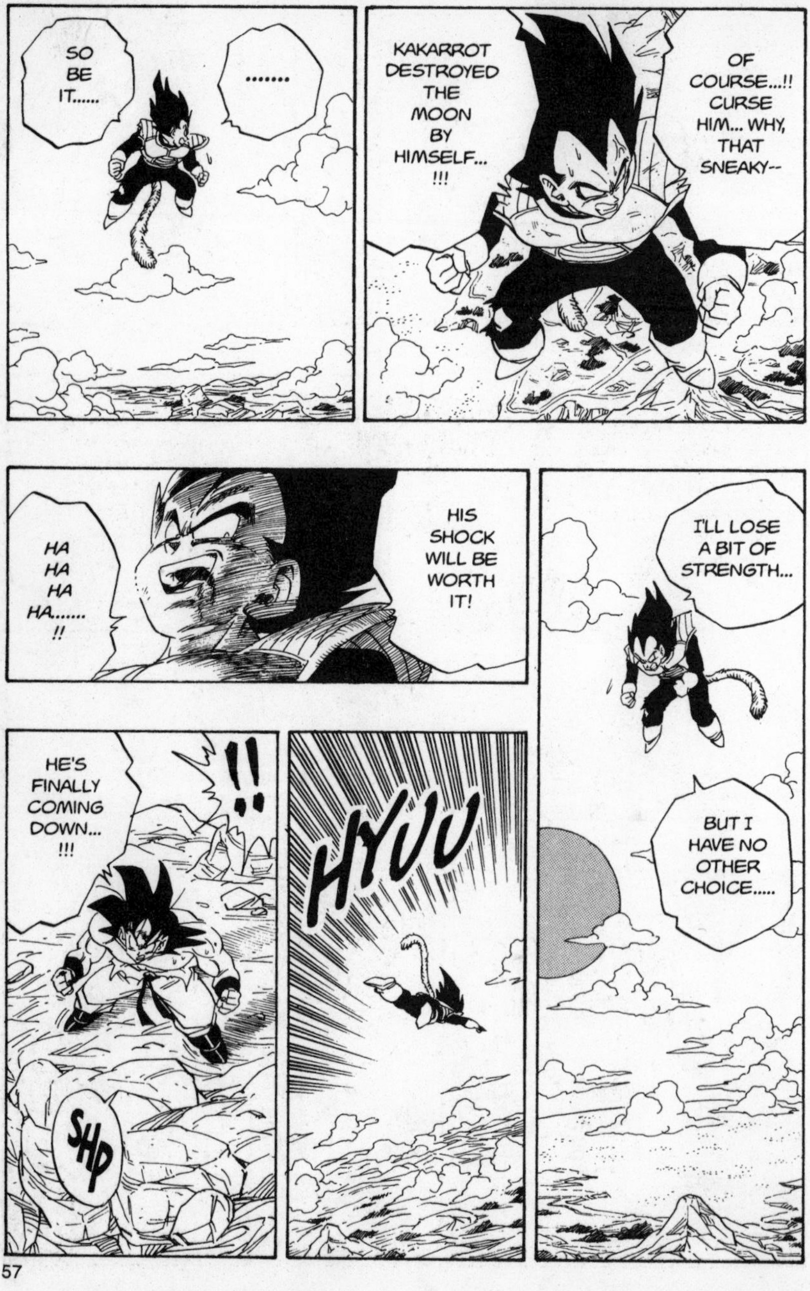
KAKARROT DESTROYED THE MOON BY HIMSELF... !!!
OF COURSE...!! CURSE HIM... WHY, THAT SNEAKY--
....
SO BE IT......
I'LL LOSE A BIT OF STRENGTH...
BUT I HAVE NO OTHER CHOICE.....
HIS SHOCK WILL BE WORTH IT!
HA HA HA HA...... !!
HYUU
!!
HE'S FINALLY COMING DOWN... !!!
SHP

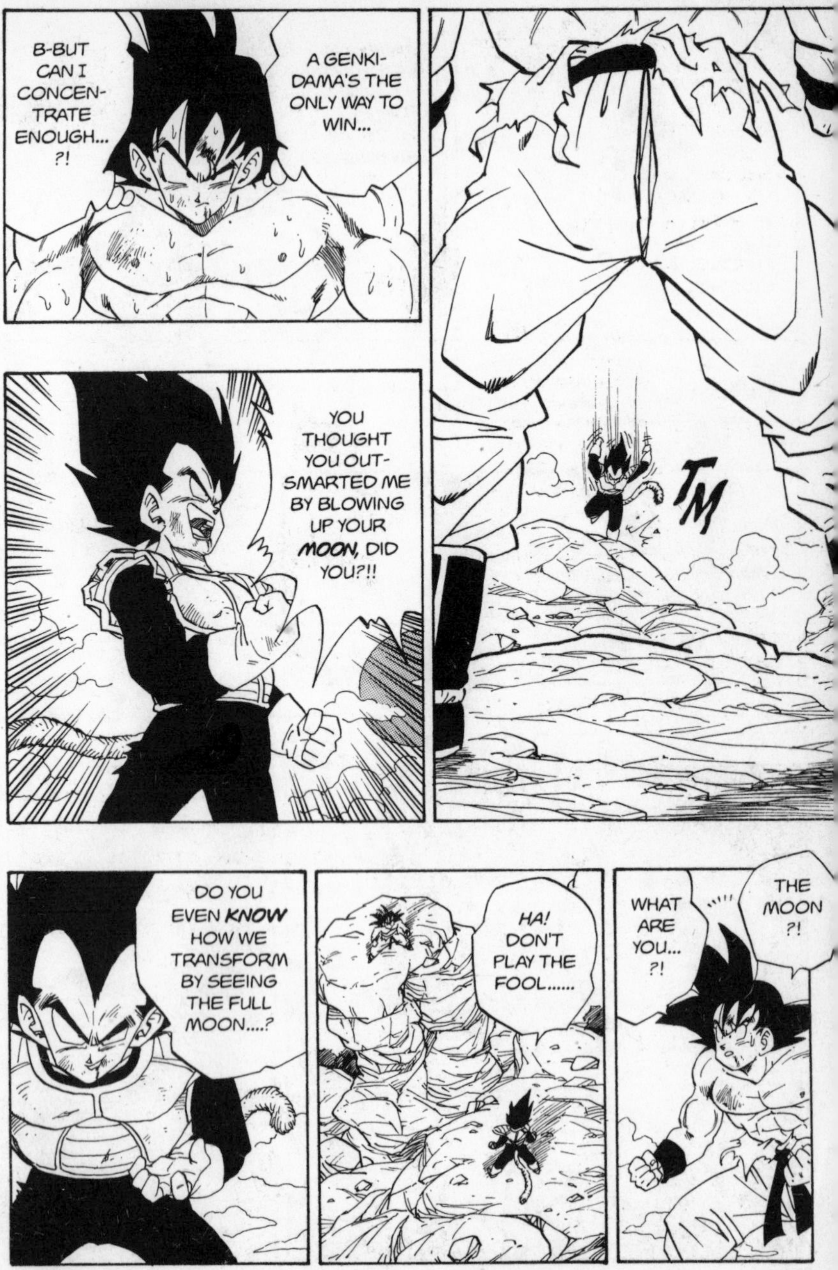
TM
A GENKI-DAMA'S THE ONLY WAY TO WIN...
B-BUT CAN I CONCENTRATE ENOUGH...?!
YOU THOUGHT YOU OUTSMARTED ME BY BLOWING UP YOUR MOON, DID YOU?!!
THE MOON?!
WHAT ARE YOU...?!
HA! DON'T PLAY THE FOOL......
DO YOU EVEN KNOW HOW WE TRANSFORM BY SEEING THE FULL MOON....?

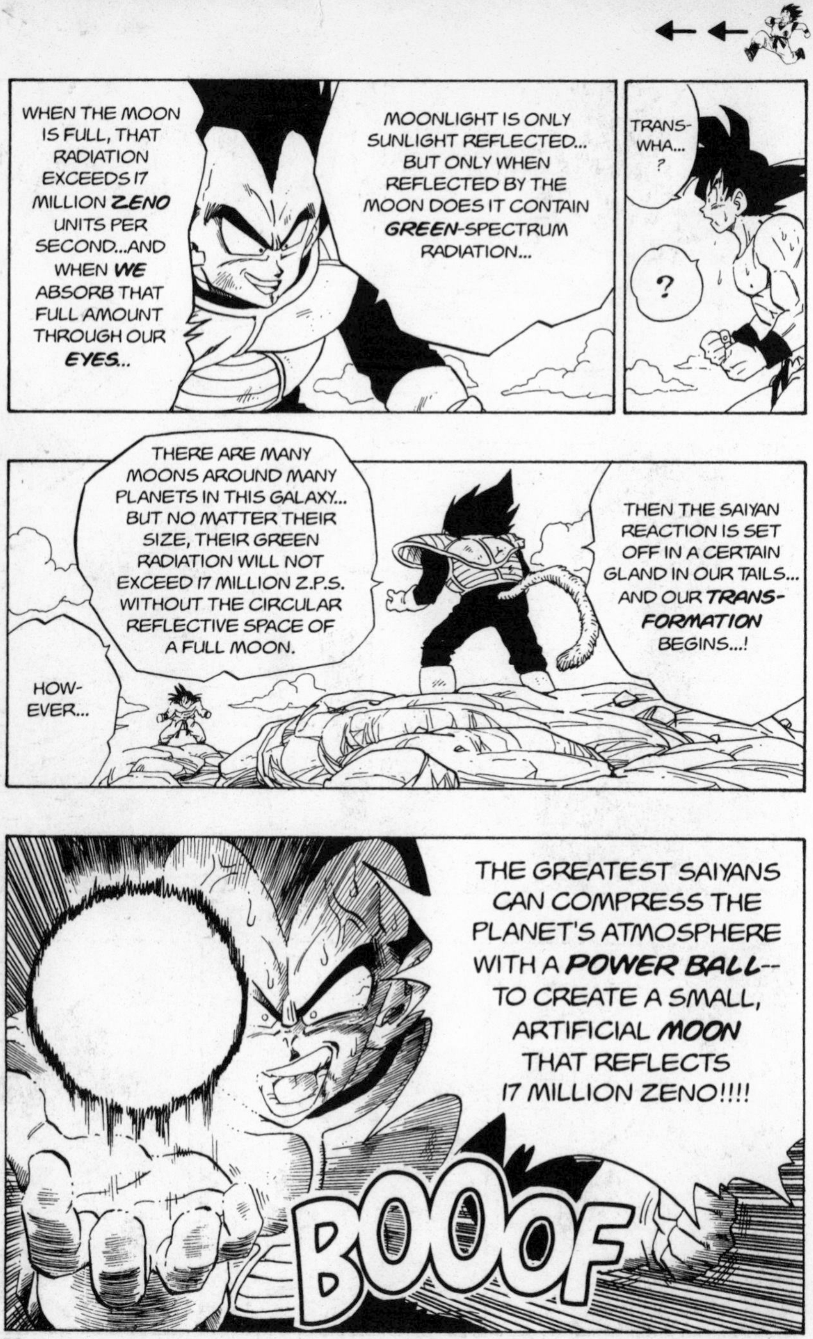
TRANS-WHA... ?
?
MOONLIGHT IS ONLY SUNLIGHT REFLECTED... BUT ONLY WHEN REFLECTED BY THE MOON DOES IT CONTAIN GREEN-SPECTRUM RADIATION...
WHEN THE MOON IS FULL, THAT RADIATION EXCEEDS 17 MILLION ZENO UNITS PER SECOND...AND WHEN WE ABSORB THAT FULL AMOUNT THROUGH OUR EYES...
THEN THE SAIYAN REACTION IS SET OFF IN A CERTAIN GLAND IN OUR TAILS... AND OUR TRANSFORMATION BEGINS...!
THERE ARE MANY MOONS AROUND MANY PLANETS IN THIS GALAXY... BUT NO MATTER THEIR SIZE, THEIR GREEN RADIATION WILL NOT EXCEED 17 MILLION Z.P.S. WITHOUT THE CIRCULAR REFLECTIVE SPACE OF A FULL MOON.
HOW-EVER...
THE GREATEST SAIYANS CAN COMPRESS THE PLANET'S ATMOSPHERE WITH A POWER BALL-- TO CREATE A SMALL, ARTIFICIAL MOON THAT REFLECTS 17 MILLION ZENO!!!!
BOOOF

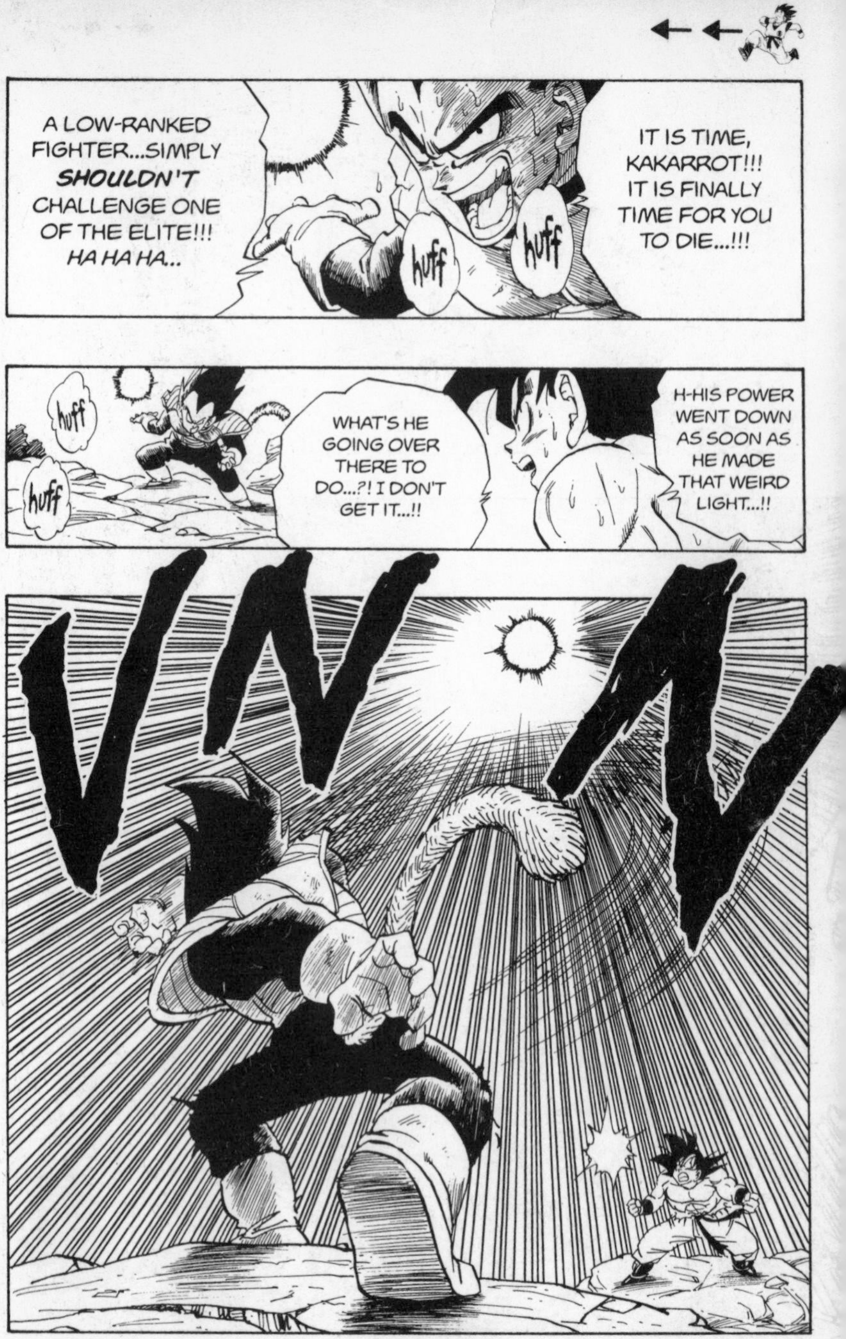
IT IS TIME, KAKARROT!!! IT IS FINALLY TIME FOR YOU TO DIE...!!!
huff
huff
A LOW-RANKED FIGHTER...SIMPLY **SHOULDN'T** CHALLENGE ONE OF THE ELITE!!! *HA HA HA...*
H-HIS POWER WENT DOWN AS SOON AS HE MADE THAT WEIRD LIGHT...!!
WHAT'S HE GOING OVER THERE TO DO...?! I DON'T GET IT...!!
huff
huff
VNN

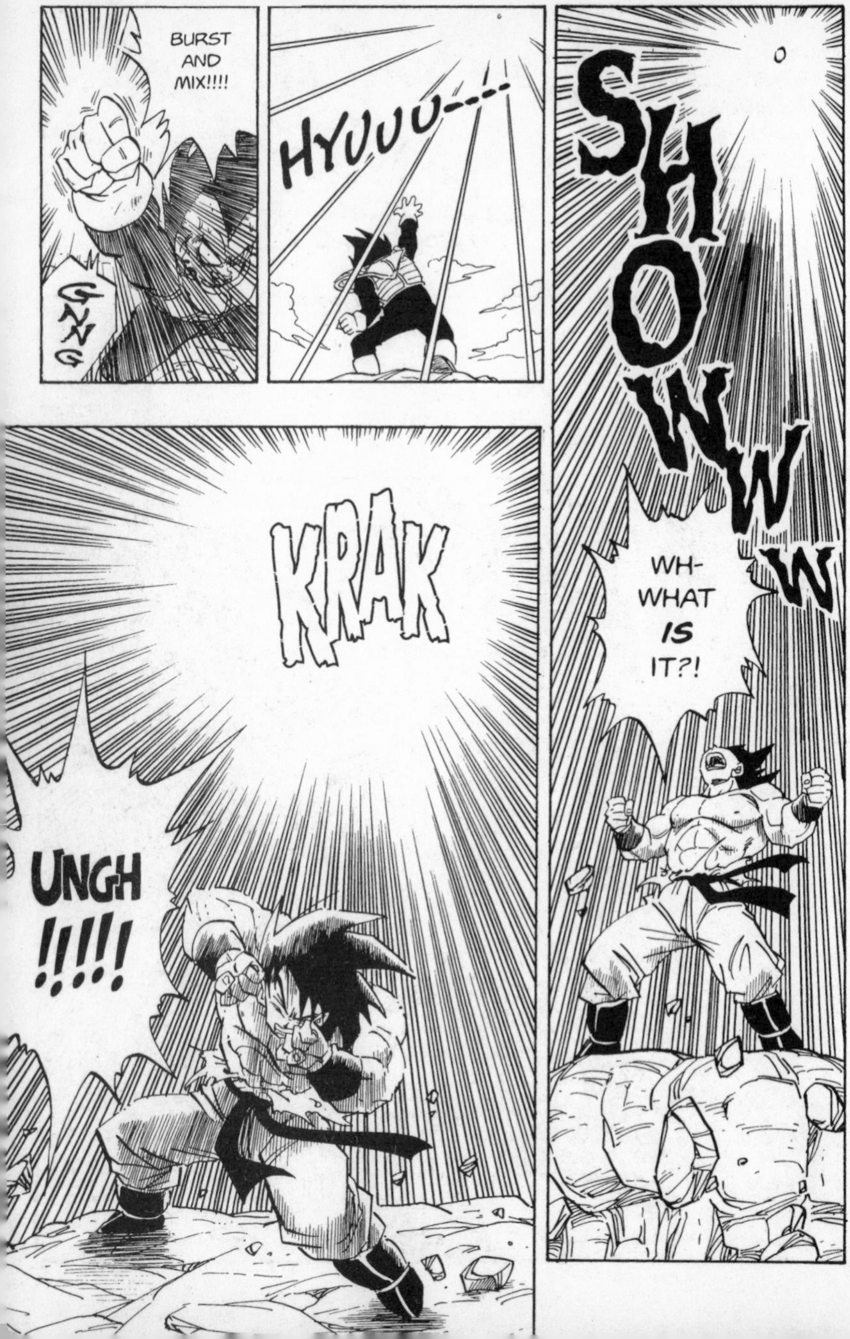
SHOWWW
WH- WHAT IS IT?!
HYUUU---!
BURST AND MIX!!!!
GNNG
KRAK
UNGH !!!!!

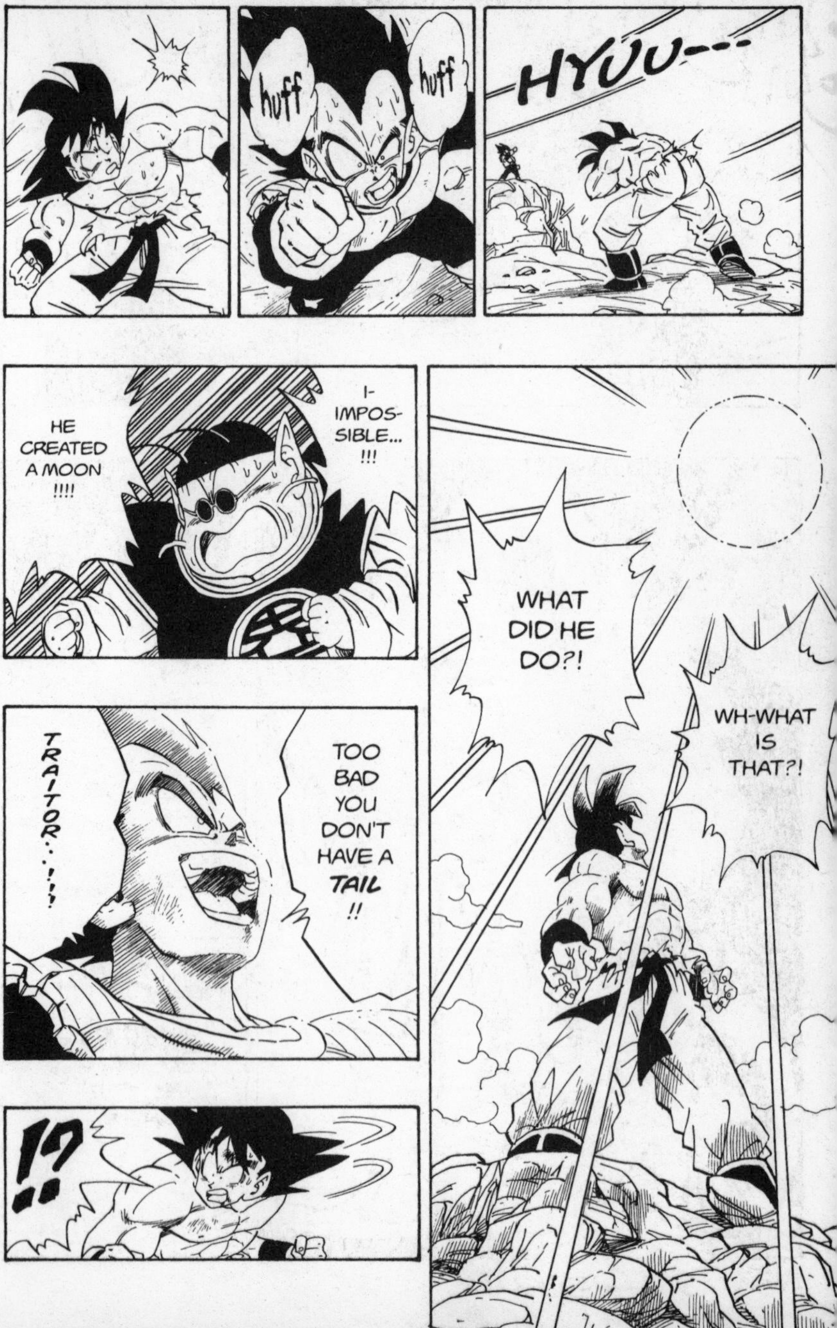
HYUU---
huff
huff
WHAT DID HE DO?!
WH-WHAT IS THAT?!
I- IMPOSSIBLE... !!!
HE CREATED A MOON !!!!
TOO BAD YOU DON'T HAVE A TAIL !!
TRAITOR...!!
!?

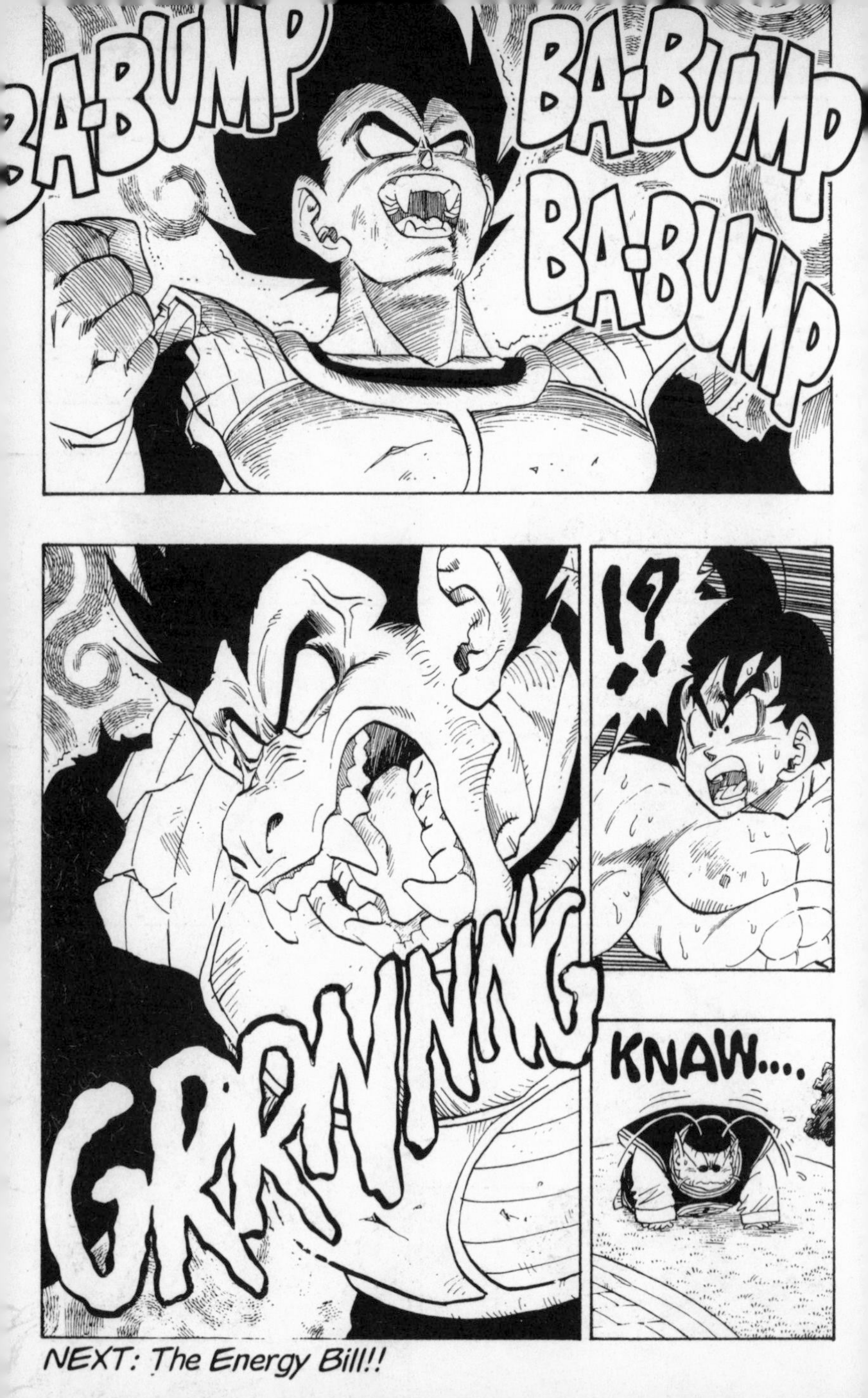
BA-BUMP
BA-BUMP
BA-BUMP
!?
KNAW....
GRAWNNG

NEXT: The Energy Bill!!

DBZ:39 • The Energy Sphere

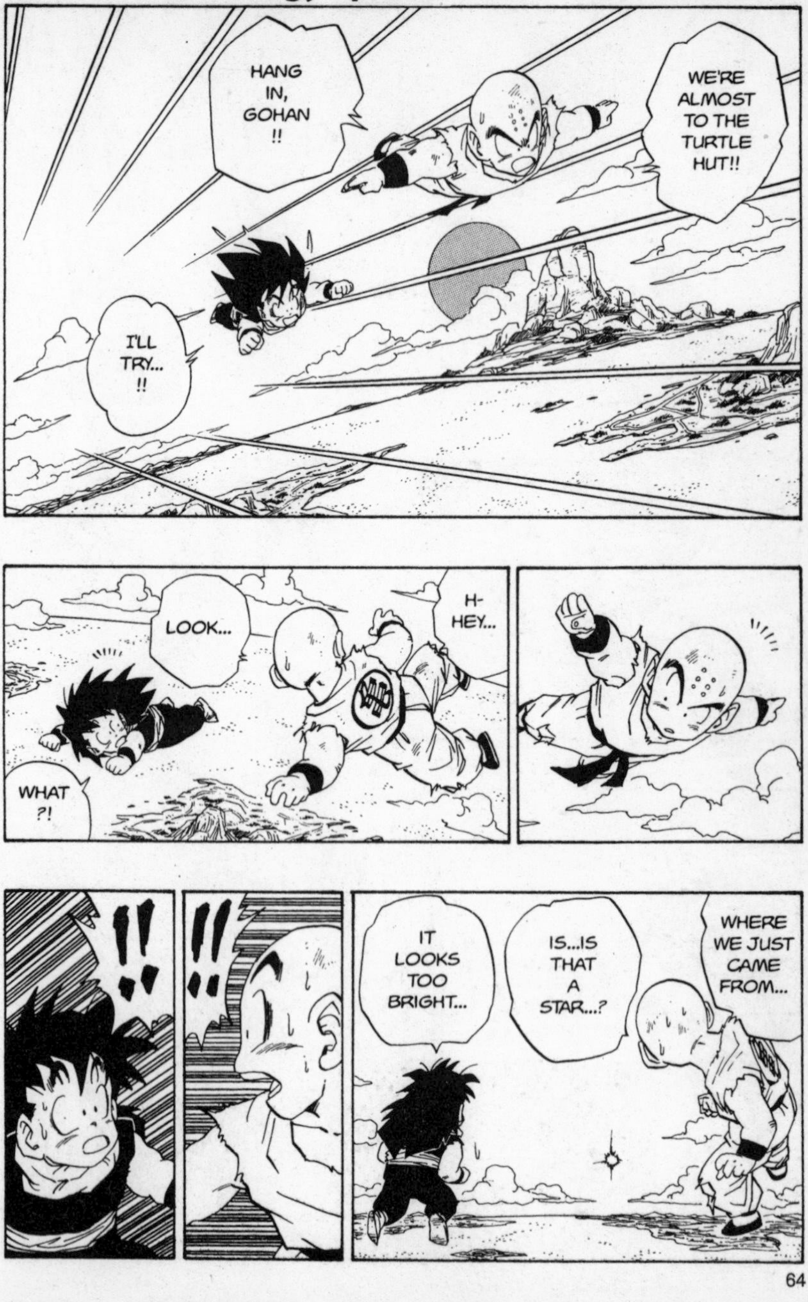
WE'RE ALMOST TO THE TURTLE HUT!!
HANG IN, GOHAN !!
I'LL TRY... !!
H- HEY...
LOOK...
WHAT ?!
WHERE WE JUST CAME FROM...
IS...IS THAT A STAR...?
IT LOOKS TOO BRIGHT...
!!
!!

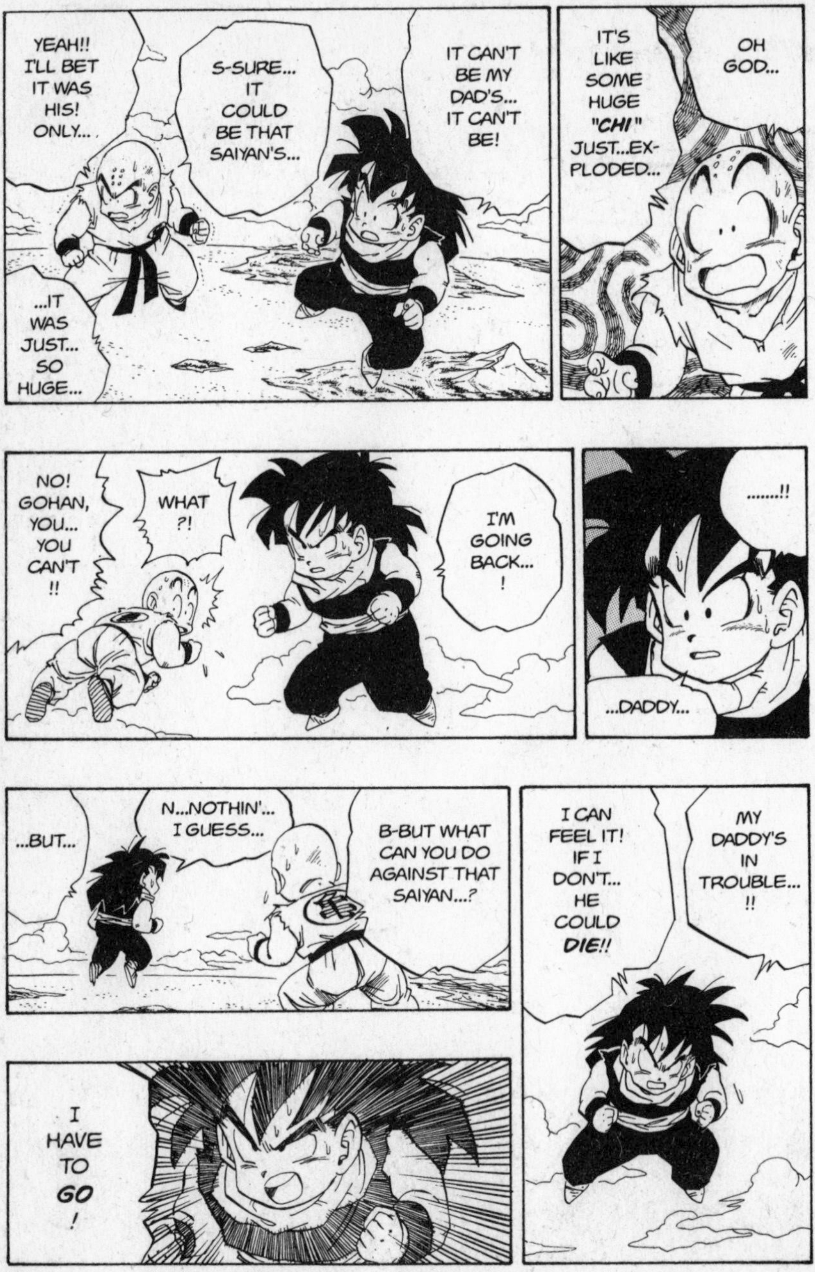
OH GOD...
IT'S LIKE SOME HUGE "CHI" JUST...EXPLODED...
IT CAN'T BE MY DAD'S... IT CAN'T BE!
S-SURE... IT COULD BE THAT SAIYAN'S...
YEAH!! I'LL BET IT WAS HIS! ONLY...
...IT WAS JUST... SO HUGE...
......!!
...DADDY...
I'M GOING BACK...!
WHAT?!
NO! GOHAN, YOU... YOU CAN'T!!
MY DADDY'S IN TROUBLE...!!
I CAN FEEL IT! IF I DON'T... HE COULD DIE!!
B-BUT WHAT CAN YOU DO AGAINST THAT SAIYAN...?
N...NOTHIN'... I GUESS...
...BUT...
I HAVE TO GO!

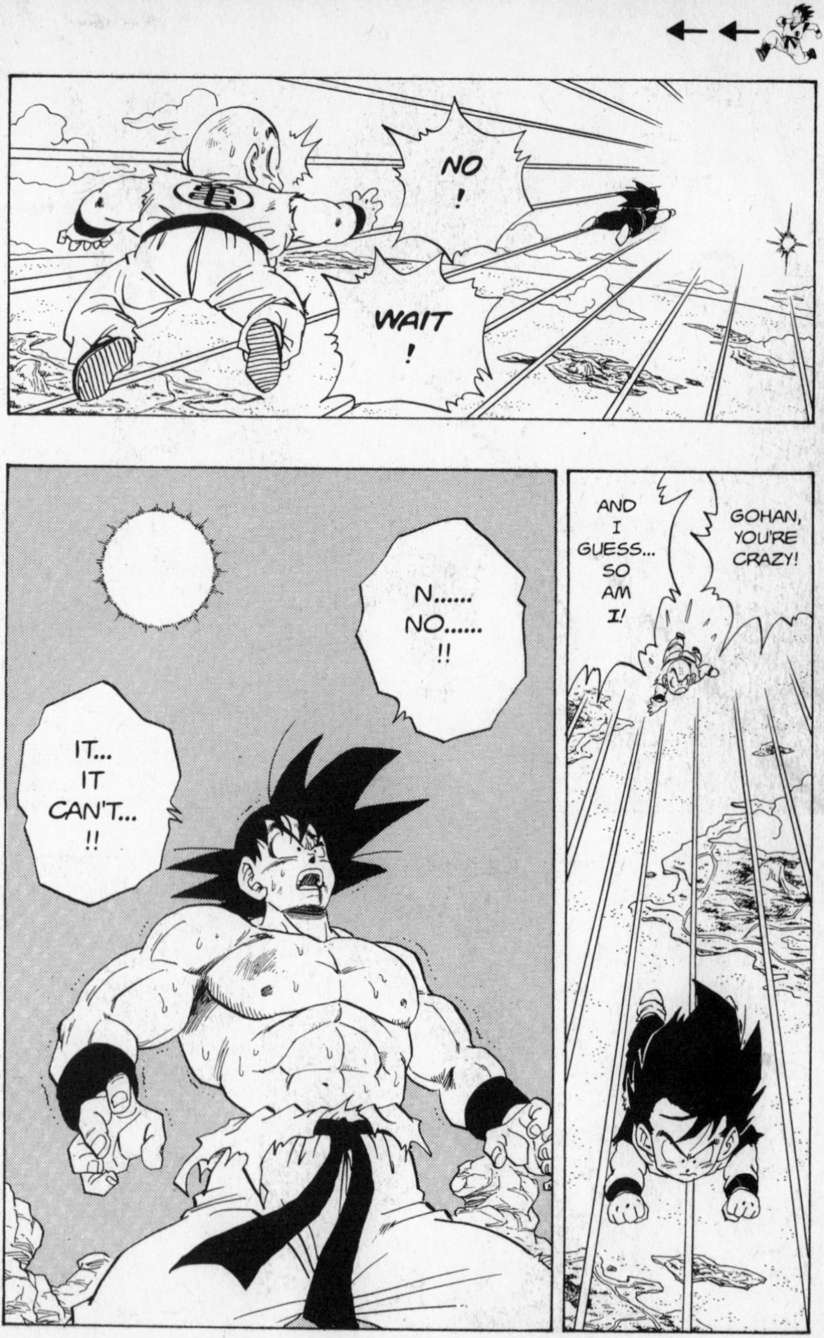
NO!
WAIT!
GOHAN, YOU'RE CRAZY!
AND I GUESS... SO AM I!
N...... NO...... !!
IT... IT CAN'T... !!

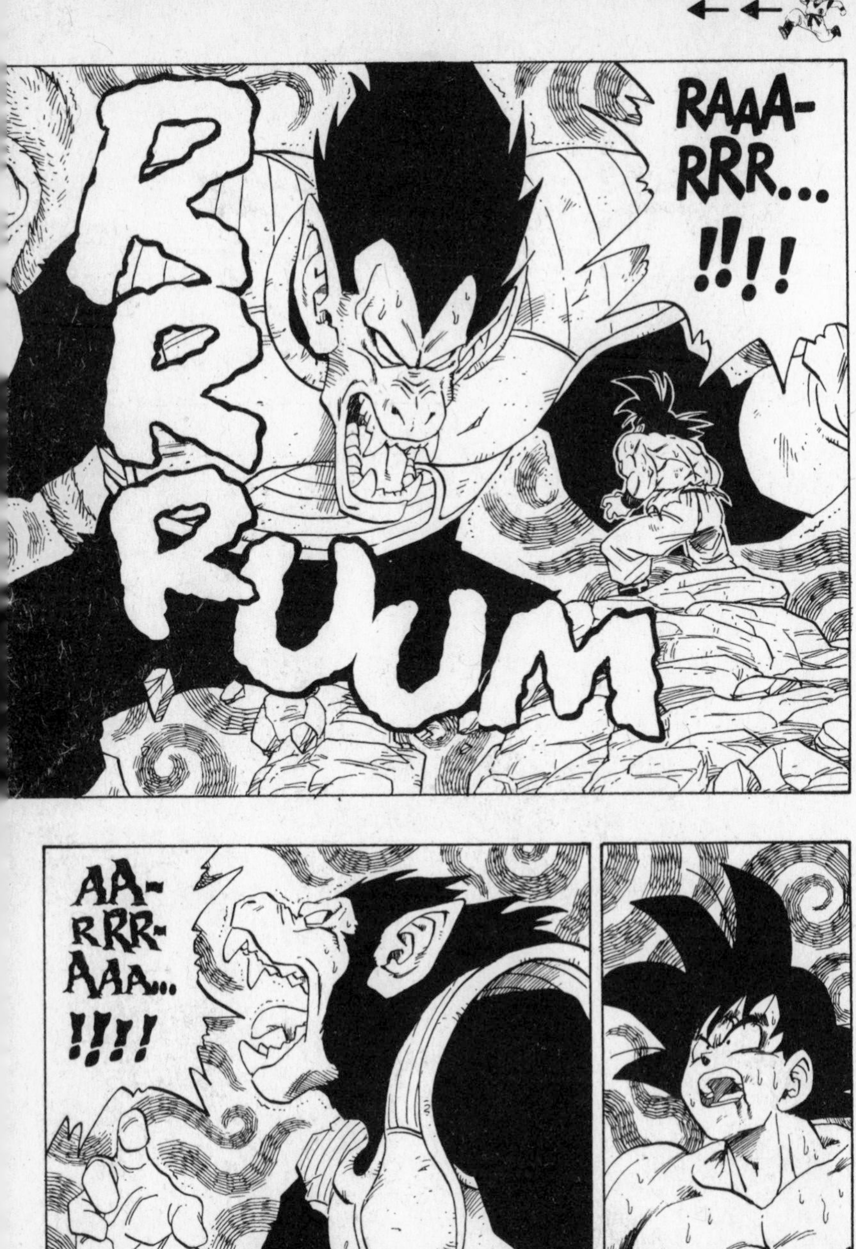

RAAA-
RRR...
!!!!
RRRUUM
AA-
RRR-
AAA...
!!!!

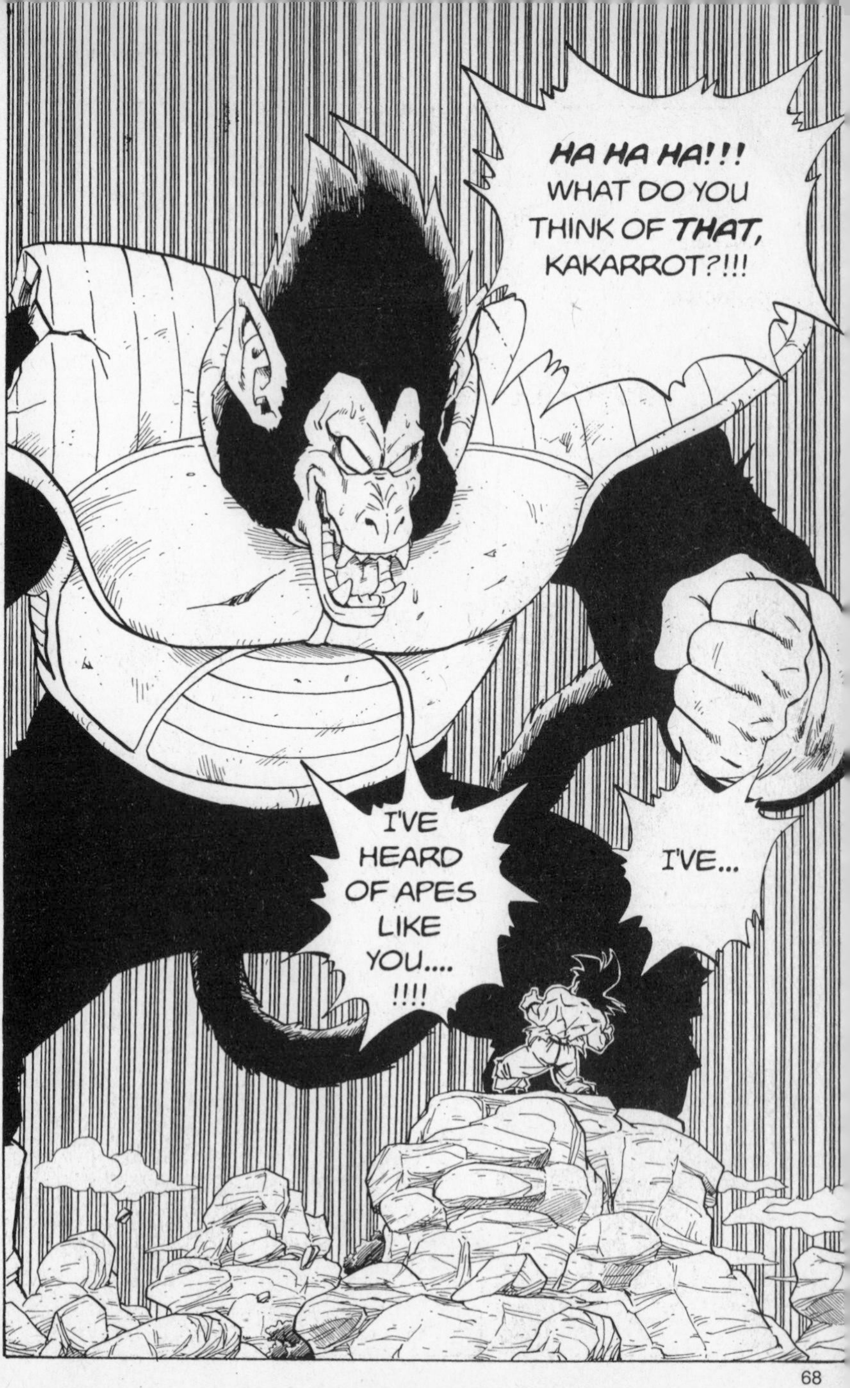
HA HA HA!!! WHAT DO YOU THINK OF **THAT,** KAKARROT?!!!
I'VE...
I'VE HEARD OF APES LIKE YOU.... !!!!

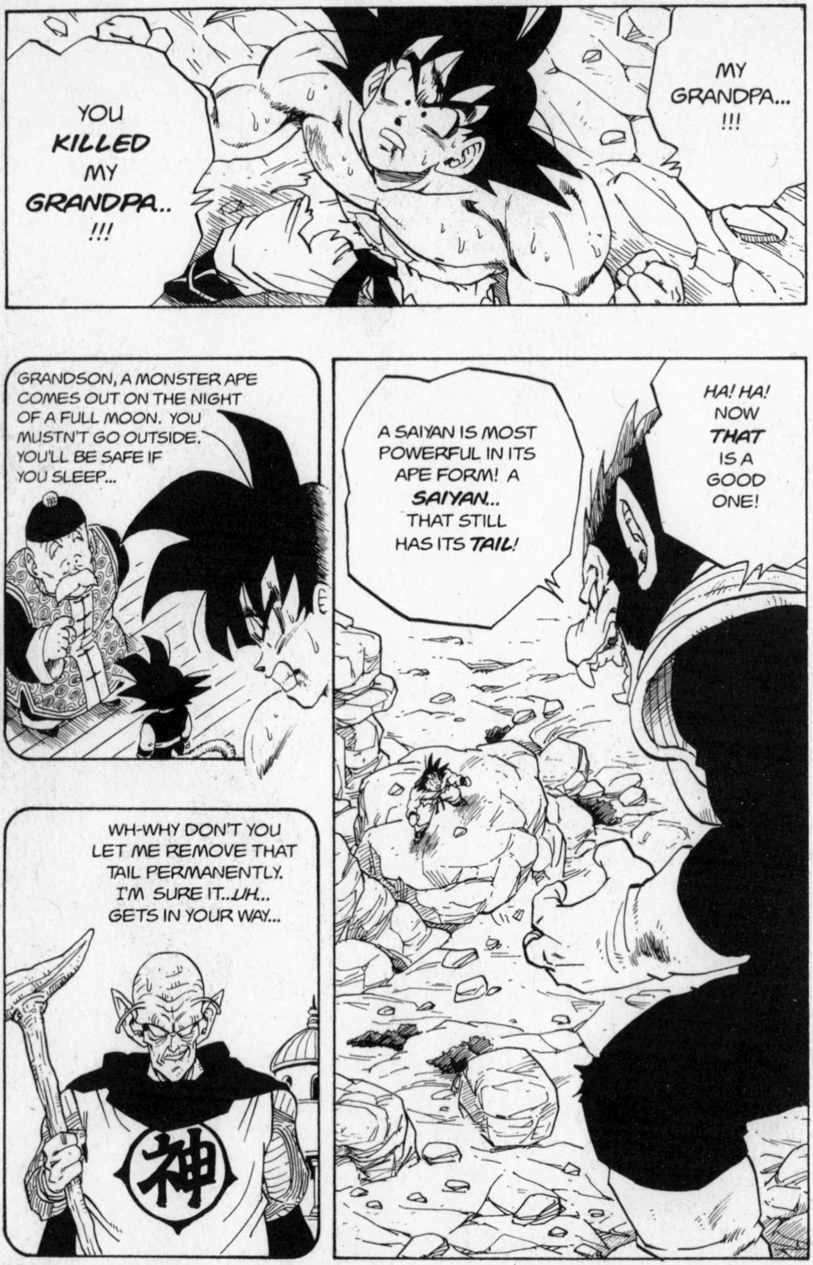
MY GRANDPA... !!!
YOU KILLED MY GRANDPA.. !!!
HA! HA! NOW THAT IS A GOOD ONE!
A SAIYAN IS MOST POWERFUL IN ITS APE FORM! A SAIYAN... THAT STILL HAS ITS TAIL!
GRANDSON, A MONSTER APE COMES OUT ON THE NIGHT OF A FULL MOON. YOU MUSTN'T GO OUTSIDE. YOU'LL BE SAFE IF YOU SLEEP...
WH-WHY DON'T YOU LET ME REMOVE THAT TAIL PERMANENTLY. I'M SURE IT...UH... GETS IN YOUR WAY...
神

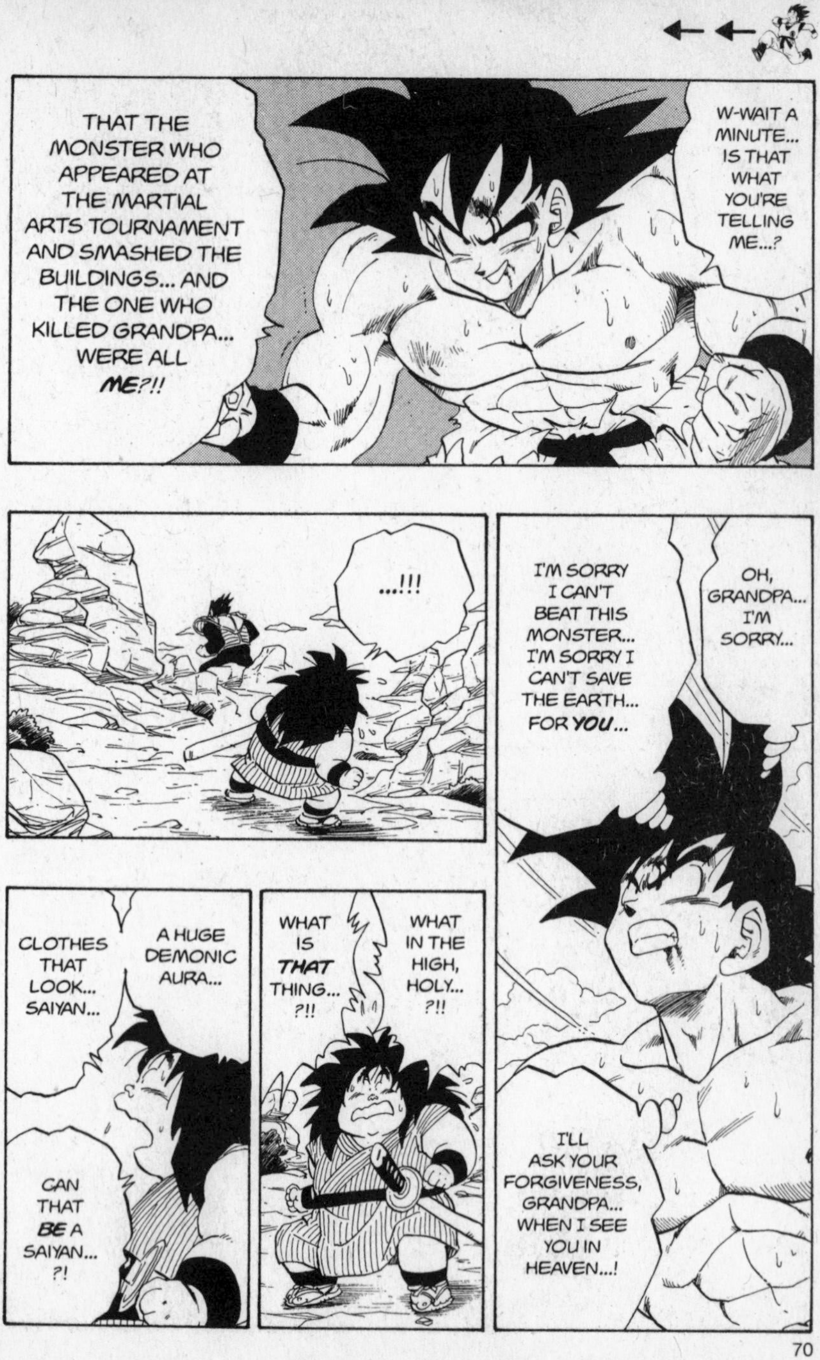
W-WAIT A MINUTE... IS THAT WHAT YOU'RE TELLING ME...?
THAT THE MONSTER WHO APPEARED AT THE MARTIAL ARTS TOURNAMENT AND SMASHED THE BUILDINGS... AND THE ONE WHO KILLED GRANDPA... WERE ALL *ME*?!!
OH, GRANDPA... I'M SORRY...
I'M SORRY I CAN'T BEAT THIS MONSTER... I'M SORRY I CAN'T SAVE THE EARTH... FOR *YOU*...
I'LL ASK YOUR FORGIVENESS, GRANDPA... WHEN I SEE YOU IN HEAVEN...!
...!!!
WHAT IN THE HIGH, HOLY... ?!!
WHAT IS *THAT* THING... ?!!
A HUGE DEMONIC AURA...
CLOTHES THAT LOOK... SAIYAN...
CAN THAT *BE* A SAIYAN... ?!

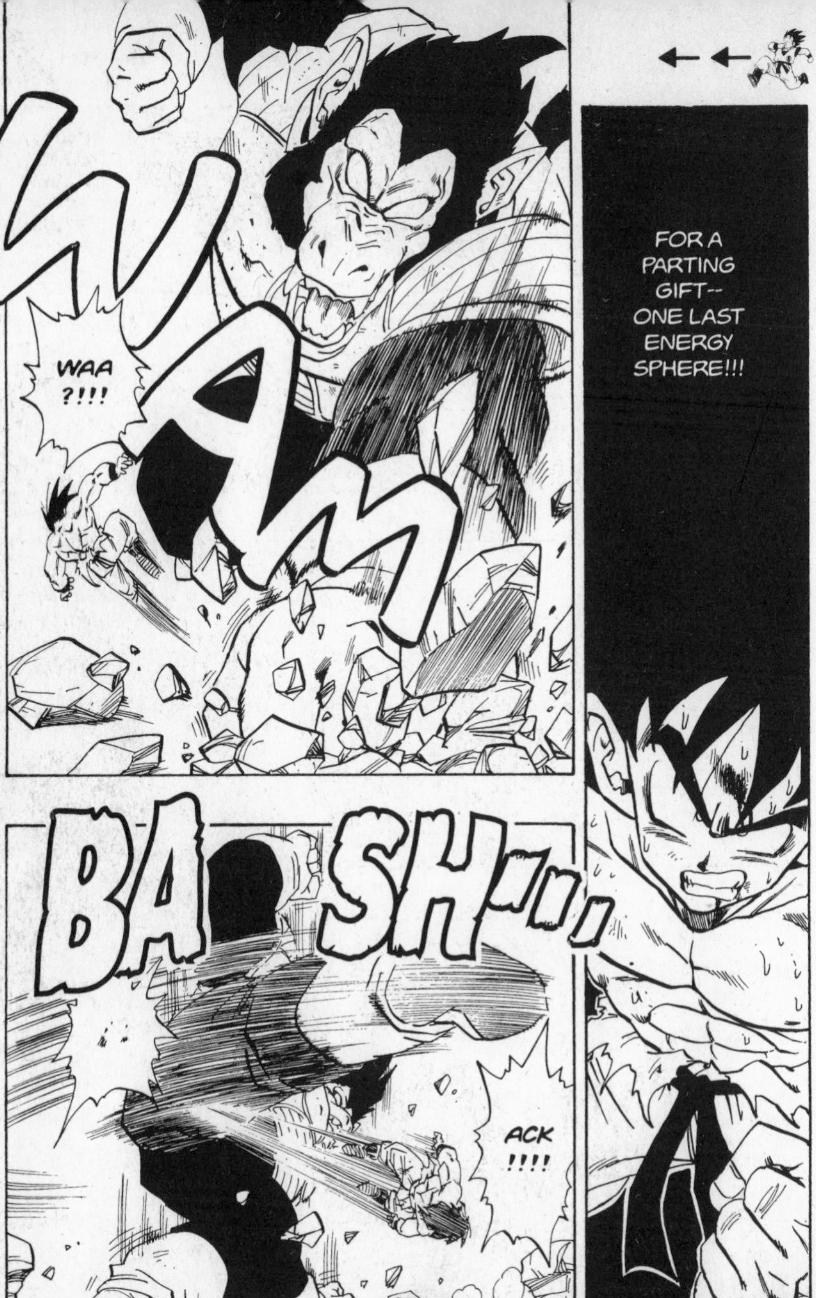
FOR A PARTING GIFT-- ONE LAST ENERGY SPHERE!!!
WAM
WAA ?!!!
BASH...
ACK !!!!

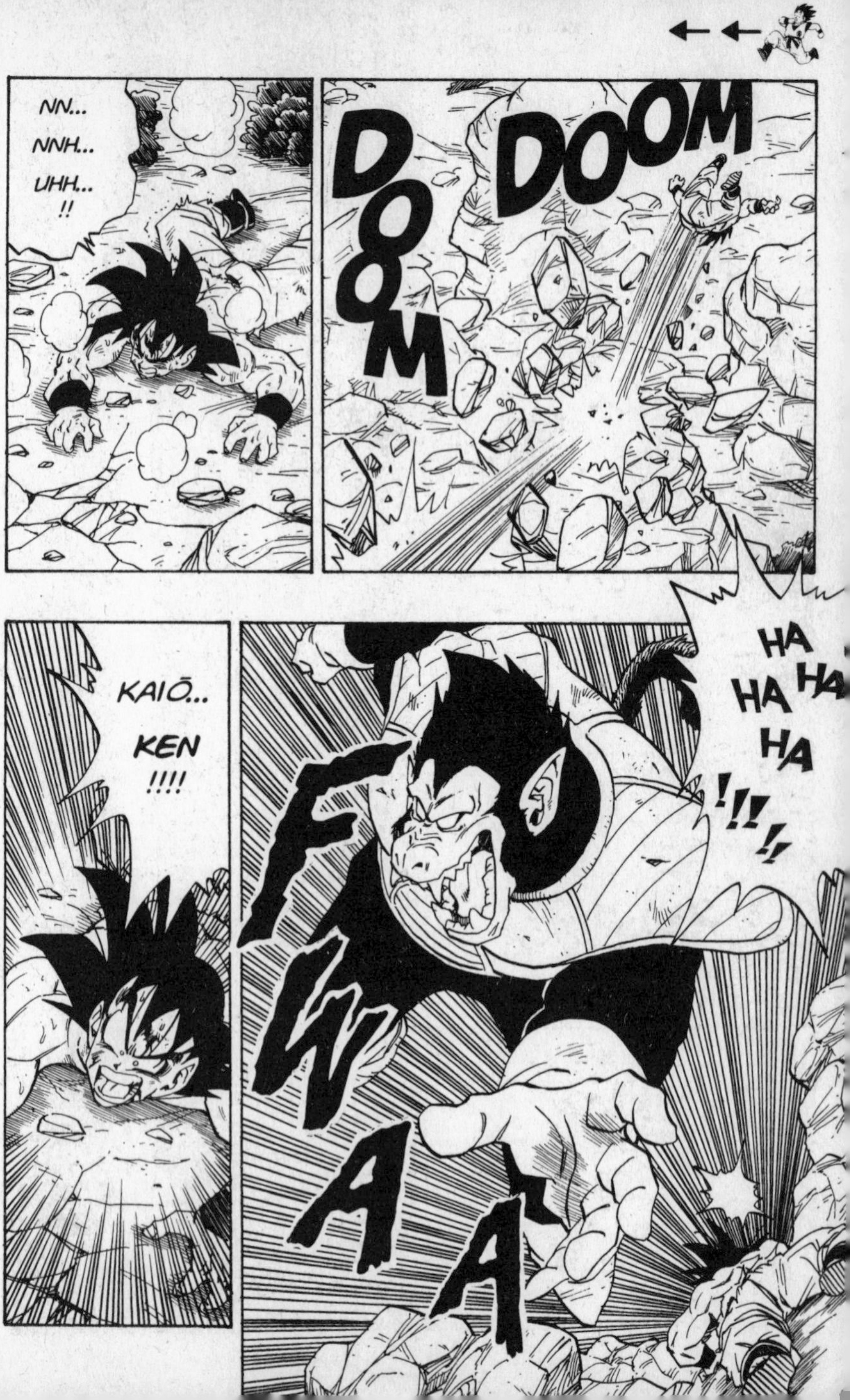
DOOM
DOOM
NN... NNH... UHH... !!
HA HA HA HA !!!!
FWAA
KAIŌ... KEN !!!!

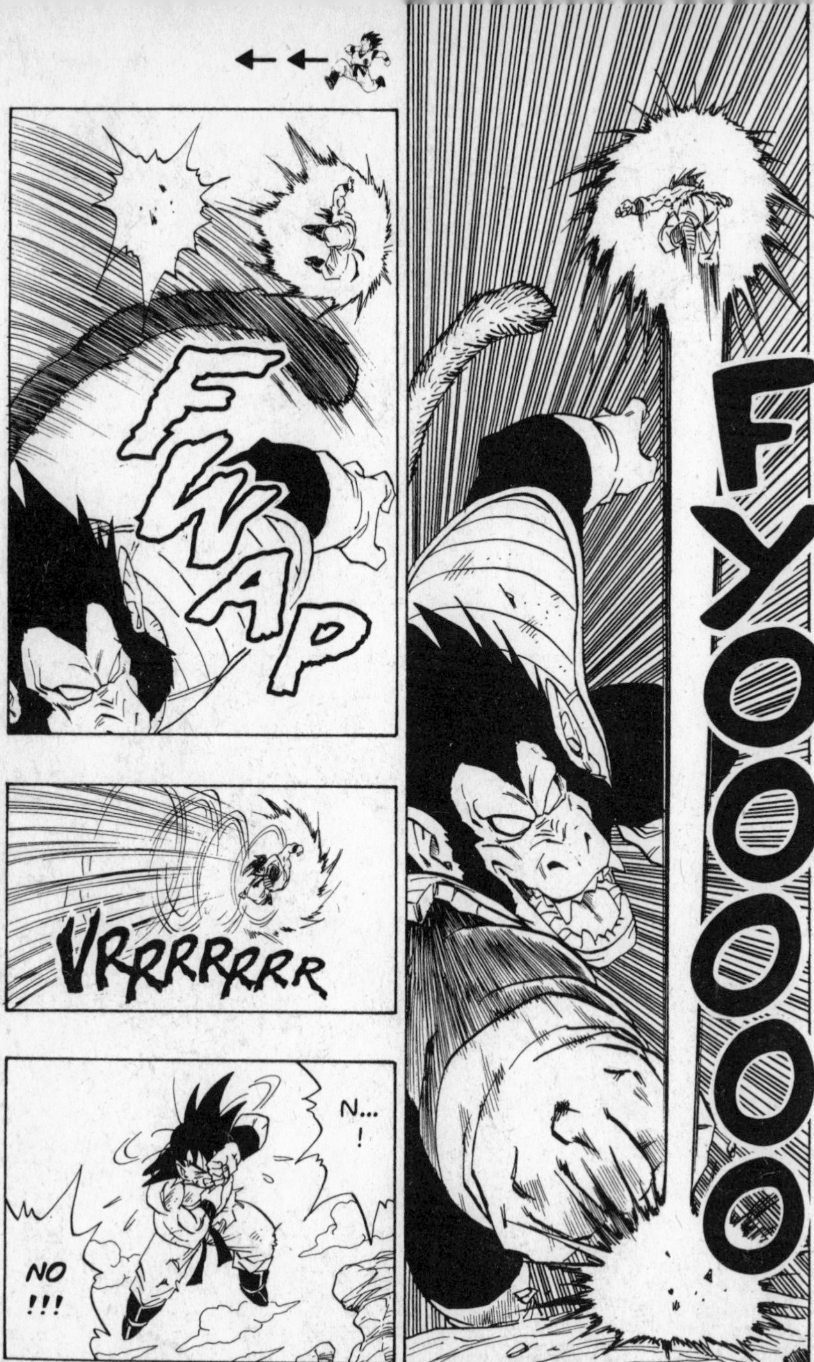
FYOOOOO
FWAP
VRRRRRRR
N... !
NO !!!

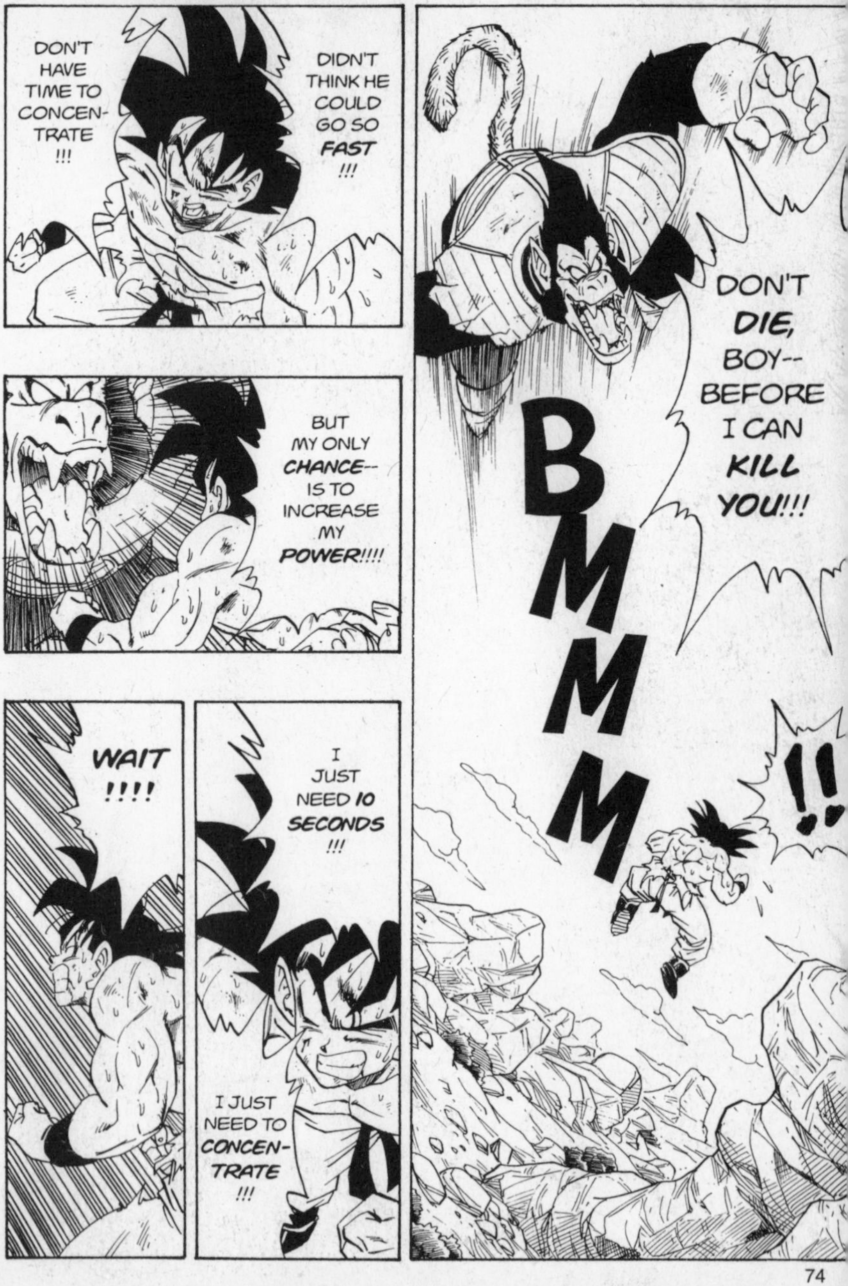
DON'T DIE, BOY-- BEFORE I CAN KILL YOU!!!
BMMM
!!
DIDN'T THINK HE COULD GO SO FAST!!!
DON'T HAVE TIME TO CONCEN-TRATE!!!
BUT MY ONLY CHANCE-- IS TO INCREASE MY POWER!!!!
I JUST NEED 10 SECONDS!!!
I JUST NEED TO CONCEN-TRATE!!!
WAIT!!!!

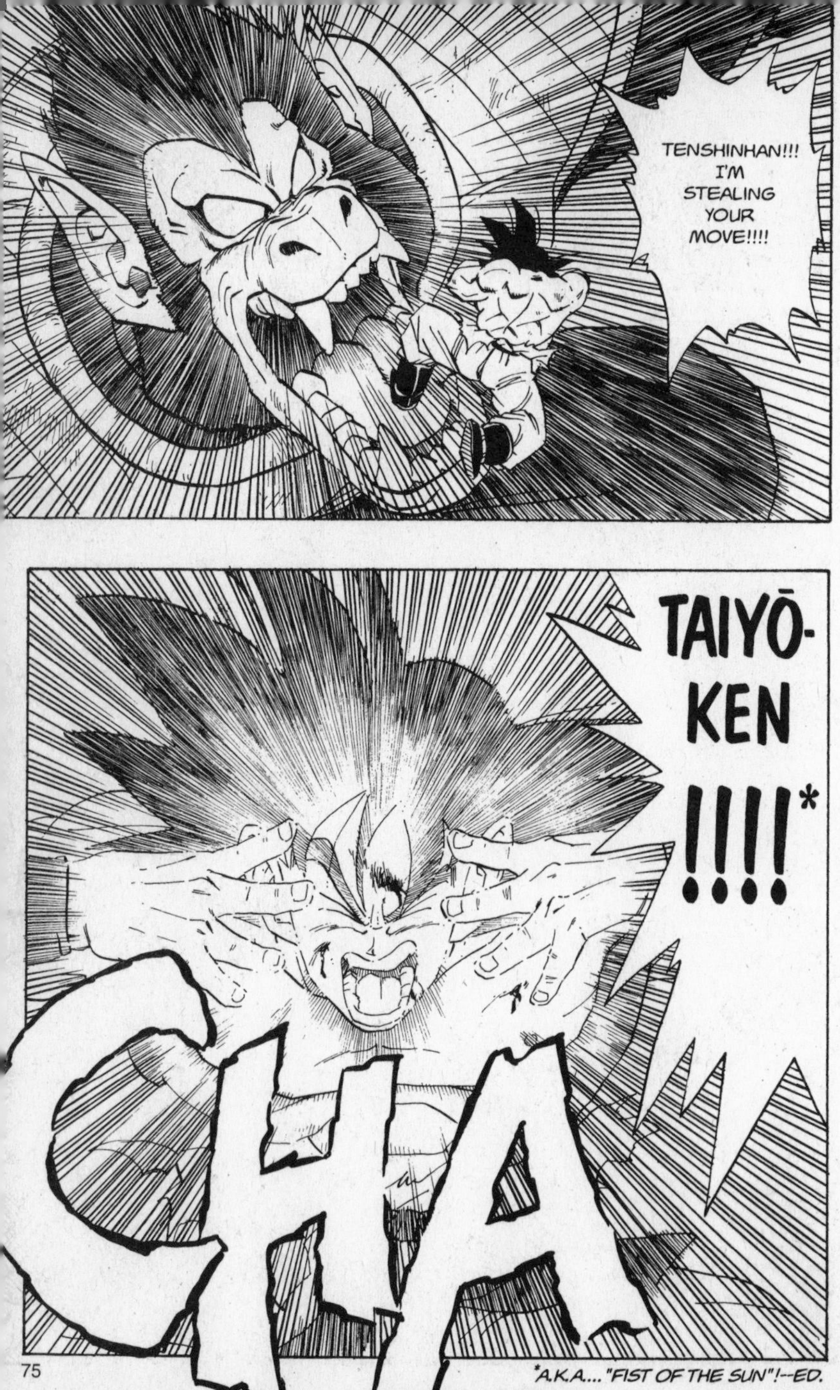
TENSHINHAN!!! I'M STEALING YOUR MOVE!!!!
TAIYŌ-KEN !!!!*
CHA

*A.K.A.... "FIST OF THE SUN"!--ED.

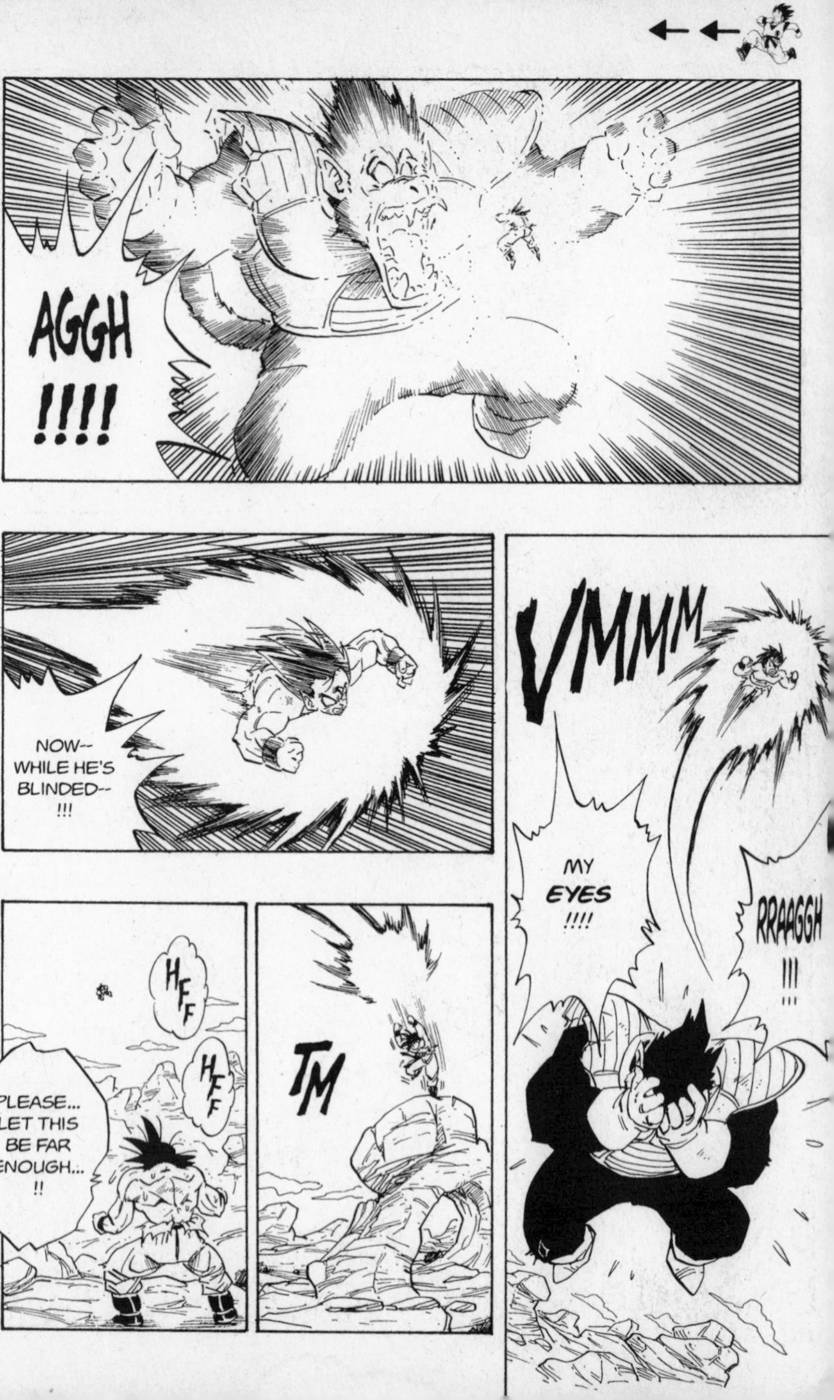

AGGH !!!!
VMMM
RRAAGGH !!!
MY EYES !!!!
NOW-- WHILE HE'S BLINDED-- !!!
TM
HFF
HFF
PLEASE... LET THIS BE FAR ENOUGH... !!

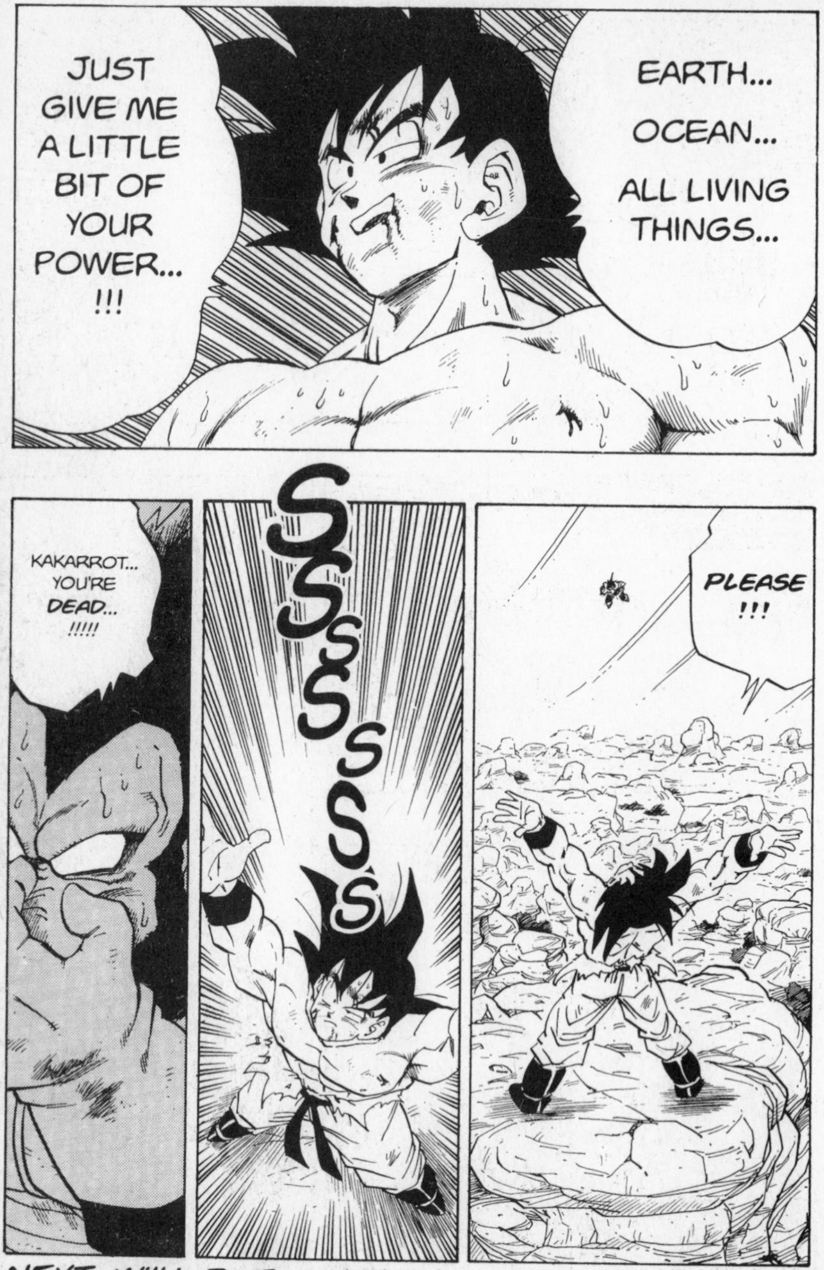
EARTH... OCEAN... ALL LIVING THINGS...
JUST GIVE ME A LITTLE BIT OF YOUR POWER... !!!
PLEASE !!!
SSSSSSSS
KAKARROT... YOU'RE DEAD... !!!!!

NEXT: Will It Be Enough?!

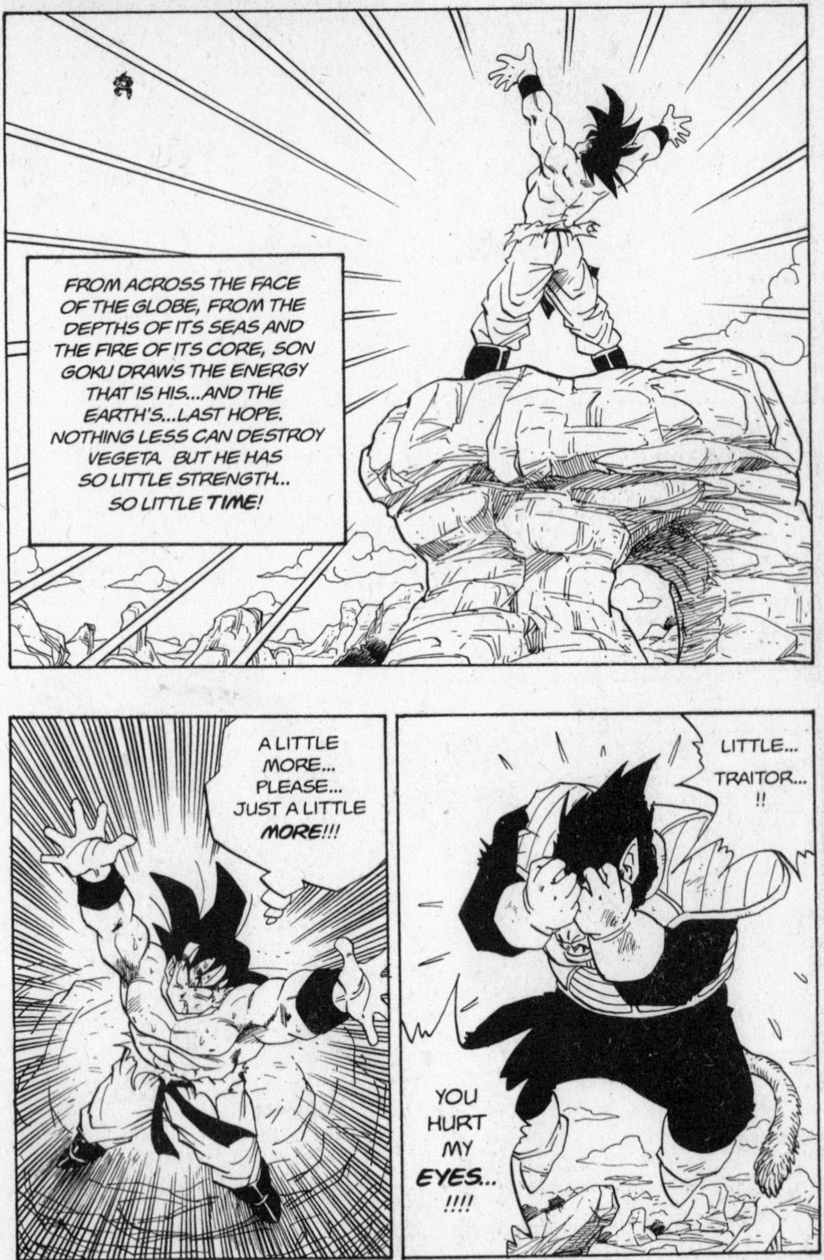
FROM ACROSS THE FACE OF THE GLOBE, FROM THE DEPTHS OF ITS SEAS AND THE FIRE OF ITS CORE, SON GOKU DRAWS THE ENERGY THAT IS HIS...AND THE EARTH'S...LAST HOPE. NOTHING LESS CAN DESTROY VEGETA. BUT HE HAS SO LITTLE STRENGTH... SO LITTLE TIME!
LITTLE... TRAITOR... !!
YOU HURT MY EYES... !!!!
A LITTLE MORE... PLEASE... JUST A LITTLE MORE!!!

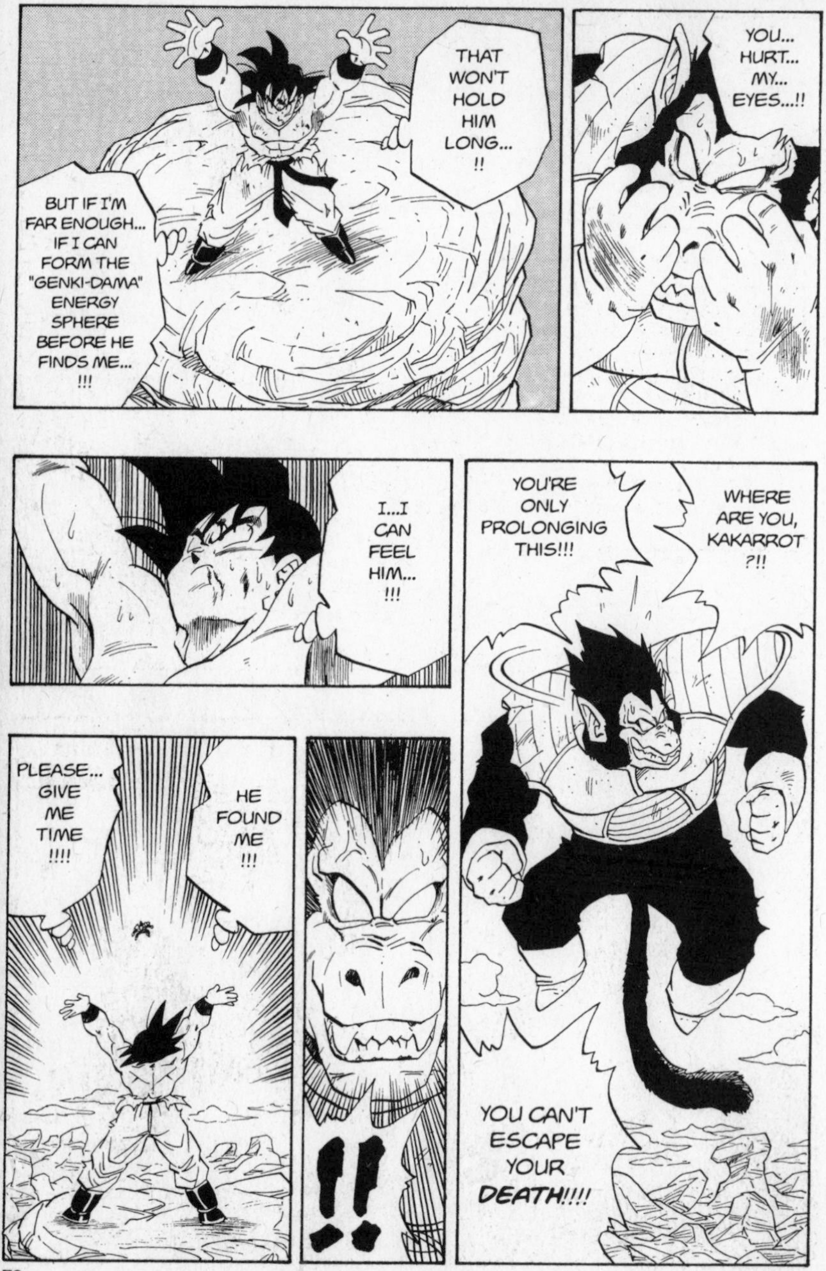
YOU... HURT... MY... EYES...!!
THAT WON'T HOLD HIM LONG... !!
BUT IF I'M FAR ENOUGH... IF I CAN FORM THE "GENKI-DAMA" ENERGY SPHERE BEFORE HE FINDS ME... !!!
WHERE ARE YOU, KAKARROT ?!!
YOU'RE ONLY PROLONGING THIS!!!
YOU CAN'T ESCAPE YOUR **DEATH**!!!!
I...I CAN FEEL HIM... !!!
!!
HE FOUND ME !!!
PLEASE... GIVE ME TIME !!!!

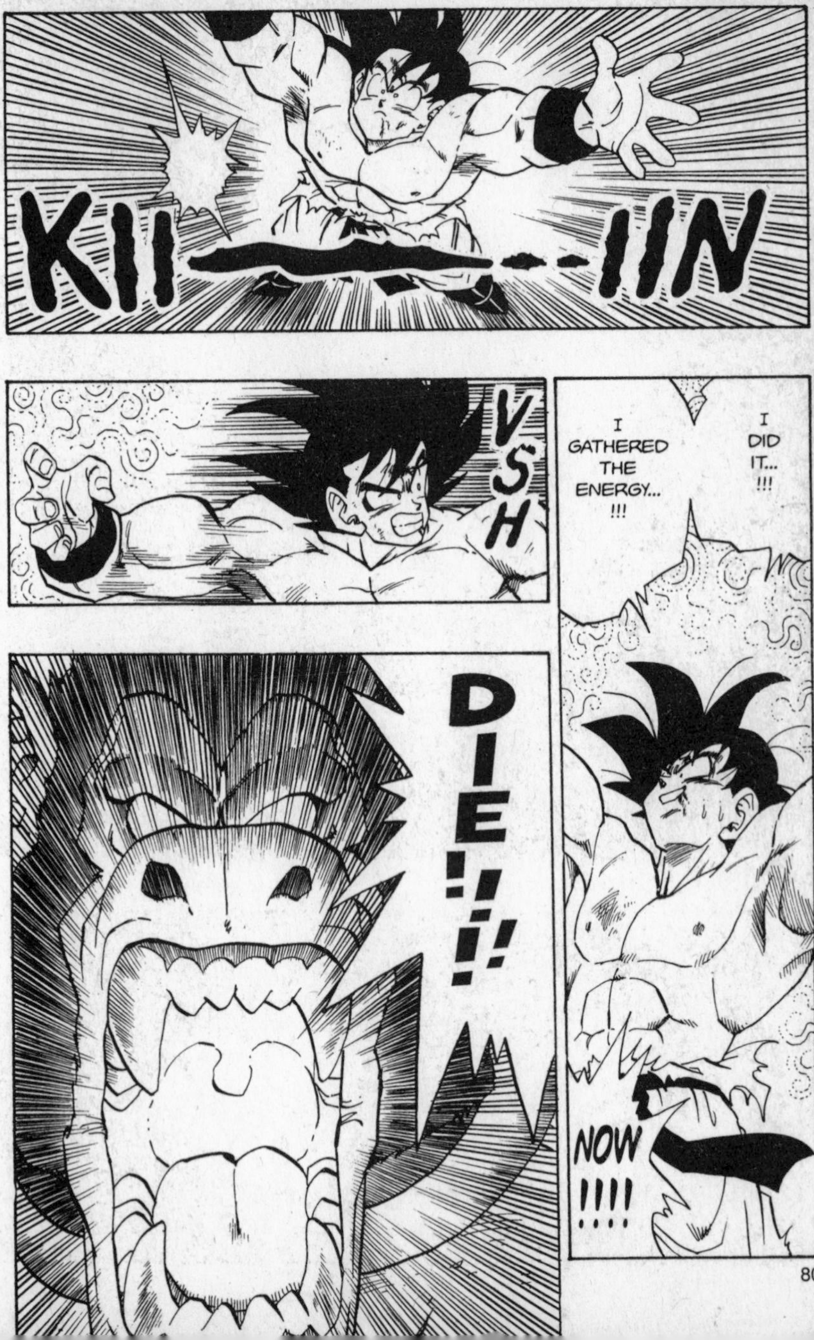

KII——--IIN
I DID IT...!!!
I GATHERED THE ENERGY...!!!
NOW!!!!
VSH
DIE!!!!!

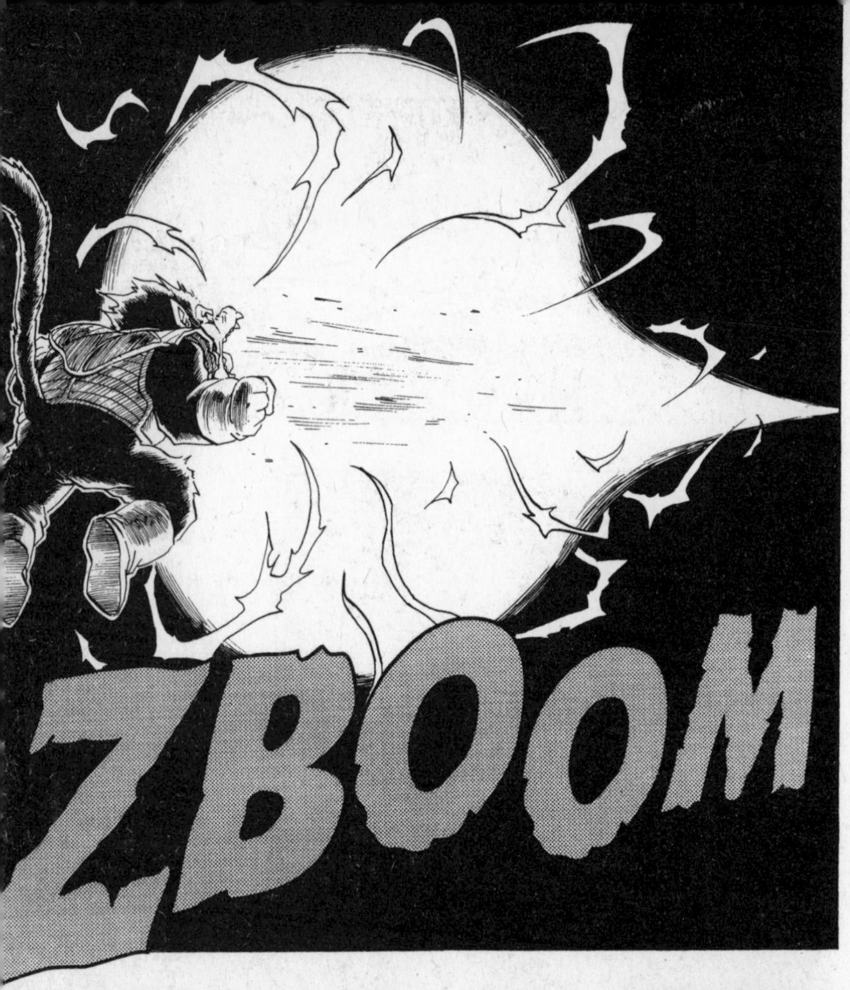
ZBOOM

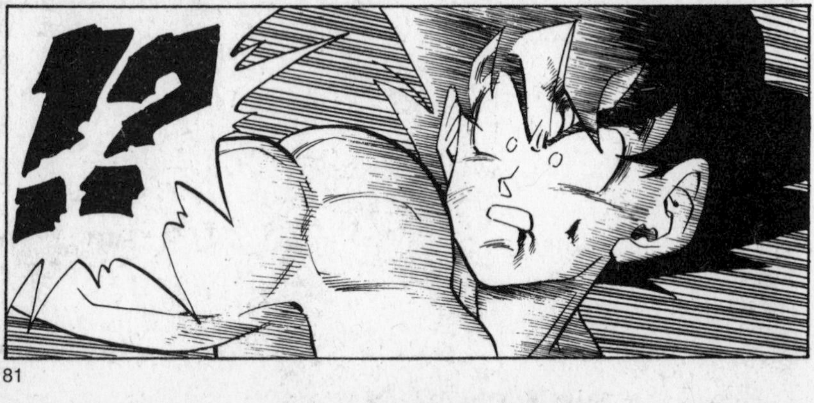
!?

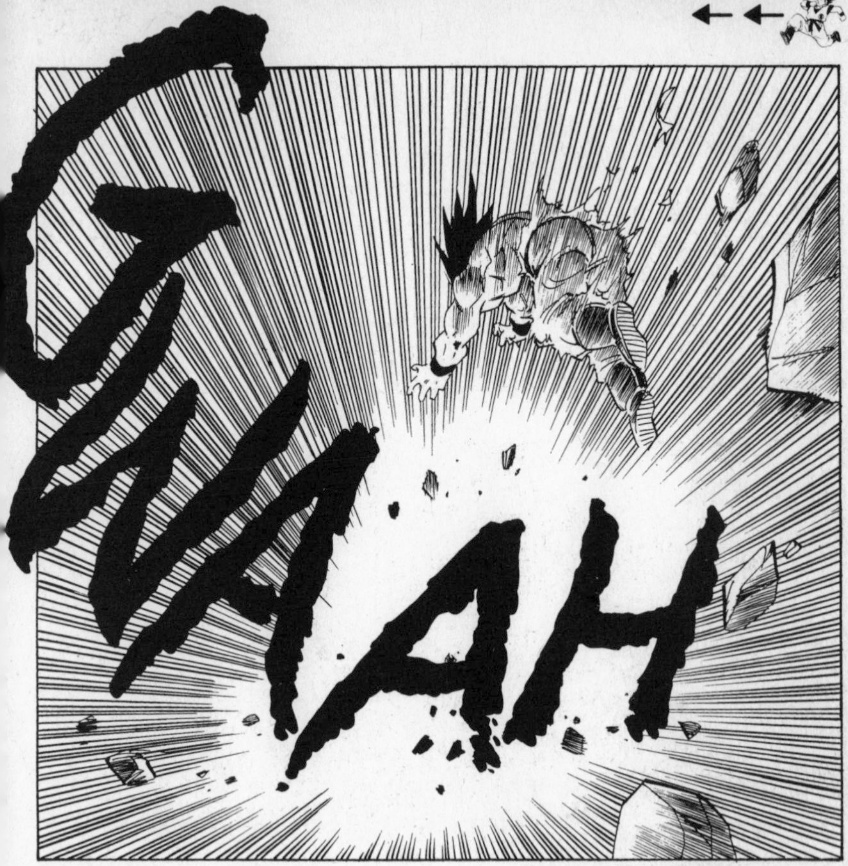
GWAAH

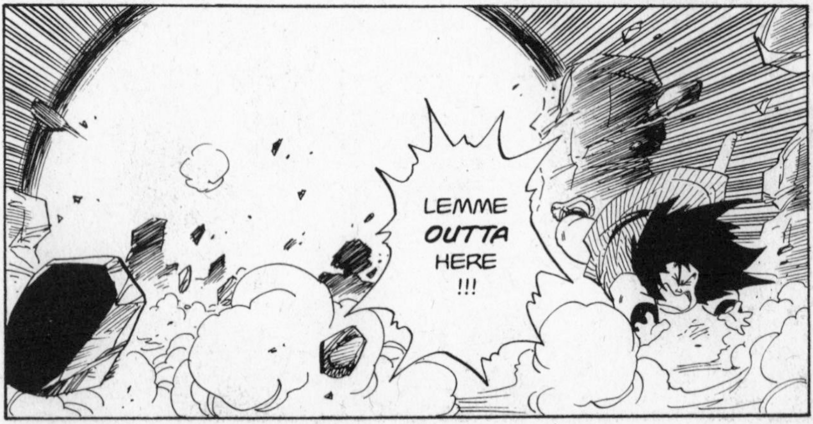
LEMME *OUTTA* HERE !!!

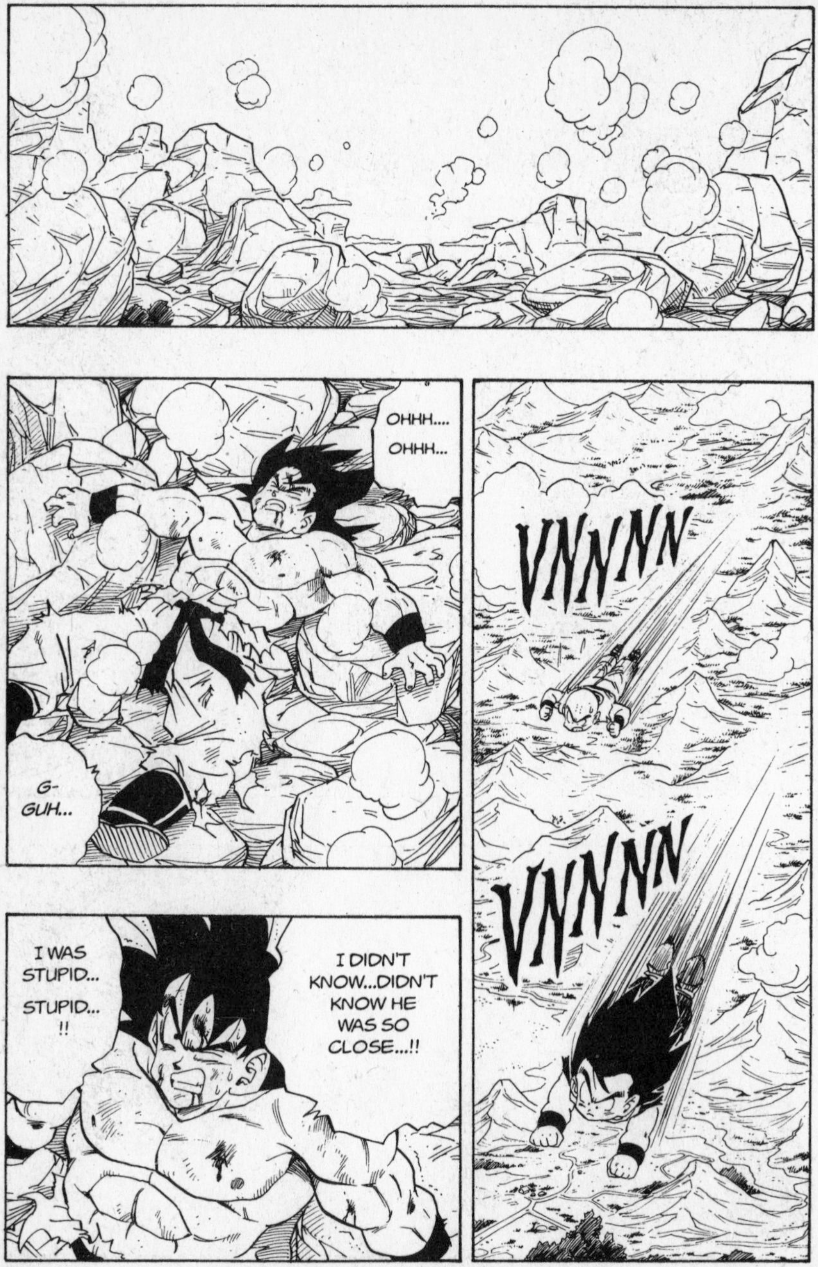
VNNNN
VNNNN
OHHH....
OHHH...
G-
GUH...
I DIDN'T KNOW...DIDN'T KNOW HE WAS SO CLOSE...!!
I WAS STUPID...
STUPID...
!!

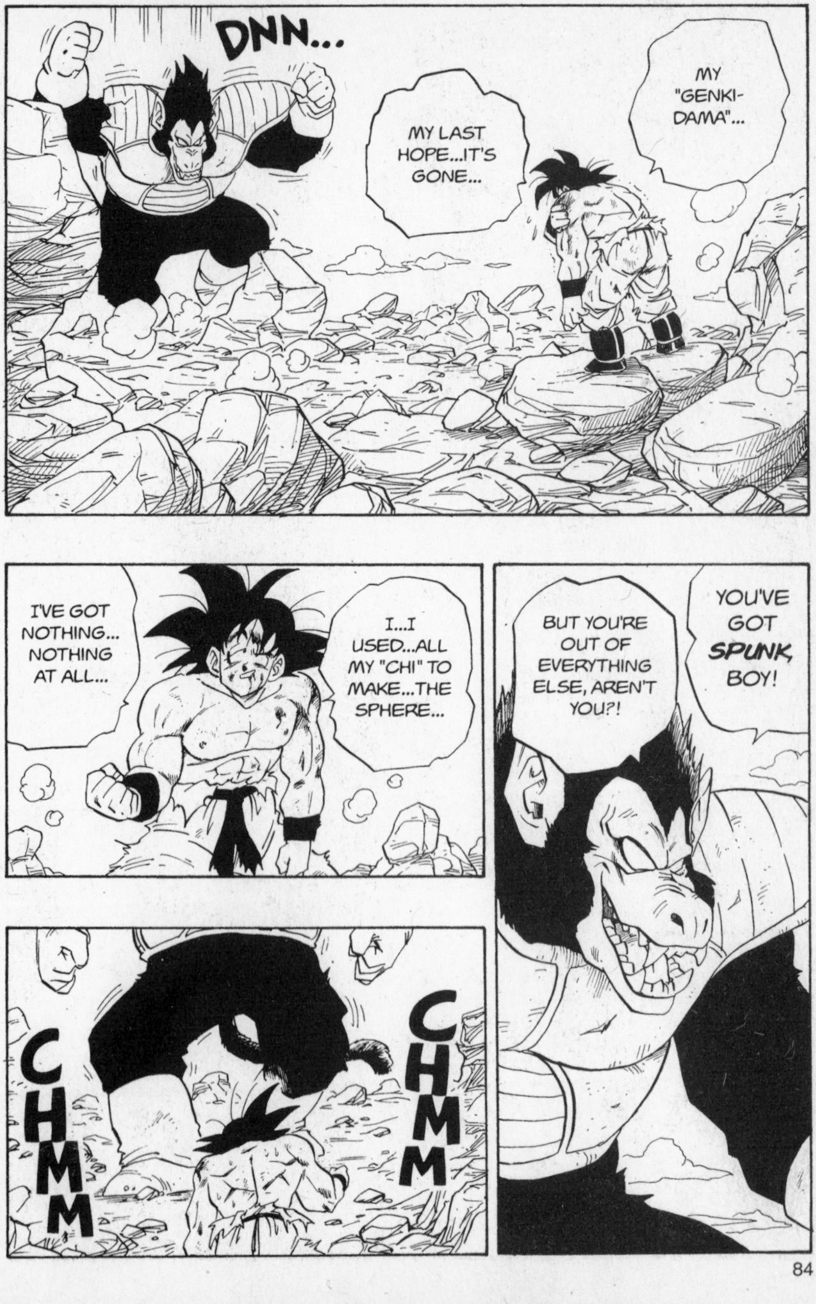
MY "GENKI-DAMA"...
MY LAST HOPE...IT'S GONE...
DNN...
YOU'VE GOT SPUNK, BOY!
BUT YOU'RE OUT OF EVERYTHING ELSE, AREN'T YOU?!
I...I USED...ALL MY "CHI" TO MAKE...THE SPHERE...
I'VE GOT NOTHING... NOTHING AT ALL...
CHMM
CHMM

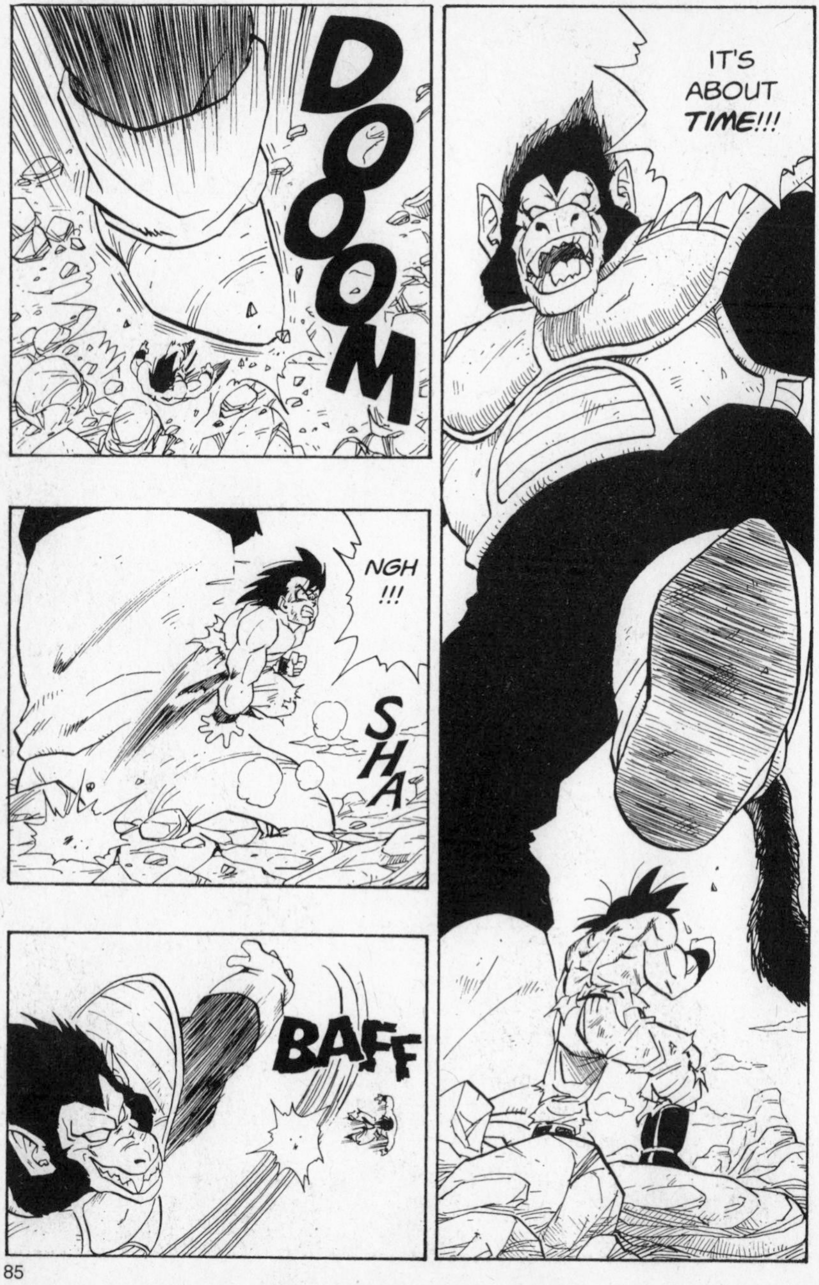
IT'S ABOUT TIME!!!
DOOOM
NGH !!!
SHA
BAFF

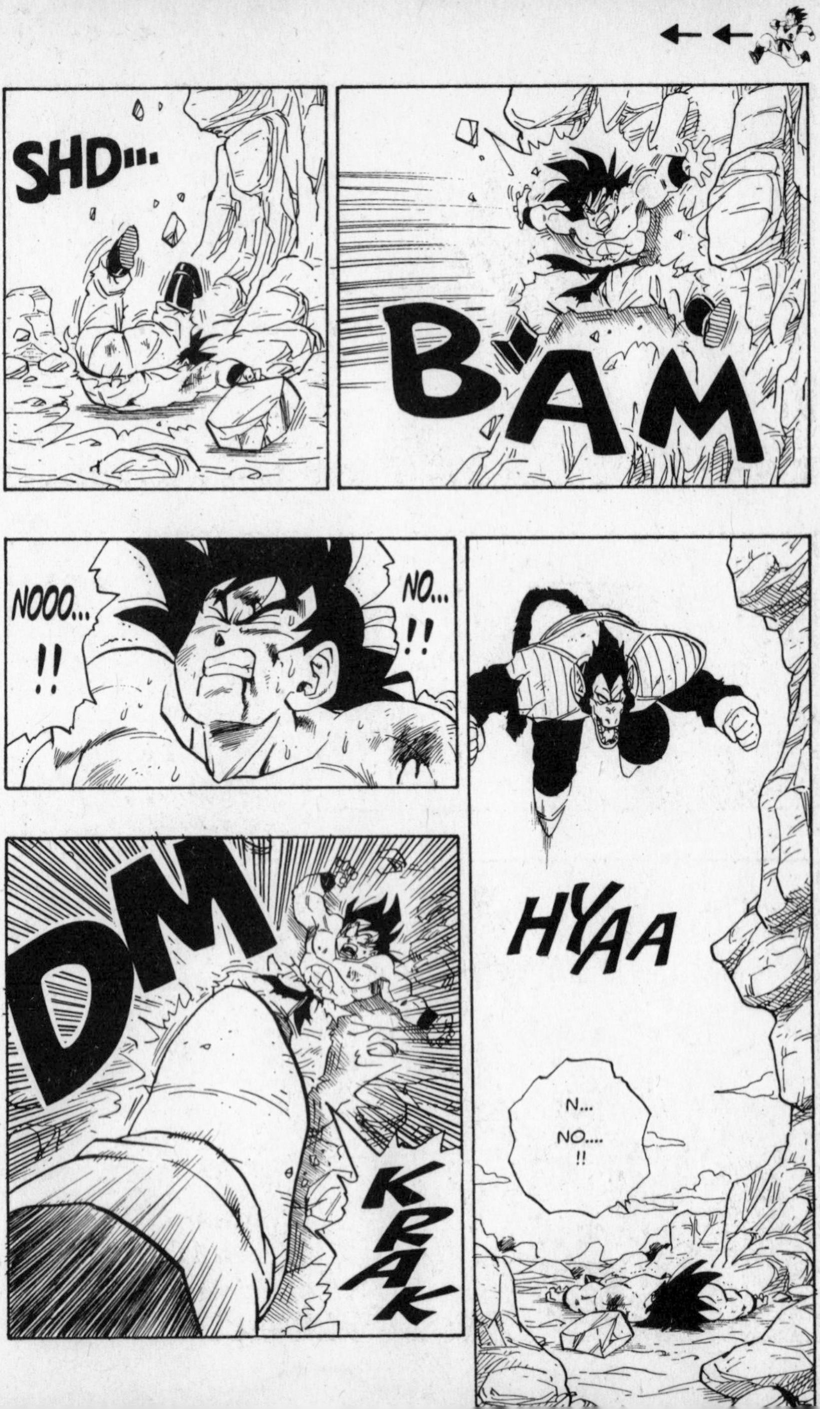
BAM
SHD...
HYAA
N... NO.... !!
NO... !!
NOOO... !!
DM
KRAK

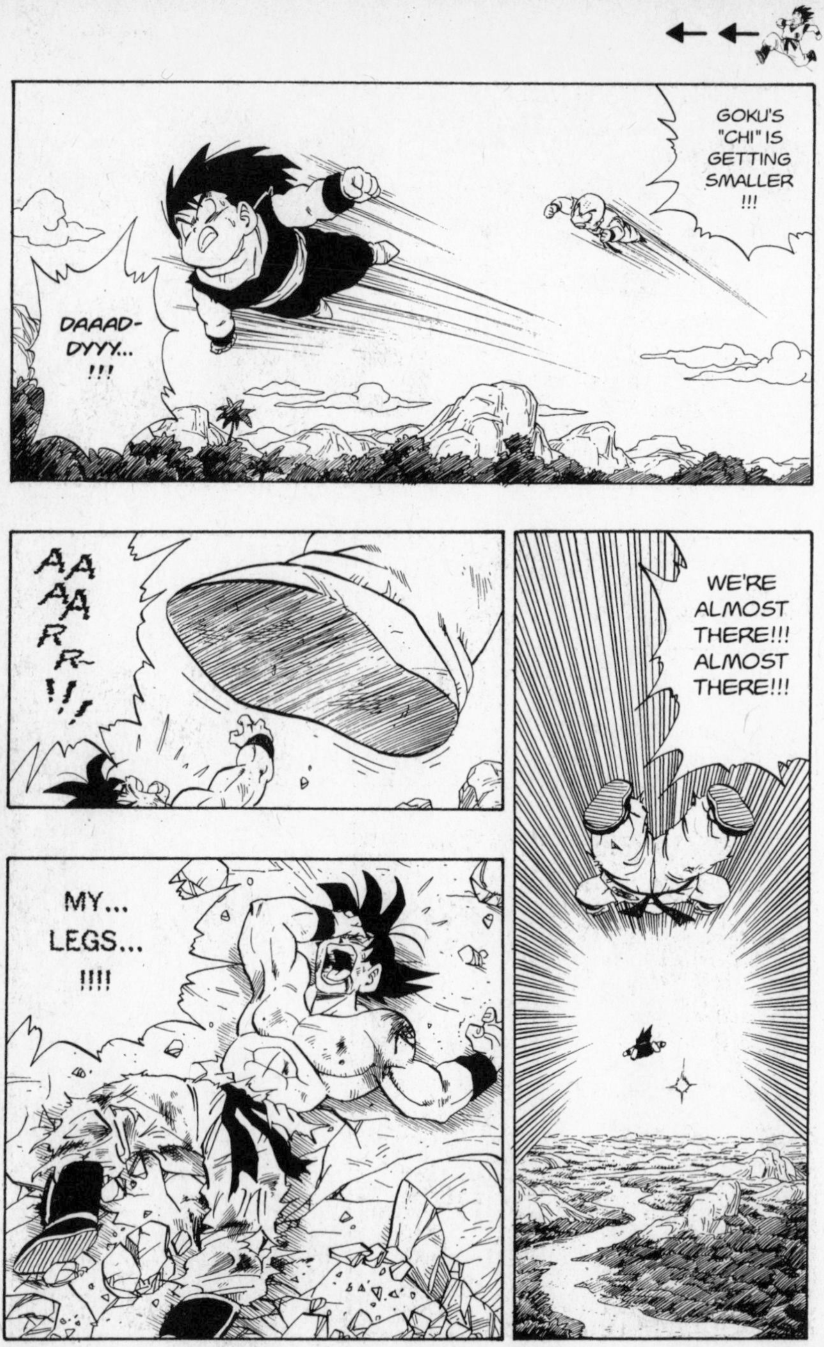
GOKU'S "CHI" IS GETTING SMALLER !!!
DAAAD-DYYY... !!!
WE'RE ALMOST THERE!!! ALMOST THERE!!!
AAAARR~!!!
MY... LEGS... !!!!

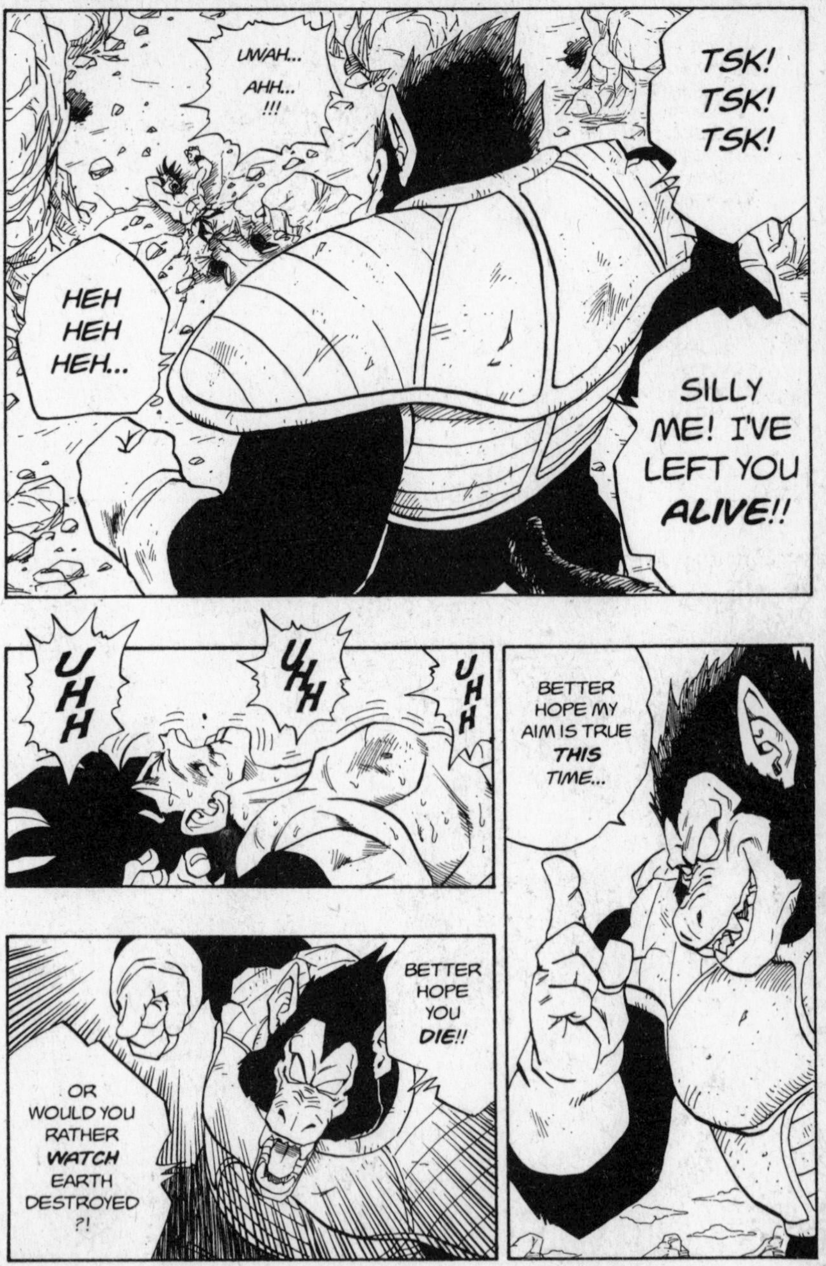
TSK! TSK! TSK!
UWAH... AHH... !!!
SILLY ME! I'VE LEFT YOU ALIVE!!
HEH HEH HEH...
BETTER HOPE MY AIM IS TRUE THIS TIME...
UHH
UHH
UHH
BETTER HOPE YOU DIE!!
OR WOULD YOU RATHER WATCH EARTH DESTROYED ?!

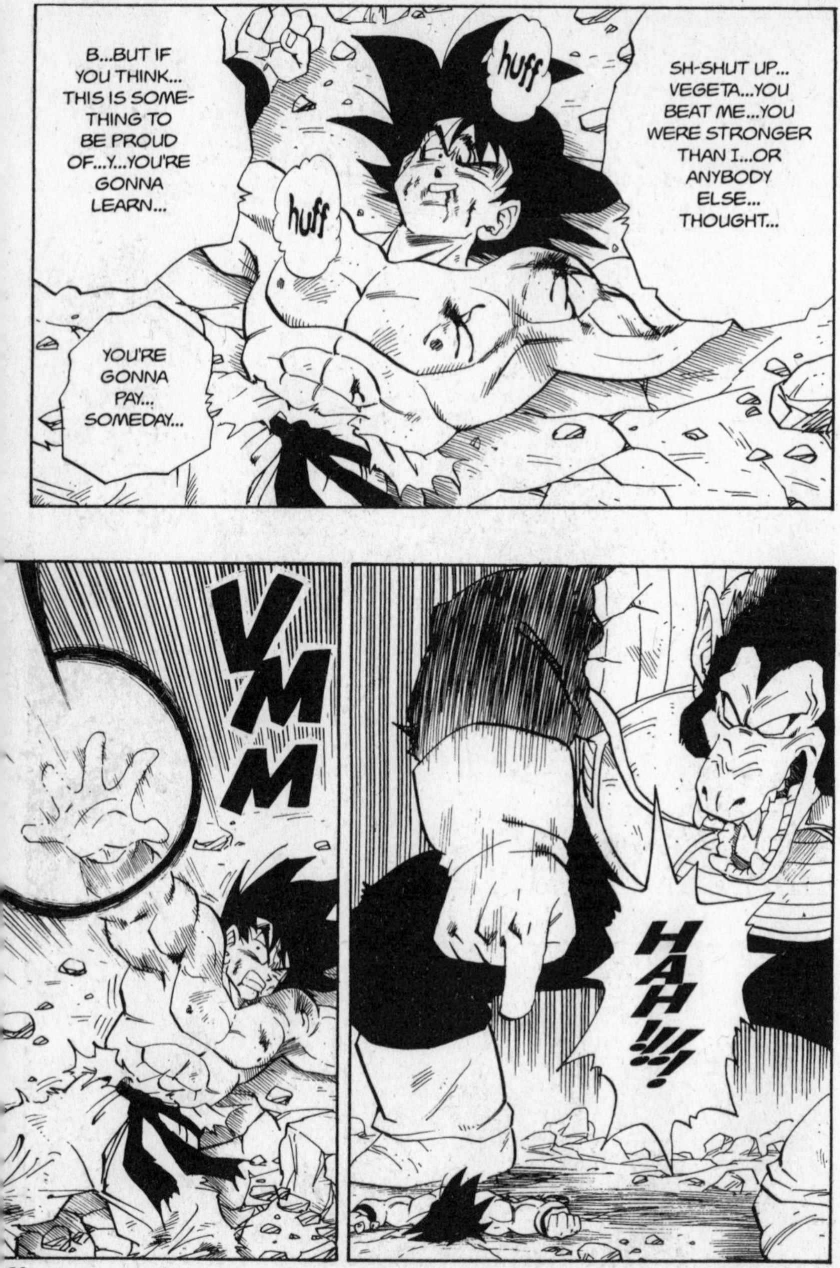
SH-SHUT UP... VEGETA...YOU BEAT ME...YOU WERE STRONGER THAN I...OR ANYBODY ELSE... THOUGHT...
huff
huff
B...BUT IF YOU THINK... THIS IS SOME-THING TO BE PROUD OF...Y...YOU'RE GONNA LEARN...
YOU'RE GONNA PAY... SOMEDAY...
HAH!!!!
VMM

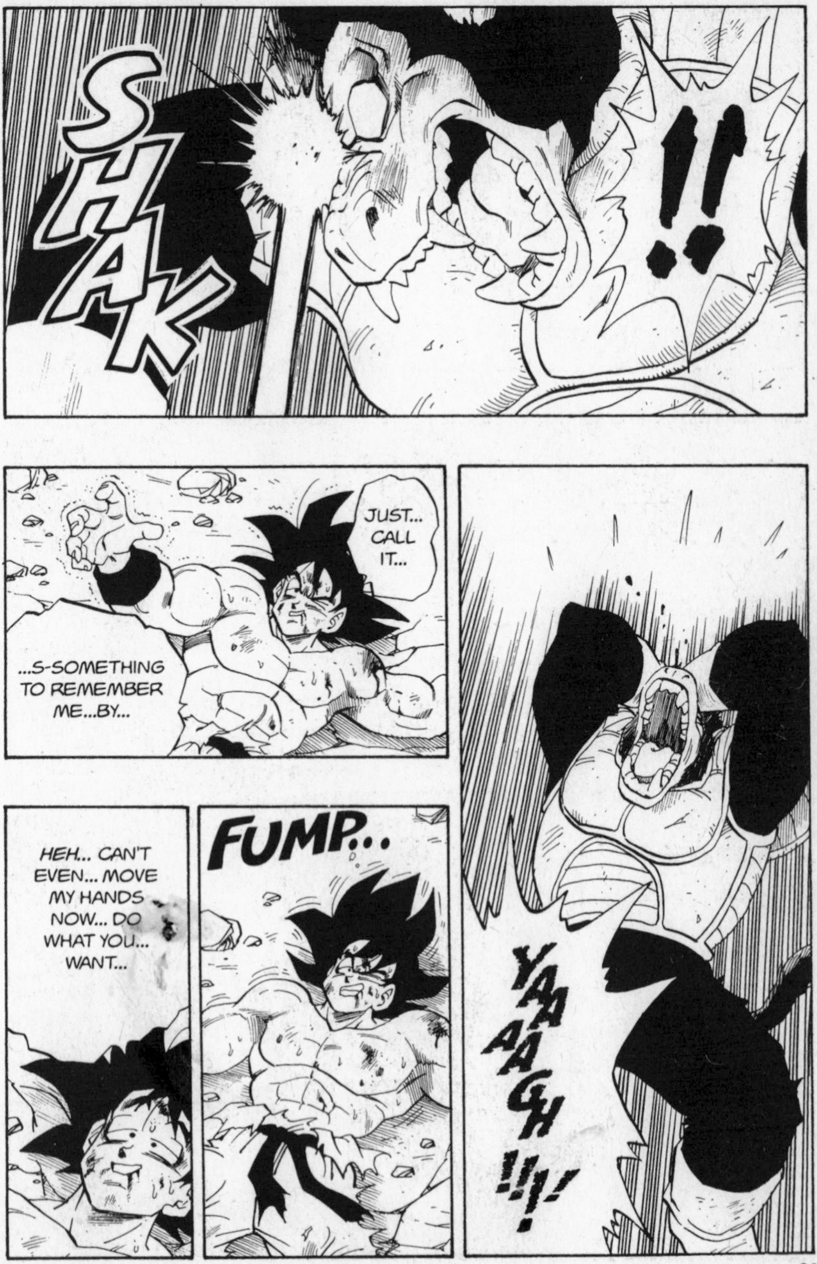
!!
SHAK
YAAAAGH!!!!
JUST... CALL IT...
...S-SOMETHING TO REMEMBER ME...BY...
FUMP...
HEH... CAN'T EVEN... MOVE MY HANDS NOW... DO WHAT YOU... WANT...

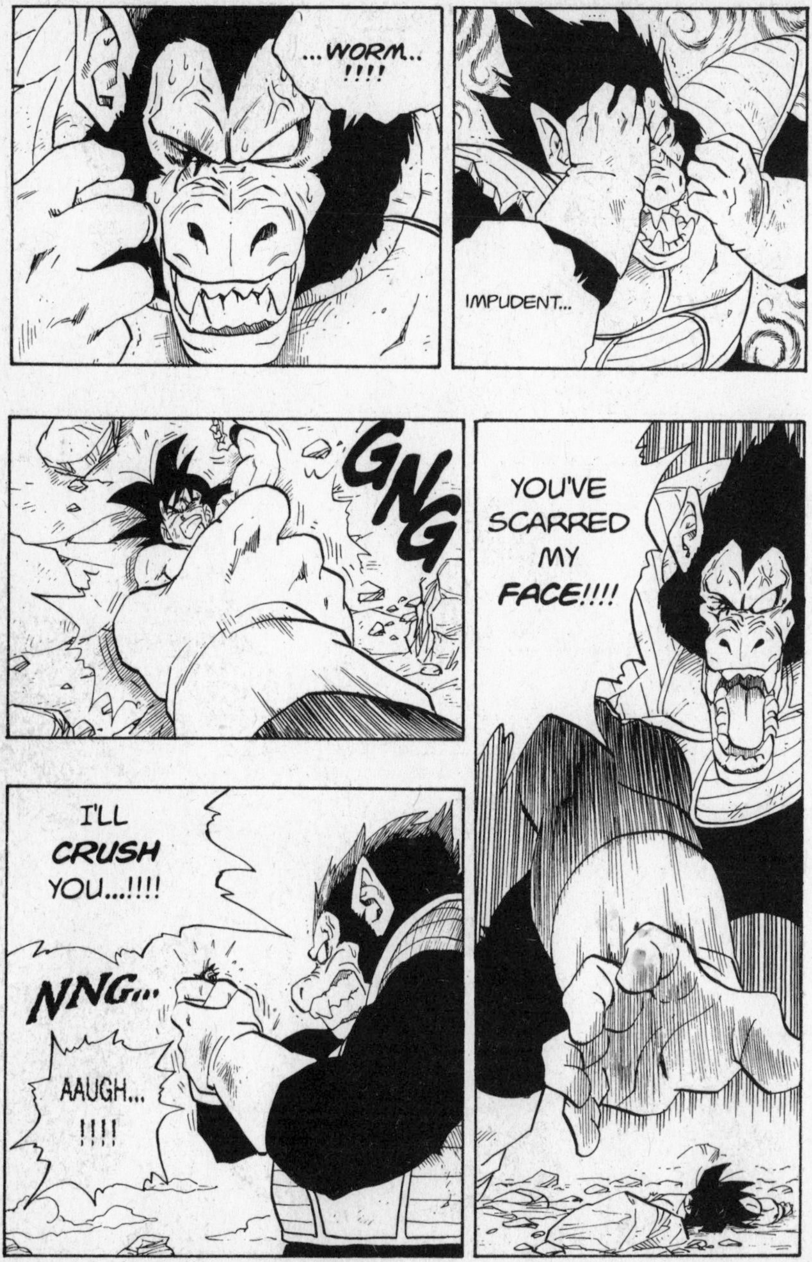
IMPUDENT...
...WORM..!!!!
YOU'VE SCARRED MY FACE!!!!
GNG
I'LL CRUSH YOU...!!!!
NNG...
AAUGH...!!!!

NEXT: The Last Heartbeat!

DBZ:41 • The Last Heartbeat

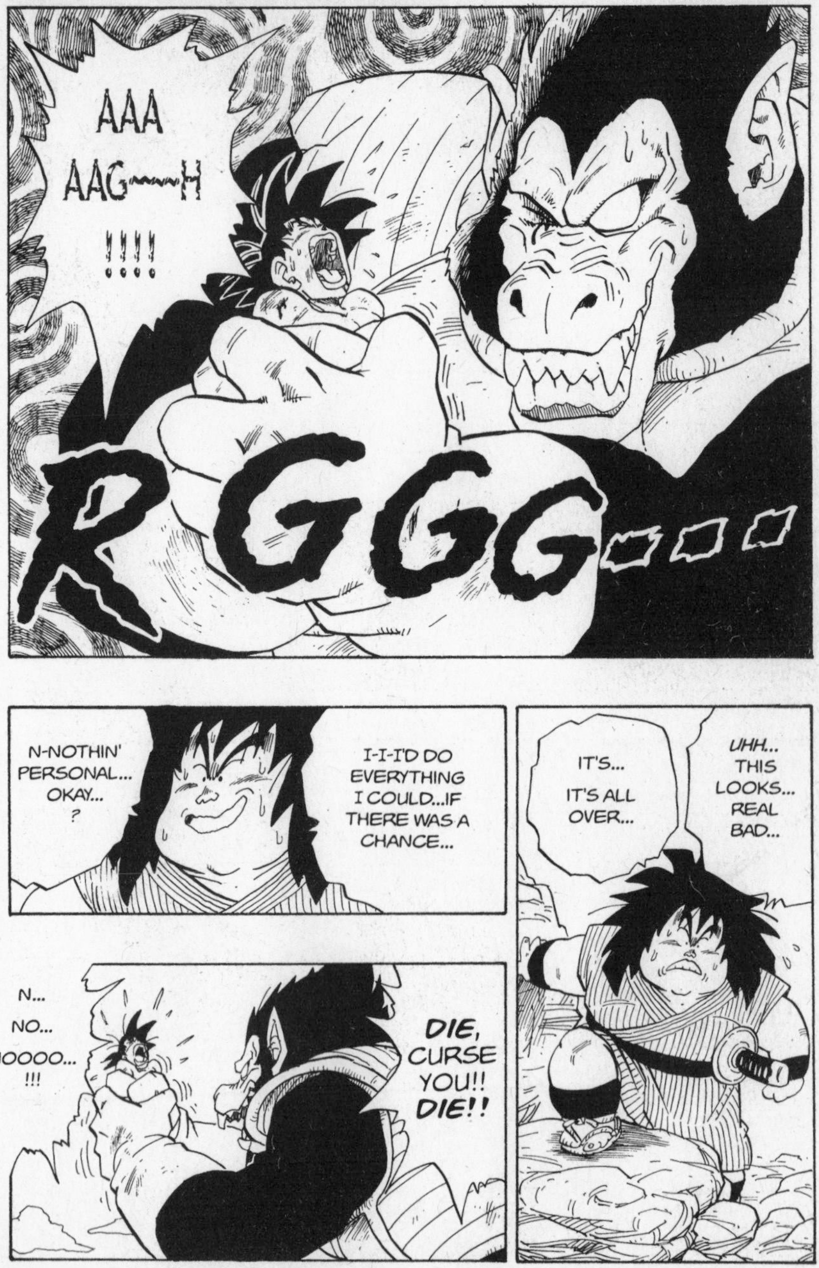
AAA AAG~~~H !!!!!
RGGG...
UHH... THIS LOOKS... REAL BAD...
IT'S... IT'S ALL OVER...
I-I-I'D DO EVERYTHING I COULD...IF THERE WAS A CHANCE...
N-NOTHIN' PERSONAL... OKAY... ?
DIE, CURSE YOU!! DIE!!
N... NO... NOOOO... !!!

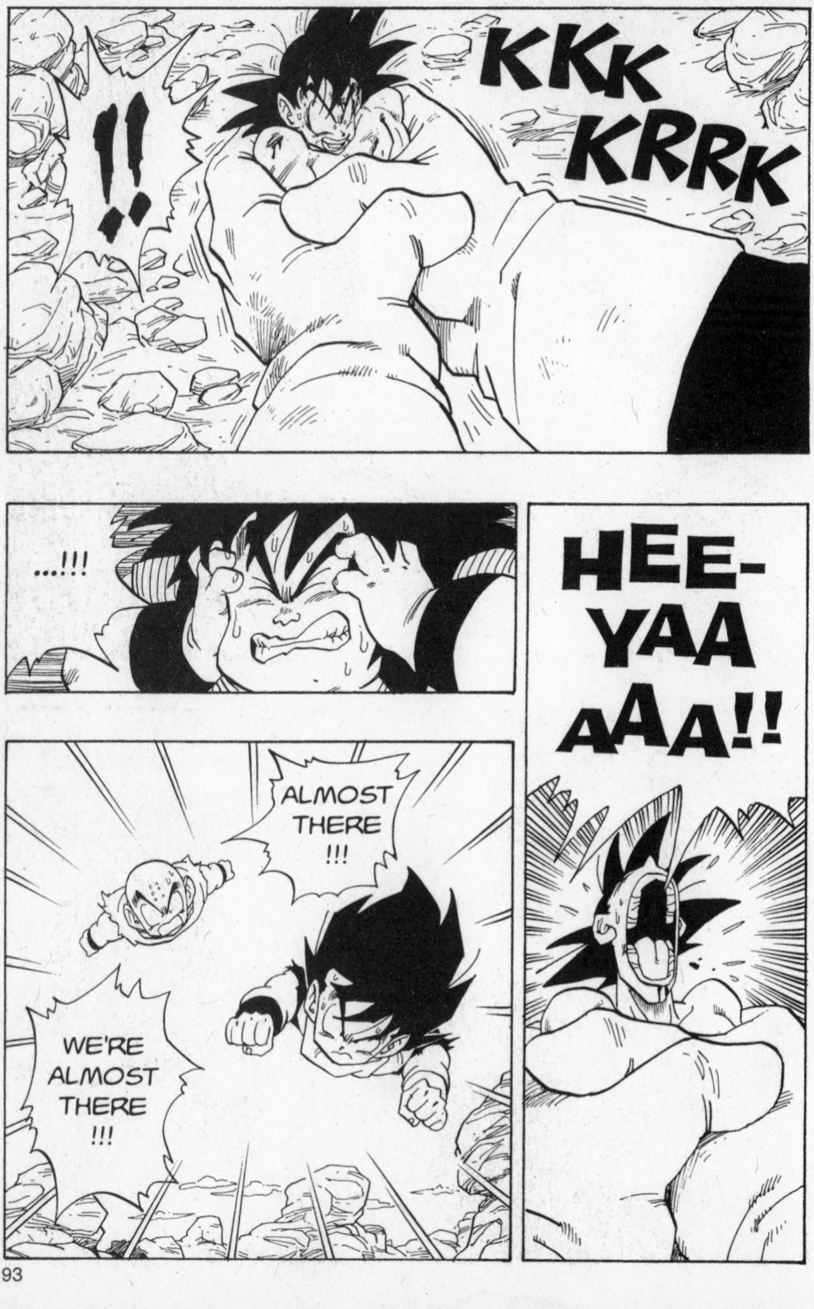
KKK KRRRK
!!
HEE-YAA AAA!!
...!!!
ALMOST THERE !!!
WE'RE ALMOST THERE !!!

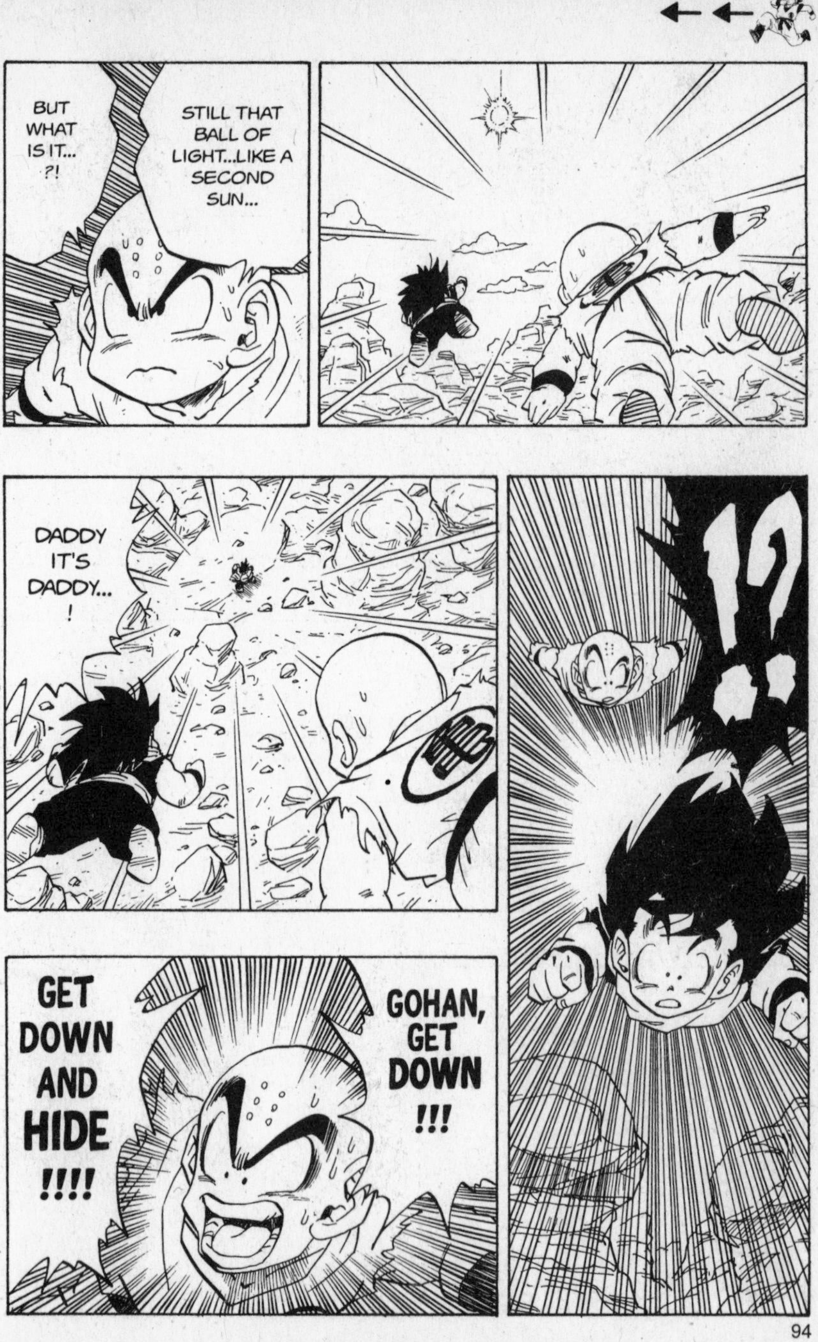
STILL THAT BALL OF LIGHT...LIKE A SECOND SUN...
BUT WHAT IS IT...?!
!?
DADDY IT'S DADDY...!
GOHAN, GET DOWN!!!
GET DOWN AND HIDE!!!!

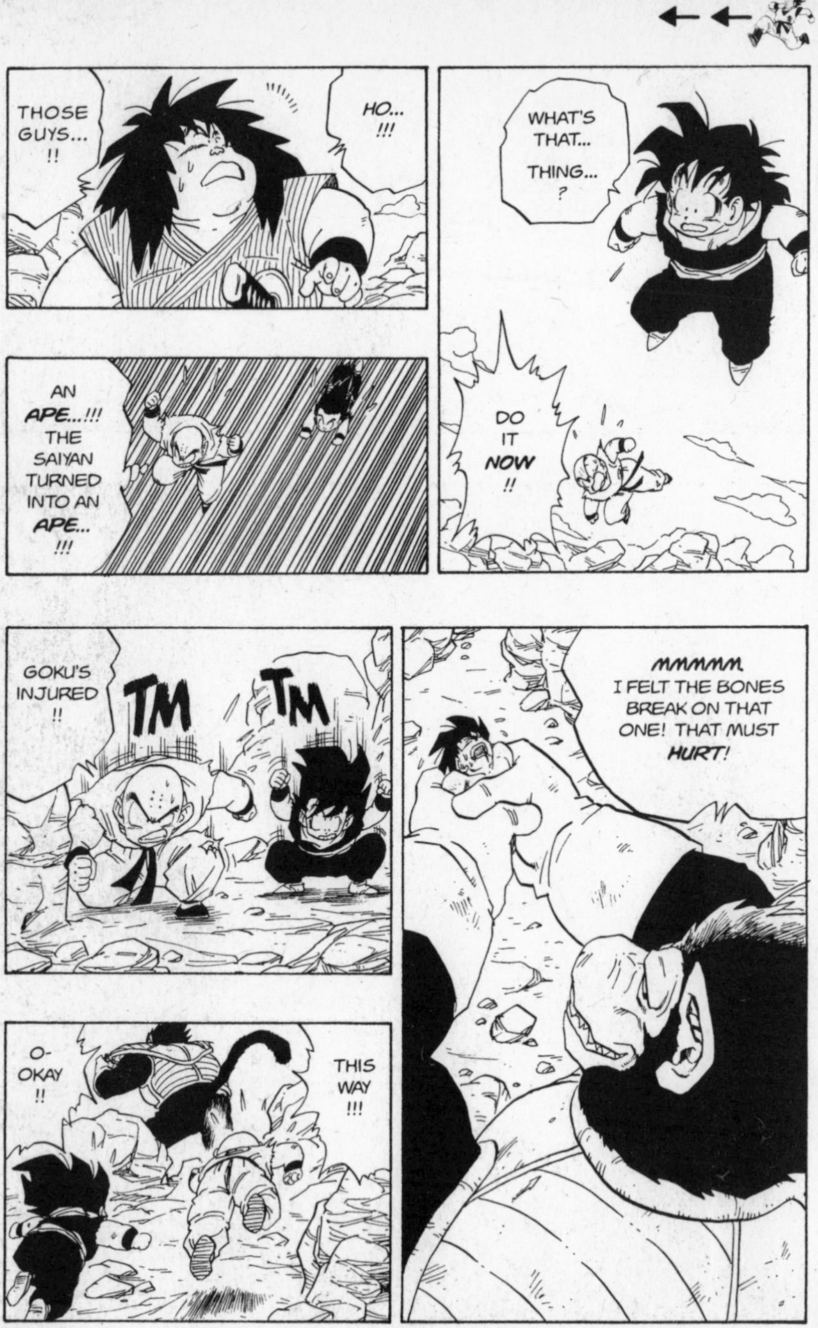
WHAT'S THAT... THING...?
DO IT NOW!!
HO...!!!
THOSE GUYS...!!
AN APE...!!! THE SAIYAN TURNED INTO AN APE...!!!
MMMMM. I FELT THE BONES BREAK ON THAT ONE! THAT MUST HURT!
TM
TM
GOKU'S INJURED!!
THIS WAY!!!
O-OKAY!!

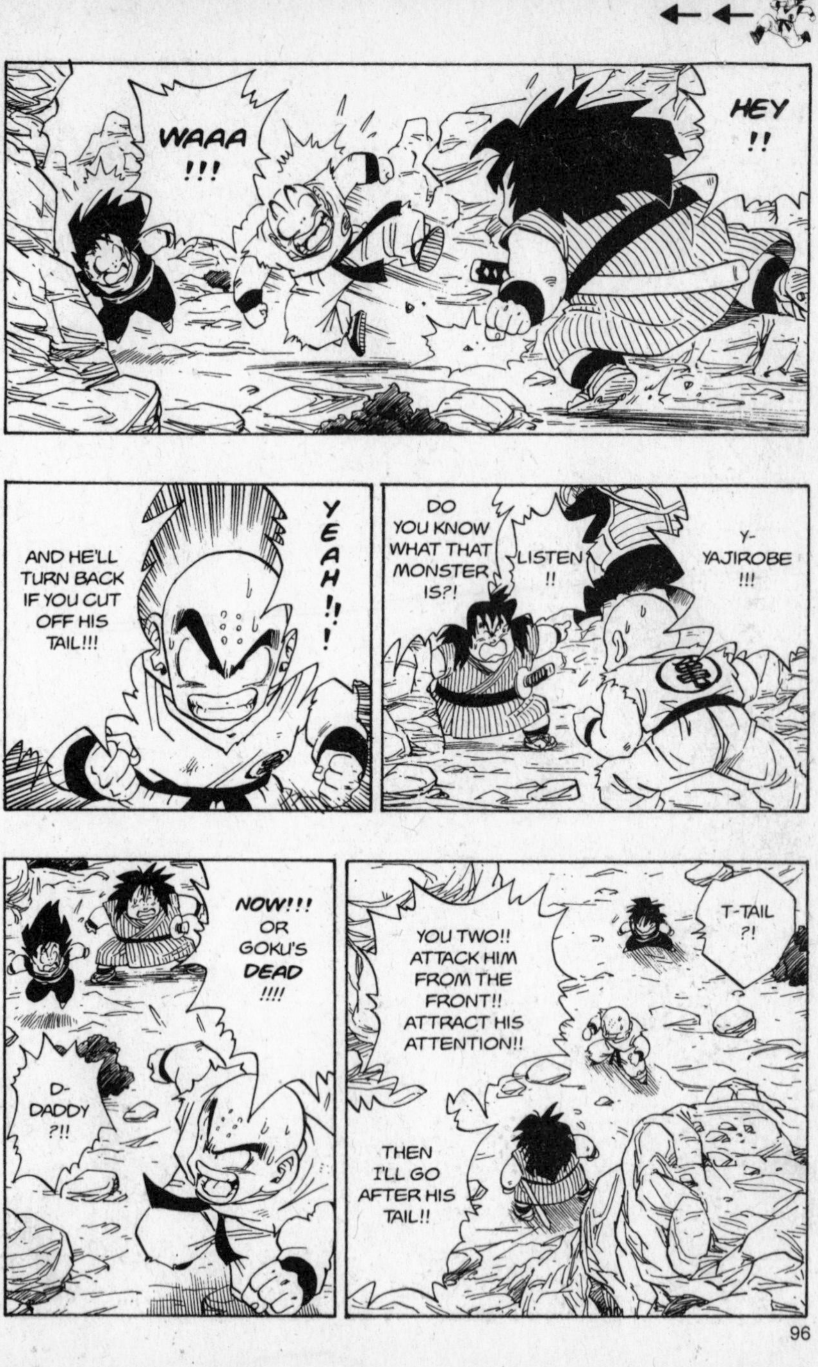
HEY!!
WAAA!!!
Y-YAJIROBE!!!
LISTEN!!
DO YOU KNOW WHAT THAT MONSTER IS?!
YEAH!!!
AND HE'LL TURN BACK IF YOU CUT OFF HIS TAIL!!!
T-TAIL?!
YOU TWO!! ATTACK HIM FROM THE FRONT!! ATTRACT HIS ATTENTION!!
THEN I'LL GO AFTER HIS TAIL!!
NOW!!! OR GOKU'S DEAD!!!!
D-DADDY?!!

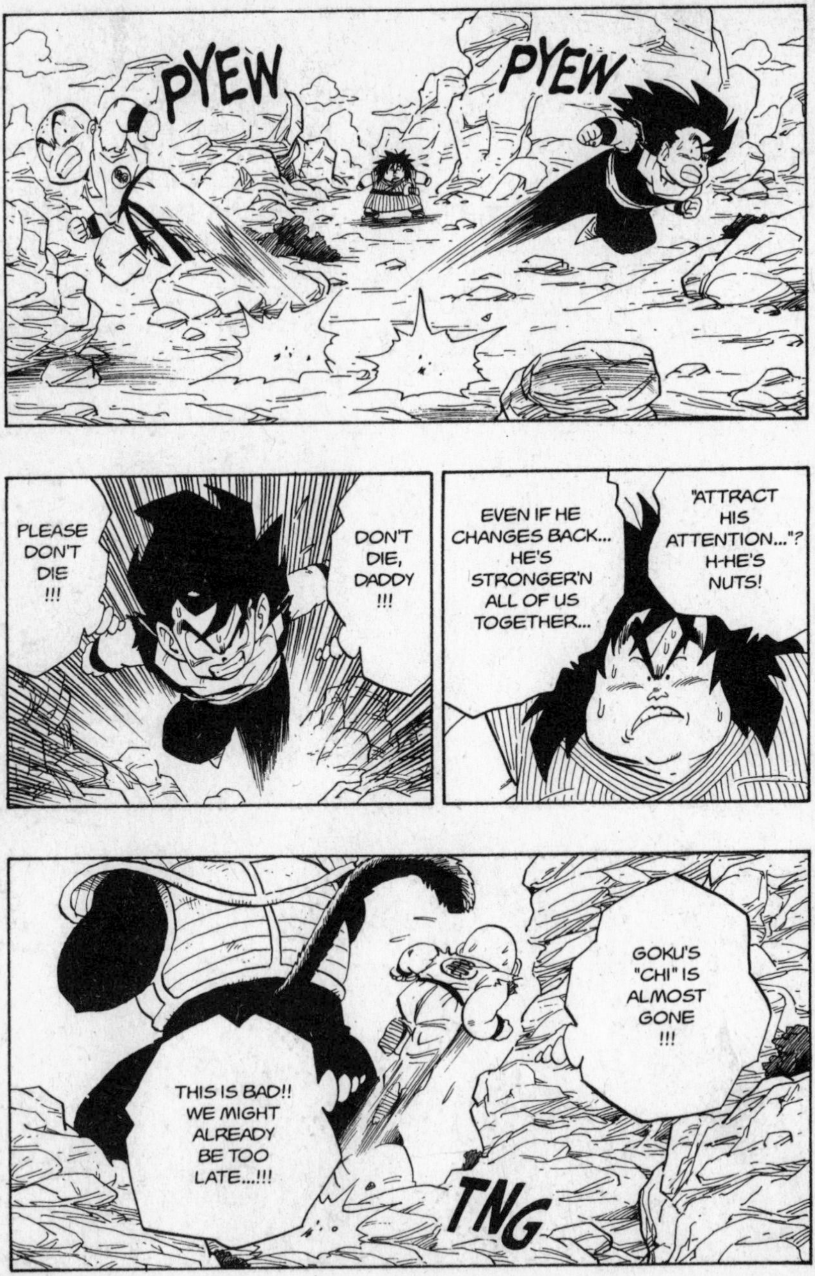
PYEW
PYEW
"ATTRACT HIS ATTENTION..."? H-HE'S NUTS!
EVEN IF HE CHANGES BACK... HE'S STRONGER'N ALL OF US TOGETHER...
DON'T DIE, DADDY !!!
PLEASE DON'T DIE !!!
GOKU'S "CHI" IS ALMOST GONE !!!
THIS IS BAD!! WE MIGHT ALREADY BE TOO LATE...!!!
TNG

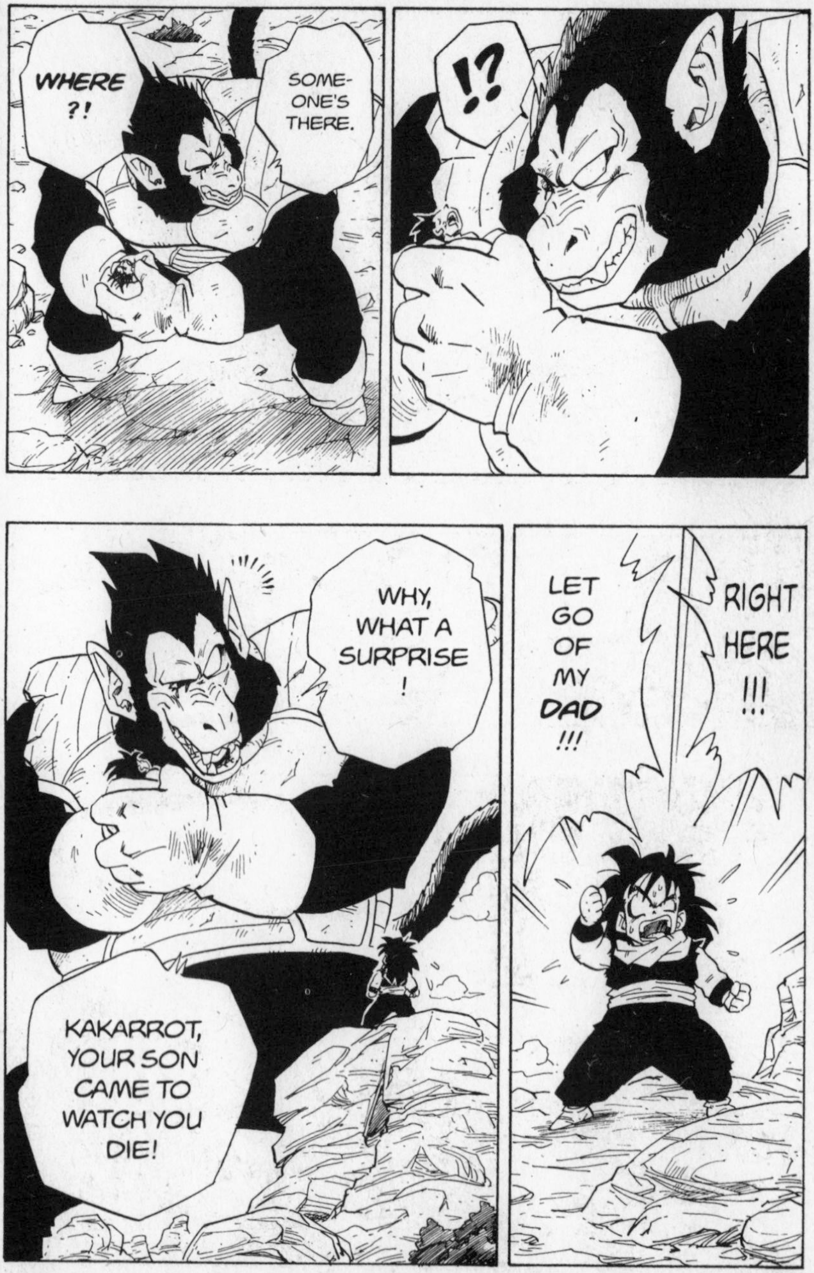
!?
SOME-ONE'S THERE.
WHERE ?!
RIGHT HERE !!!
LET GO OF MY DAD !!!
WHY, WHAT A SURPRISE !
KAKARROT, YOUR SON CAME TO WATCH YOU DIE!

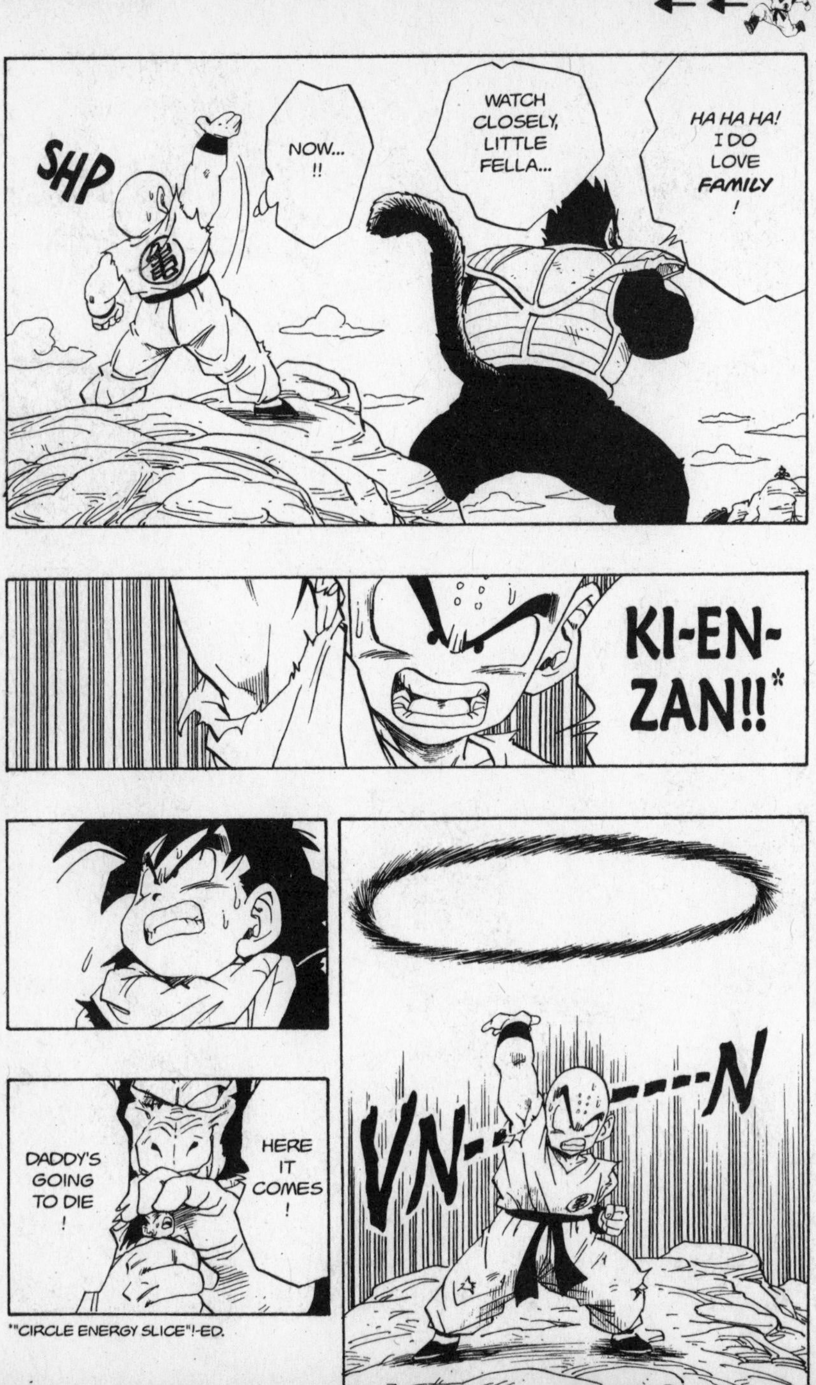
HA HA HA! I DO LOVE FAMILY!
WATCH CLOSELY, LITTLE FELLA...
NOW...!!
SHP
KI-EN-ZAN!!*
VN----N
HERE IT COMES!
DADDY'S GOING TO DIE!

*"CIRCLE ENERGY SLICE"!-ED.

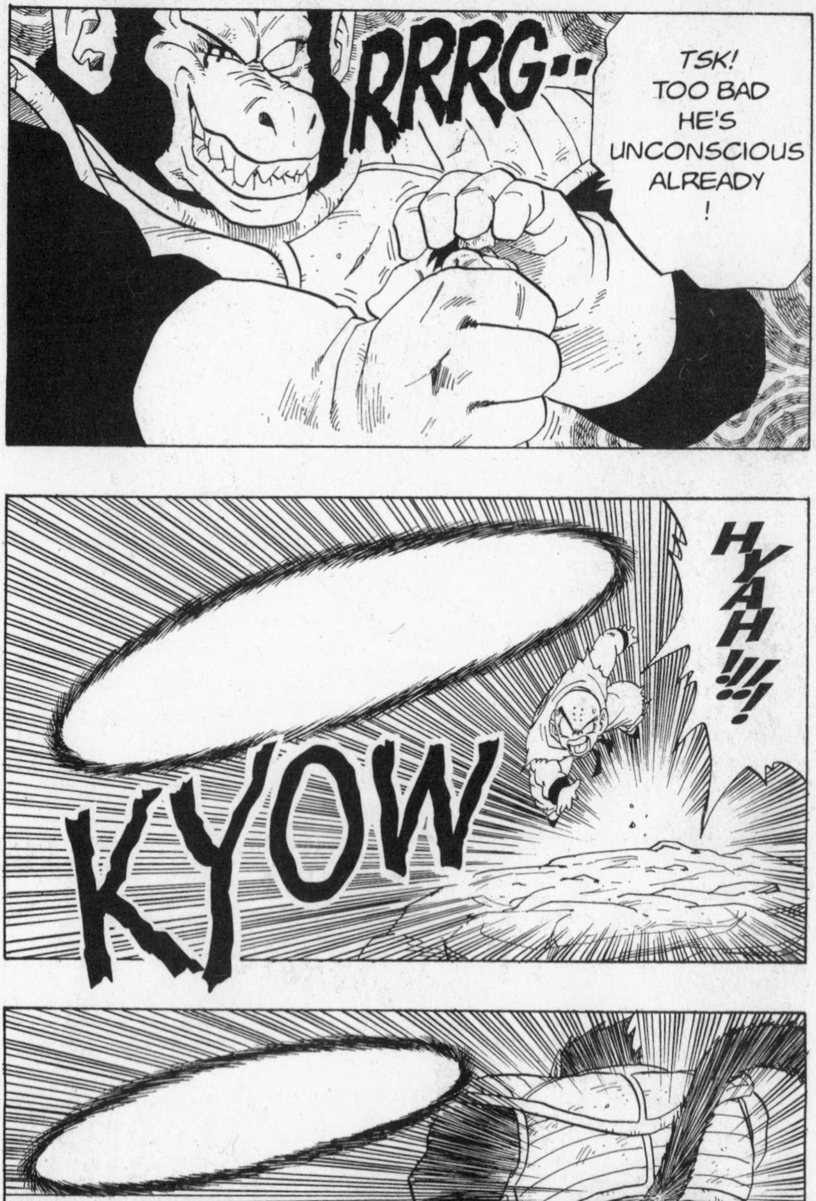
RRRG..
TSK! TOO BAD HE'S UNCONSCIOUS ALREADY!
HYAH!!!
KYOW

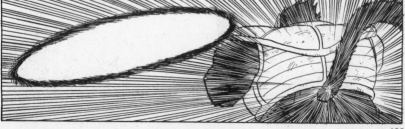

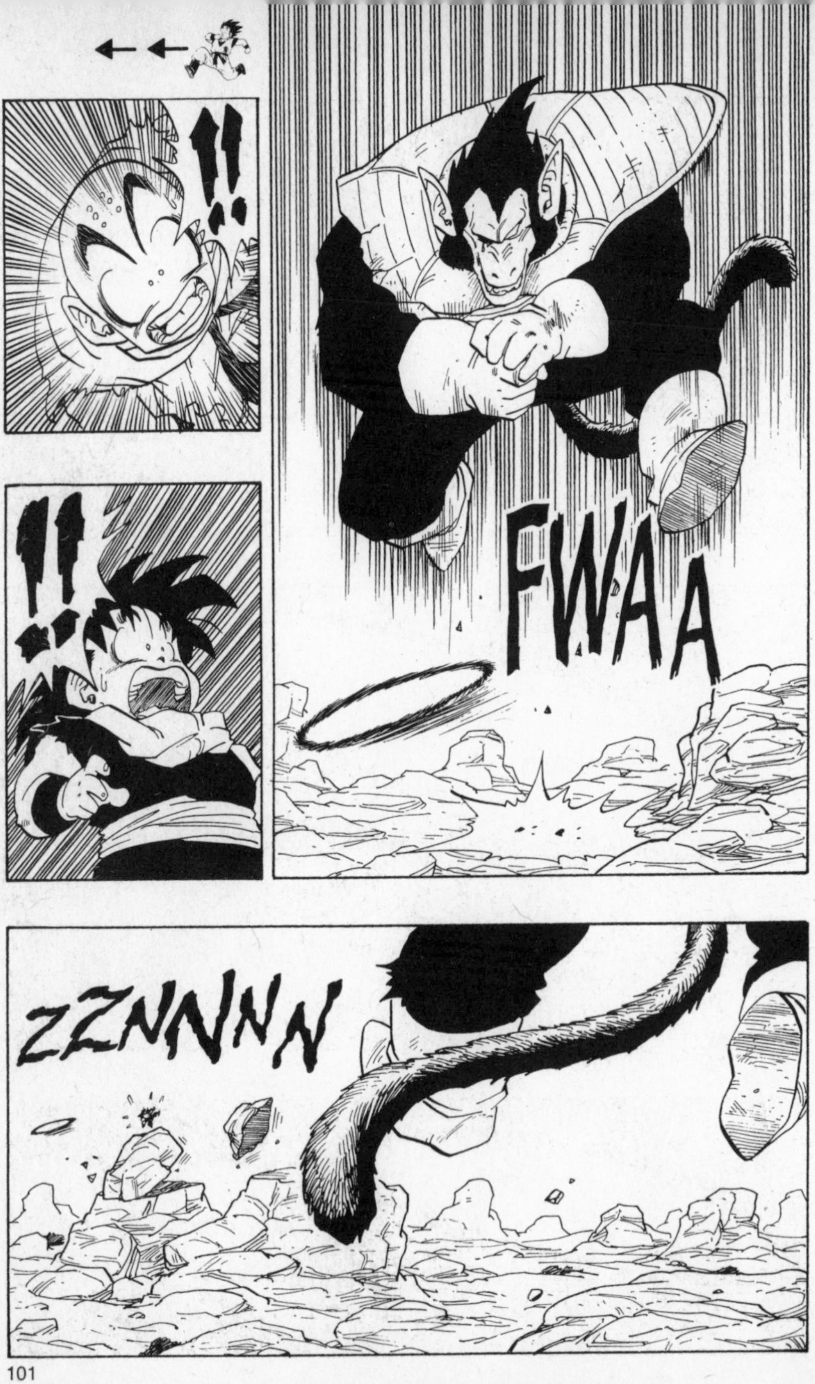
FWAA
!!
!!
ZZNNNN

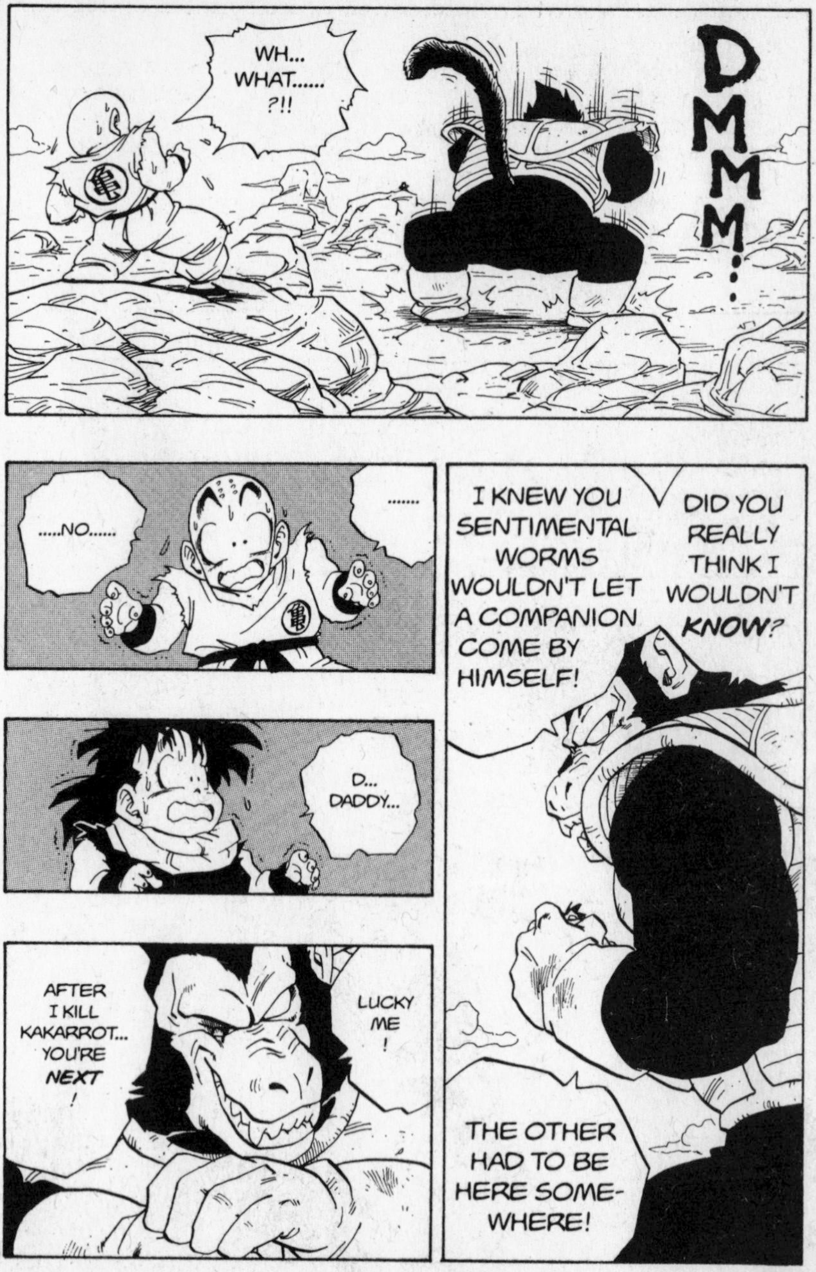
DMMM...
WH... WHAT......?!!
DID YOU REALLY THINK I WOULDN'T KNOW?
I KNEW YOU SENTIMENTAL WORMS WOULDN'T LET A COMPANION COME BY HIMSELF!
THE OTHER HAD TO BE HERE SOME-WHERE!
....
.....NO......
D... DADDY...
LUCKY ME!
AFTER I KILL KAKARROT... YOU'RE NEXT!

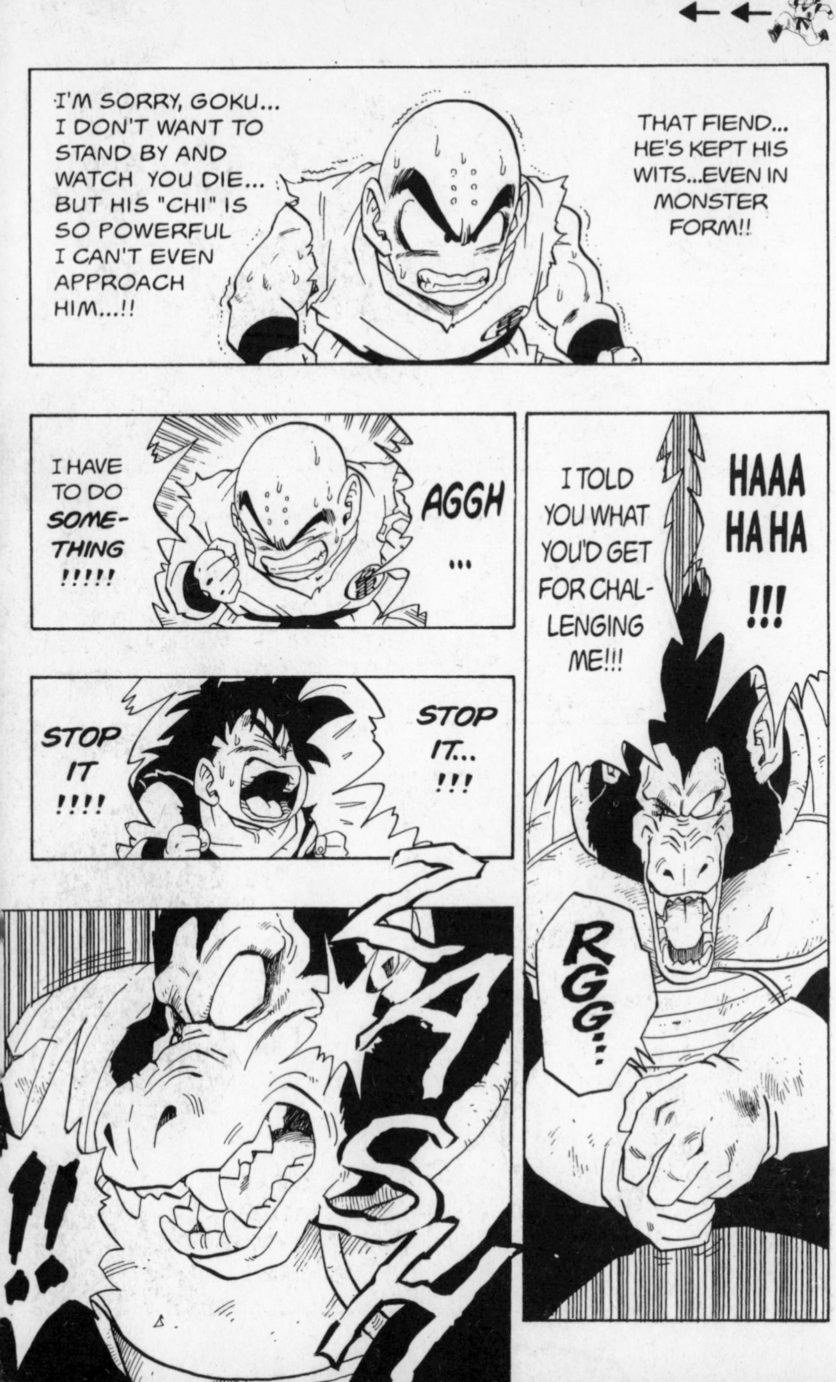

THAT FIEND... HE'S KEPT HIS WITS...EVEN IN MONSTER FORM!!
I'M SORRY, GOKU... I DON'T WANT TO STAND BY AND WATCH YOU DIE... BUT HIS "CHI" IS SO POWERFUL I CAN'T EVEN APPROACH HIM...!!
HAAA HA HA !!!
I TOLD YOU WHAT YOU'D GET FOR CHAL-LENGING ME!!!
RGG...
AGGH ...
I HAVE TO DO SOME-THING !!!!!
STOP IT... !!!
STOP IT !!!!
!!

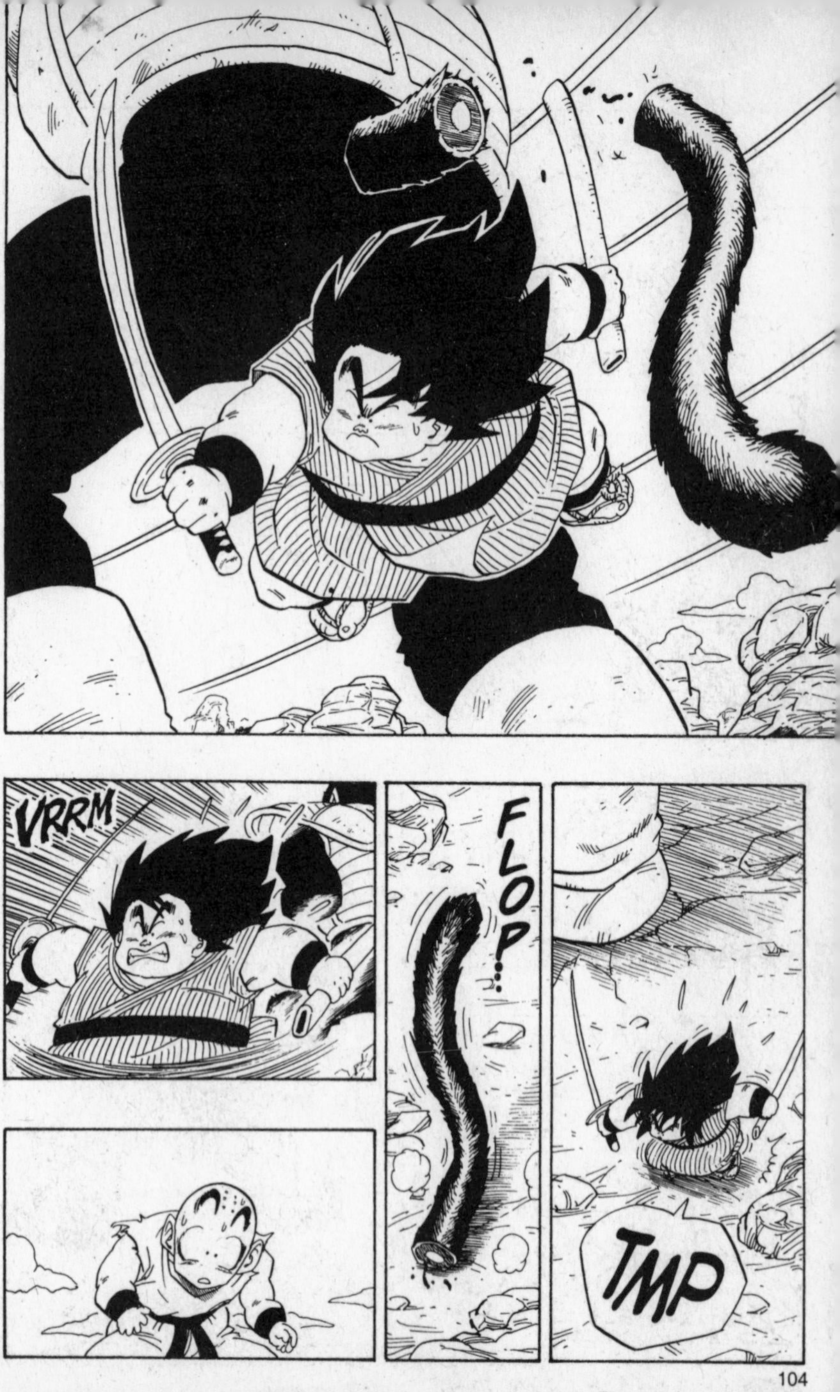
TMP
FLOP...
VRRM

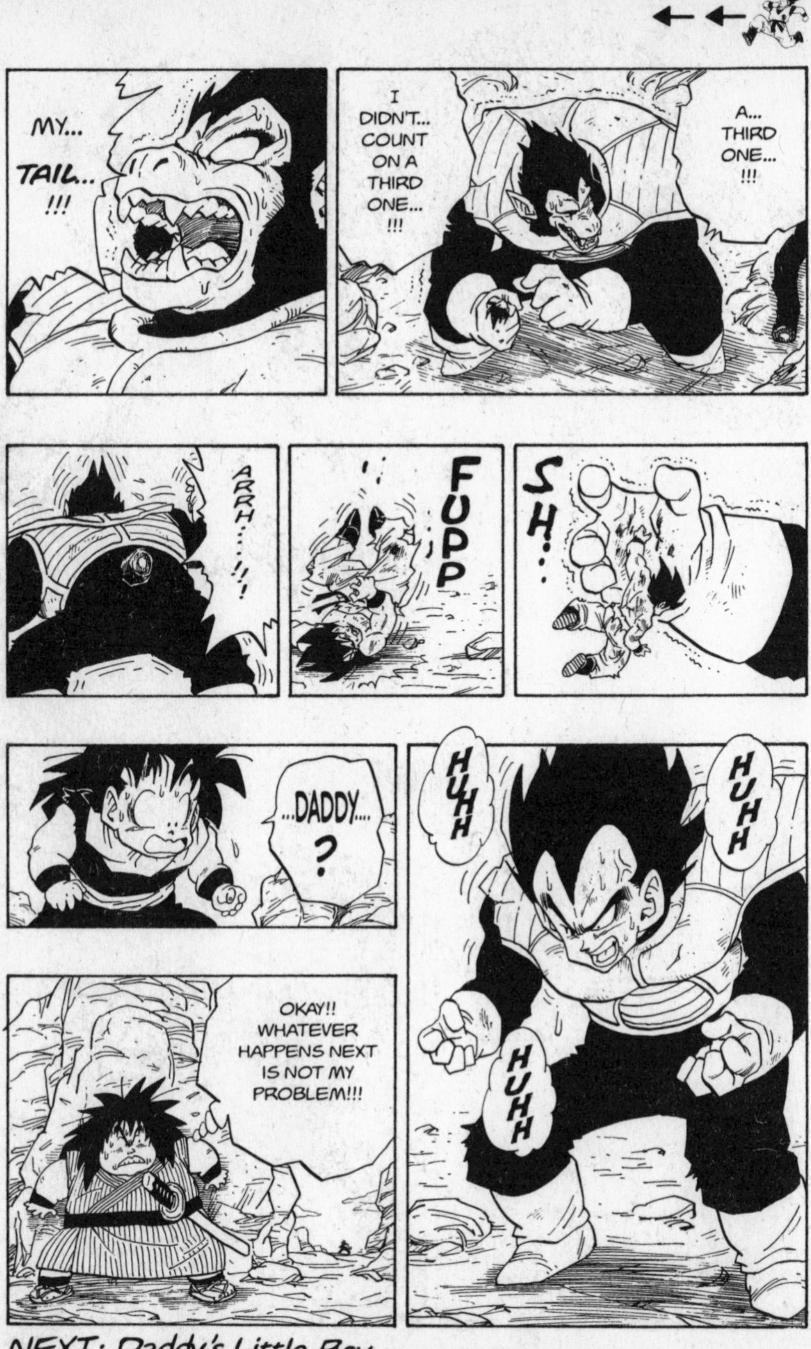
A... THIRD ONE...!!!
I DIDN'T... COUNT ON A THIRD ONE...!!!
MY... TAIL...!!!
SH...
FUPP
ARRH...!!
HUHH
HUHH
HUHH
...DADDY....?
OKAY!! WHATEVER HAPPENS NEXT IS NOT MY PROBLEM!!!

NEXT: *Daddy's Little Boy*

DBZ:42 • Least Resistance

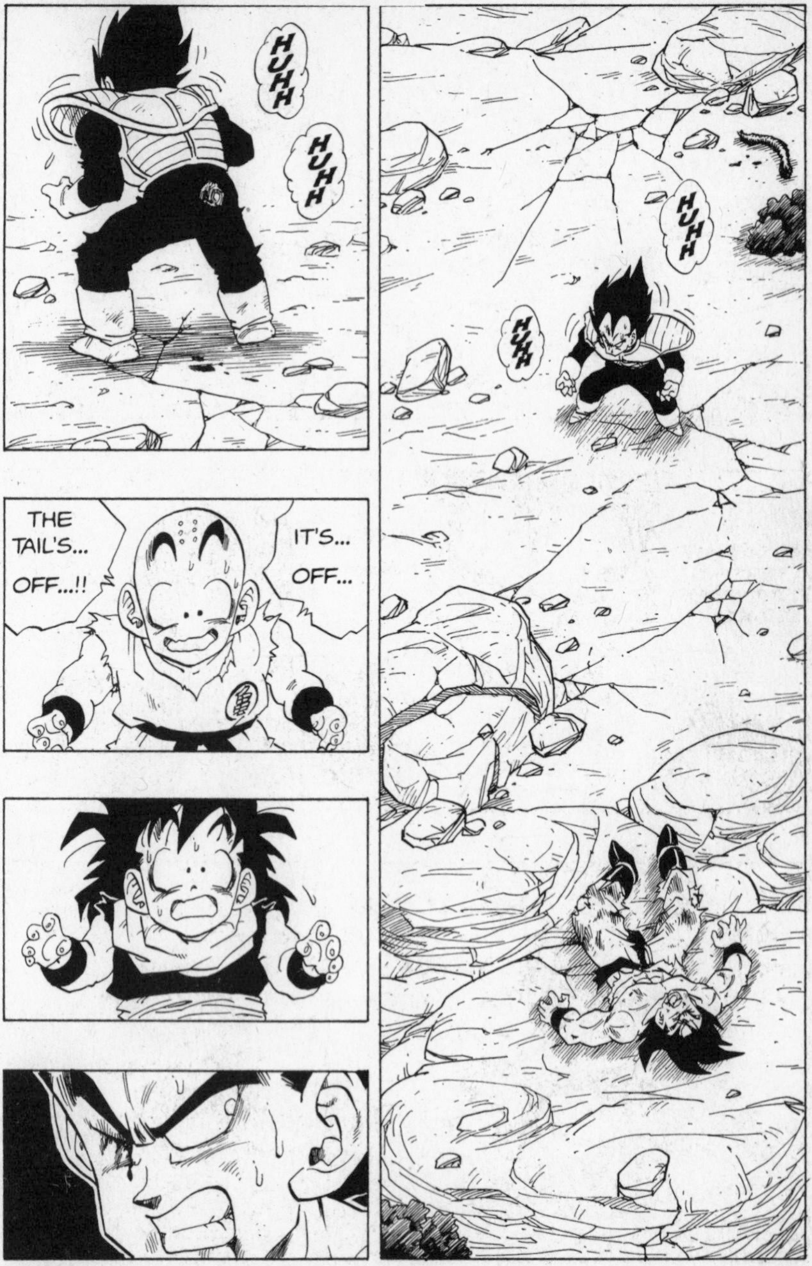
HUHH
HUHH
HUHH
HUHH
IT'S... OFF...
THE TAIL'S... OFF...!!

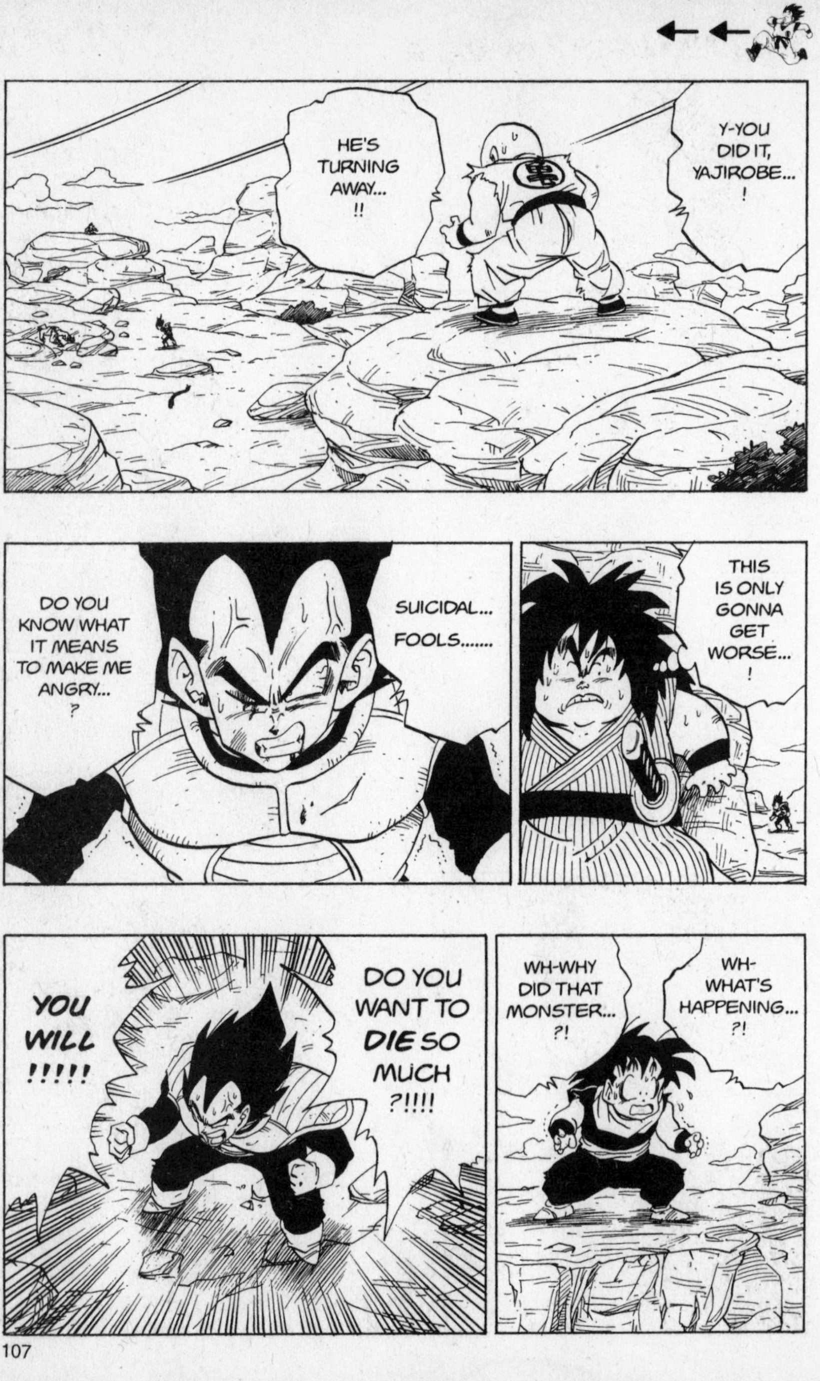
Y-YOU DID IT, YAJIROBE...!
HE'S TURNING AWAY...!!
THIS IS ONLY GONNA GET WORSE...!
SUICIDAL... FOOLS.......
DO YOU KNOW WHAT IT MEANS TO MAKE ME ANGRY...?
WH-WHAT'S HAPPENING...?!
WH-WHY DID THAT MONSTER...?!
DO YOU WANT TO DIE SO MUCH?!!!!
YOU WILL!!!!!

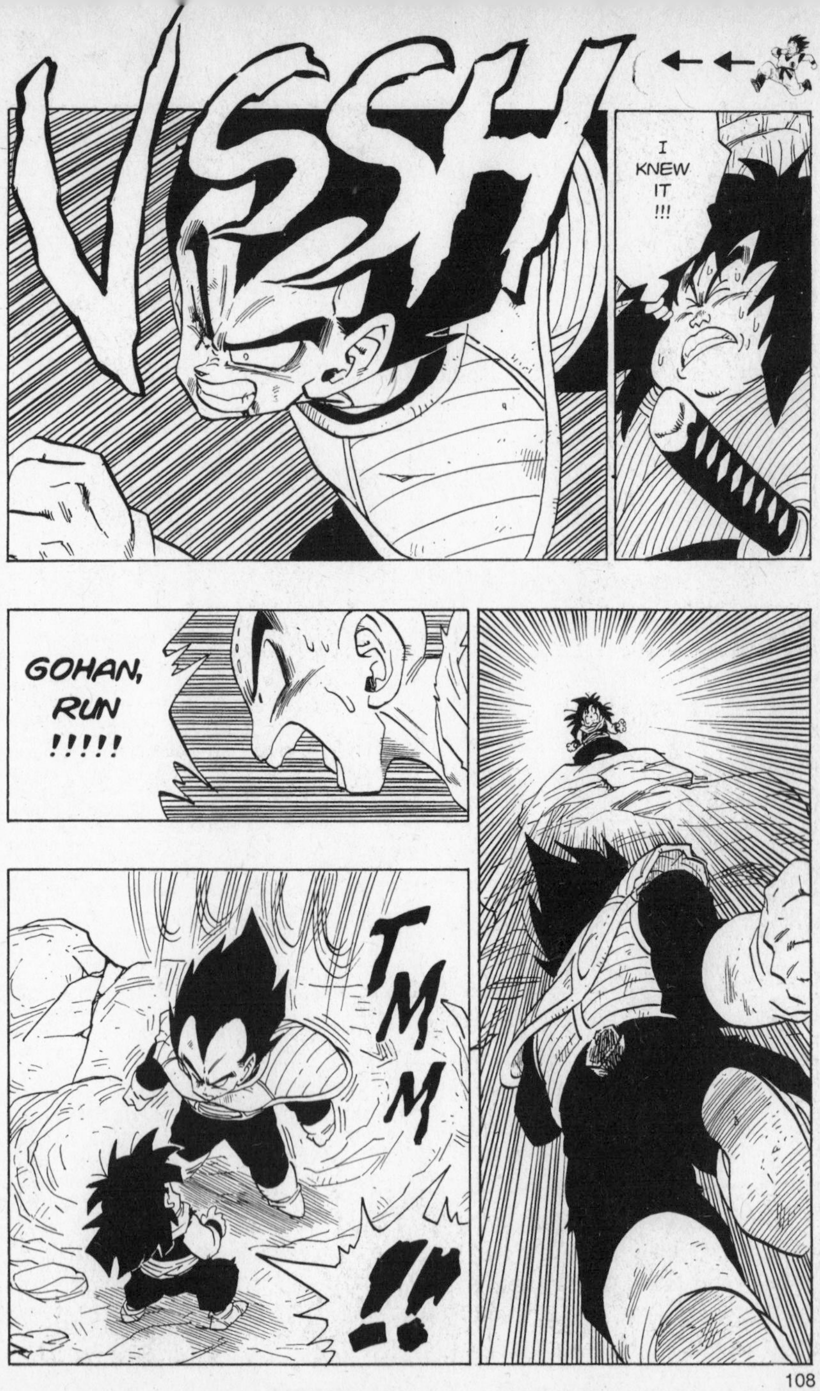
I KNEW IT !!!
VSSH
GOHAN, RUN !!!!!
TMM !!

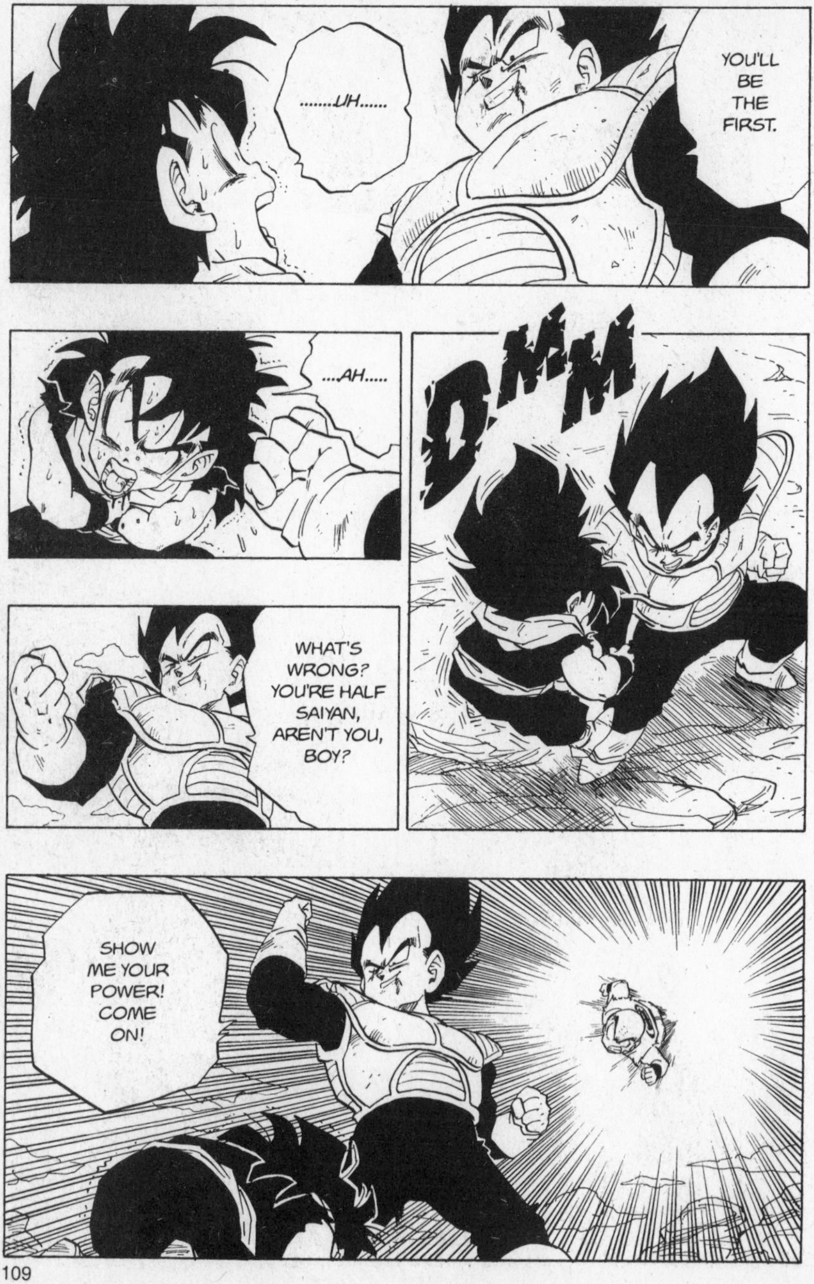
YOU'LL BE THE FIRST.
.........UH.......
DMM
....AH.....
WHAT'S WRONG? YOU'RE HALF SAIYAN, AREN'T YOU, BOY?
SHOW ME YOUR POWER! COME ON!

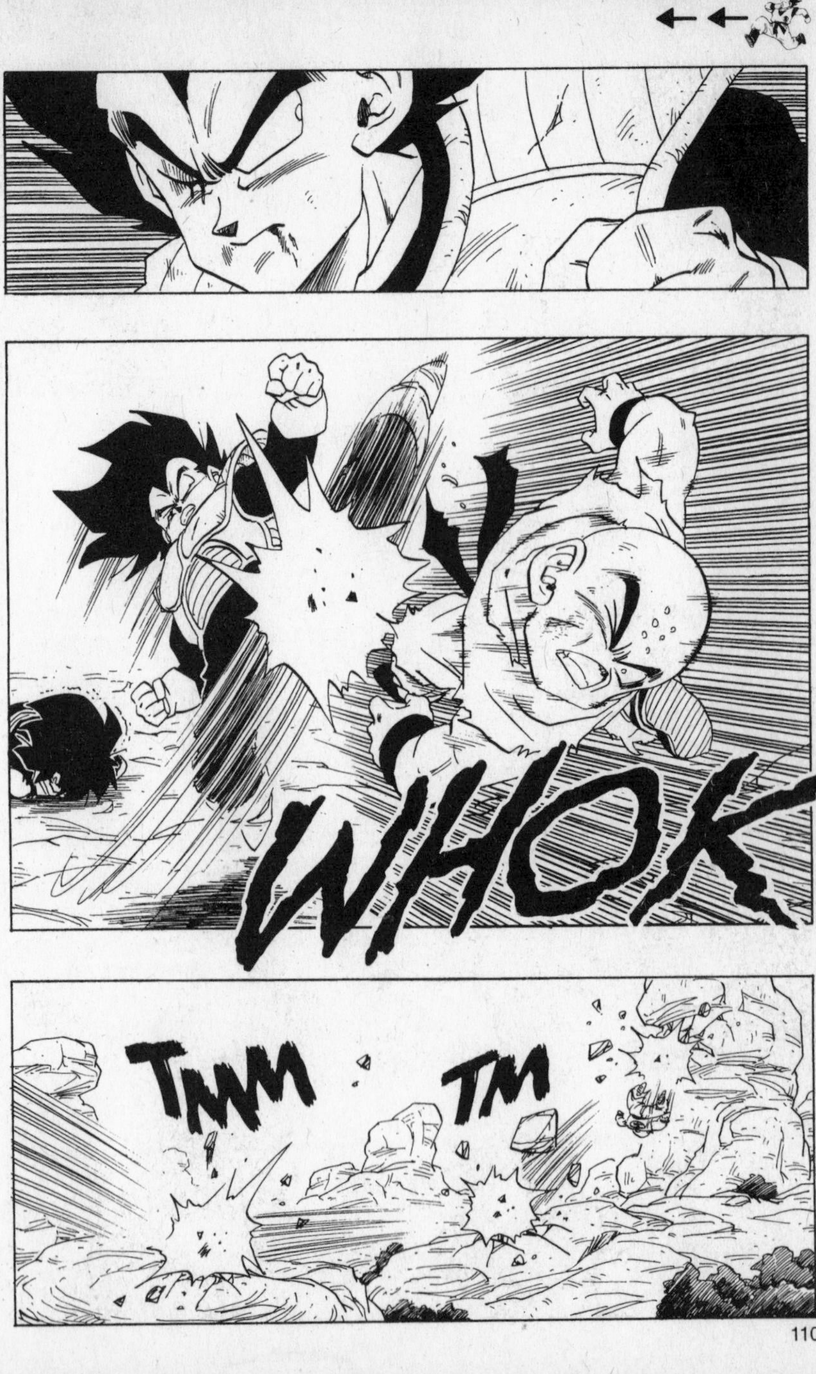
WHOK
TM
TMM

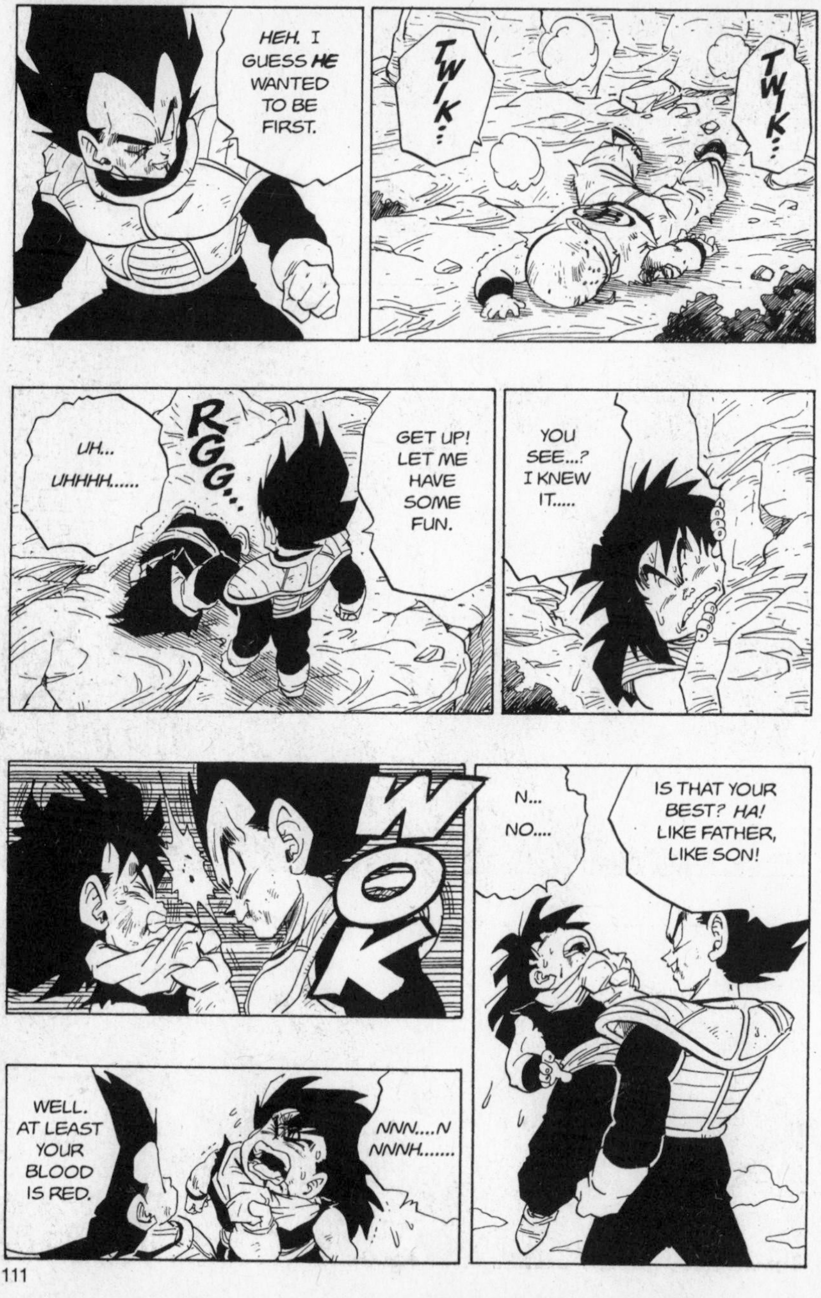
TWIK...
TWIK...
HEH. I GUESS HE WANTED TO BE FIRST.
YOU SEE...? I KNEW IT.....
GET UP! LET ME HAVE SOME FUN.
RGG...
UH... UHHHH......
IS THAT YOUR BEST? HA! LIKE FATHER, LIKE SON!
N... NO....
WOK
NNN....N NNNH......
WELL. AT LEAST YOUR BLOOD IS RED.

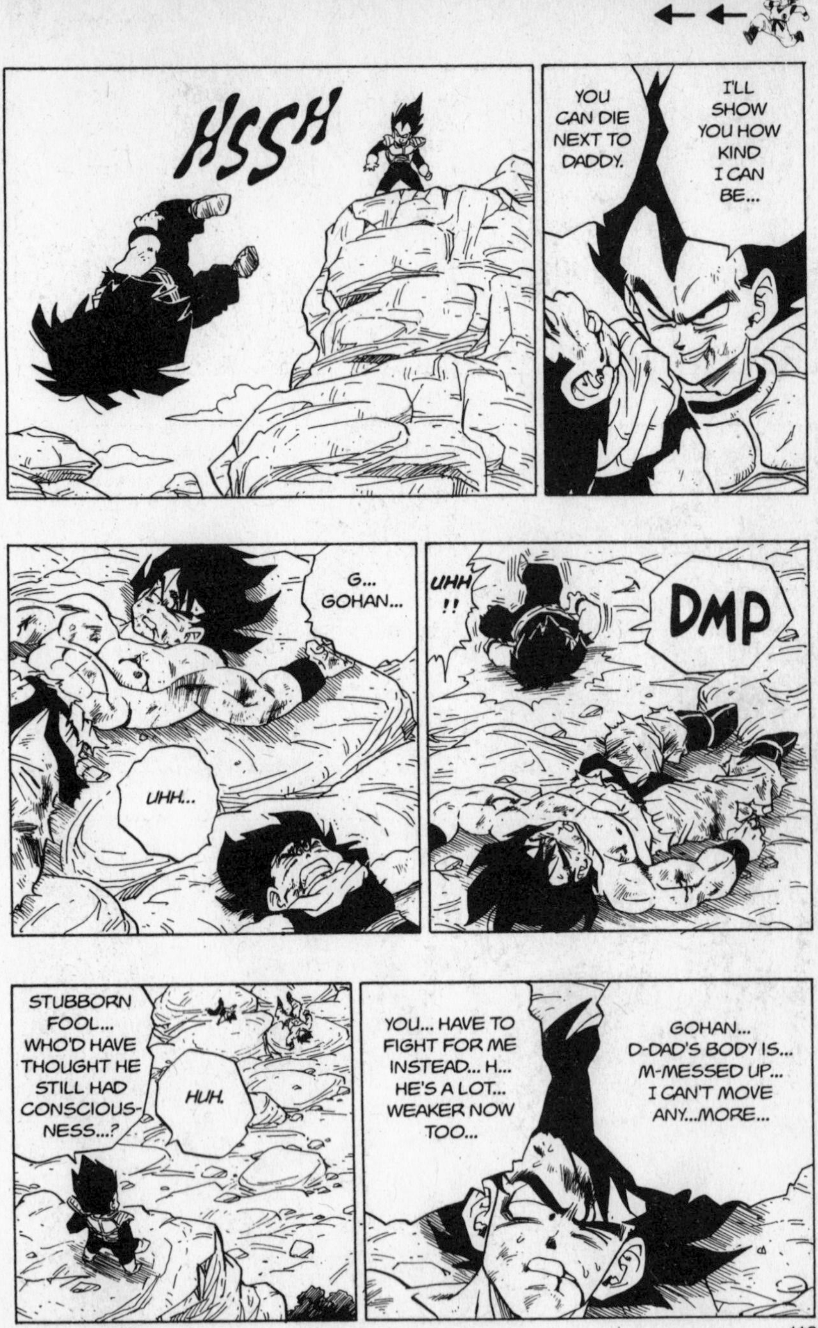
I'LL SHOW YOU HOW KIND I CAN BE...
YOU CAN DIE NEXT TO DADDY.
HSSH
DMP
UHH !!
G... GOHAN...
UHH...
GOHAN... D-DAD'S BODY IS... M-MESSED UP... I CAN'T MOVE ANY...MORE...
YOU... HAVE TO FIGHT FOR ME INSTEAD... H... HE'S A LOT... WEAKER NOW TOO...
STUBBORN FOOL... WHO'D HAVE THOUGHT HE STILL HAD CONSCIOUS-NESS...?
HUH.

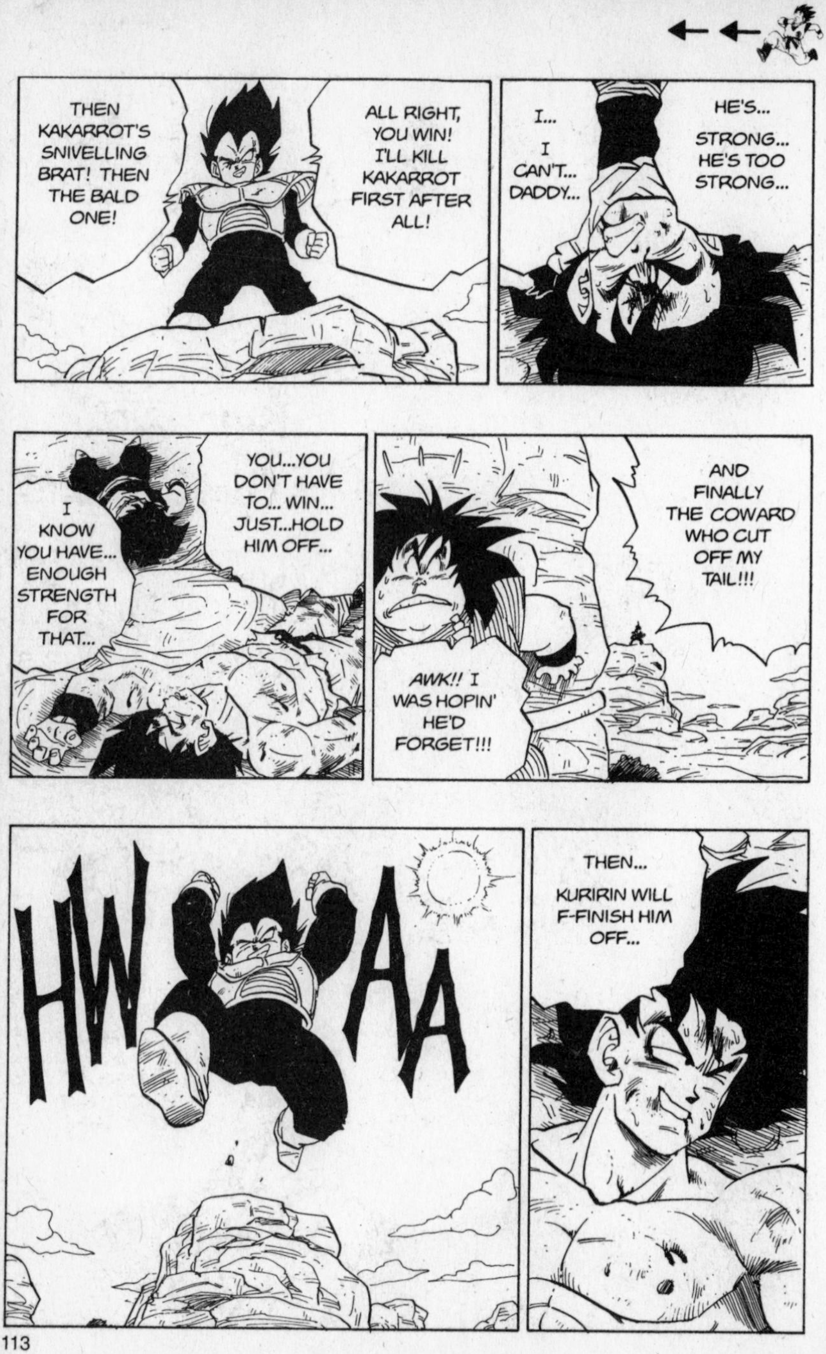
HE'S... STRONG... HE'S TOO STRONG...
I... I CAN'T... DADDY...
ALL RIGHT, YOU WIN! I'LL KILL KAKARROT FIRST AFTER ALL!
THEN KAKARROT'S SNIVELLING BRAT! THEN THE BALD ONE!
AND FINALLY THE COWARD WHO CUT OFF MY TAIL!!!
AWK!! I WAS HOPIN' HE'D FORGET!!!
YOU...YOU DON'T HAVE TO... WIN... JUST...HOLD HIM OFF...
I KNOW YOU HAVE... ENOUGH STRENGTH FOR THAT...
THEN... KURIRIN WILL F-FINISH HIM OFF...
HWAA

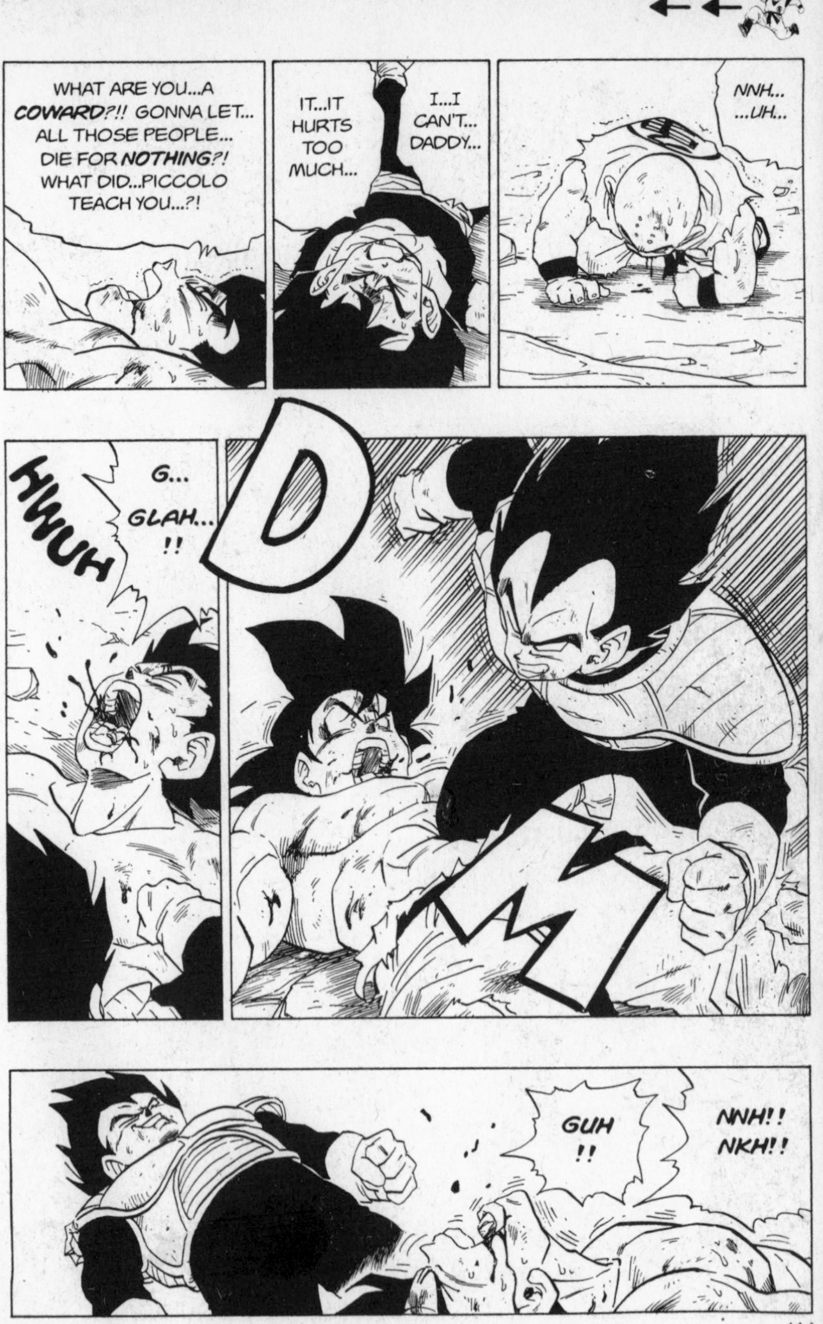
NNH...
...UH...
I...I CAN'T... DADDY...
IT...IT HURTS TOO MUCH...
WHAT ARE YOU...A *COWARD?!!* GONNA LET... ALL THOSE PEOPLE... DIE FOR *NOTHING?!* WHAT DID...PICCOLO TEACH YOU...?!
D
M
G... GLAH...!!
HWUH
NNH!! NKH!!
GUH!!

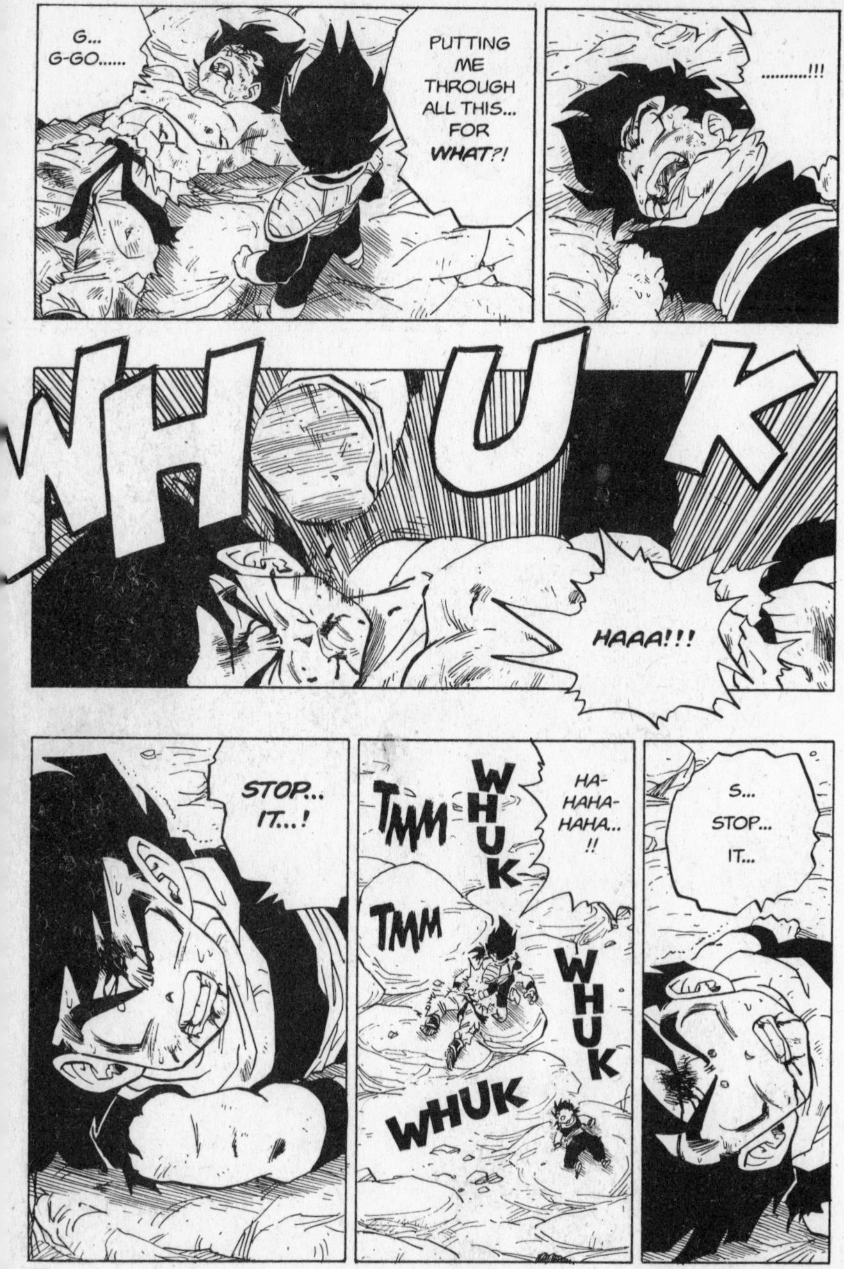

..........!!!
PUTTING ME THROUGH ALL THIS... FOR WHAT?!
G... G-GO......
WHUK
HAAA!!!
S... STOP... IT...
HA-HAHA-HAHA... !!
WHUK
TMM
TMM
WHUK
WHUK
STOP... IT...!

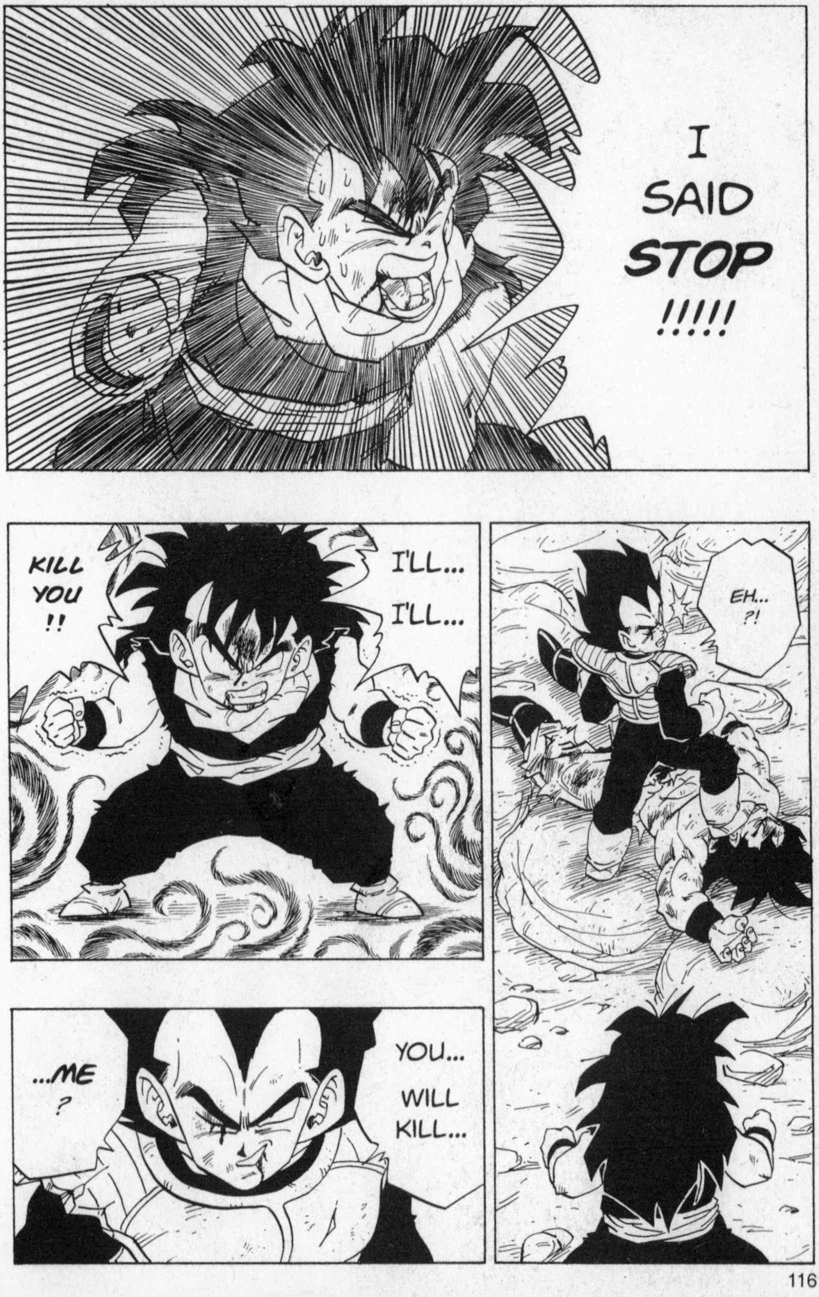
I SAID STOP!!!!!
EH...?!
I'LL... I'LL...
KILL YOU!!
YOU... WILL KILL...
...ME?

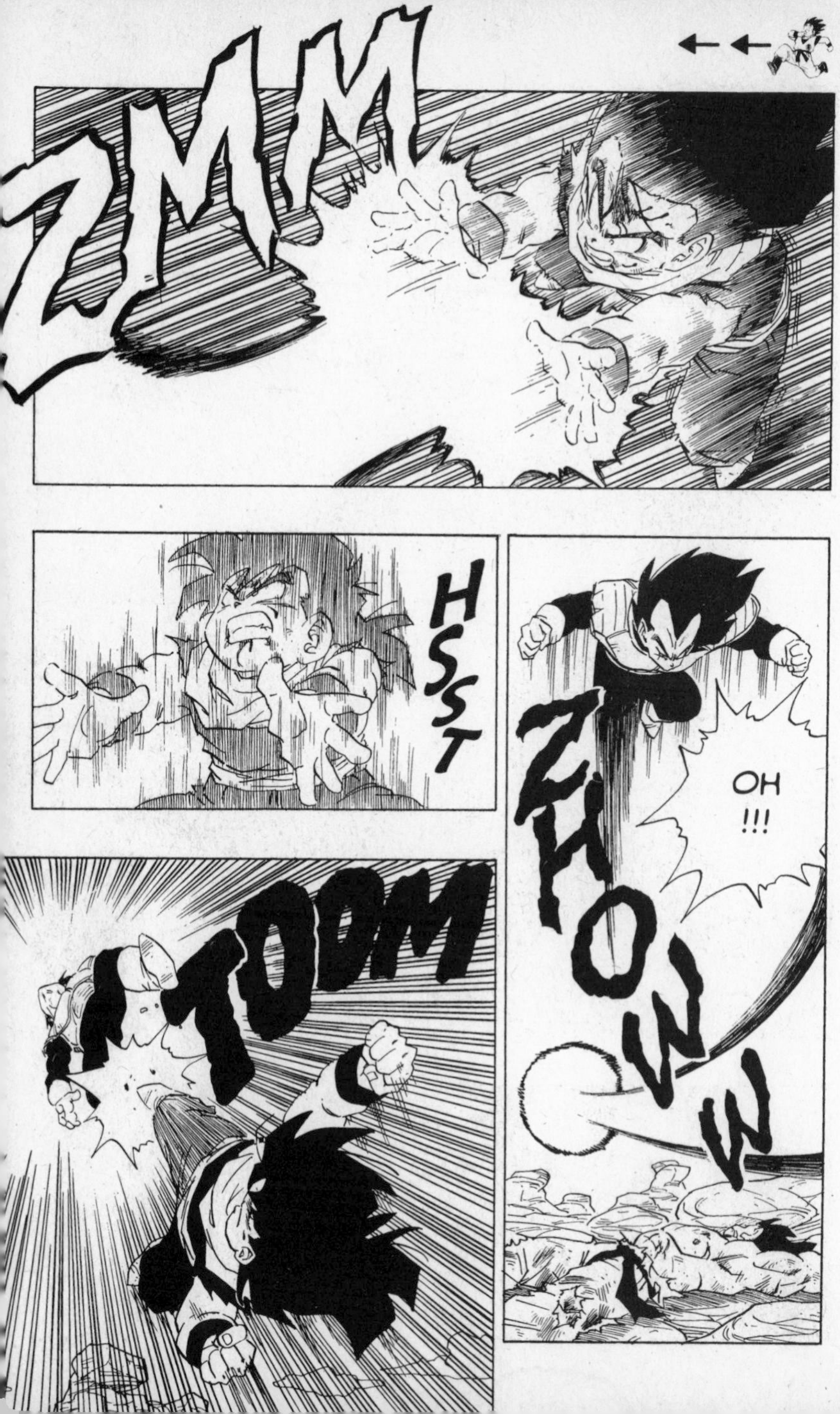
ZMM
ZHOWW
OH !!!
HSST
TOOM

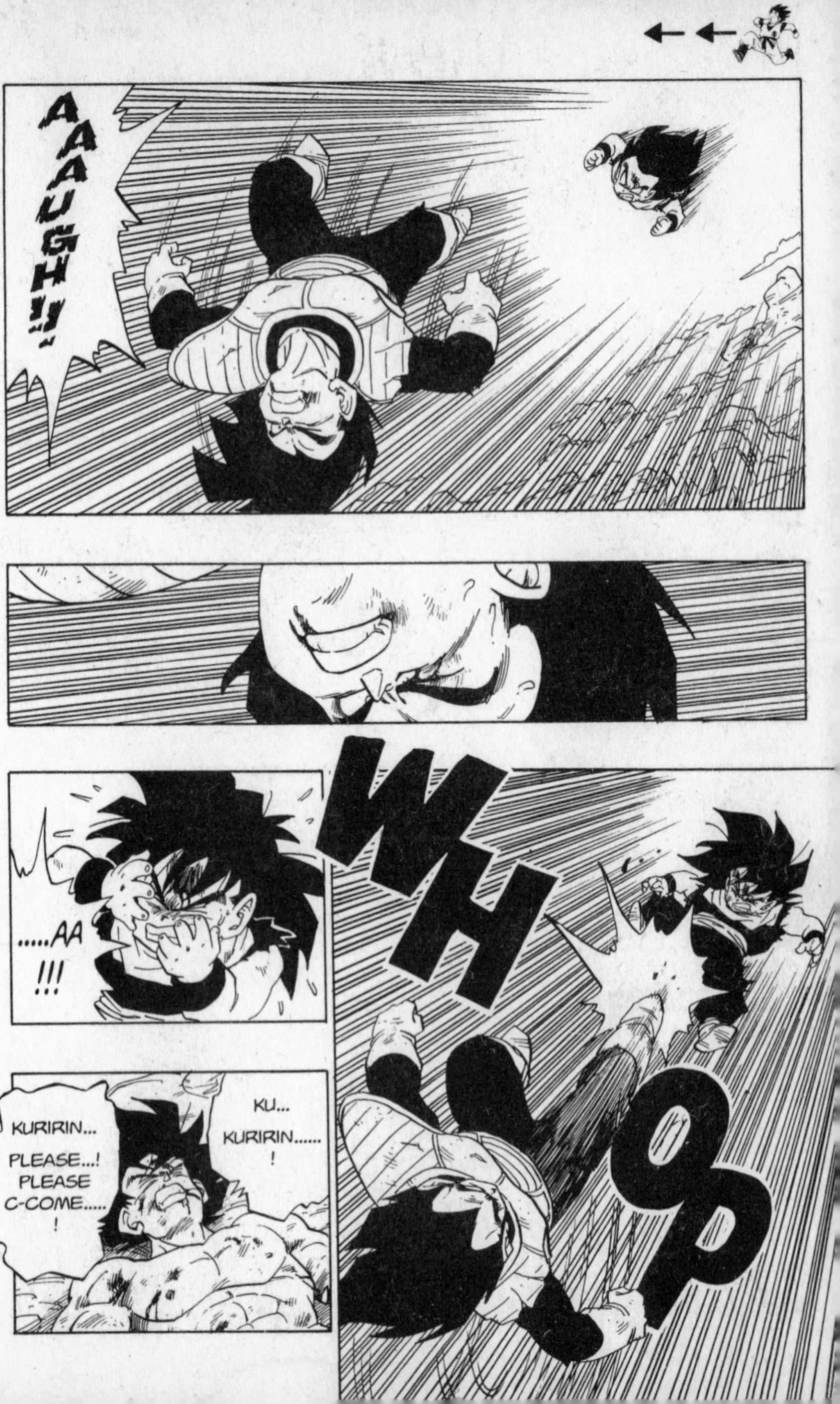
AAAUGH!!!
WH
.....AA !!!
KU... KURIRIN...... !
KURIRIN... PLEASE...! PLEASE C-COME..... !

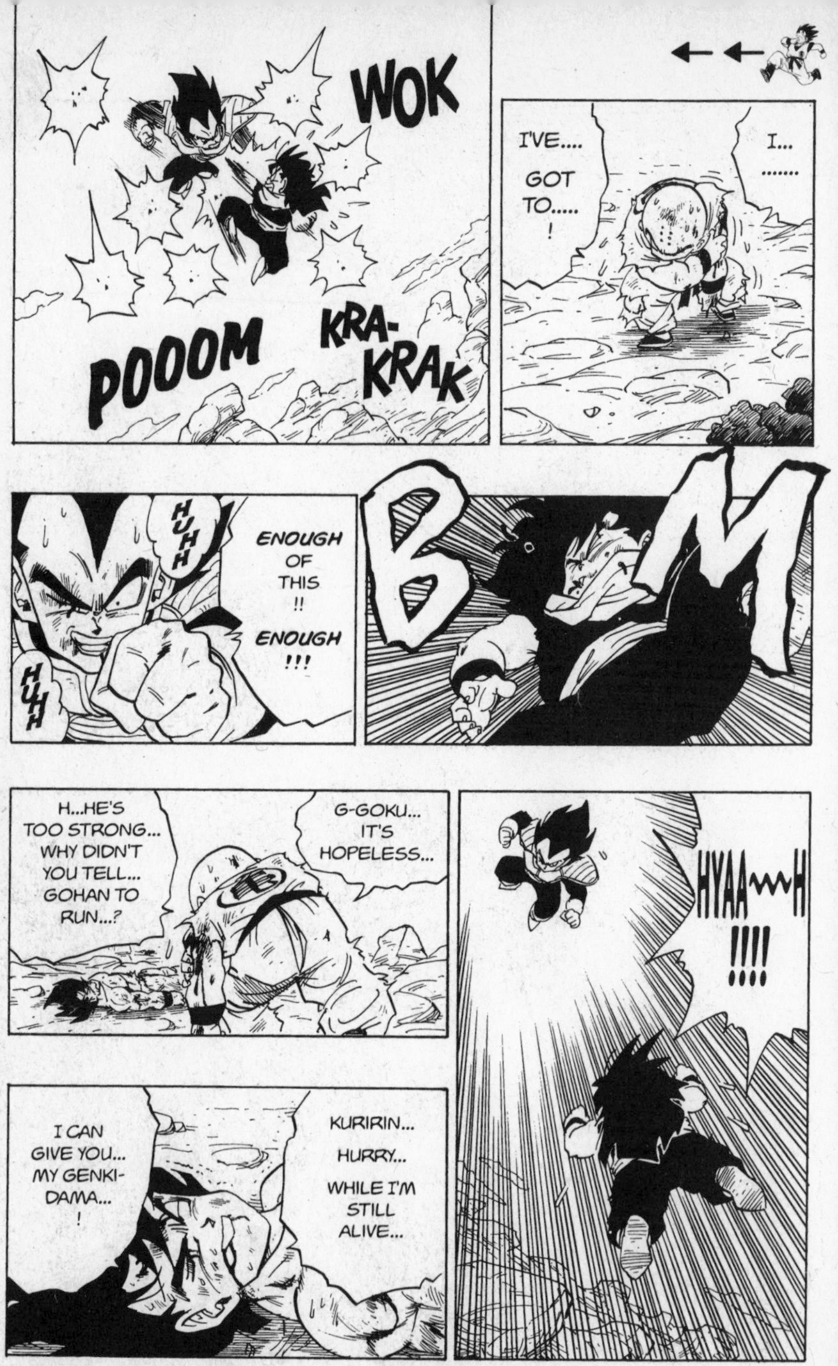
I... ....
I'VE.... GOT TO..... !
WOK
KRA-KRAK
POOOM
BM
HUHH
ENOUGH OF THIS !!
ENOUGH !!!
HUHH
HYAA~~H !!!!
G-GOKU... IT'S HOPELESS...
H...HE'S TOO STRONG... WHY DIDN'T YOU TELL... GOHAN TO RUN...?
KURIRIN...
HURRY...
WHILE I'M STILL ALIVE...
I CAN GIVE YOU... MY GENKI-DAMA... !

NEXT: Once More... the Sphere!

DBZ:43 • Once More…the Sphere!

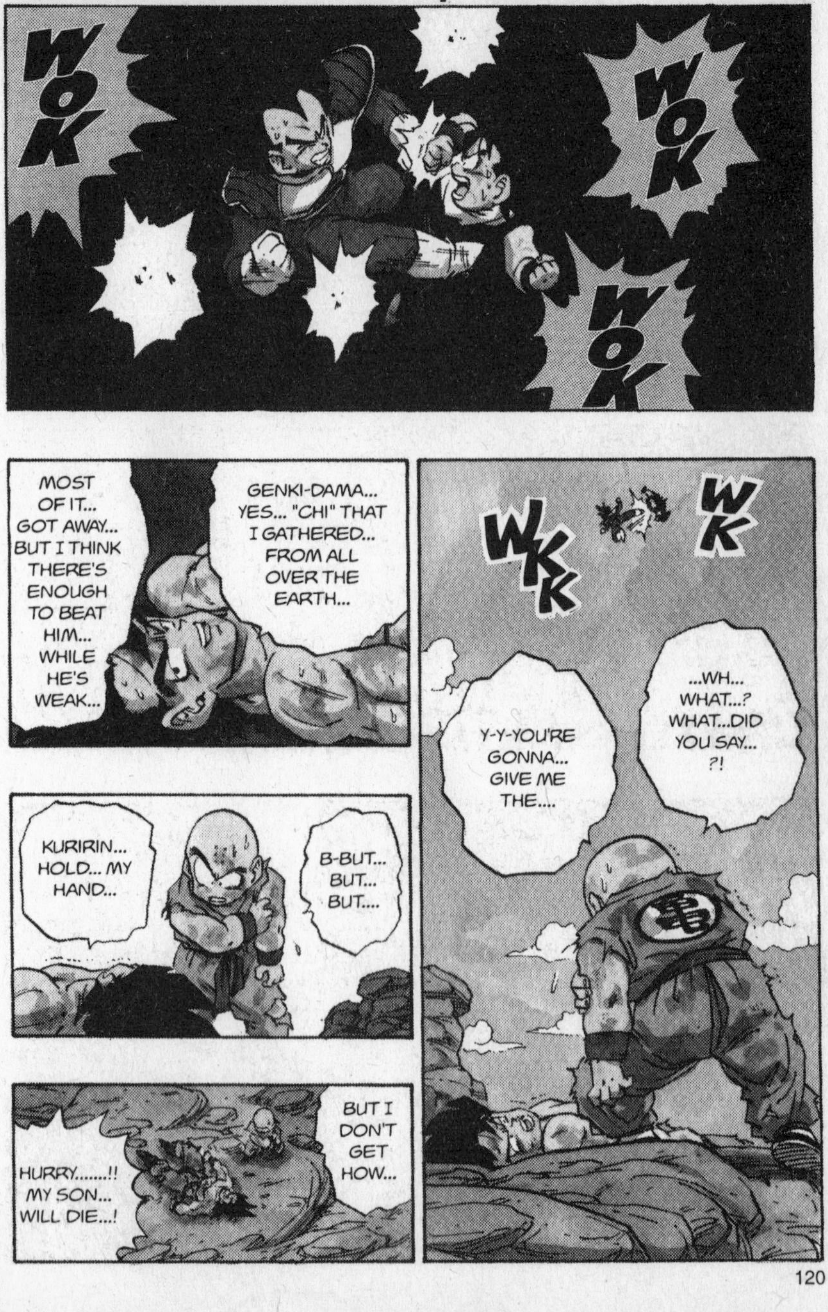

WOK
WOK
WOK
WK
WKK
...WH... WHAT...? WHAT...DID YOU SAY... ?!
Y-Y-YOU'RE GONNA... GIVE ME THE....
GENKI-DAMA... YES... "CHI" THAT I GATHERED... FROM ALL OVER THE EARTH...
MOST OF IT... GOT AWAY... BUT I THINK THERE'S ENOUGH TO BEAT HIM... WHILE HE'S WEAK...
B-BUT... BUT... BUT....
KURIRIN... HOLD... MY HAND...
BUT I DON'T GET HOW...
HURRY.......!! MY SON... WILL DIE...!

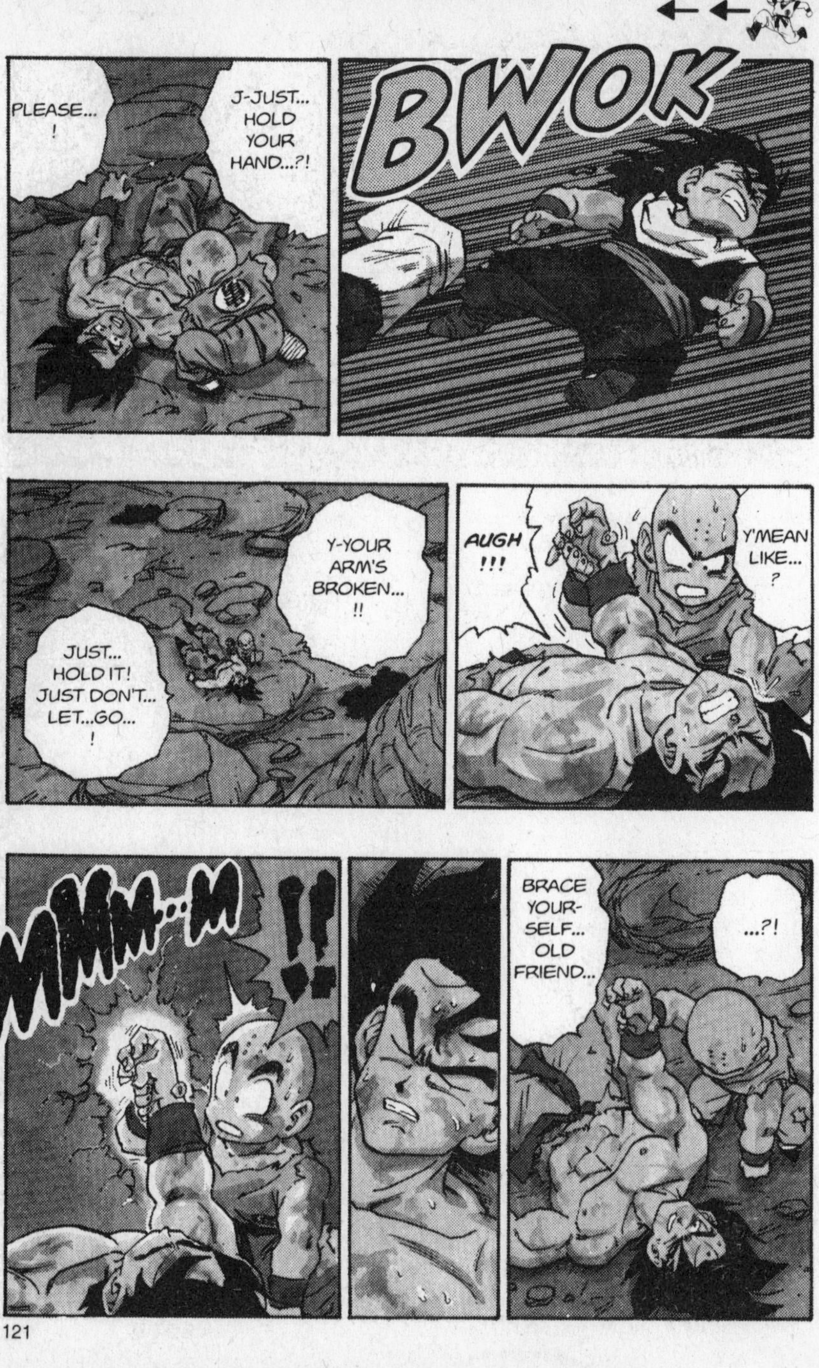
BWOK
J-JUST... HOLD YOUR HAND...?!
PLEASE... !
Y'MEAN LIKE... ?
AUGH !!!
Y-YOUR ARM'S BROKEN... !!
JUST... HOLD IT! JUST DON'T... LET...GO... !
...?!
BRACE YOUR-SELF... OLD FRIEND...
MMM...M
!!

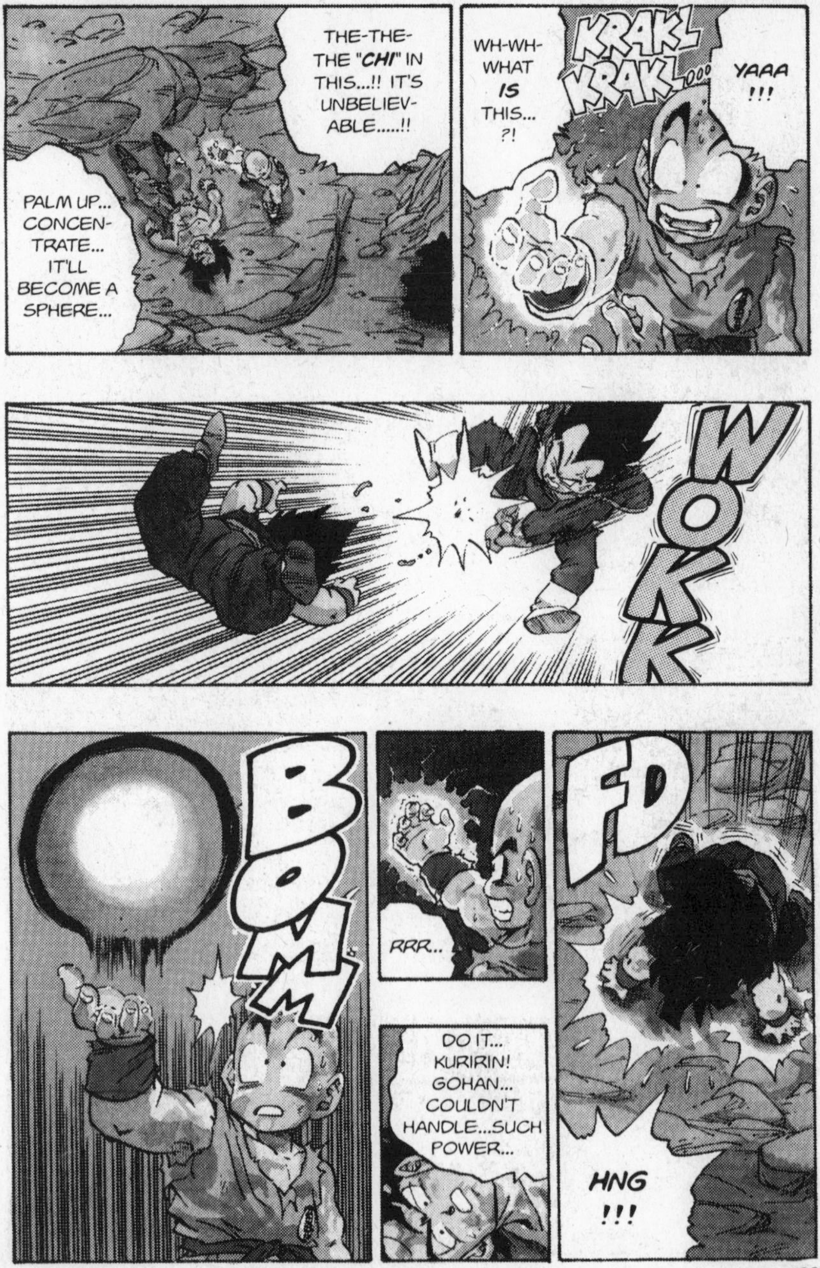
YAAA !!!
KRAKL KRAKL...
WH-WH-WHAT IS THIS... ?!
THE-THE-THE "CHI" IN THIS...!! IT'S UNBELIEVABLE.....!!
PALM UP... CONCENTRATE... IT'LL BECOME A SPHERE...
WOKK
FD
HNG !!!
RRR...
DO IT... KURIRIN! GOHAN... COULDN'T HANDLE...SUCH POWER...
BOMM

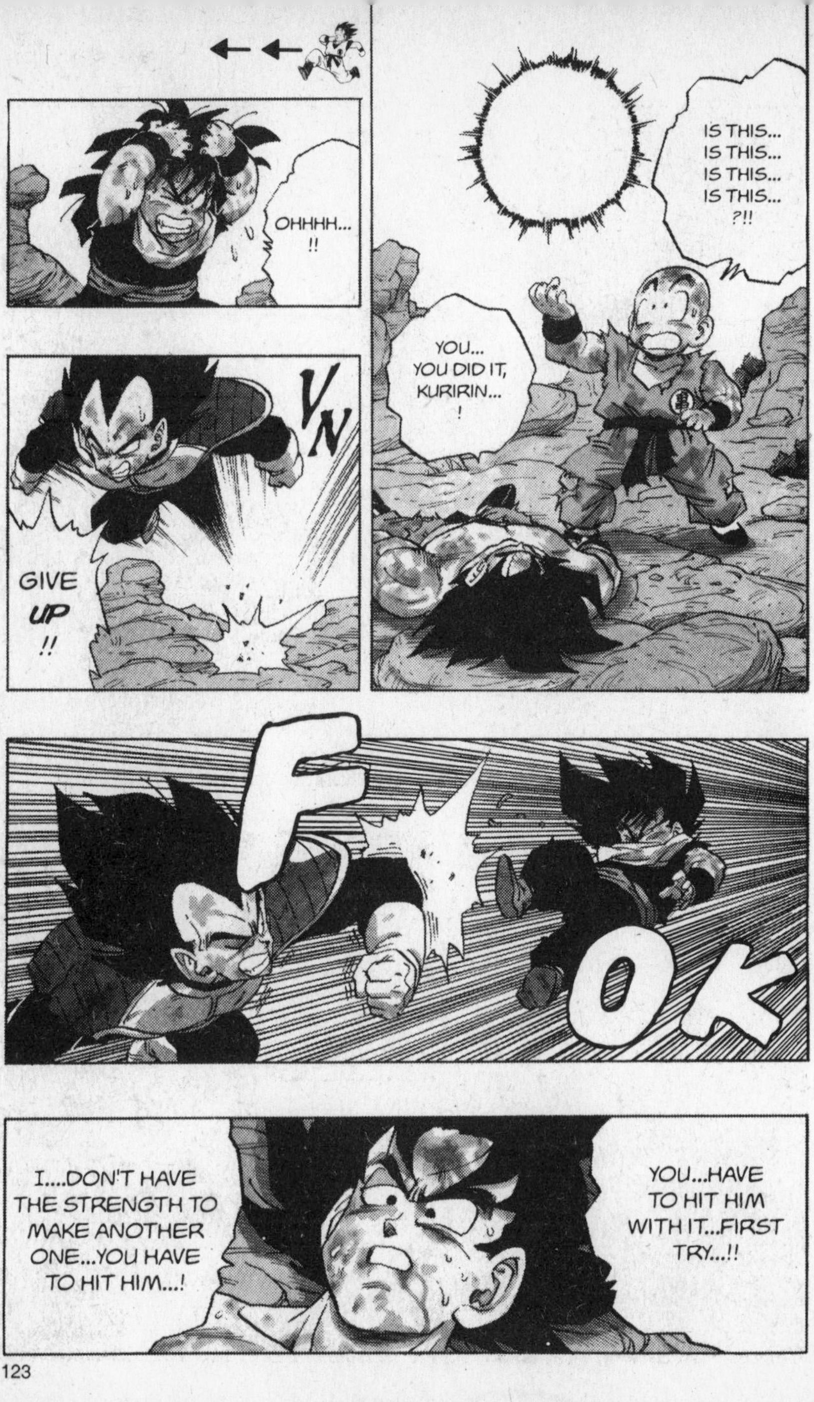
IS THIS... IS THIS... IS THIS... IS THIS... ?!!
YOU... YOU DID IT, KURIRIN... !
OHHHH... !!
VN
GIVE UP !!
F
OK
YOU...HAVE TO HIT HIM WITH IT...FIRST TRY...!!
I....DON'T HAVE THE STRENGTH TO MAKE ANOTHER ONE...YOU HAVE TO HIT HIM...!

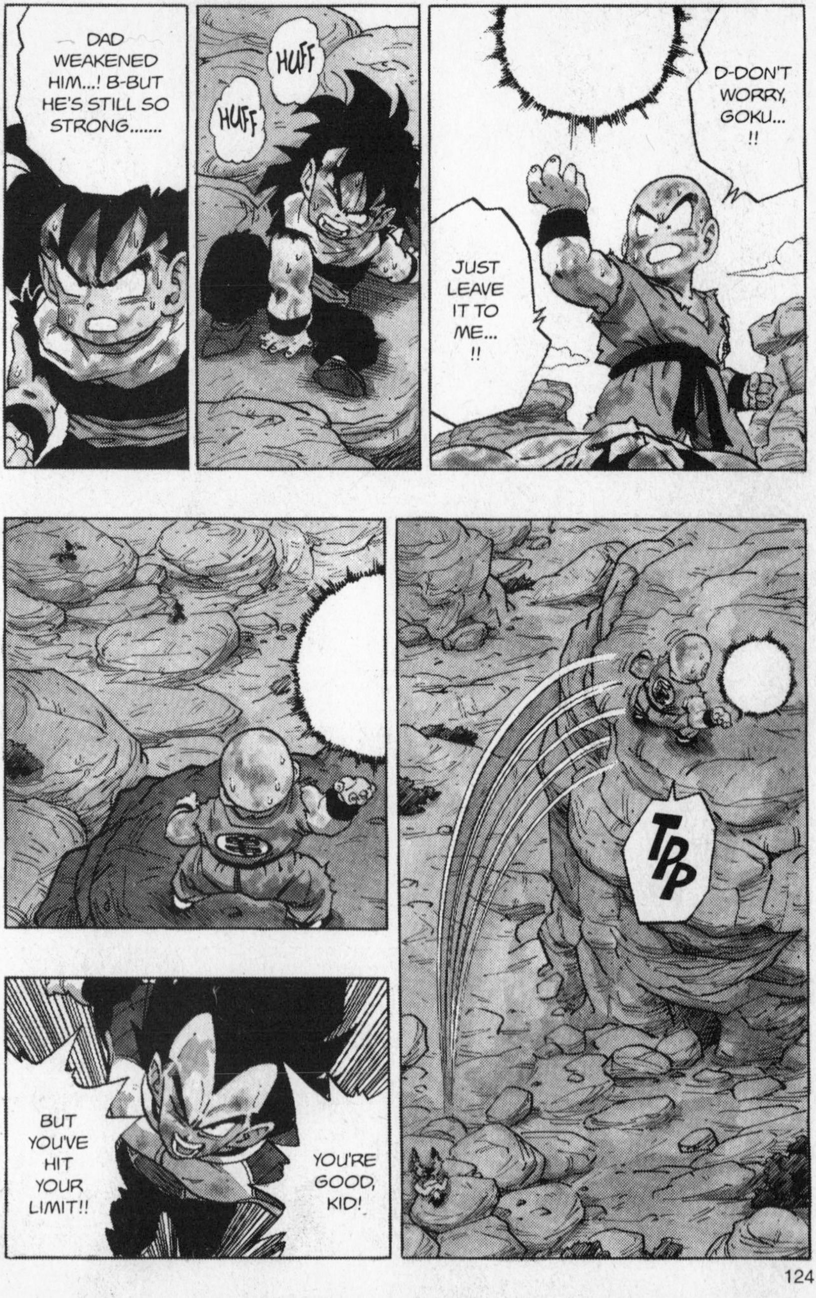
D-DON'T WORRY, GOKU...!!
JUST LEAVE IT TO ME...!!
HUFF
HUFF
DAD WEAKENED HIM...! B-BUT HE'S STILL SO STRONG.......
TPP
YOU'RE GOOD, KID!
BUT YOU'VE HIT YOUR LIMIT!!

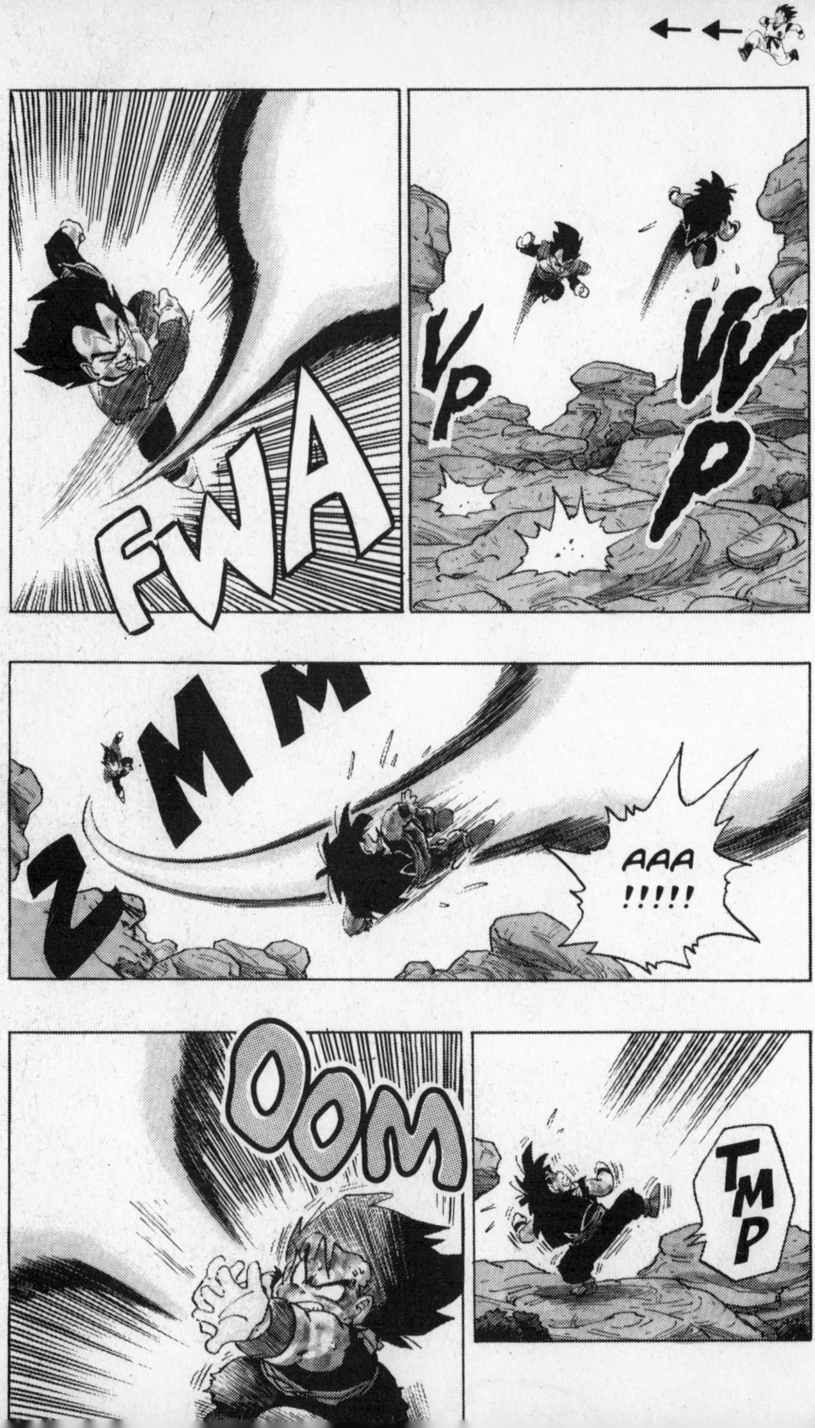
VP
WWP
FWA
ZMMM
AAA !!!!!
TMP
OOM

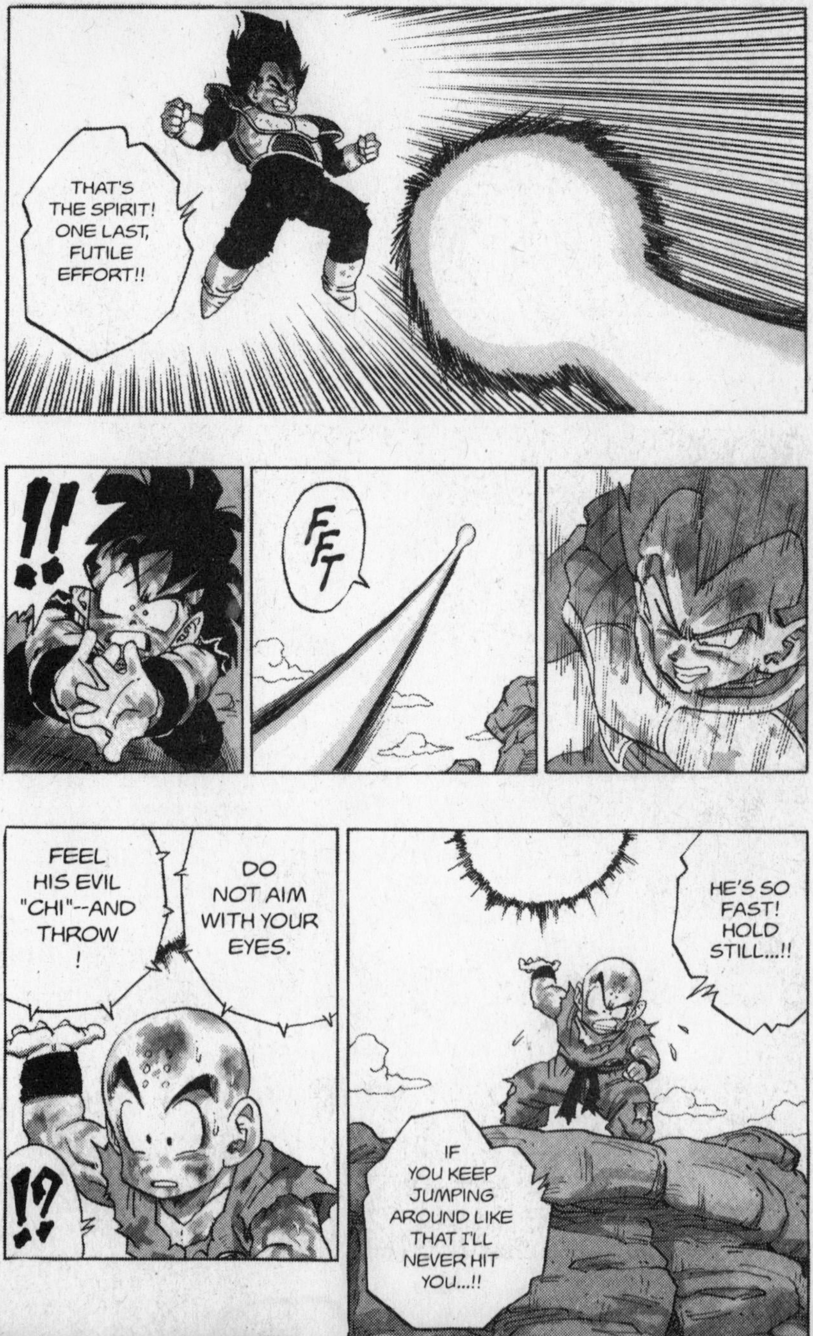
THAT'S THE SPIRIT! ONE LAST, FUTILE EFFORT!!
FFT
!!
HE'S SO FAST! HOLD STILL...!!
IF YOU KEEP JUMPING AROUND LIKE THAT I'LL NEVER HIT YOU...!!
DO NOT AIM WITH YOUR EYES.
FEEL HIS EVIL "CHI"--AND THROW!
!?

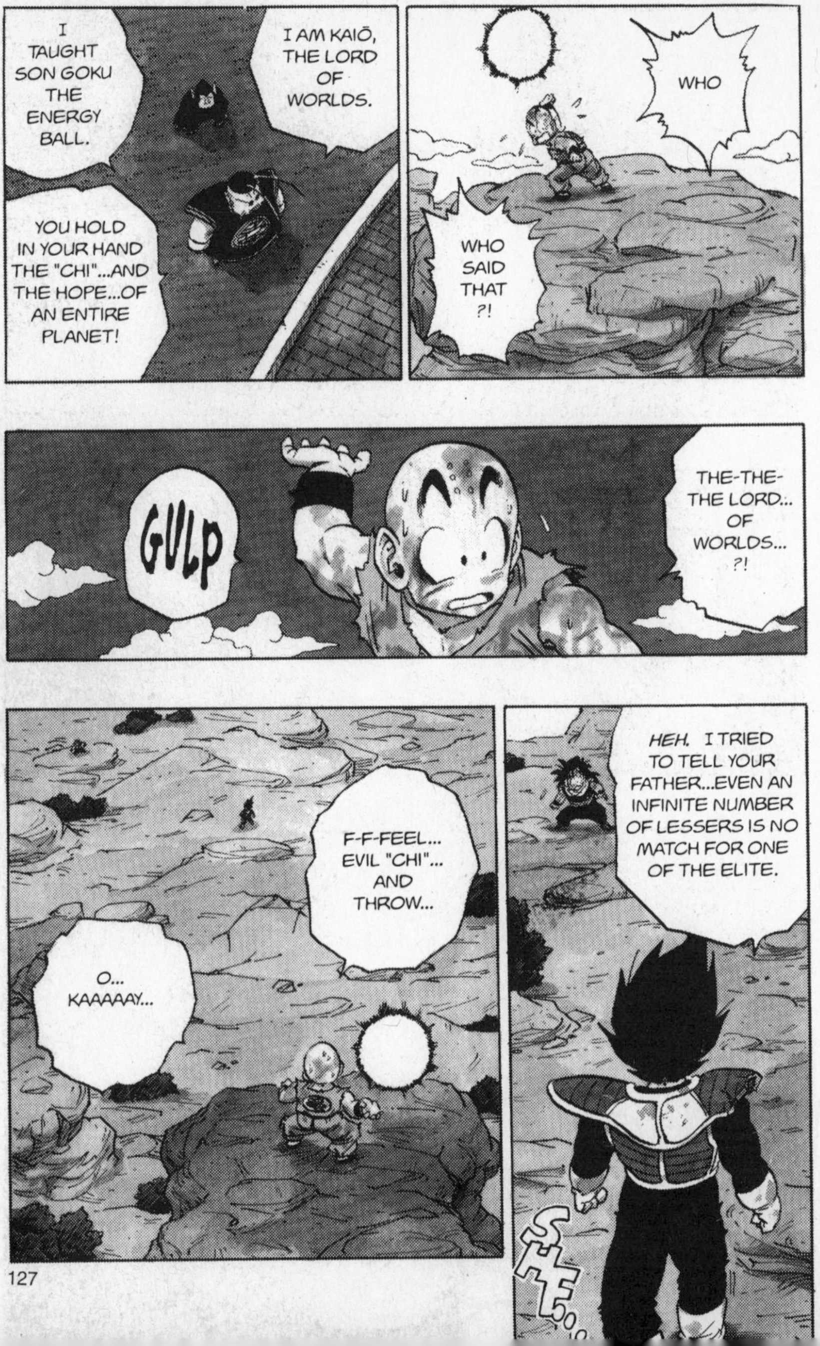
WHO
WHO SAID THAT ?!
I AM KAIŌ, THE LORD OF WORLDS.
I TAUGHT SON GOKU THE ENERGY BALL.
YOU HOLD IN YOUR HAND THE "CHI"...AND THE HOPE...OF AN ENTIRE PLANET!
THE-THE-THE LORD... OF WORLDS... ?!
GULP
HEH. I TRIED TO TELL YOUR FATHER...EVEN AN INFINITE NUMBER OF LESSERS IS NO MATCH FOR ONE OF THE ELITE.
F-F-FEEL... EVIL "CHI"... AND THROW...
O... KAAAAAY...

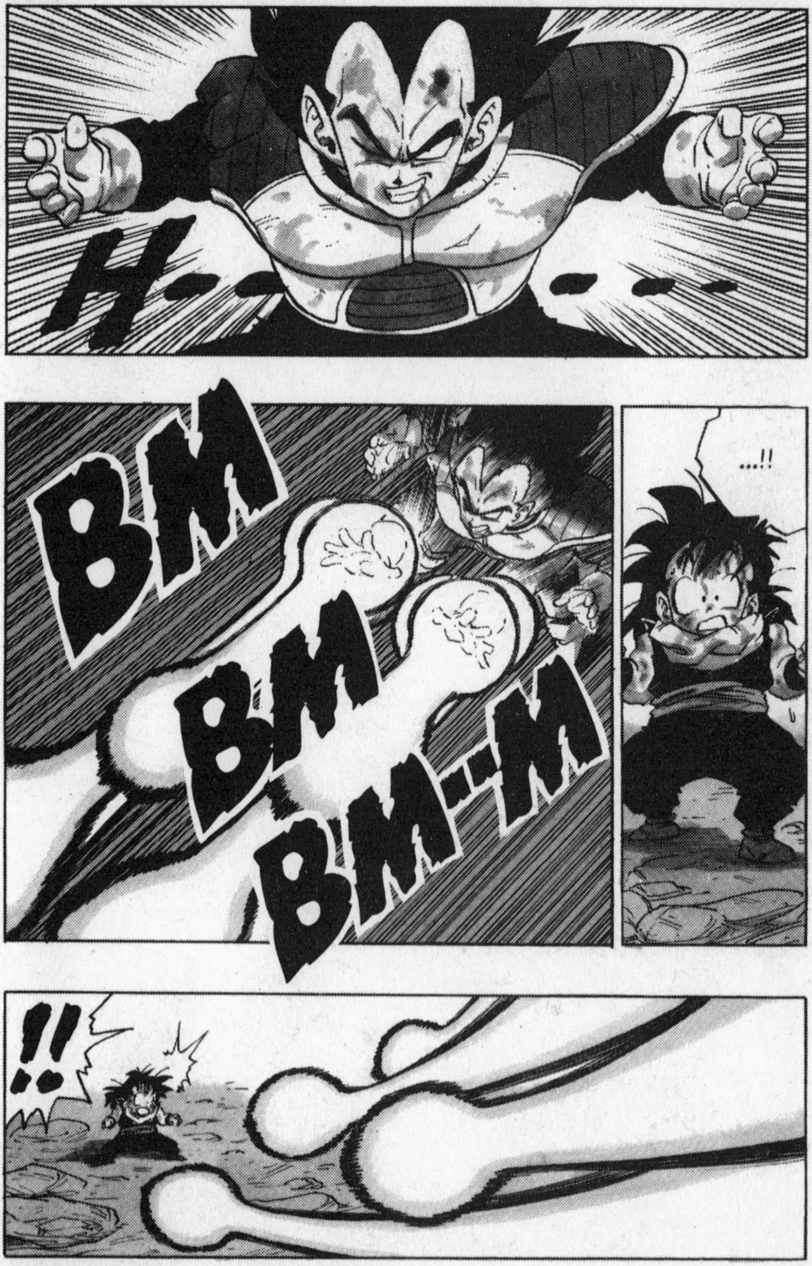
H-----
...!!
BM
BM
BM--M
!!

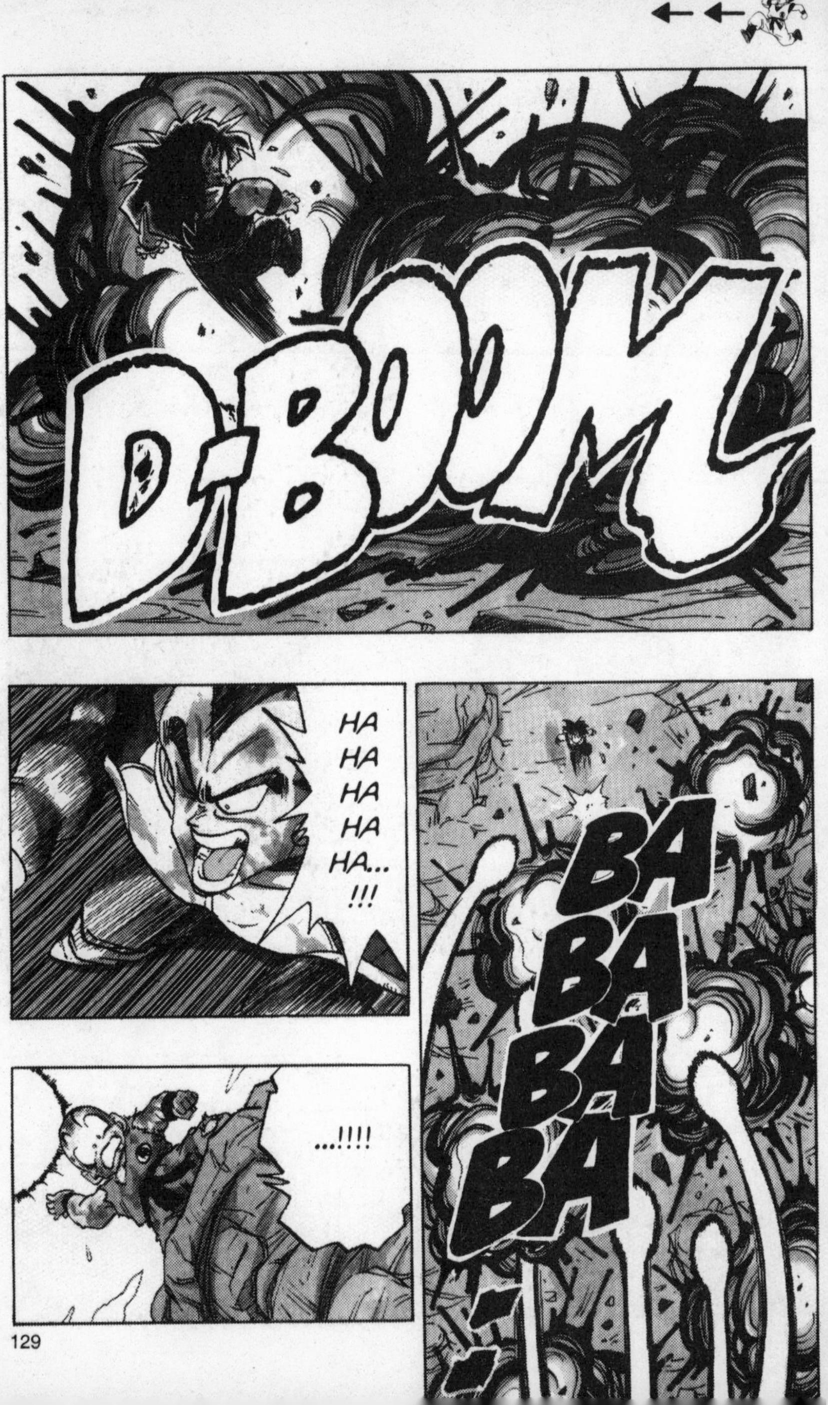
D-BOOM
HA HA HA HA HA... !!!
BA BA BA BA BA...
...!!!!

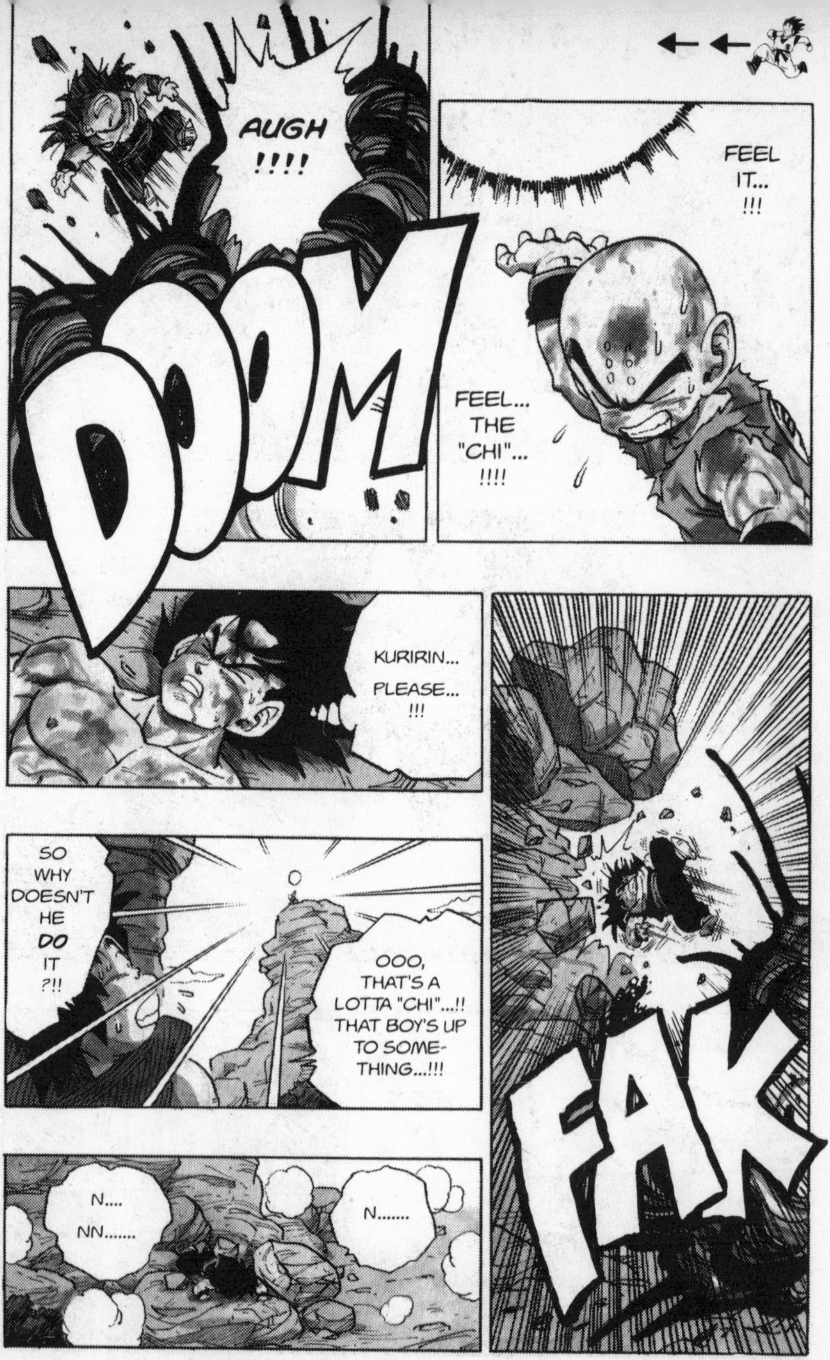
FEEL IT... !!!
FEEL... THE "CHI"... !!!!
AUGH !!!!
DOOM
FAK
KURIRIN... PLEASE... !!!
OOO, THAT'S A LOTTA "CHI"...!! THAT BOY'S UP TO SOME-THING...!!!
SO WHY DOESN'T HE *DO* IT ?!!
N.......
N.... NN.......

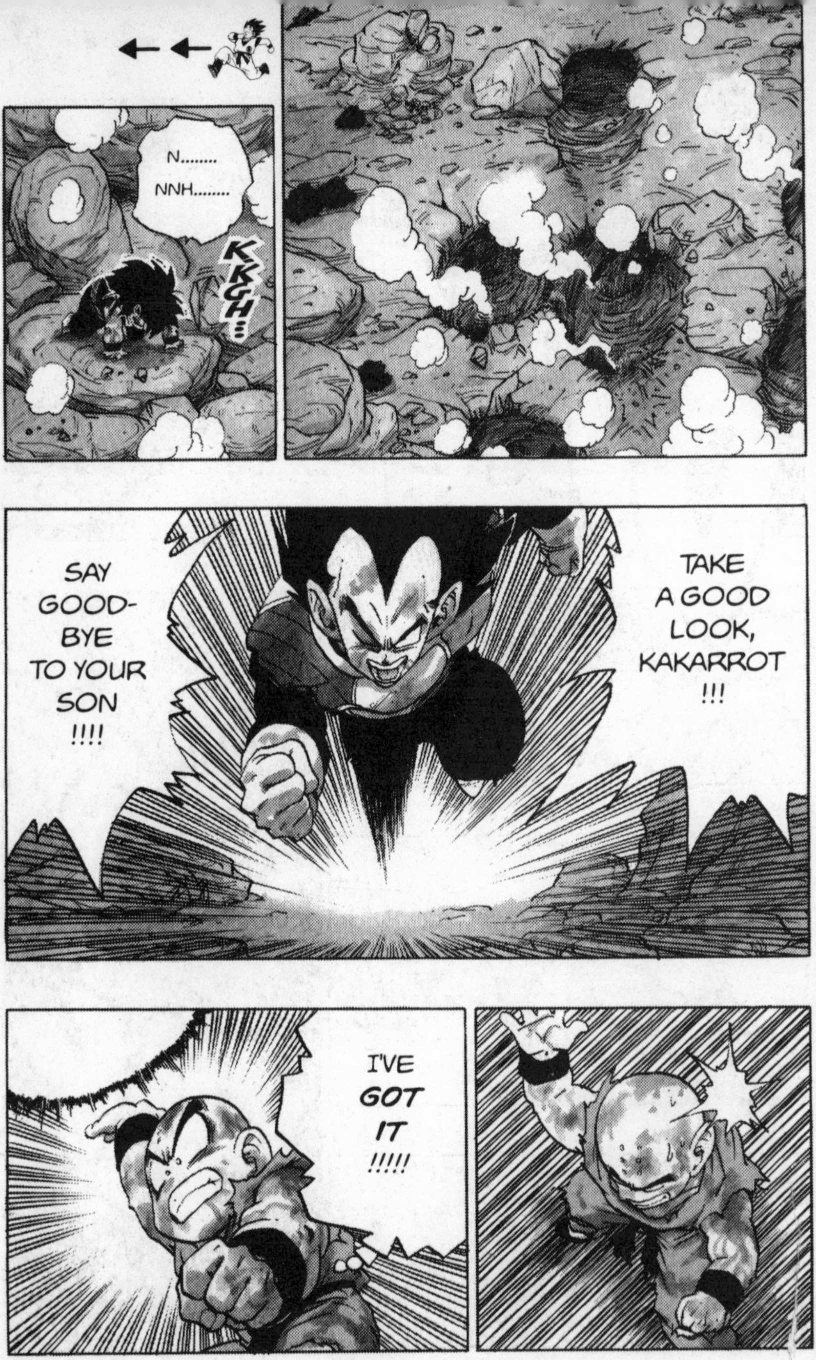
N........
NNH........
KKGH...
TAKE A GOOD LOOK, KAKARROT !!!
SAY GOOD-BYE TO YOUR SON !!!!
I'VE GOT IT !!!!!

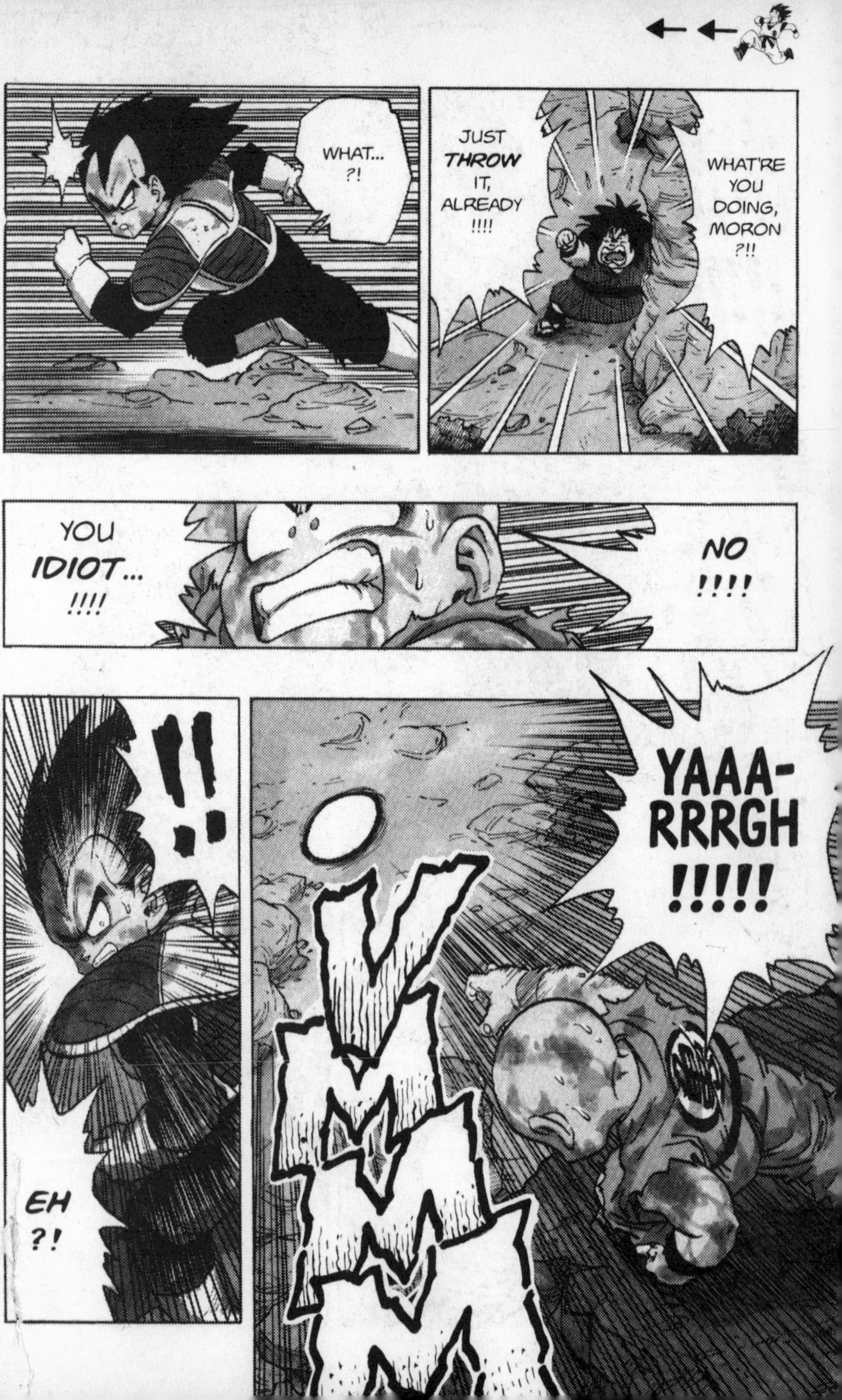
WHAT'RE YOU DOING, MORON ?!!
JUST THROW IT, ALREADY !!!!
WHAT... ?!
NO !!!!
YOU IDIOT... !!!!
YAAA-RRRGH !!!!!
!!
EH ?!

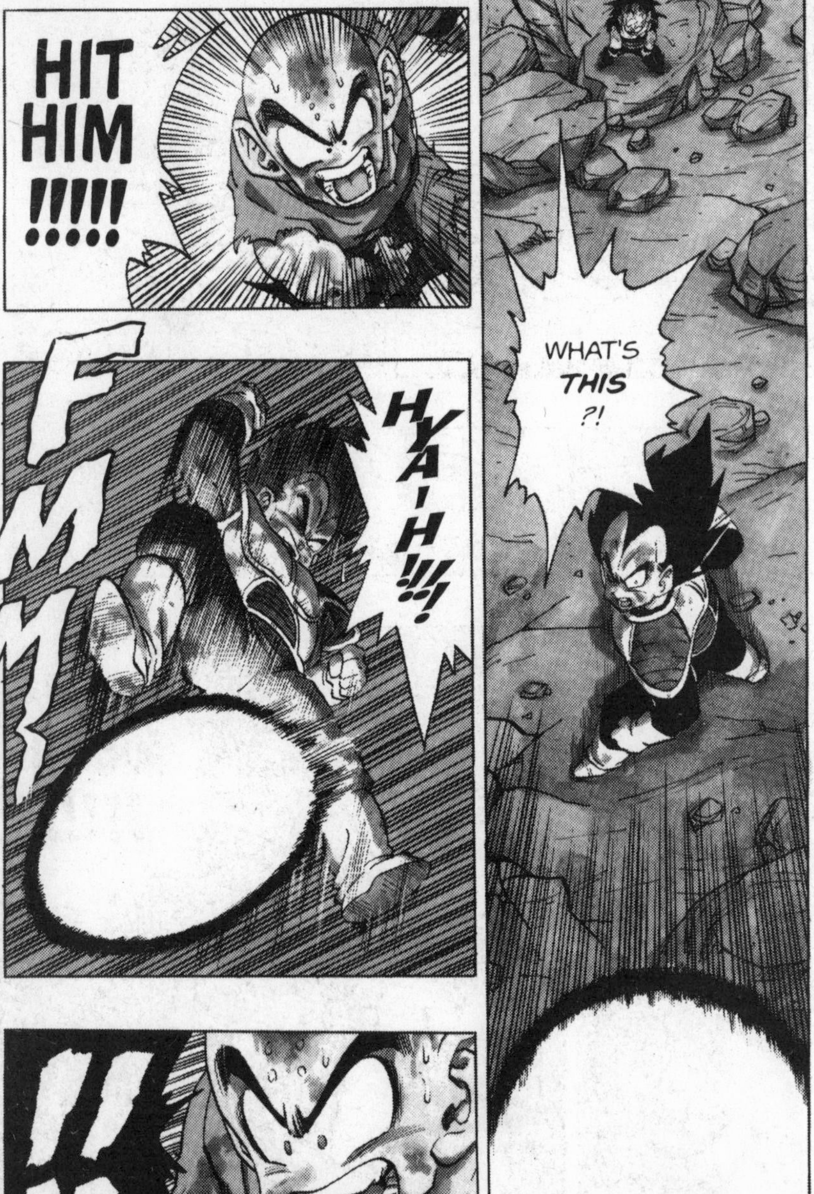
WHAT'S THIS ?!
HIT HIM!!!!!
FMM
HYAAH!!!!!
!!

NEXT: Is It... The End?!

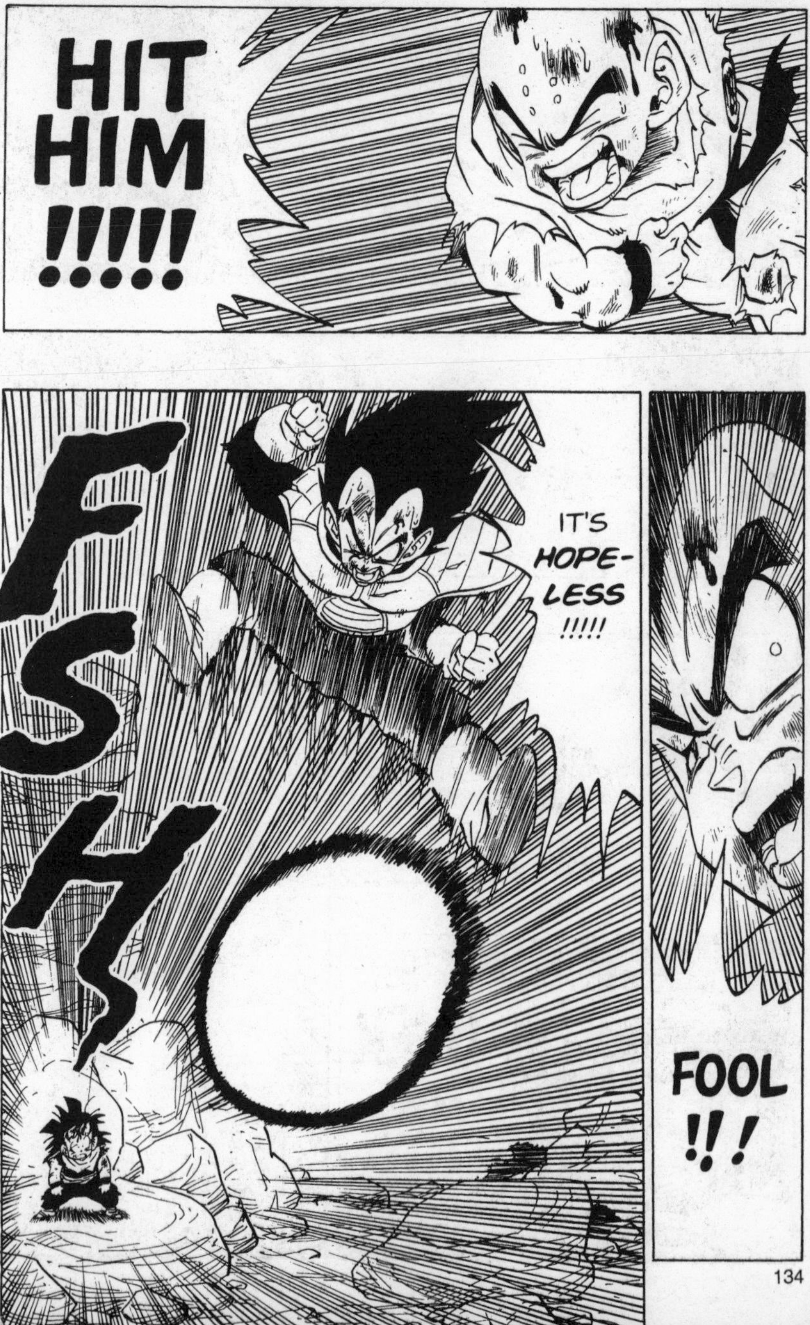
HIT HIM!!!!!
FOOL!!!
IT'S HOPELESS!!!!!
FSSH

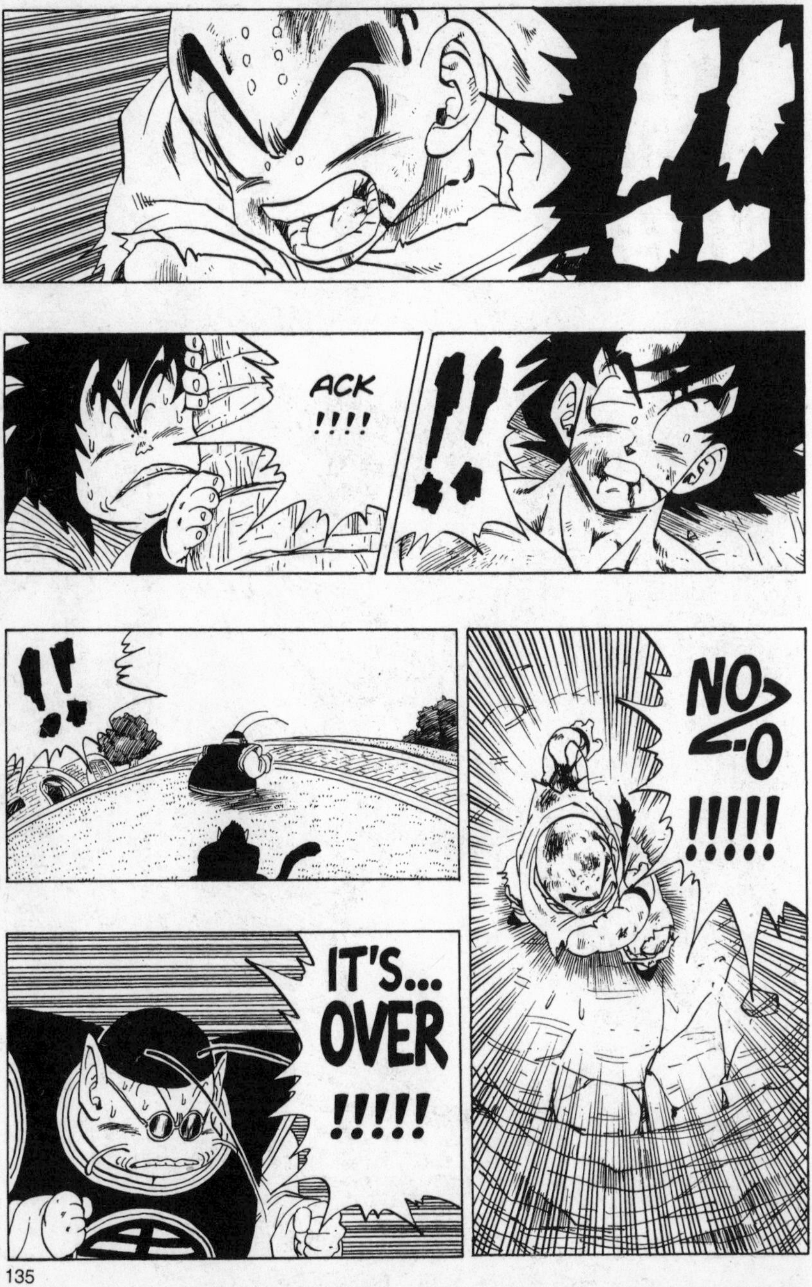
!!
ACK !!!!
NO-O !!!!!
!!
IT'S... OVER !!!!!

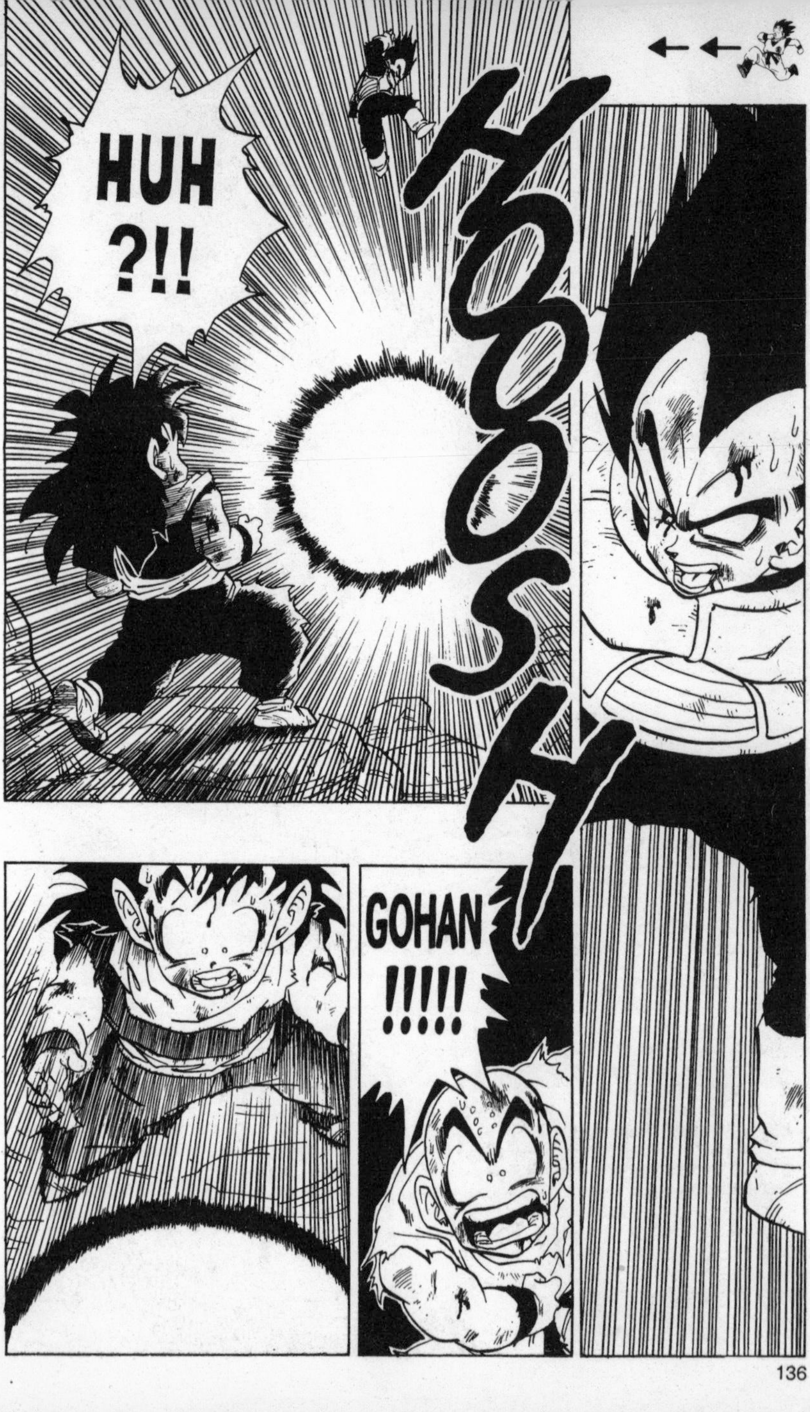
WHOOSH
HUH ?!!
GOHAN !!!!!

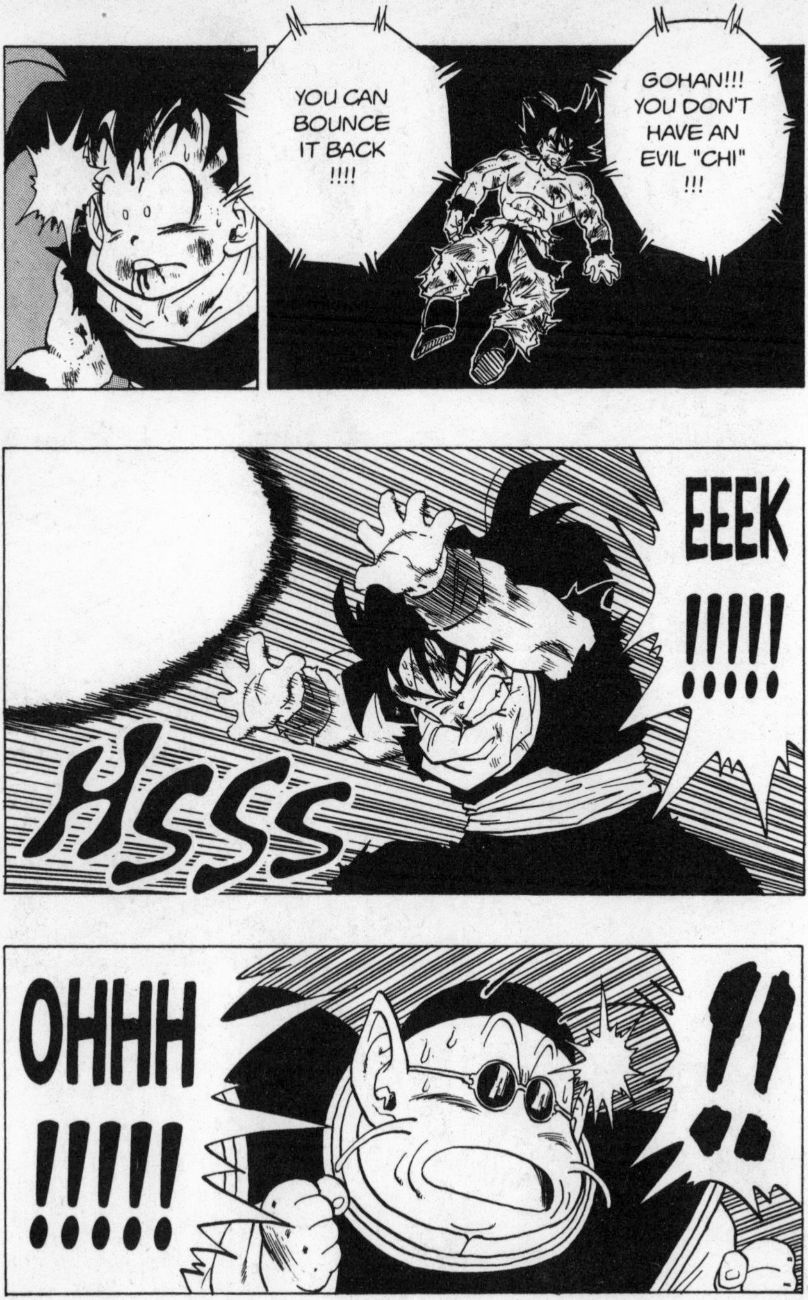
GOHAN!!! YOU DON'T HAVE AN EVIL "CHI" !!!
YOU CAN BOUNCE IT BACK !!!!
EEEK !!!!!!
HSSS
!!
OHHH !!!!!!

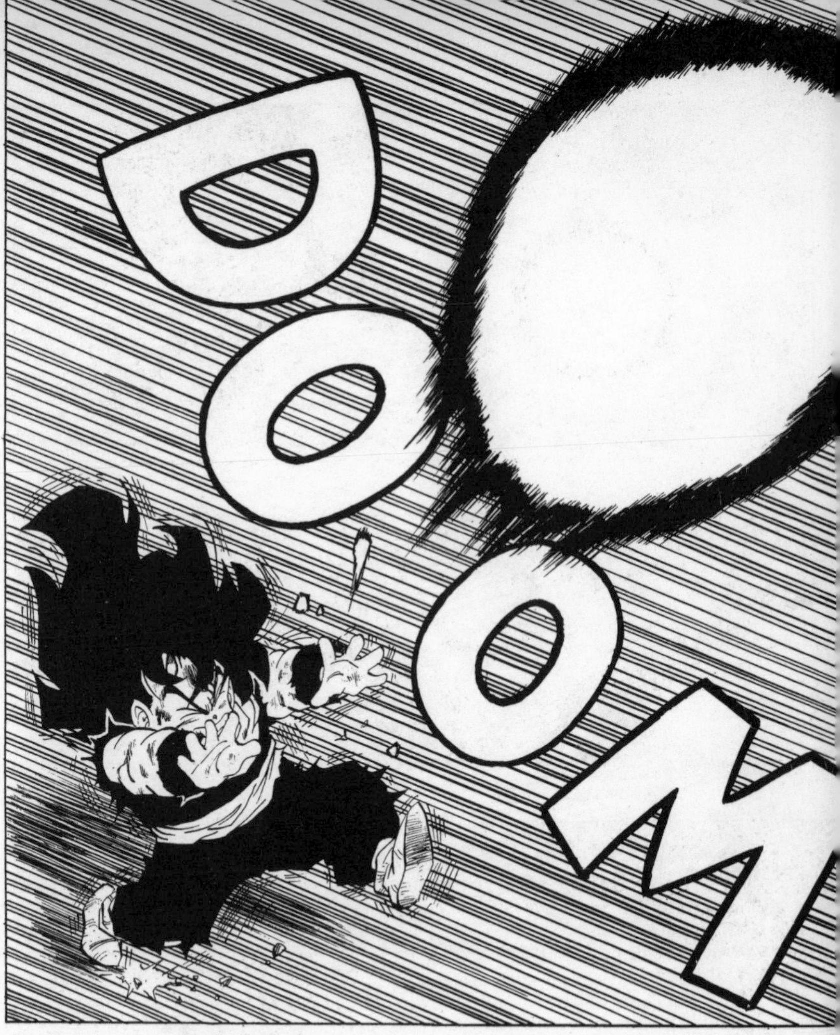
DOOOM
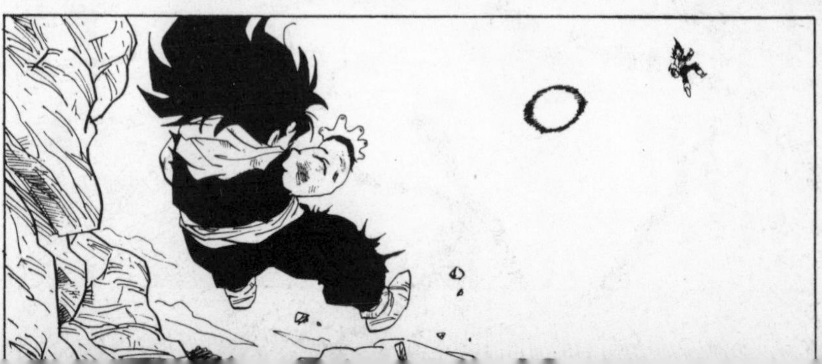

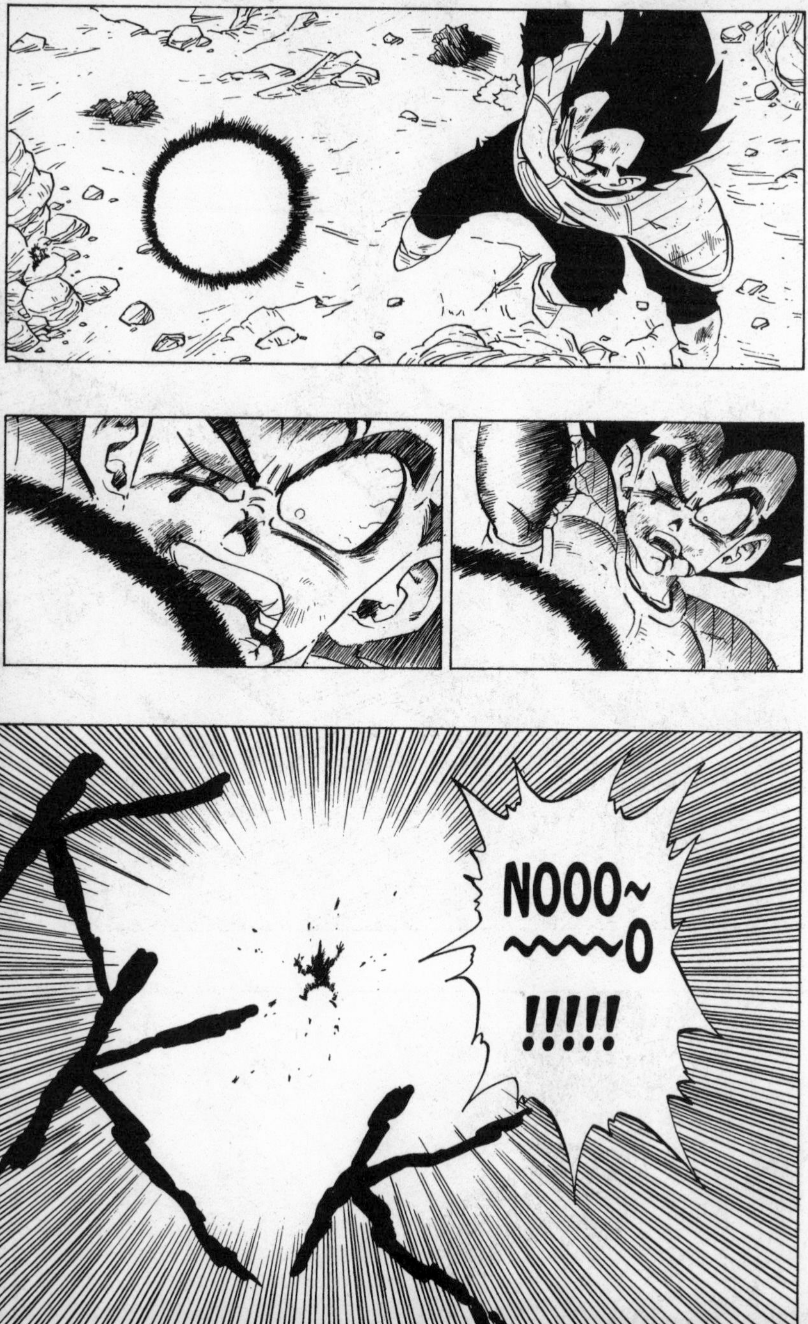
NOOO~~~~~O!!!!!

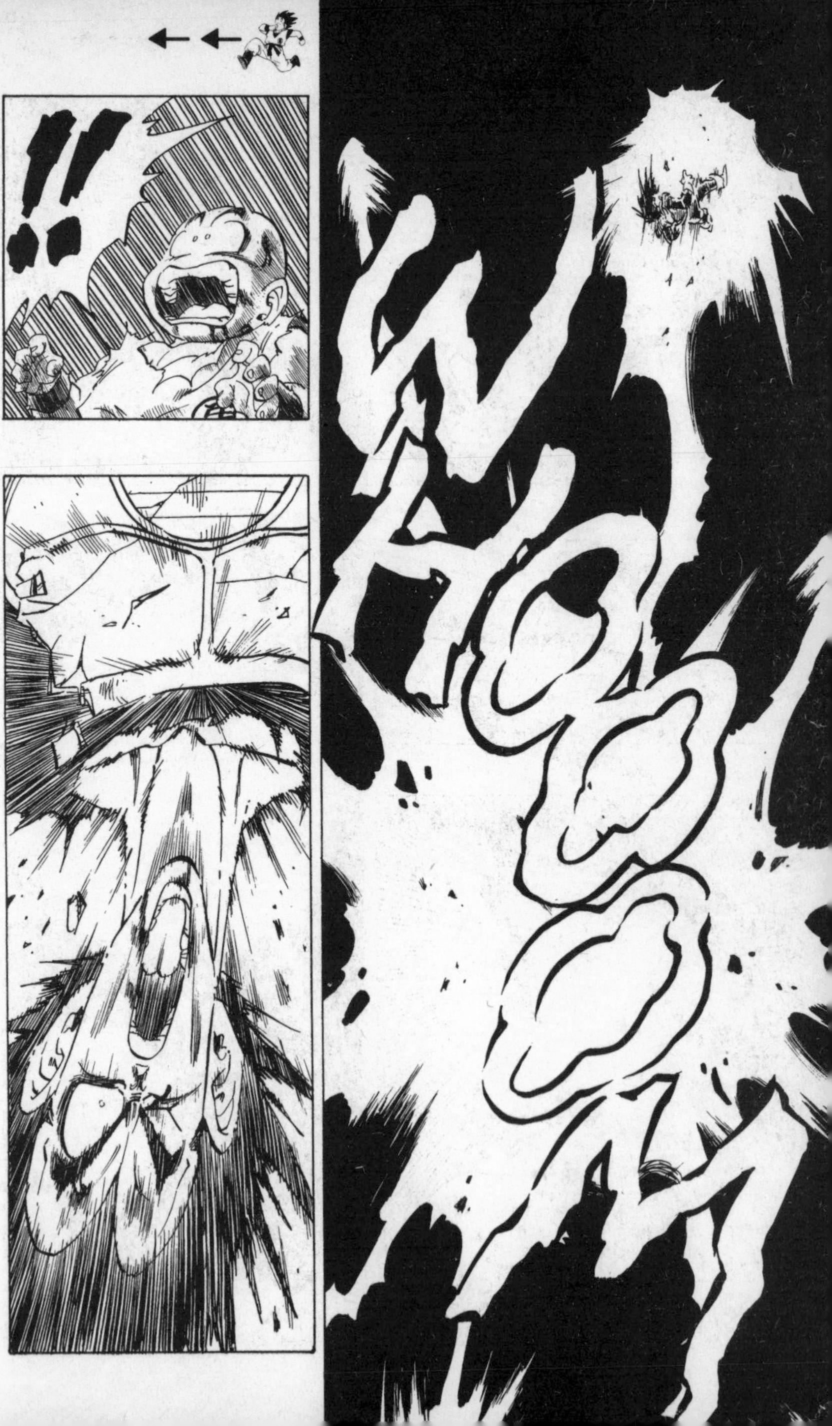
!!

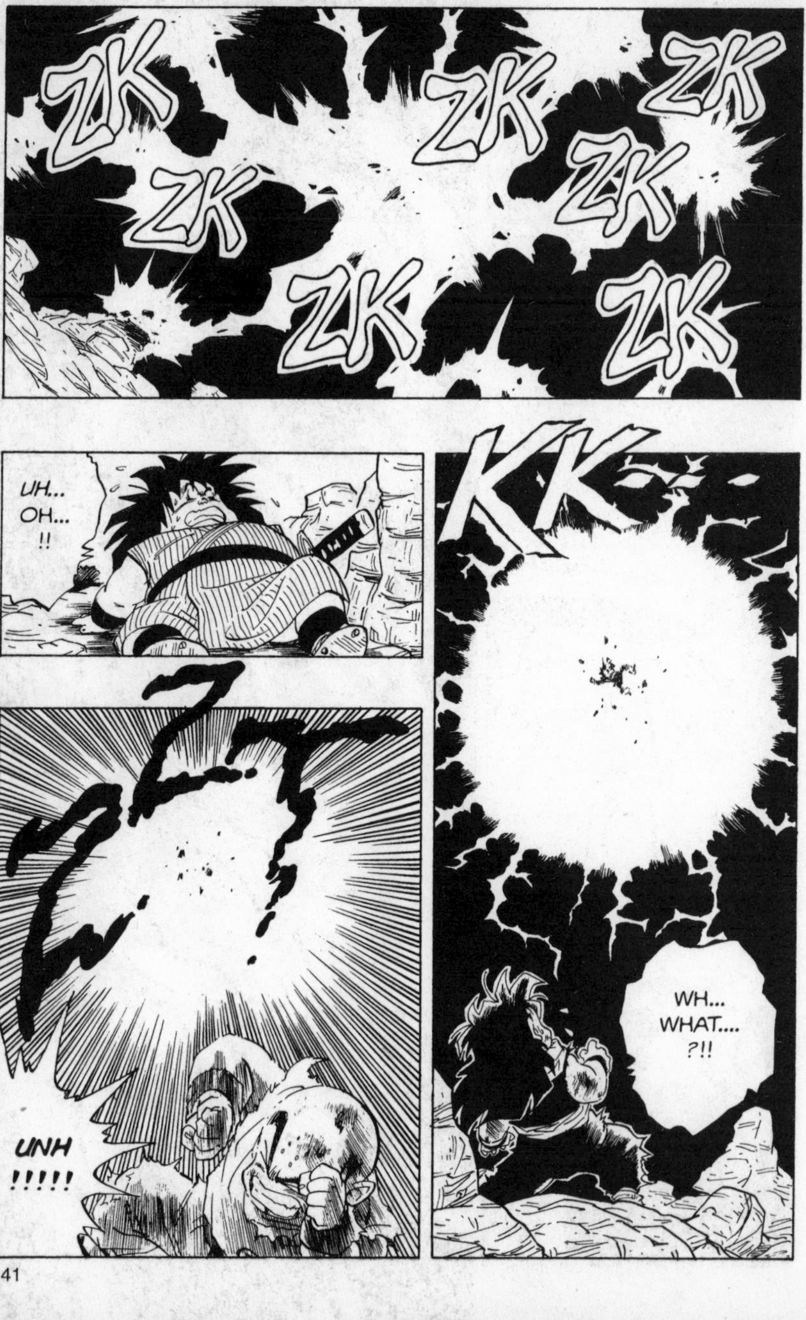
ZK
ZK
ZK
ZK
ZK
ZK
ZK
KK
WH... WHAT.... ?!!
UH... OH... !!
UNH !!!!!

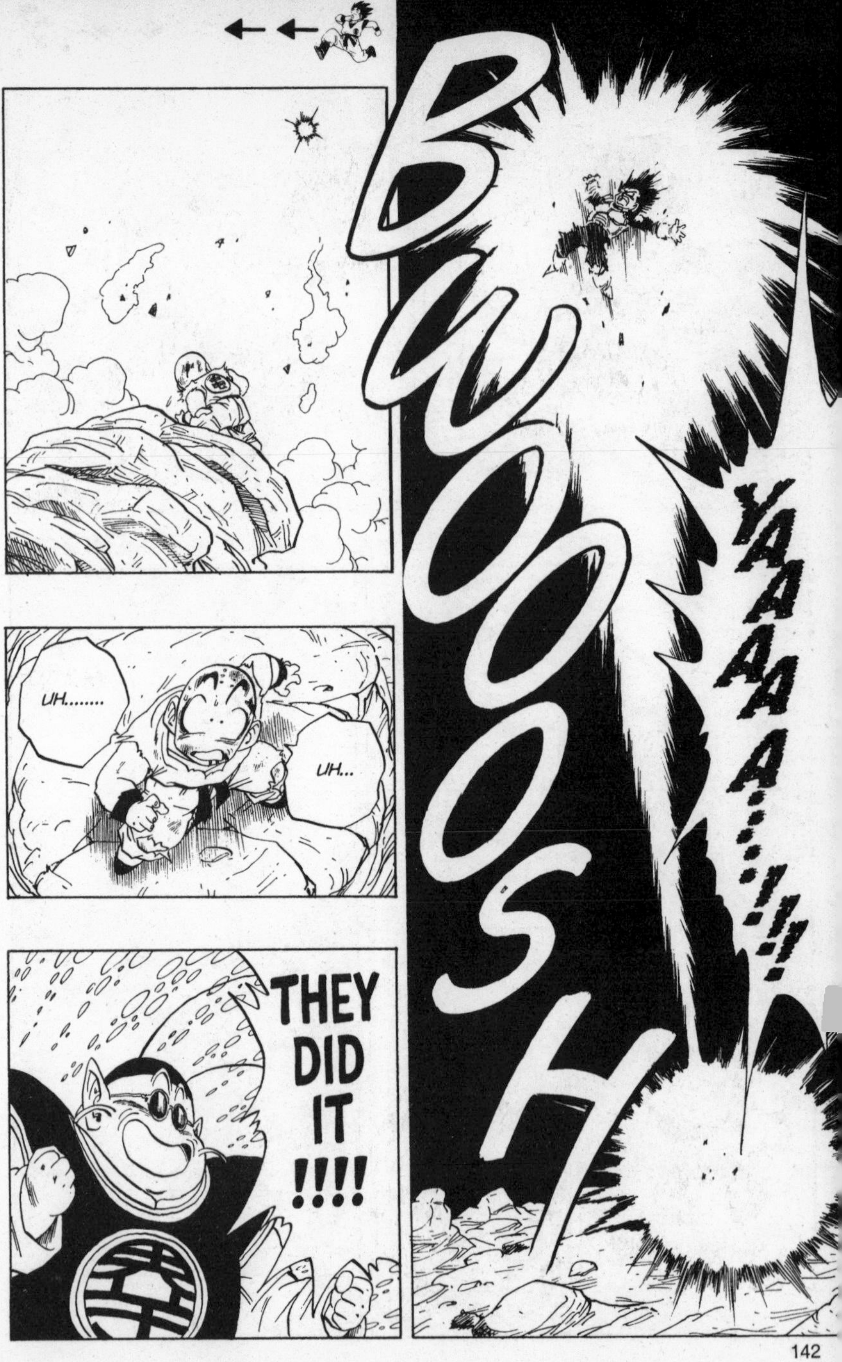
BWOOOSH
YAAAAA....!!!
UH........
UH...
THEY DID IT !!!!

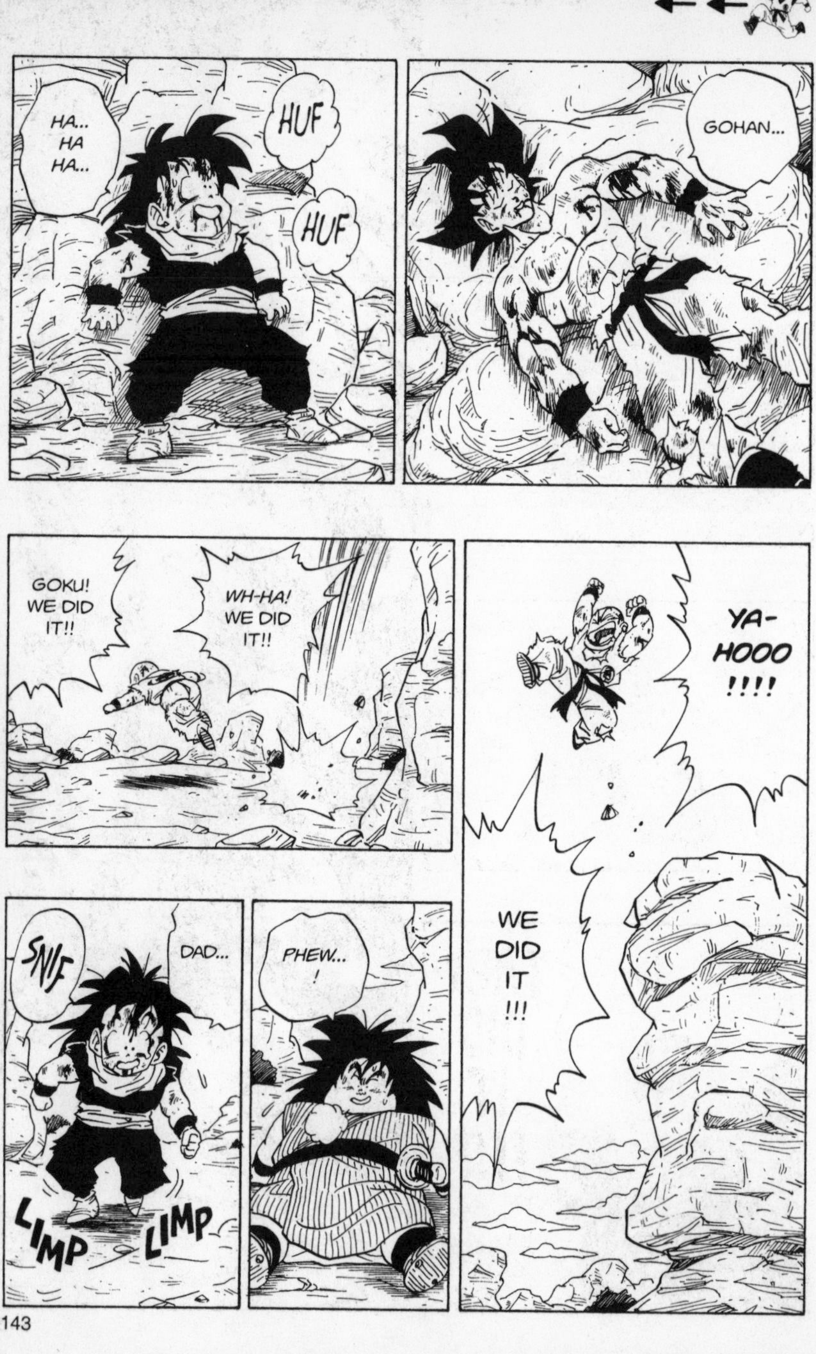
GOHAN...
HA... HA HA...
HUF
HUF
YA-HOOO!!!!
WE DID IT!!!
WH-HA! WE DID IT!!
GOKU! WE DID IT!!
PHEW... !
DAD...
SNIF
LIMP
LIMP

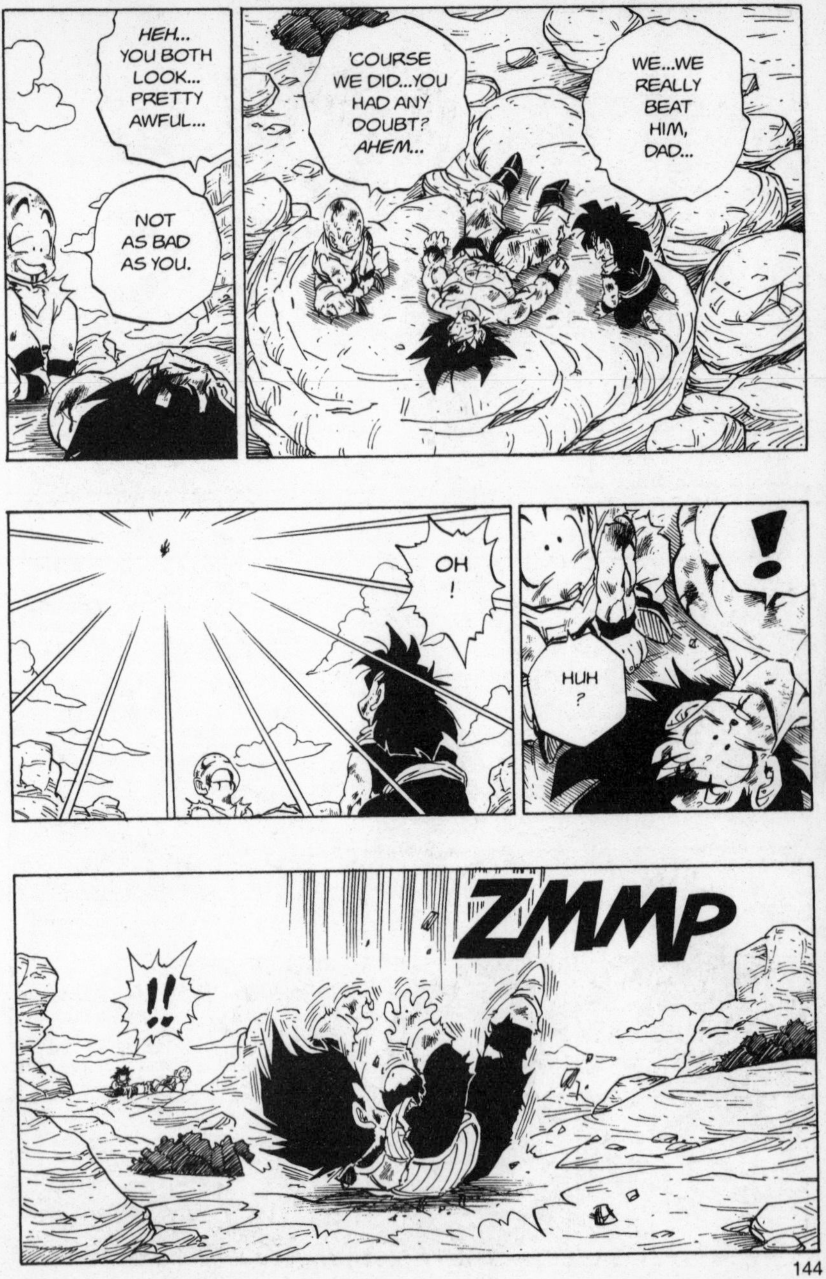
WE...WE REALLY BEAT HIM, DAD...
'COURSE WE DID...YOU HAD ANY DOUBT? *AHEM*...
HEH... YOU BOTH LOOK... PRETTY AWFUL...
NOT AS BAD AS YOU.
!
HUH ?
OH !
ZMMP
!!

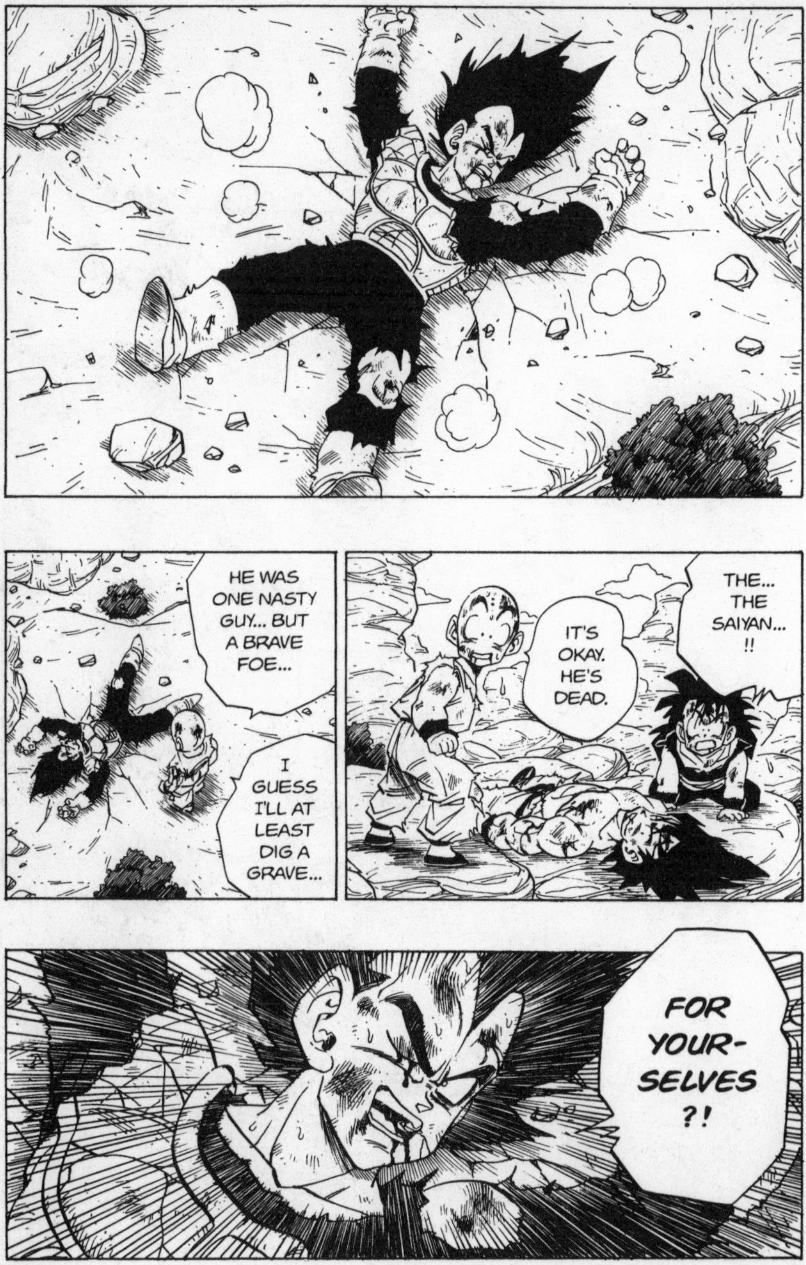
THE... THE SAIYAN... !!
IT'S OKAY. HE'S DEAD.
HE WAS ONE NASTY GUY... BUT A BRAVE FOE...
I GUESS I'LL AT LEAST DIG A GRAVE...
FOR YOUR-SELVES ?!

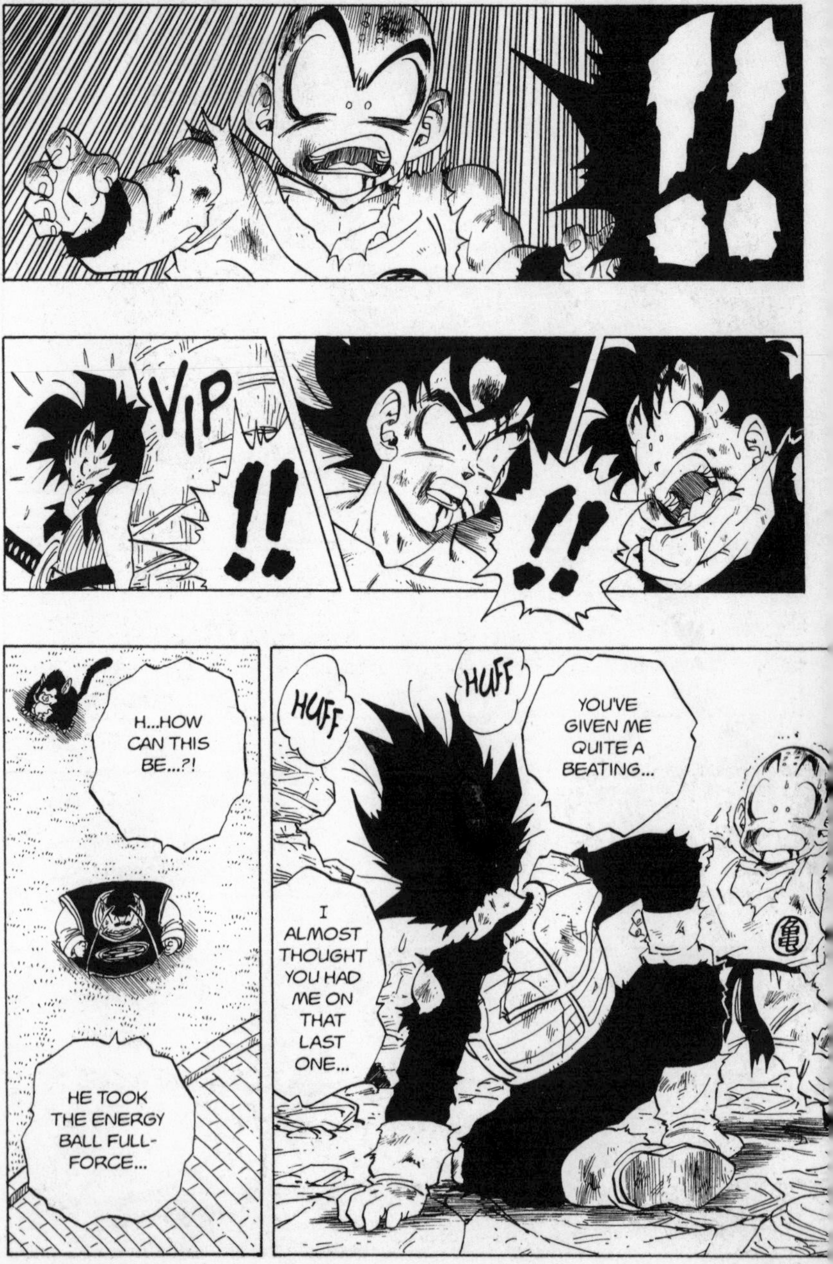
!!
VIP
!!
YOU'VE GIVEN ME QUITE A BEATING...
HUFF
HUFF
I ALMOST THOUGHT YOU HAD ME ON THAT LAST ONE...
H...HOW CAN THIS BE...?!
HE TOOK THE ENERGY BALL FULL-FORCE...

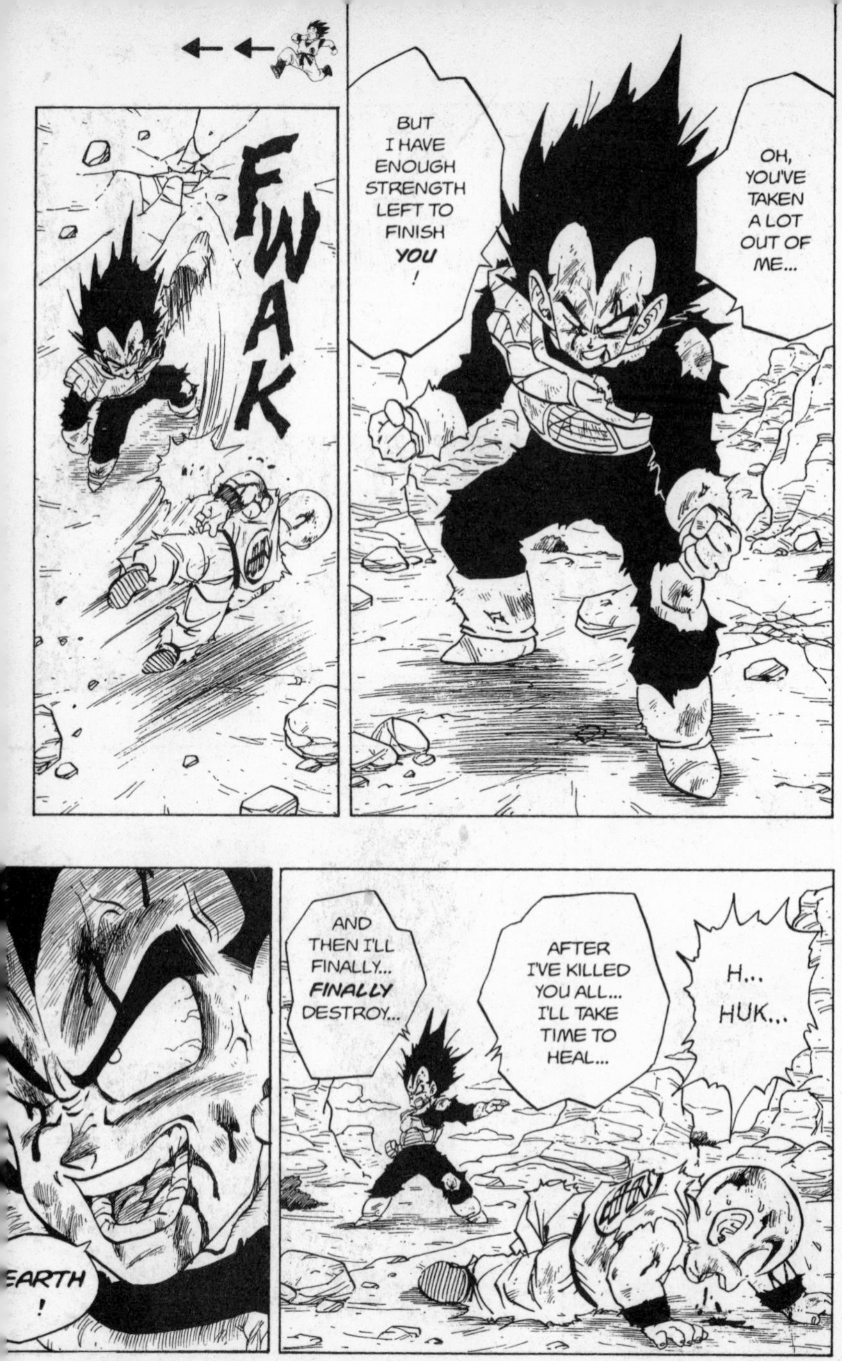

OH, YOU'VE TAKEN A LOT OUT OF ME...
BUT I HAVE ENOUGH STRENGTH LEFT TO FINISH *YOU*!
FWAK
H... HUK...
AFTER I'VE KILLED YOU ALL... I'LL TAKE TIME TO HEAL...
AND THEN I'LL FINALLY... *FINALLY* DESTROY...
EARTH!

NEXT: The Worn-Out Warriors

DBZ:45 • The Worn-Out Warriors

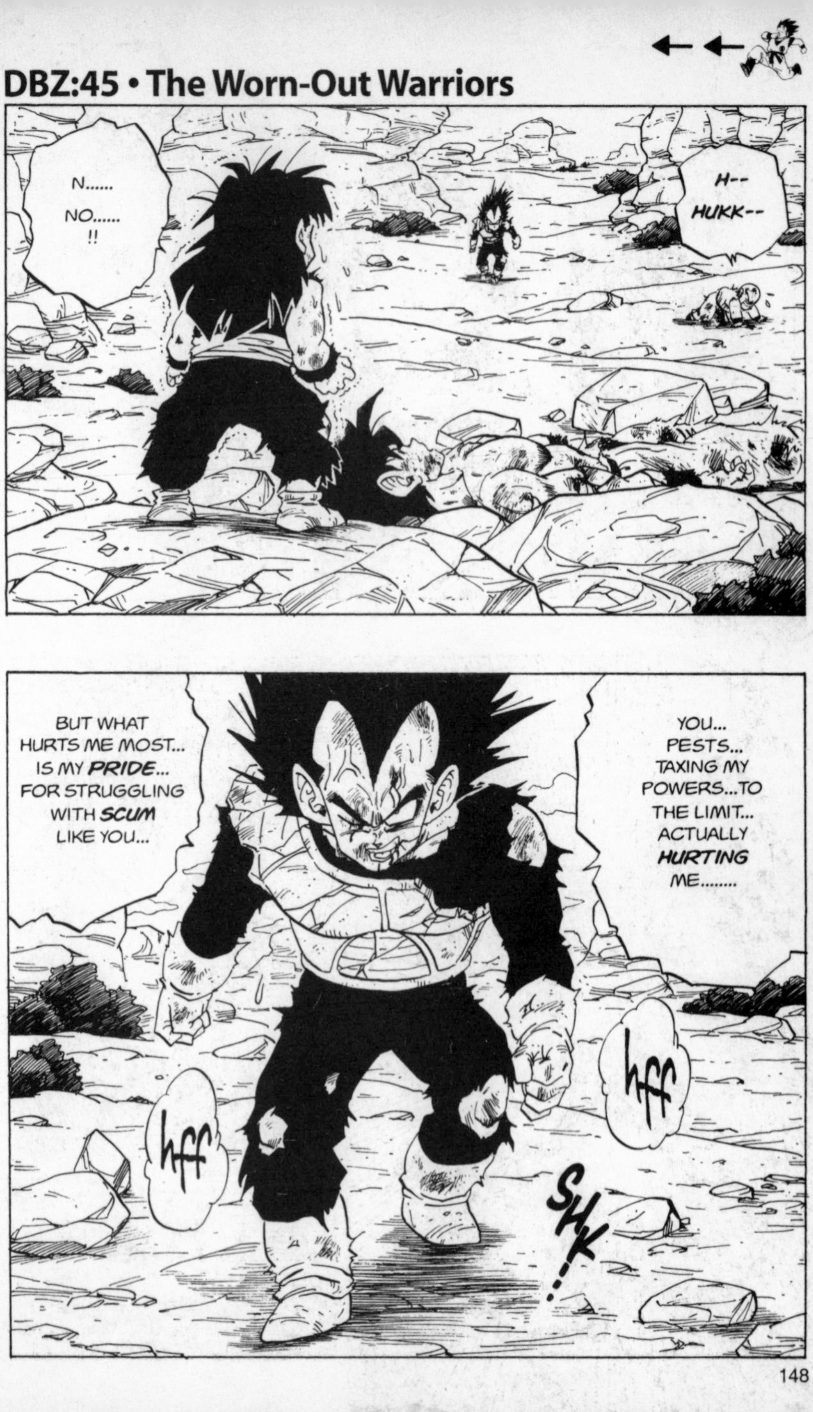
H-- HUKK--
N...... NO...... !!
YOU... PESTS... TAXING MY POWERS...TO THE LIMIT... ACTUALLY HURTING ME........
BUT WHAT HURTS ME MOST... IS MY PRIDE... FOR STRUGGLING WITH SCUM LIKE YOU...
hff
hff
SHK...

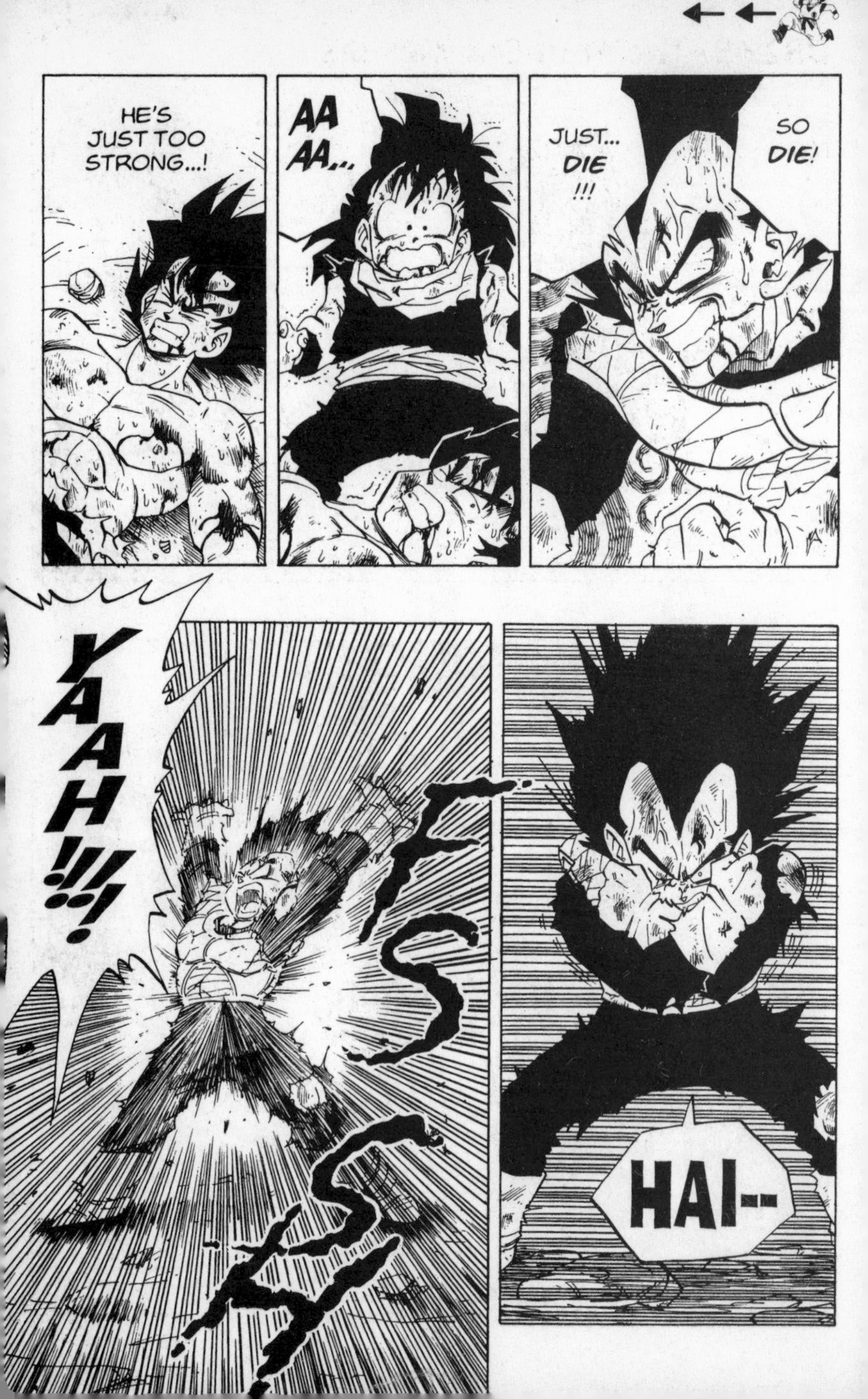
SO DIE!
JUST... DIE !!!
AA AA...
HE'S JUST TOO STRONG...!
HAI--
YAAH!!!!

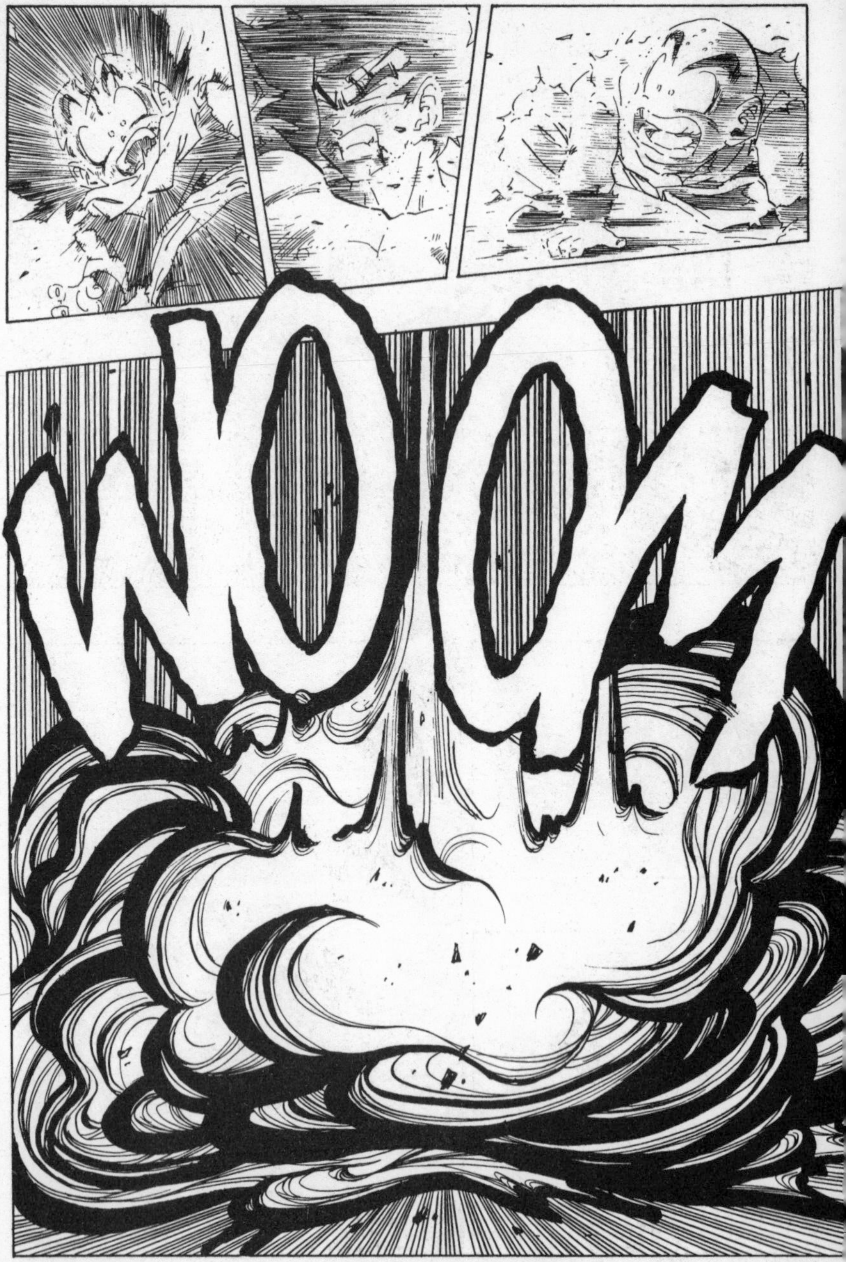
WOOM

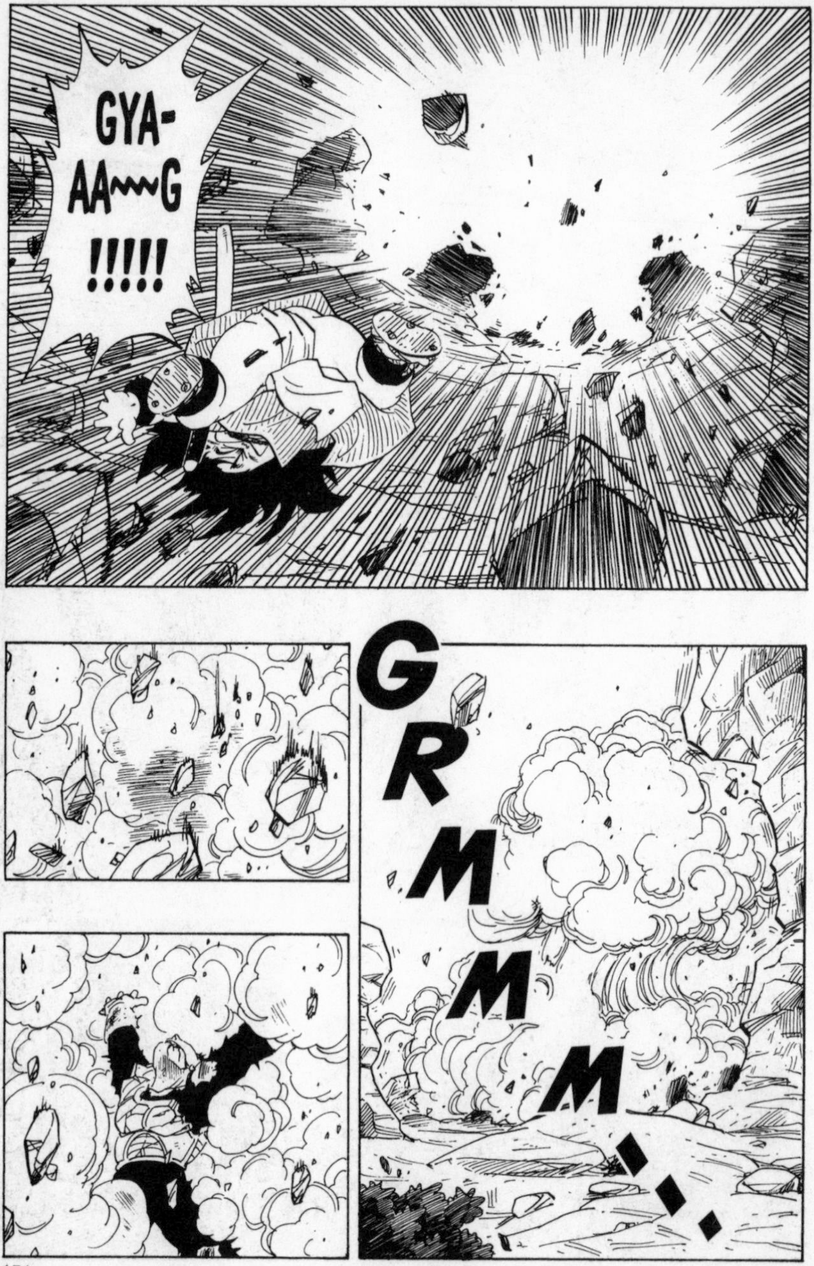
GYA-AA~~G!!!!!
GRMMM...

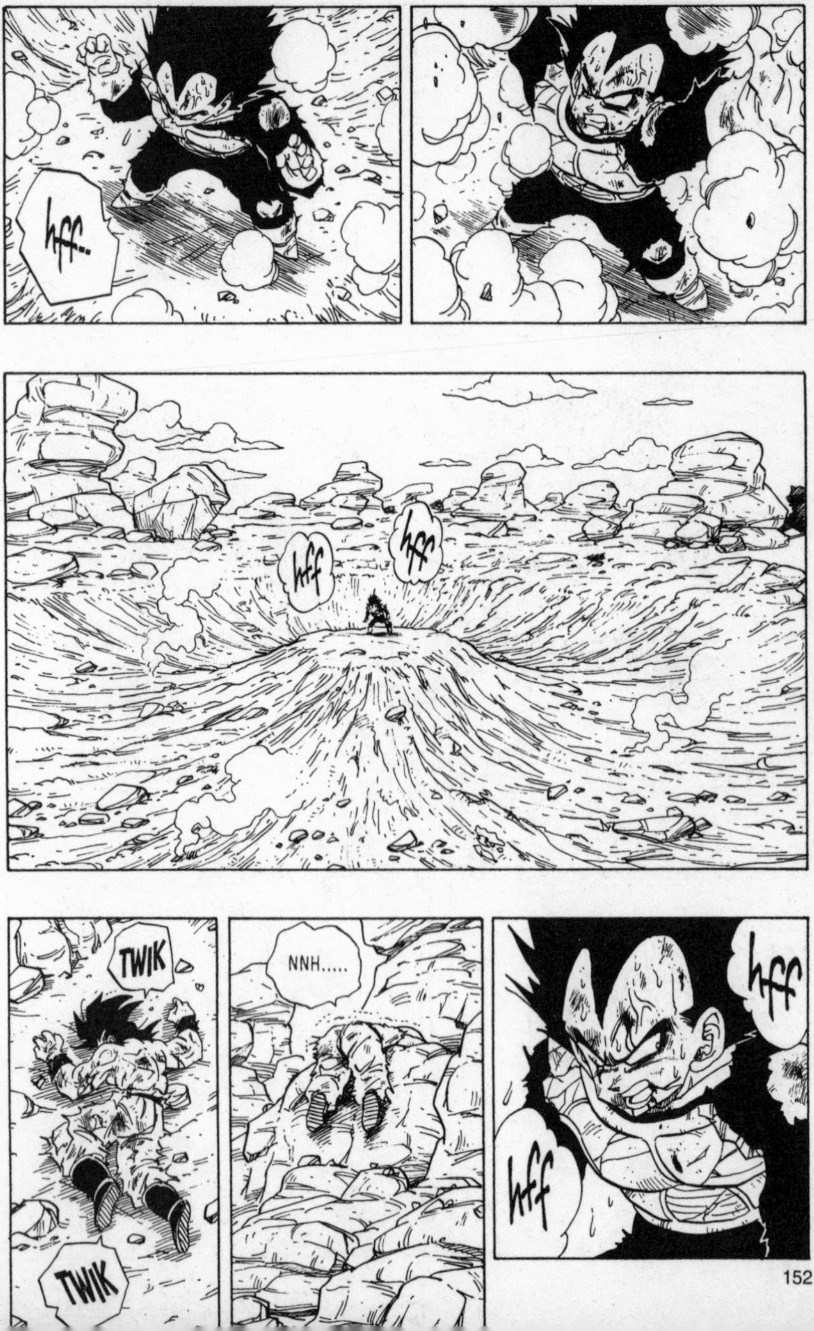
hff..
hff
hff
hff
hff
NNH.....
TWIK
TWIK

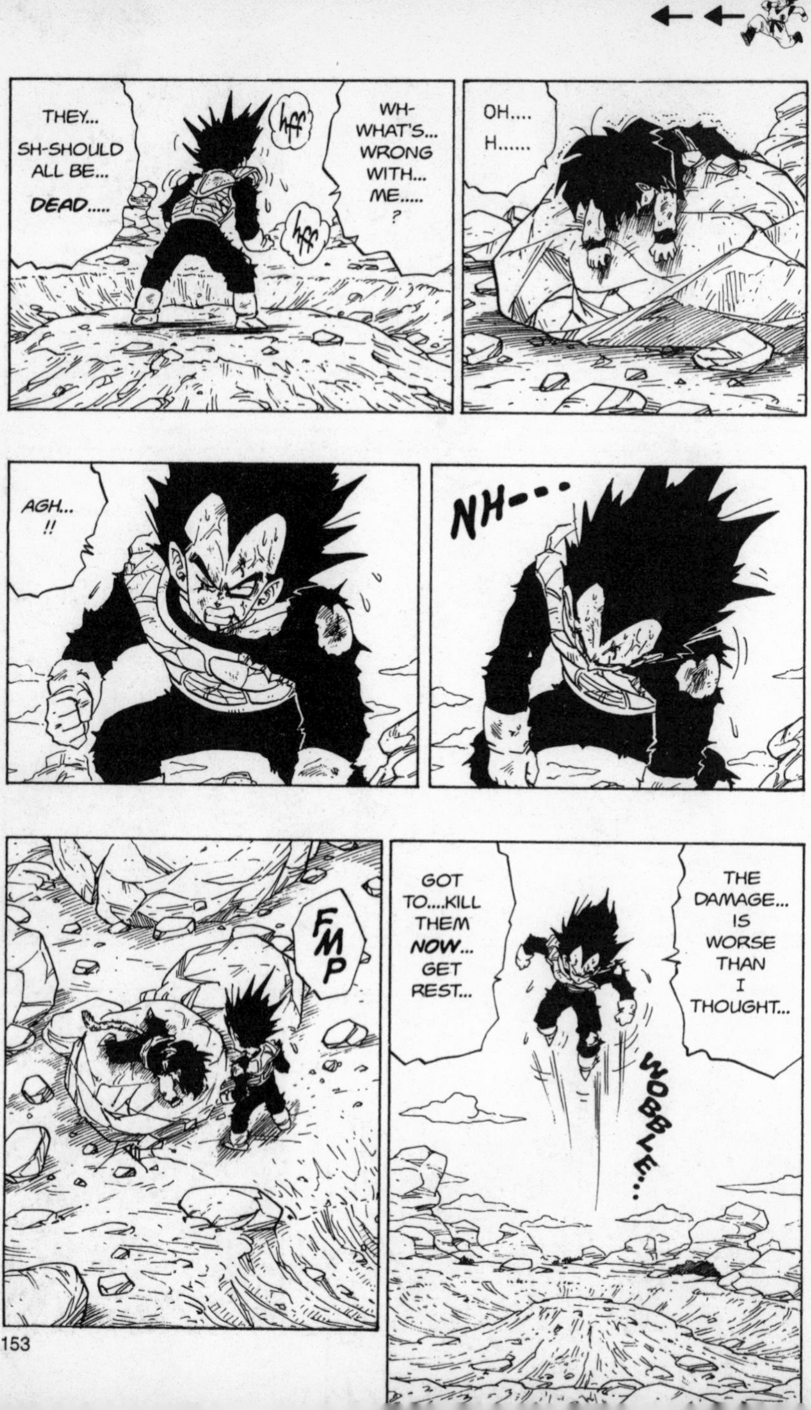
OH.... H......
WH- WHAT'S... WRONG WITH... ME..... ?
hff
hff
THEY... SH-SHOULD ALL BE... DEAD.....
NH---
AGH... !!
THE DAMAGE... IS WORSE THAN I THOUGHT...
GOT TO....KILL THEM NOW... GET REST...
WOBBLE...
FMP

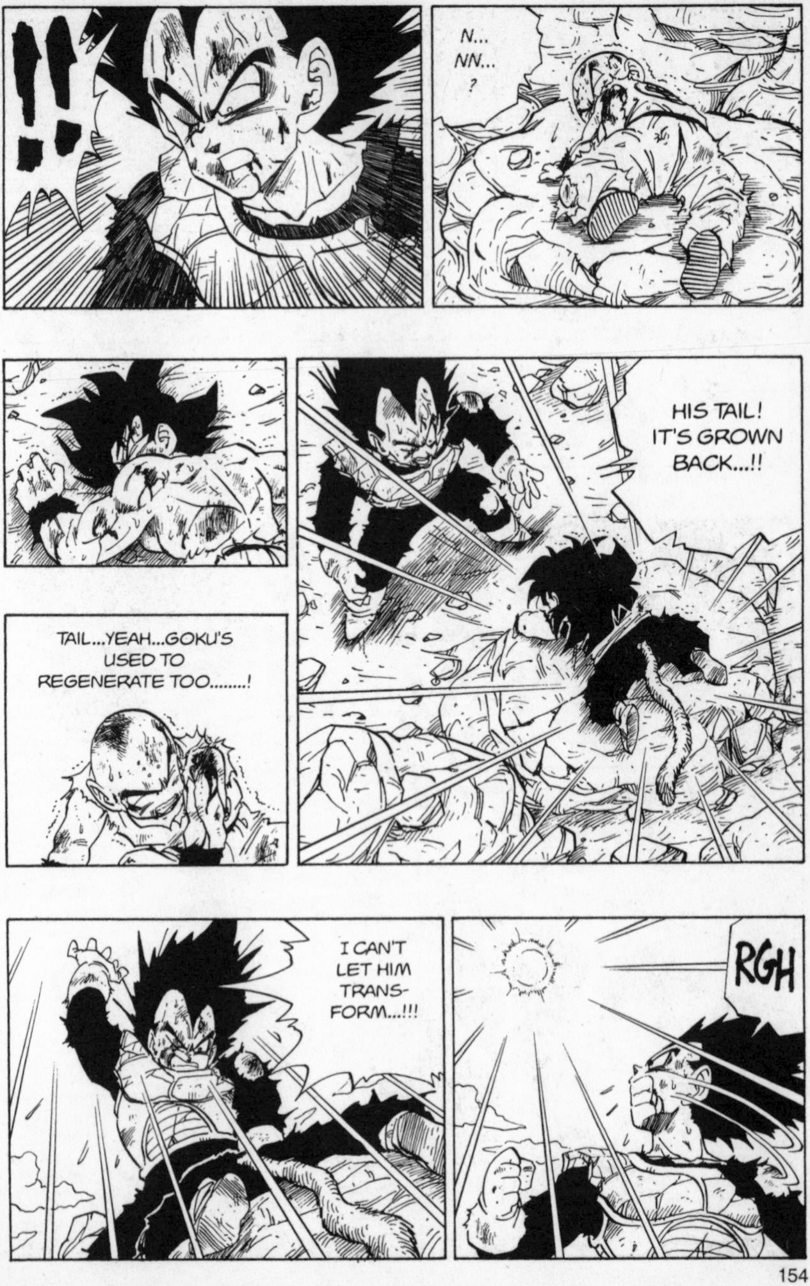

N...
NN...
?
!!
HIS TAIL! IT'S GROWN BACK...!!
TAIL...YEAH...GOKU'S USED TO REGENERATE TOO........!
RGH
I CAN'T LET HIM TRANS-FORM...!!!

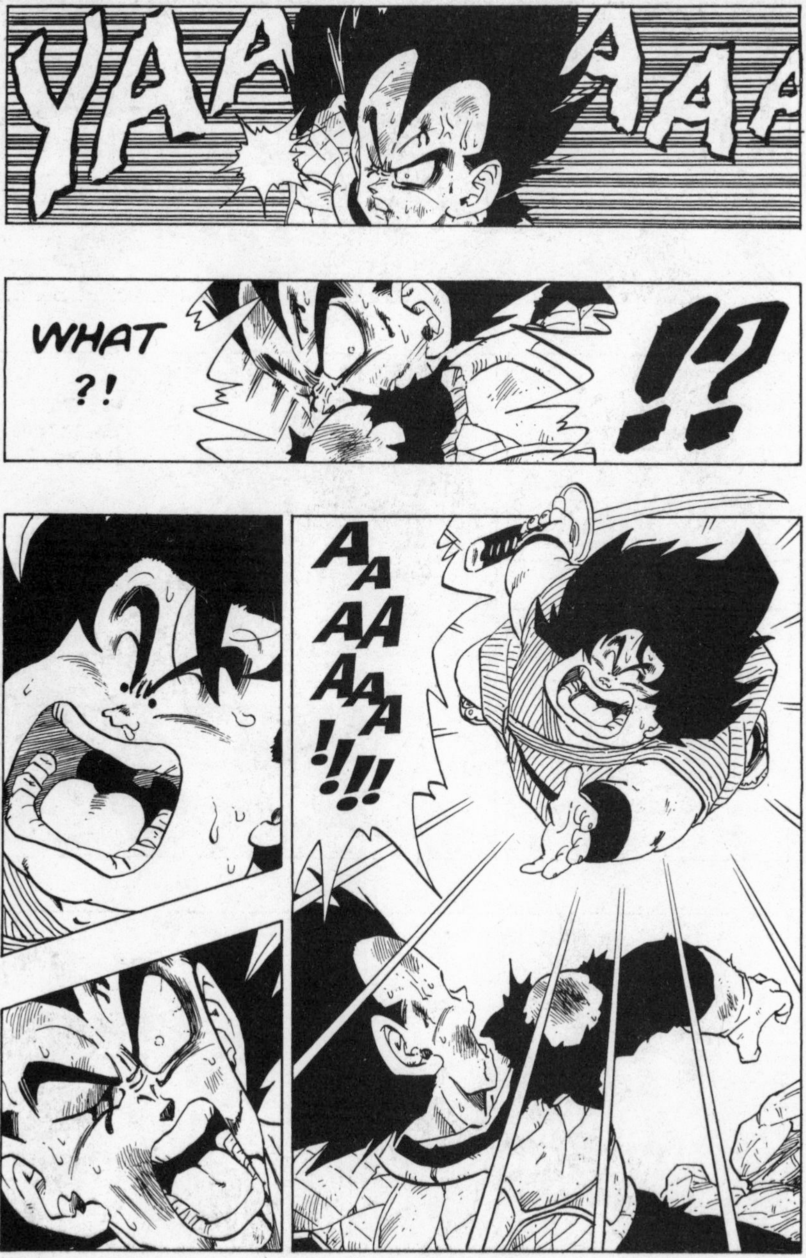
YAAAAA
WHAT ?!
!?
AAAAAAAA!!!!

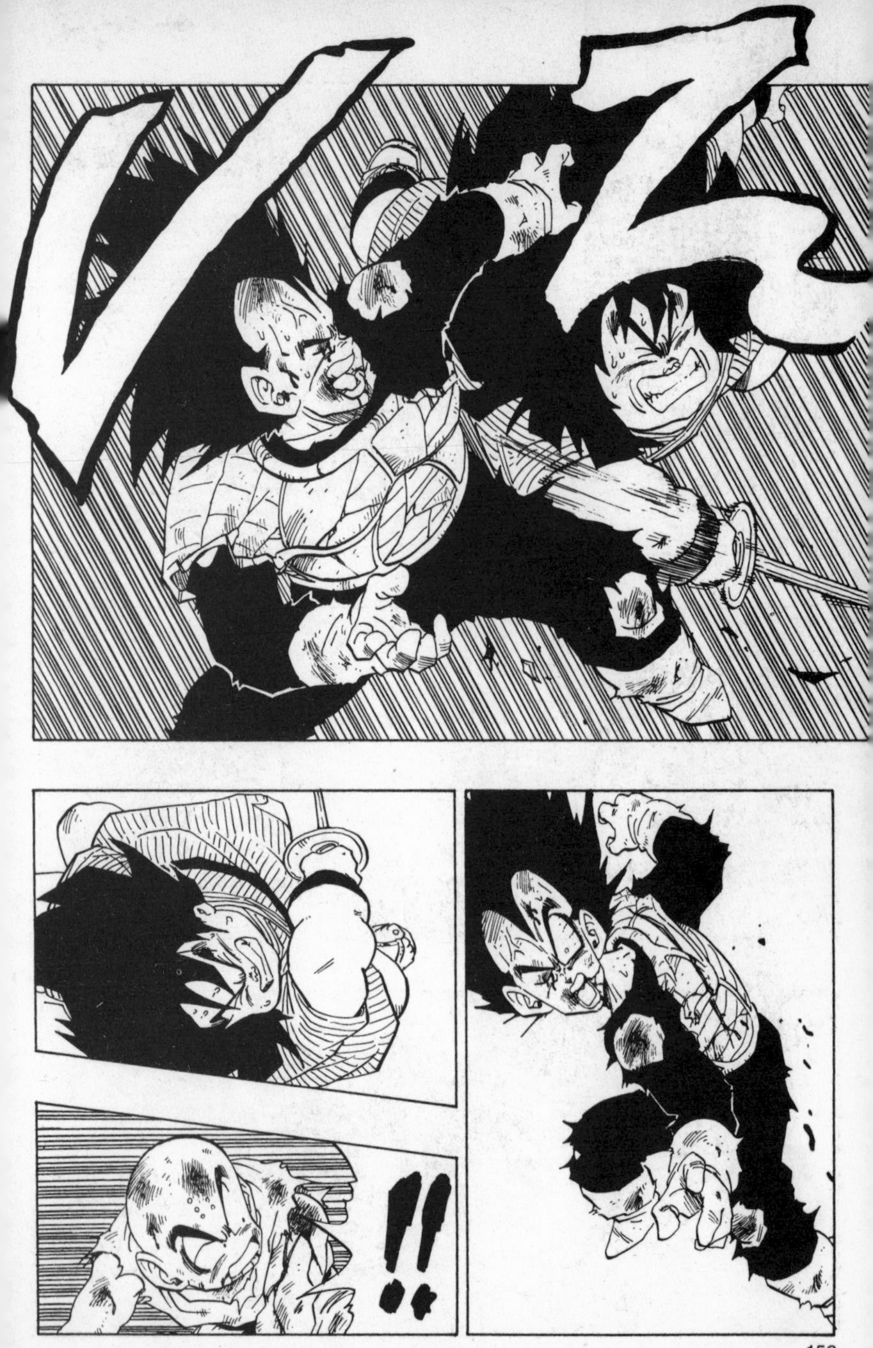
!!

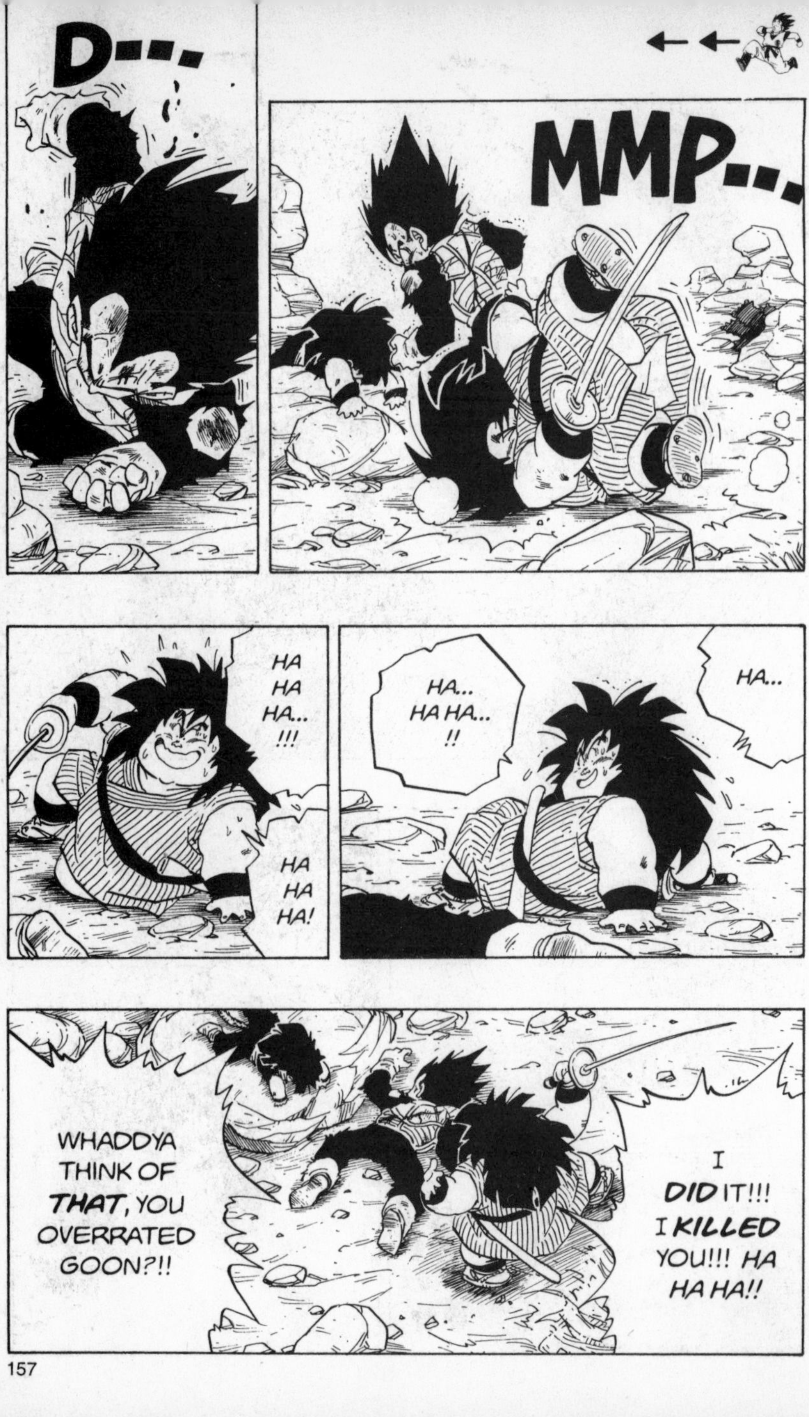
MMP...
D...
HA...
HA... HA HA... !!
HA HA HA... !!!
HA HA HA!
I DID IT!!! I KILLED YOU!!! HA HA HA!!
WHADDYA THINK OF THAT, YOU OVERRATED GOON?!!

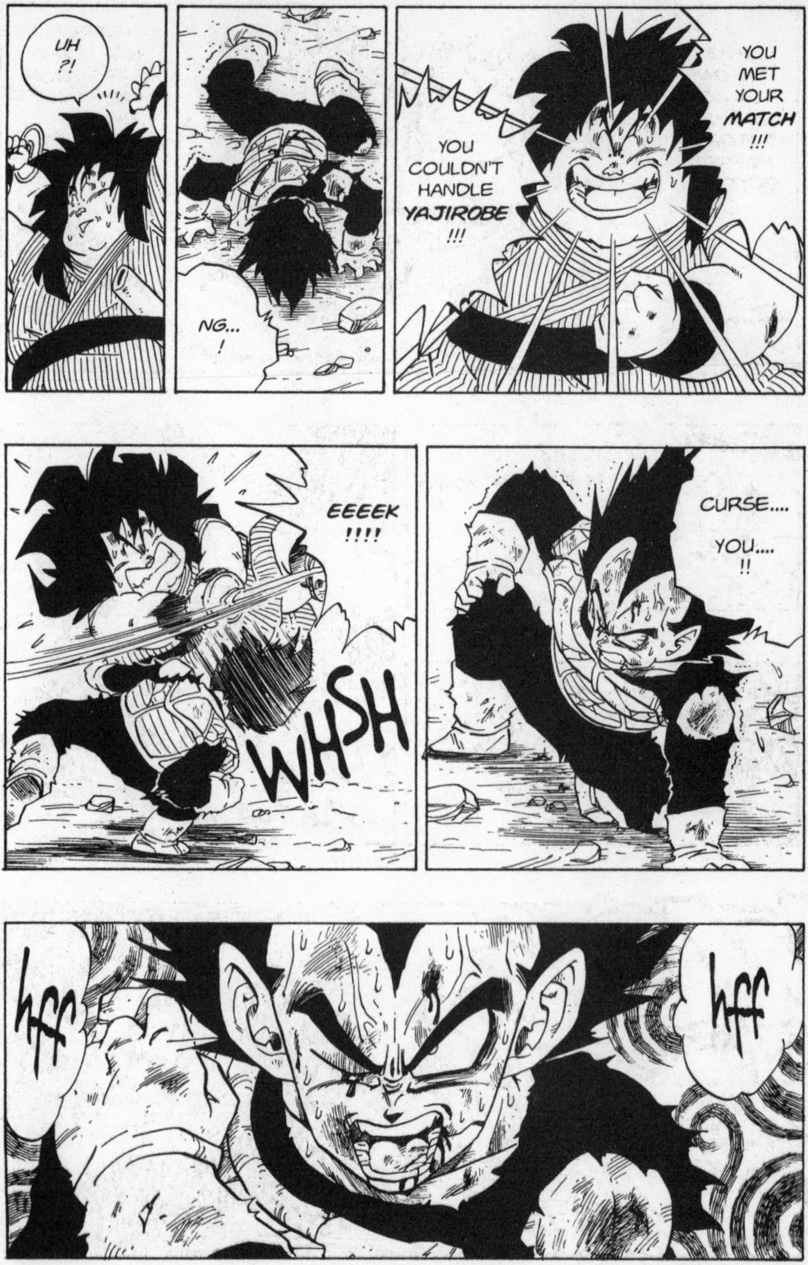
YOU MET YOUR MATCH !!!
YOU COULDN'T HANDLE YAJIROBE !!!
NG... !
UH ?!
CURSE.... YOU.... !!
EEEEK !!!!
WHSH
hff
hff

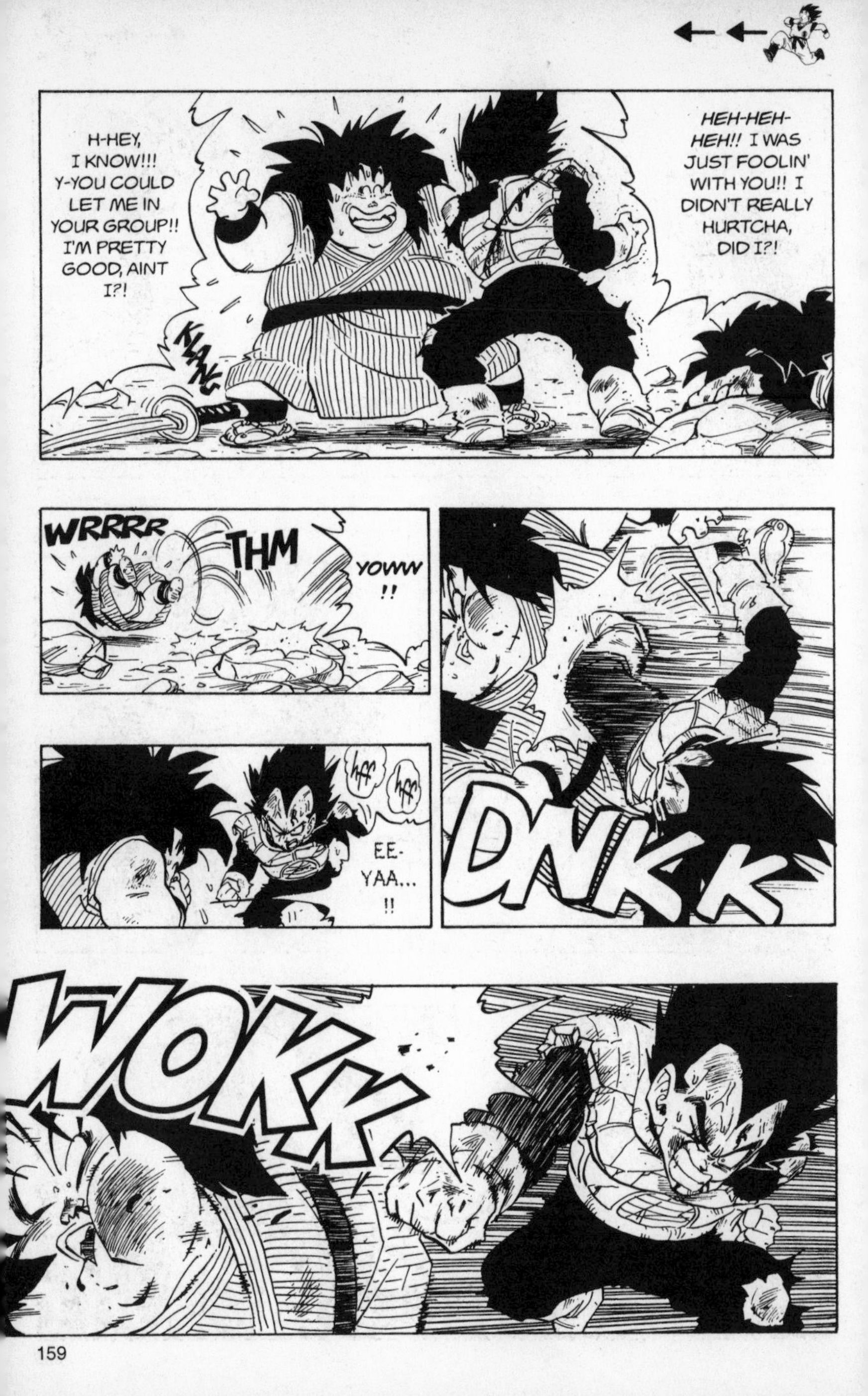
HEH-HEH-HEH!! I WAS JUST FOOLIN' WITH YOU!! I DIDN'T REALLY HURTCHA, DID I?!
H-HEY, I KNOW!!! Y-YOU COULD LET ME IN YOUR GROUP!! I'M PRETTY GOOD, AINT I?!
KLANG
DNKK
WRRRR
THM
YOWW !!
hff
hff
EE- YAA... !!
WOK

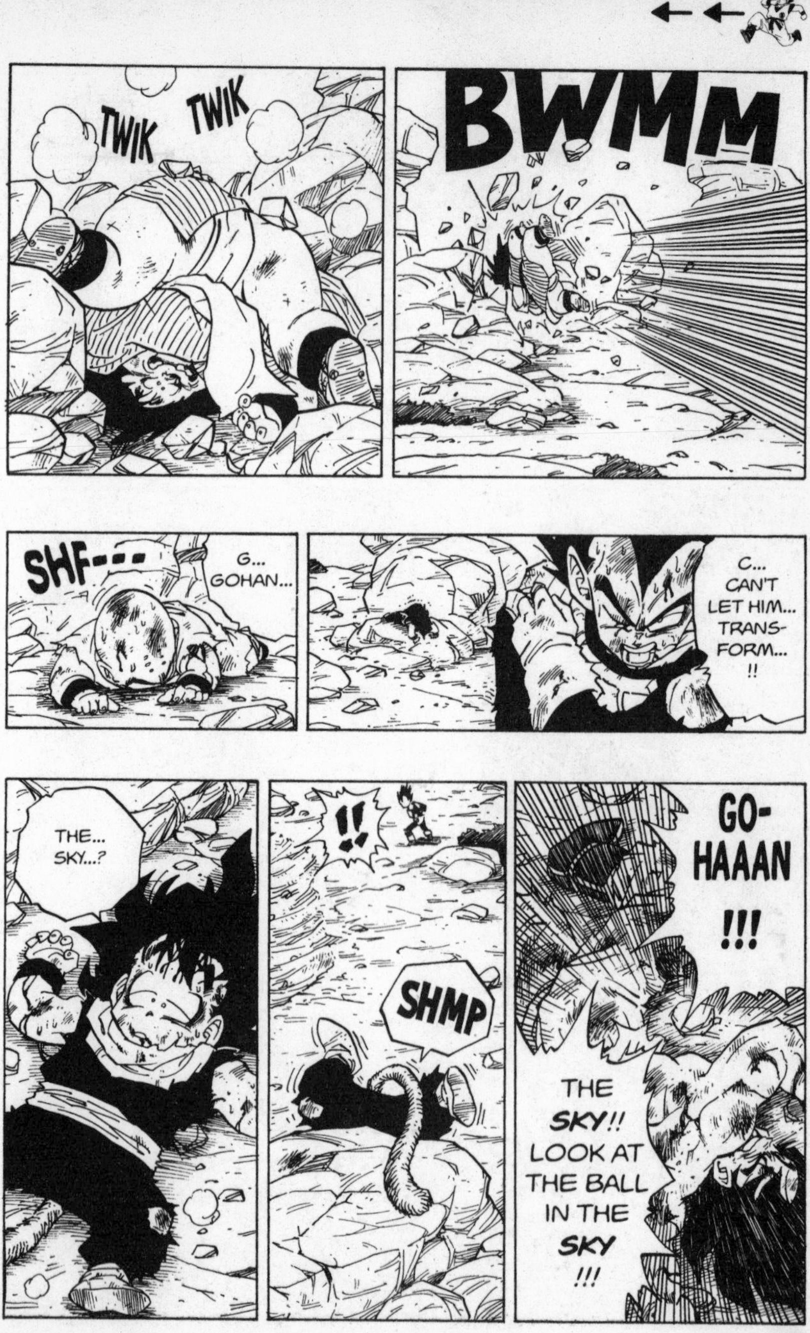
BWMM
TWIK
TWIK
C... CAN'T LET HIM... TRANS-FORM... !!
SHF---
G... GOHAN...
GO-HAAAN !!!
THE SKY!! LOOK AT THE BALL IN THE SKY !!!
!!
SHMP
THE... SKY...?

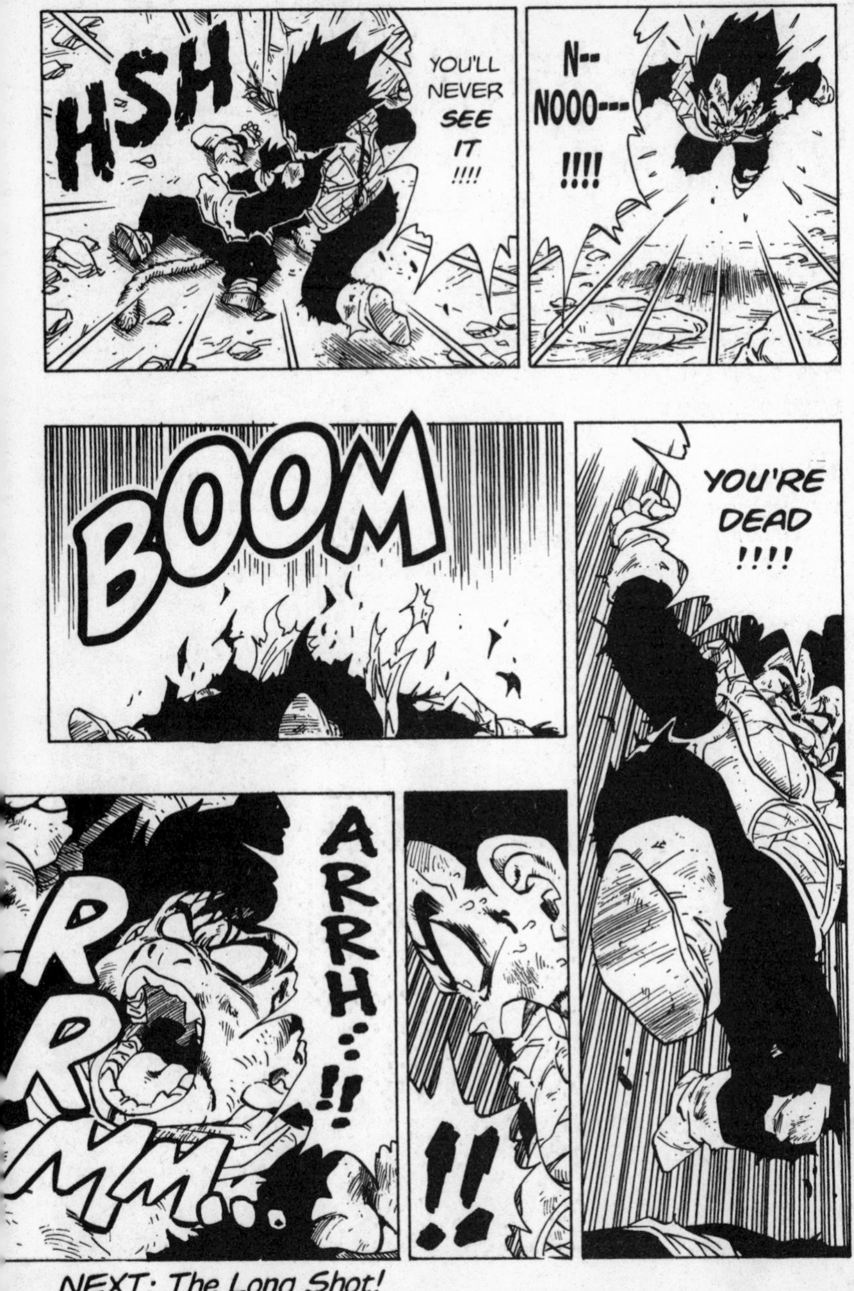

N--
NOOO---!!!!
HSH
YOU'LL NEVER SEE IT!!!!
YOU'RE DEAD!!!!
BOOM
!!
ARRH..!!
RRMM..

NEXT: The Long Shot!

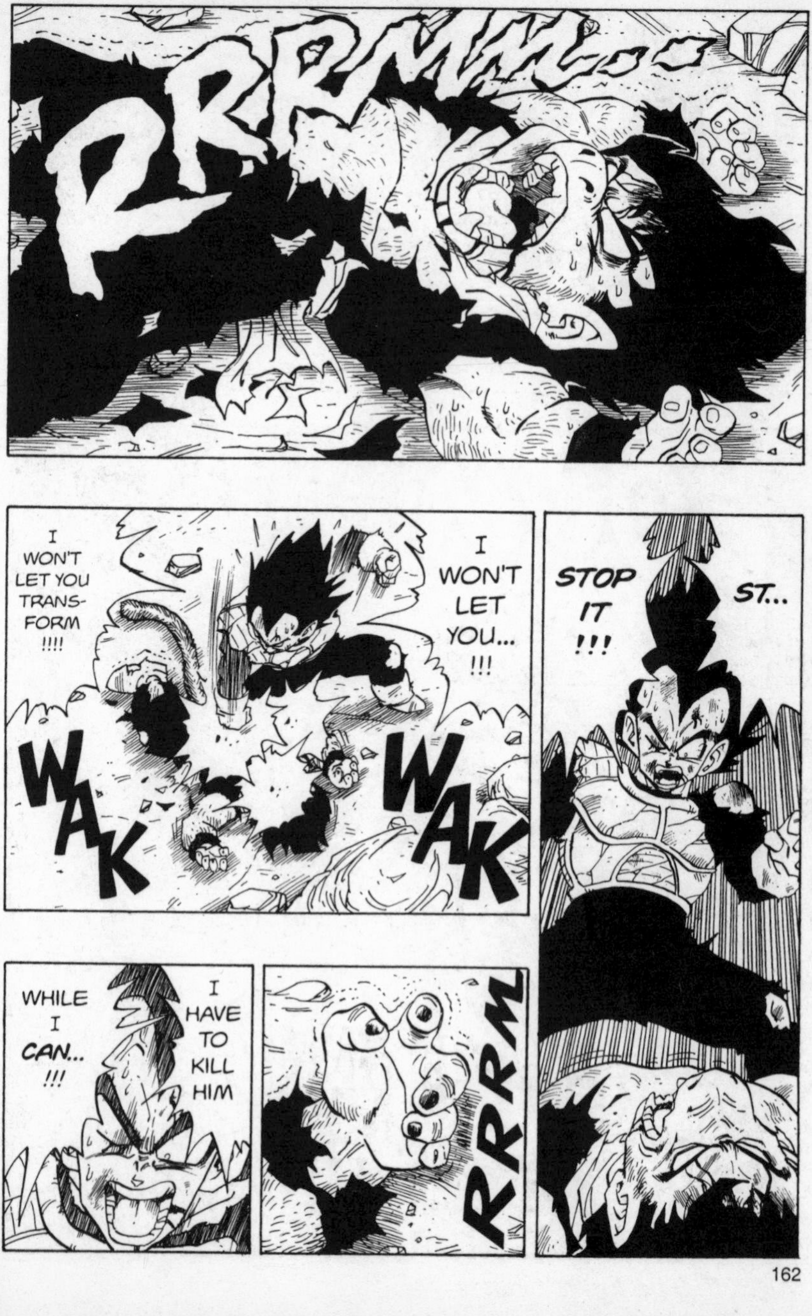
RRRMMM...
ST...
STOP IT !!!
I WON'T LET YOU... !!!
I WON'T LET YOU TRANSFORM !!!!
WAK
WAK
RRRM
I HAVE TO KILL HIM
WHILE I CAN... !!!

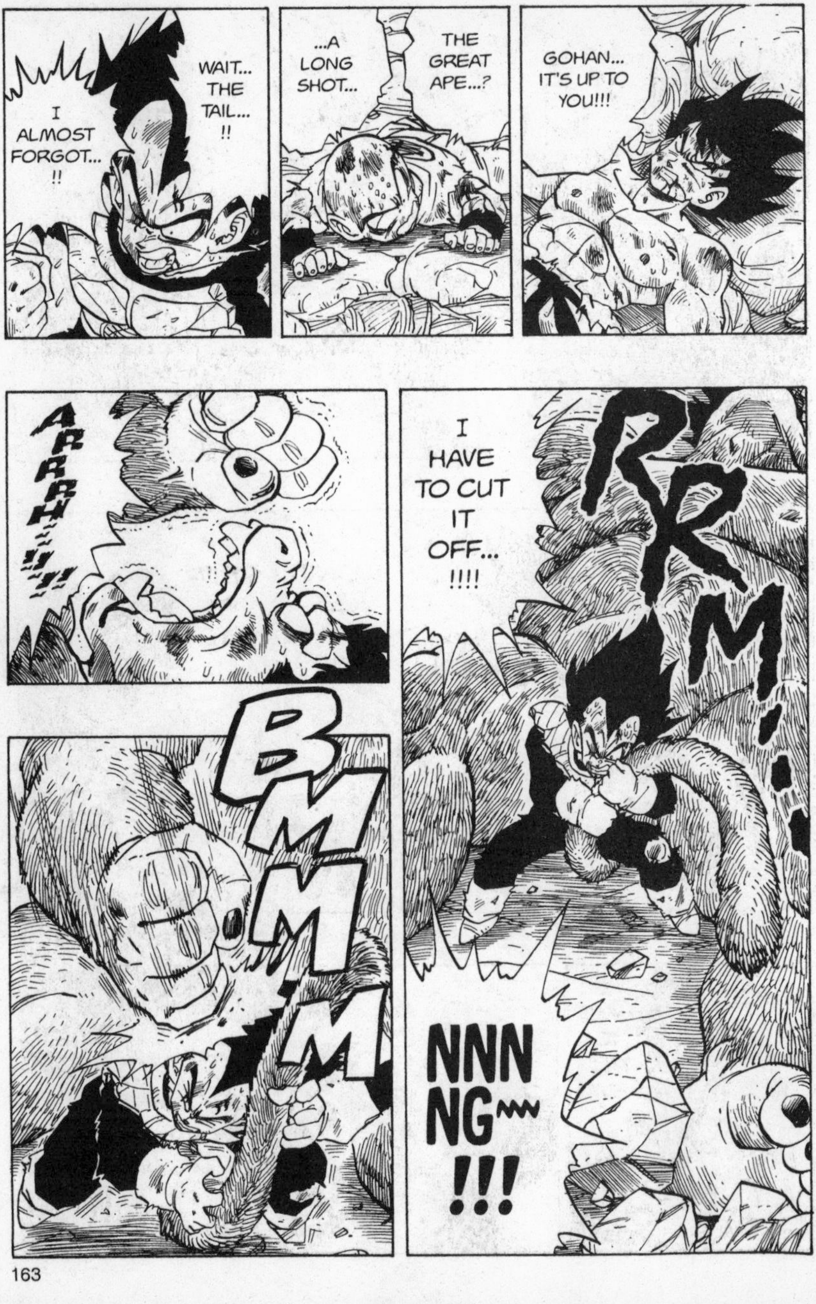

GOHAN... IT'S UP TO YOU!!!
THE GREAT APE...?
...A LONG SHOT...
WAIT... THE TAIL... !!
I ALMOST FORGOT... !!
I HAVE TO CUT IT OFF... !!!!
RRM!!
NNNNG~~ !!!
ARRRH!!!
BMMM

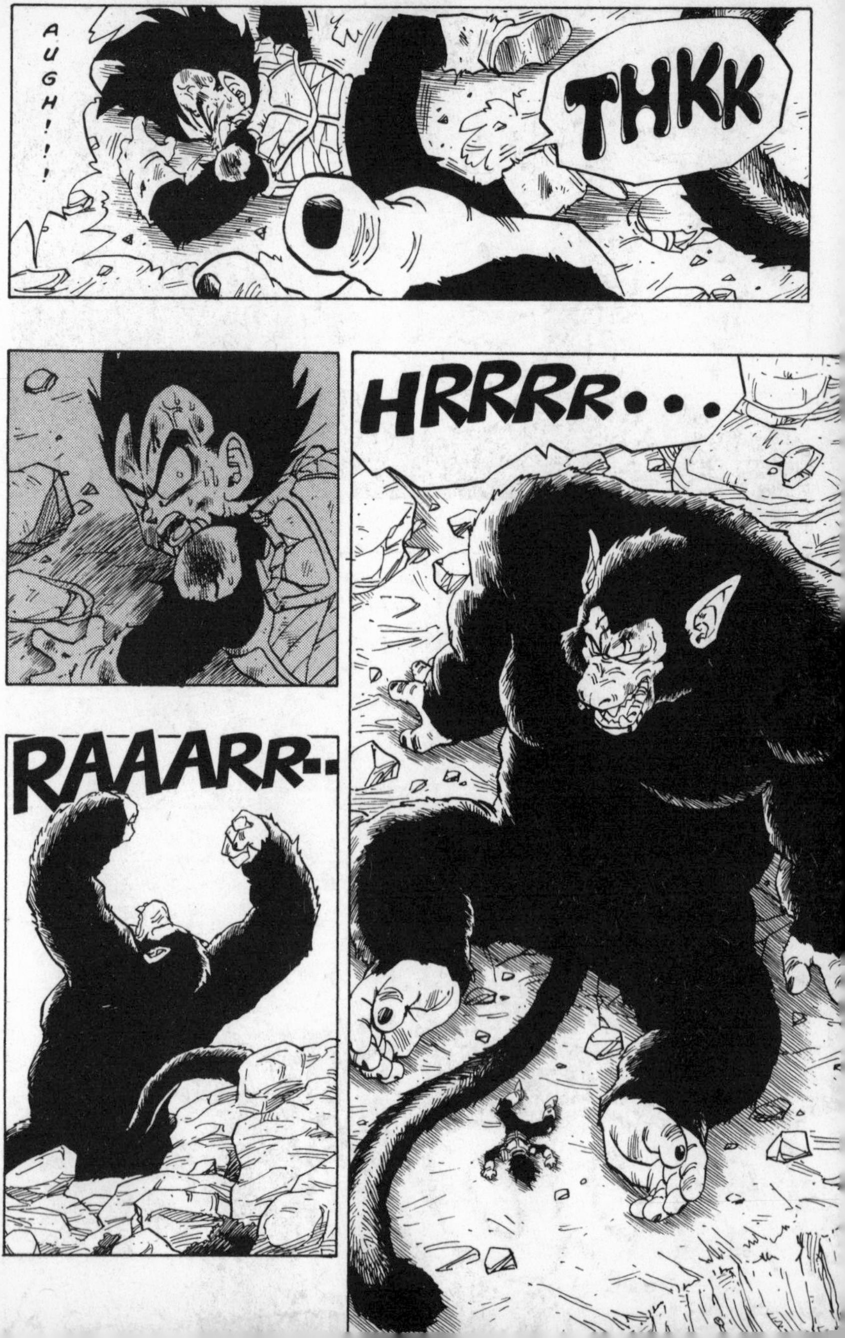
THKK
AUGH!!!
HRRRR...
RAAARR--

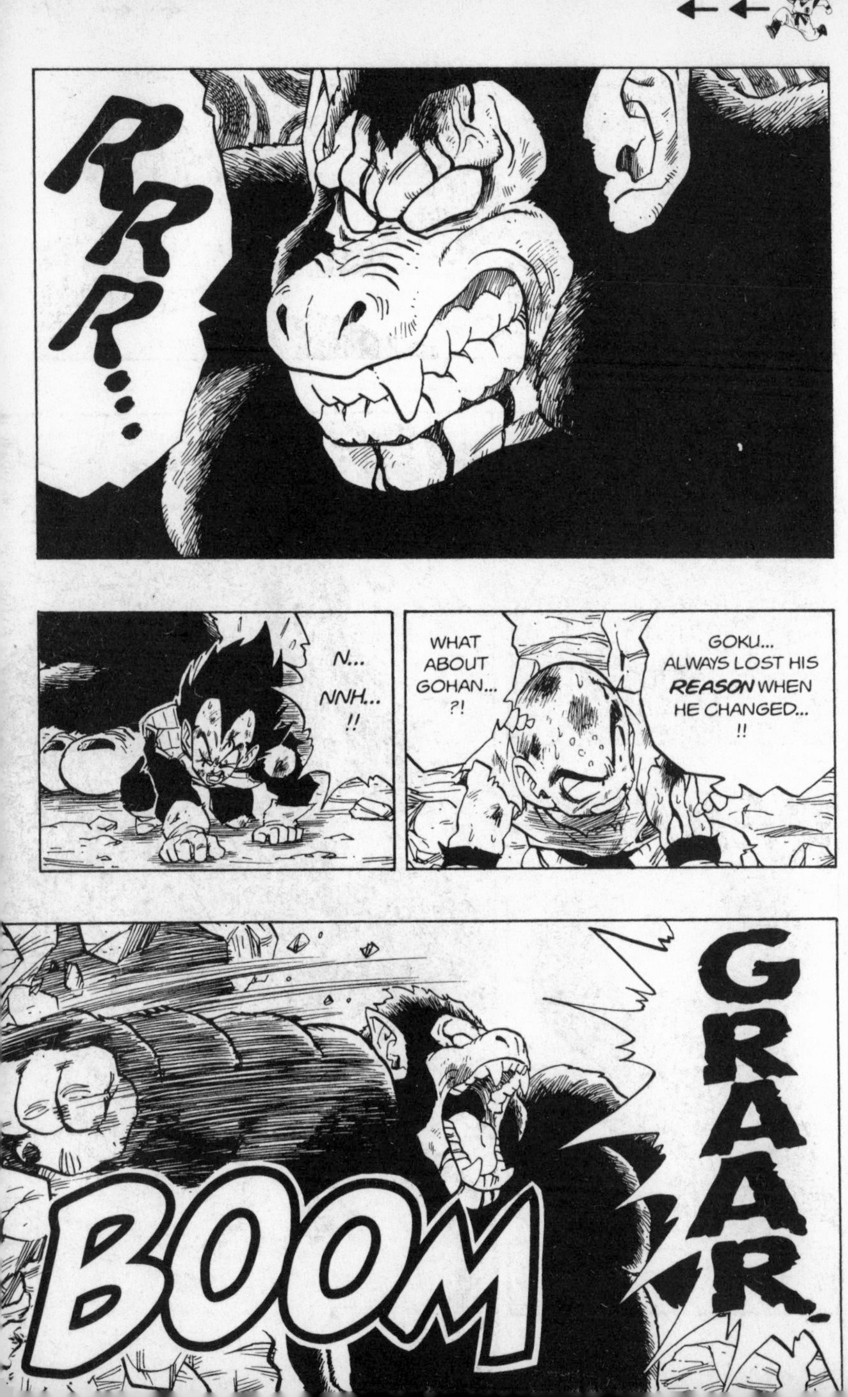
RRR...
GOKU... ALWAYS LOST HIS REASON WHEN HE CHANGED...!!
WHAT ABOUT GOHAN...?!
N... NNH...!!
GRAAR
BOOM

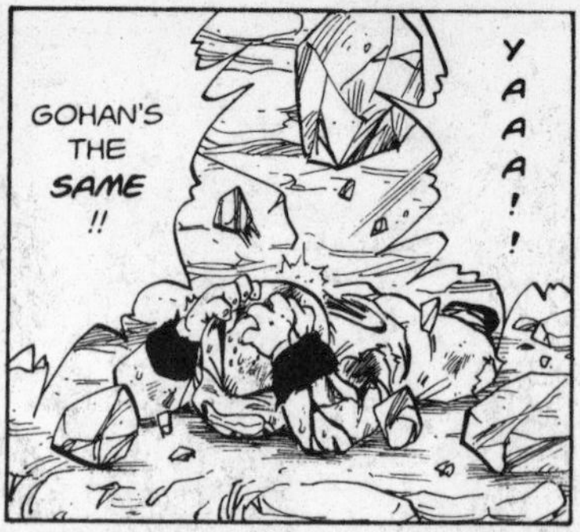
YAAAA!!
GOHAN'S THE *SAME* !!
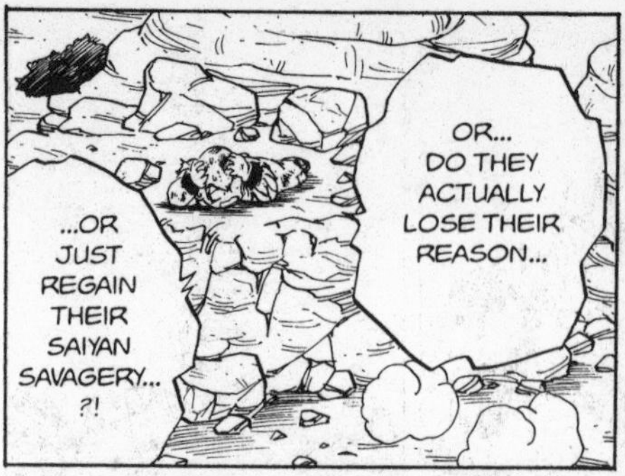
OR... DO THEY ACTUALLY LOSE THEIR REASON...
...OR JUST REGAIN THEIR SAIYAN SAVAGERY...?!
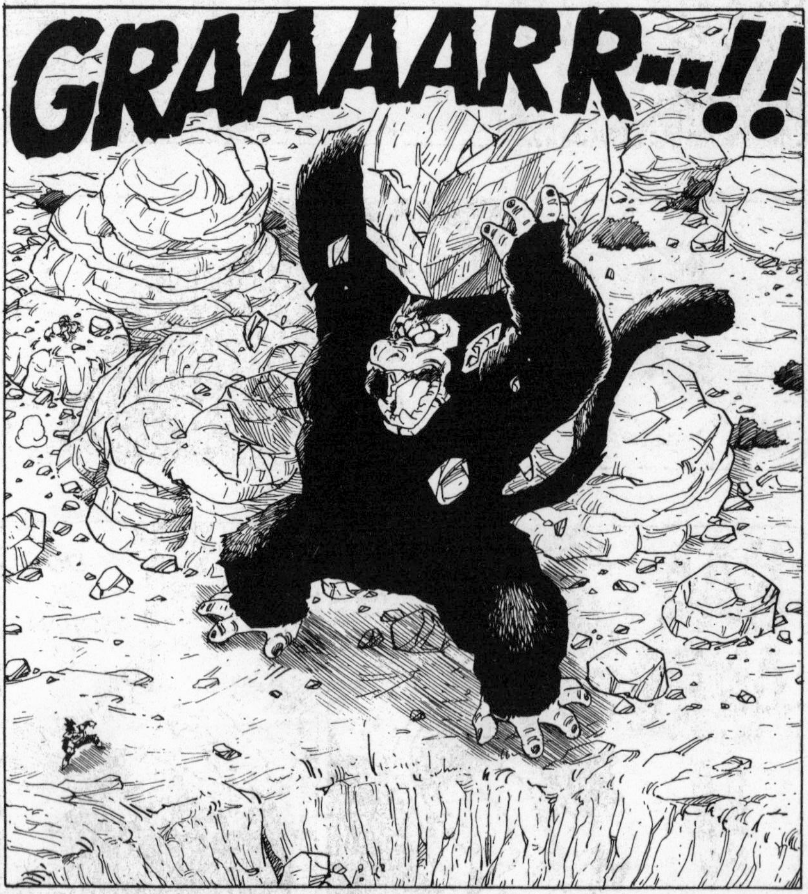
GRAAAARR..!!

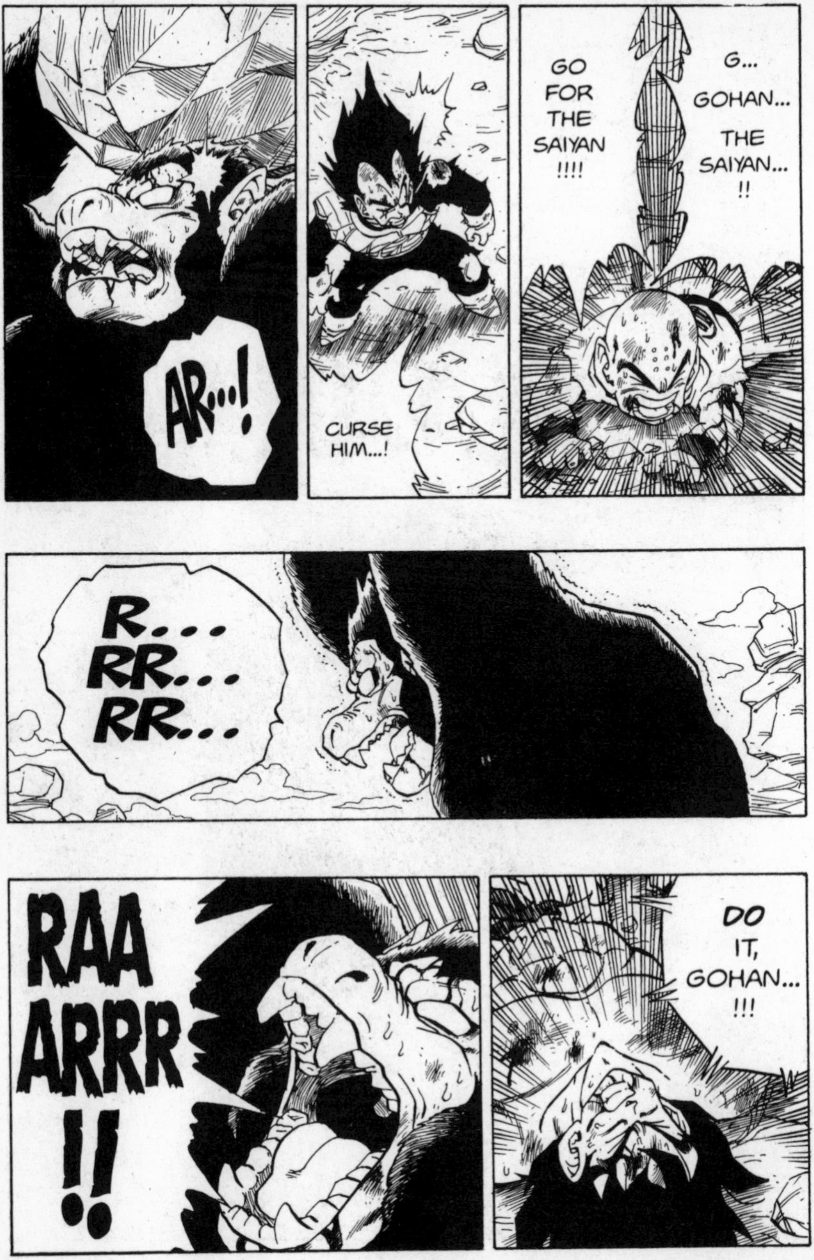
G... GOHAN... THE SAIYAN... !!
GO FOR THE SAIYAN !!!!
CURSE HIM...!
AR...!
R... RR... RR...
DO IT, GOHAN... !!!
RAA ARRR !!

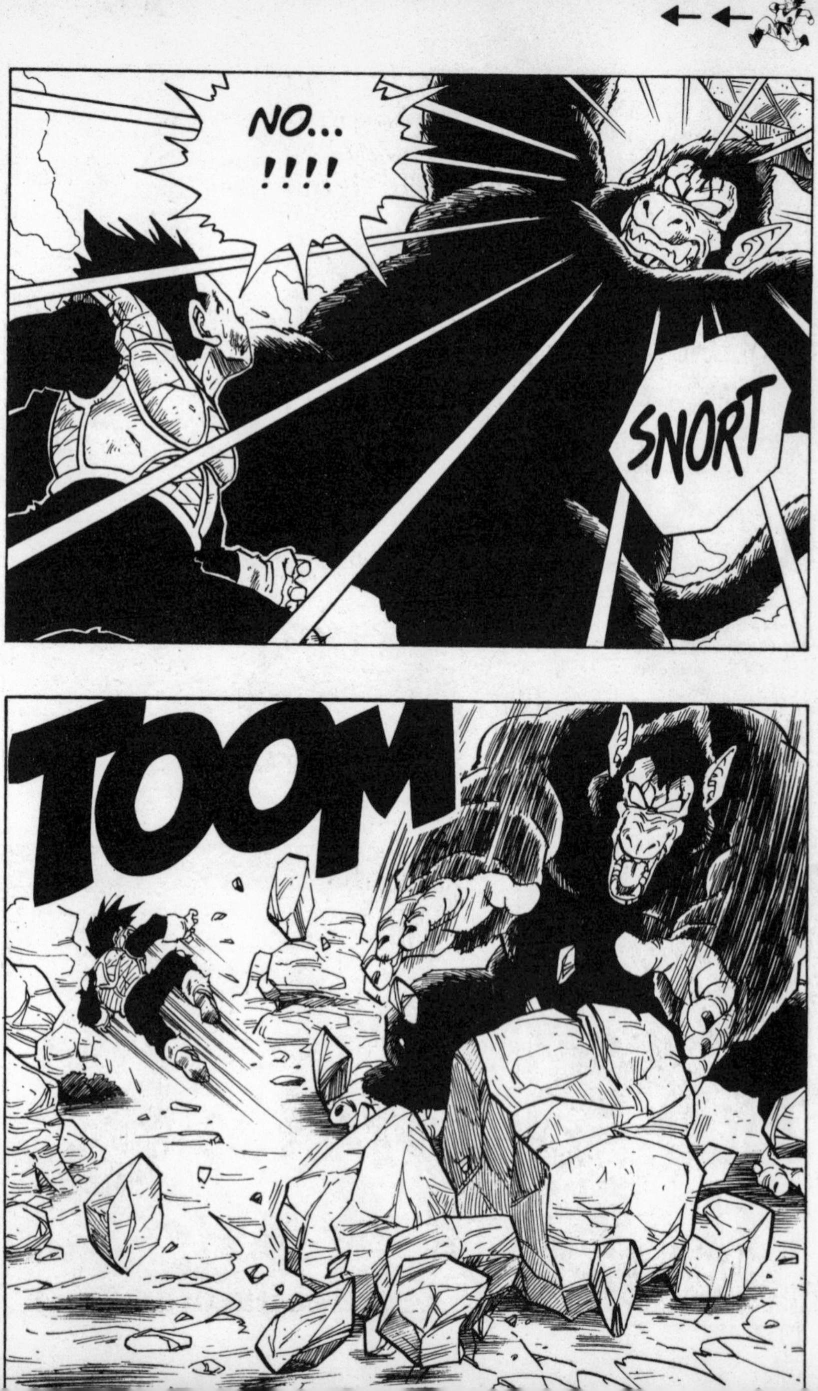
NO... !!!!
SNORT
TOOM

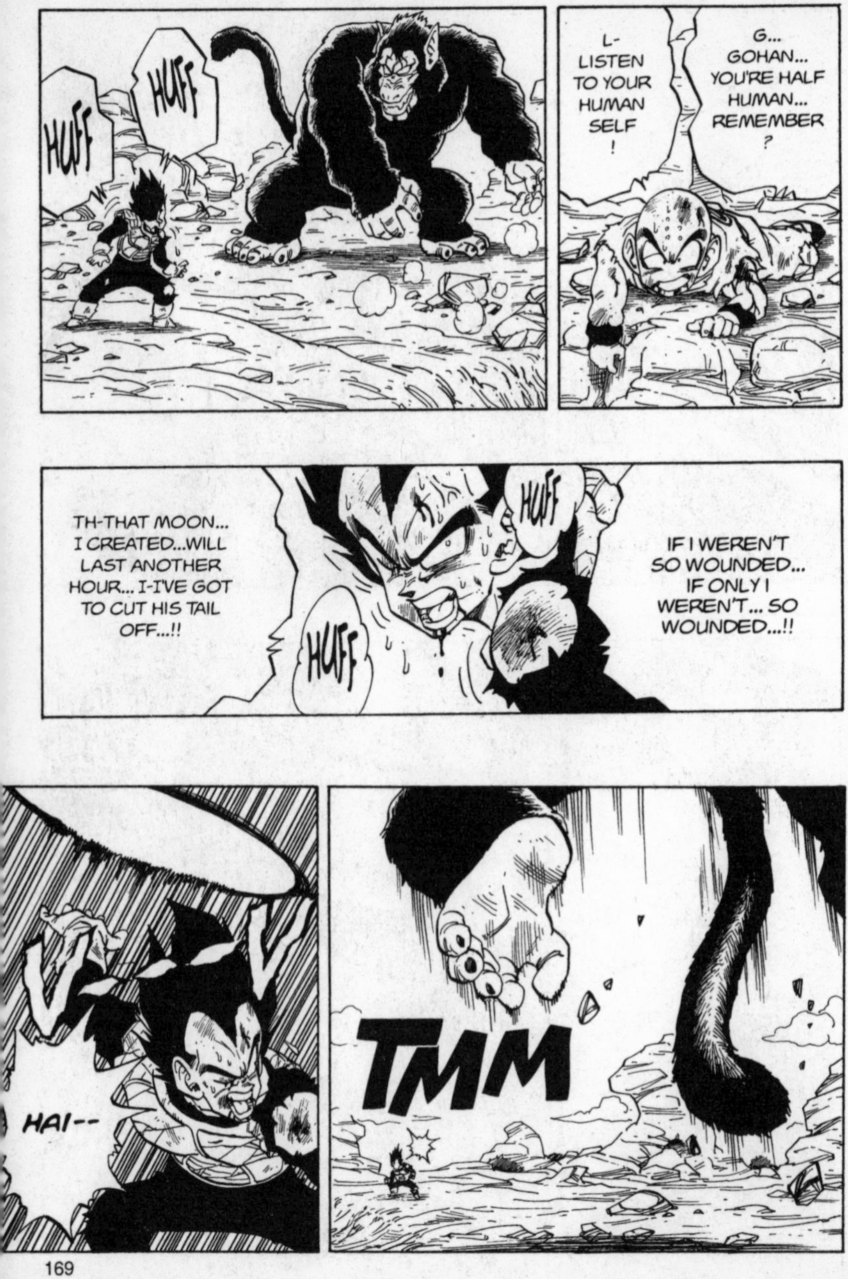
G... GOHAN... YOU'RE HALF HUMAN... REMEMBER?
L- LISTEN TO YOUR HUMAN SELF!
HUFF
HUFF
HUFF
IF I WEREN'T SO WOUNDED... IF ONLY I WEREN'T... SO WOUNDED...!!
TH-THAT MOON... I CREATED...WILL LAST ANOTHER HOUR... I-I'VE GOT TO CUT HIS TAIL OFF...!!
HUFF
TMM
HAI--

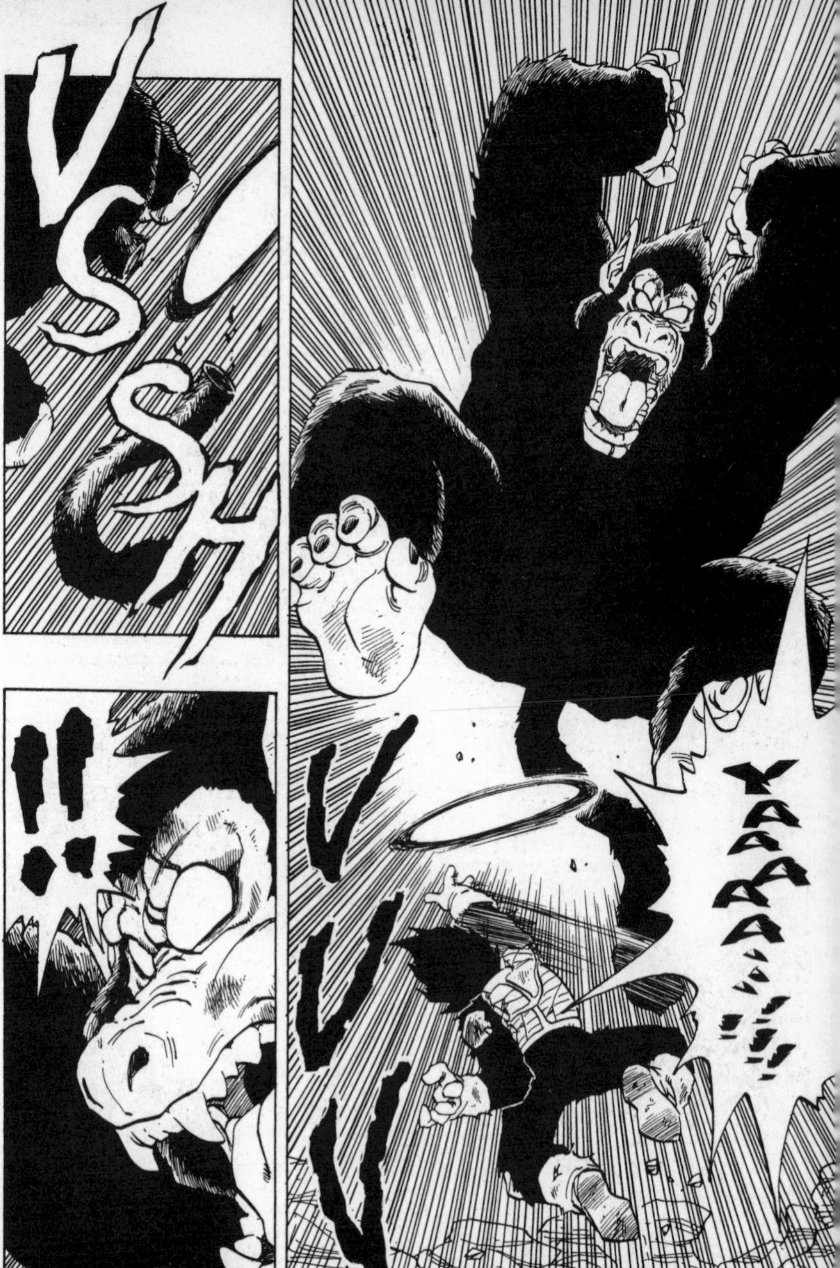
YAAAAA...!!
!!

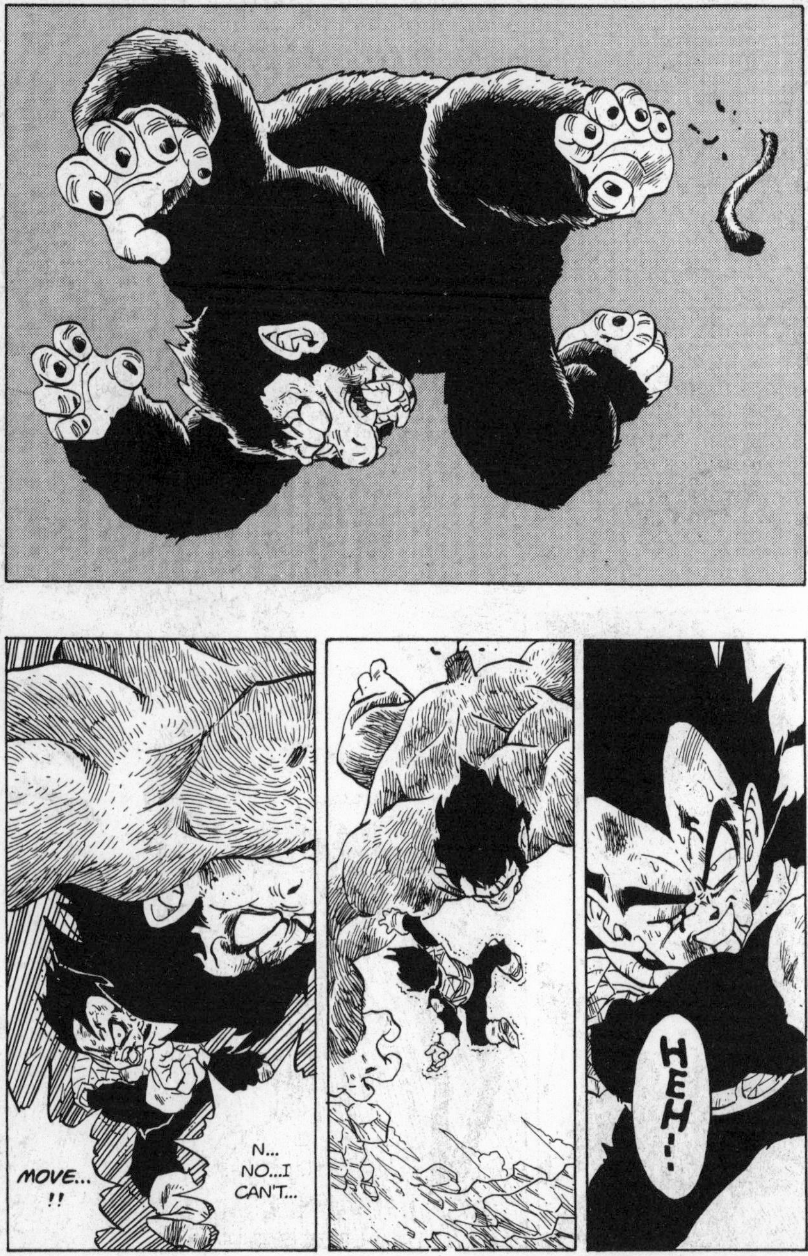
HEH...
N... NO...I CAN'T...
MOVE... !!

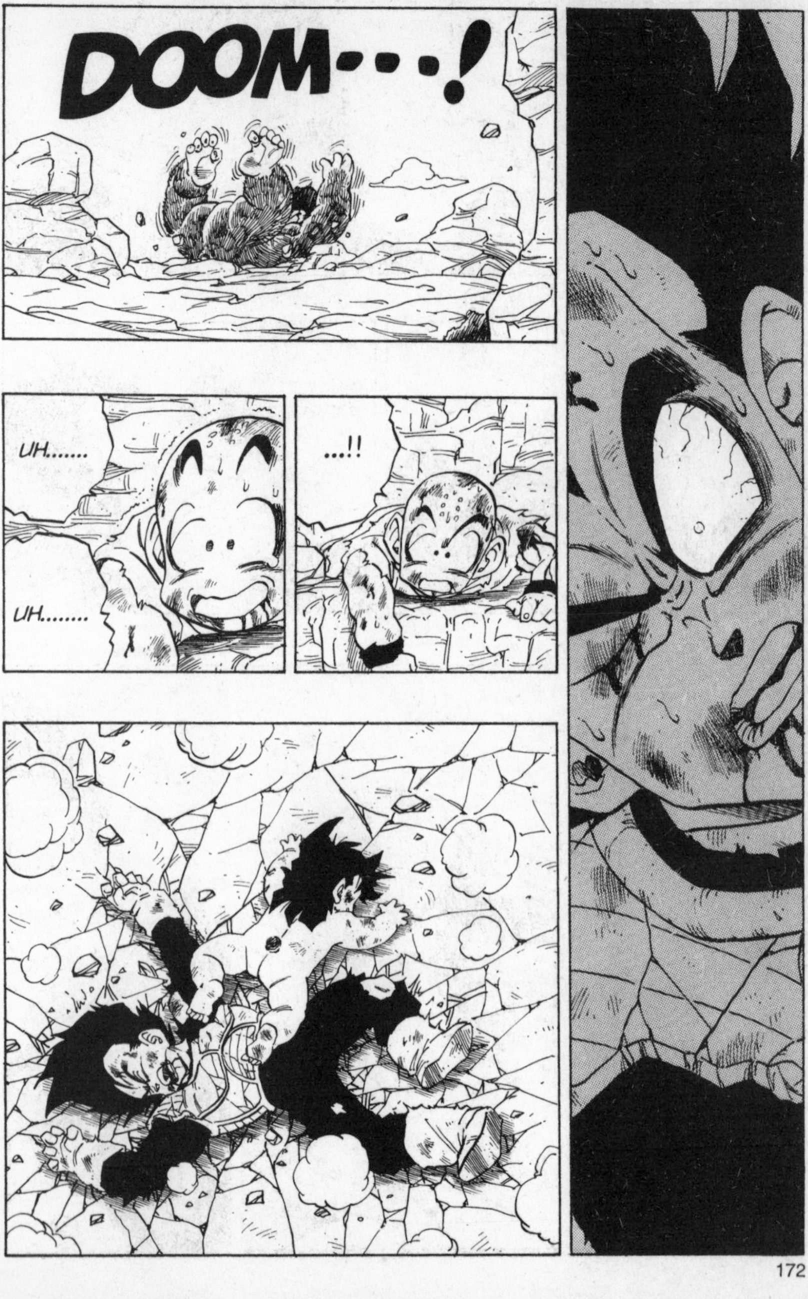
DOOM...!
...!!
UH.......
UH........

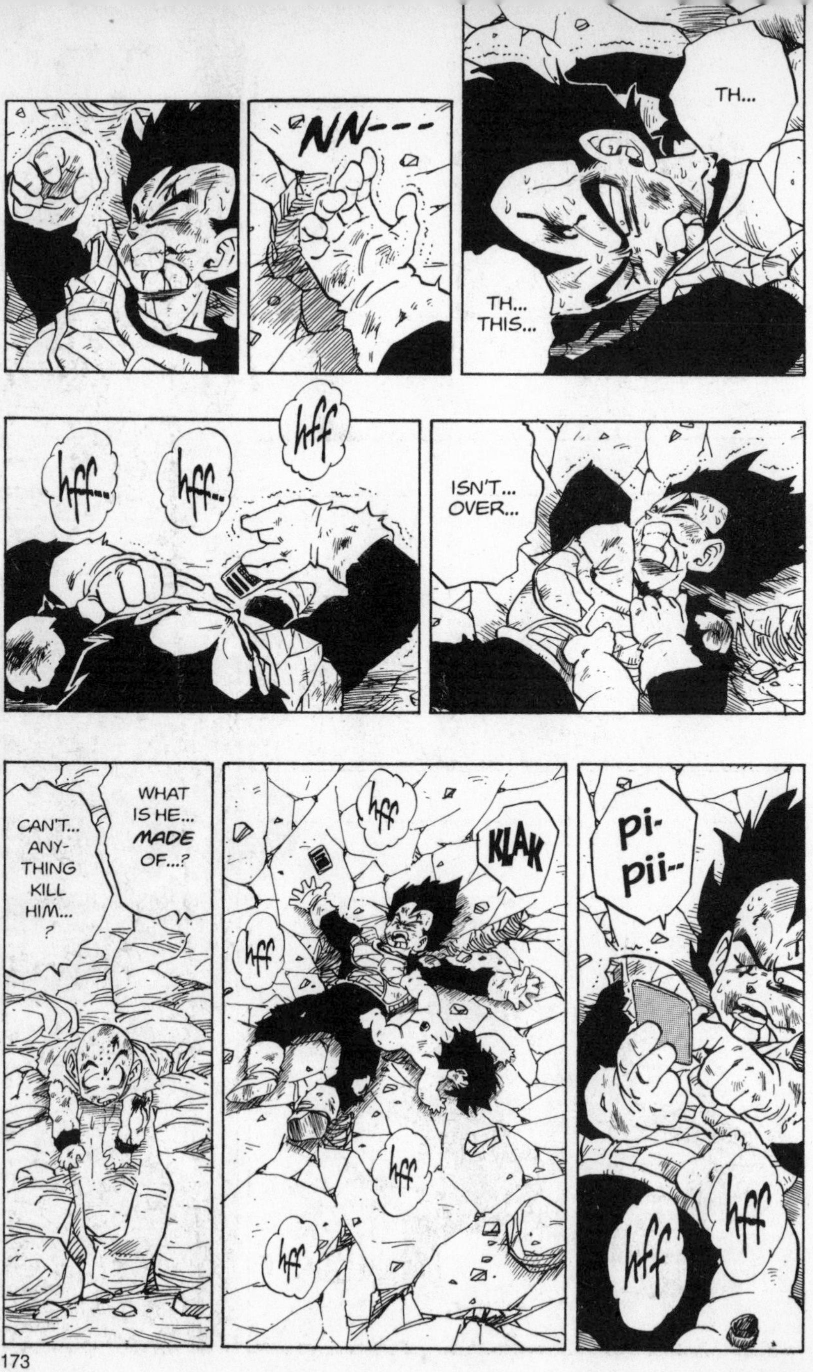
TH...
TH... THIS...
NN---
ISN'T... OVER...
hff
hff...
hff...
Pi-pii--
hff
hff
hff
KLAK
hff
hff
hff
WHAT IS HE... *MADE* OF...?
CAN'T... ANYTHING KILL HIM...?

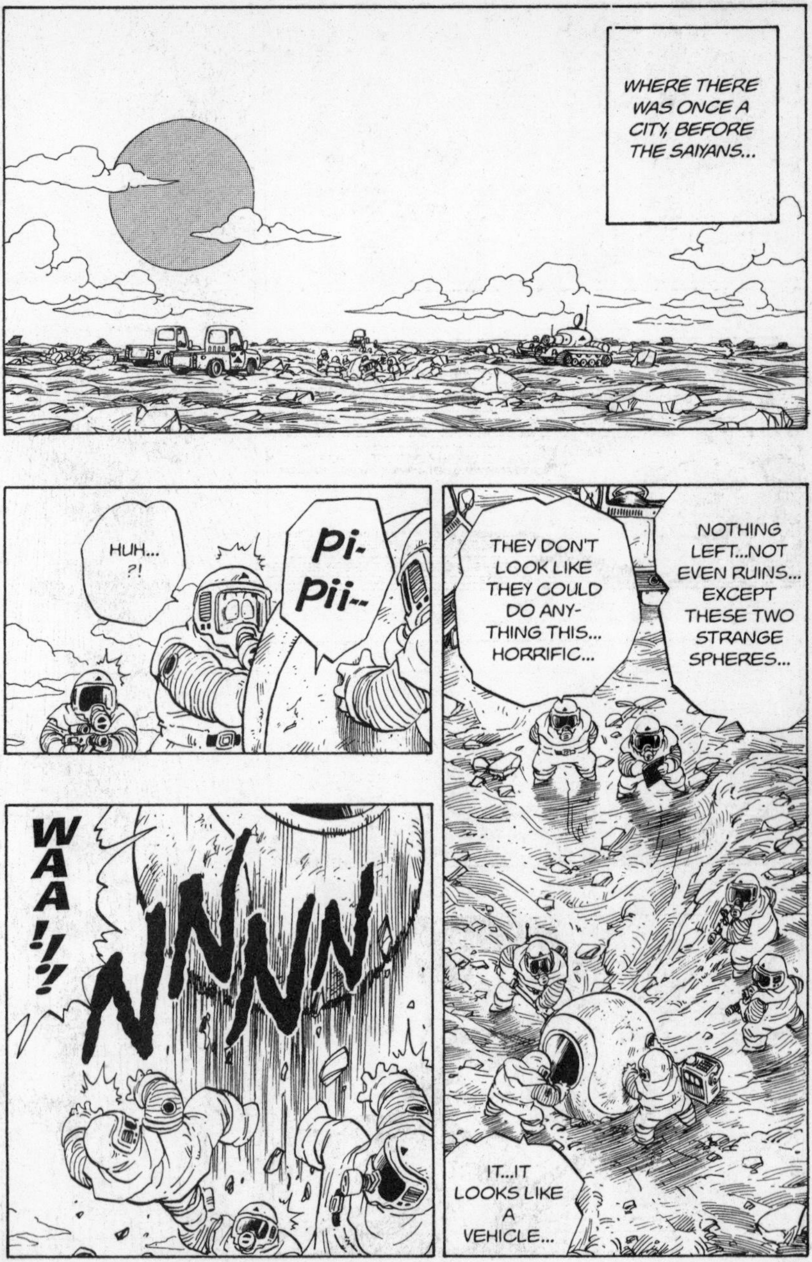
WHERE THERE WAS ONCE A CITY, BEFORE THE SAIYANS...
NOTHING LEFT...NOT EVEN RUINS... EXCEPT THESE TWO STRANGE SPHERES...
THEY DON'T LOOK LIKE THEY COULD DO ANY-THING THIS... HORRIFIC...
IT...IT LOOKS LIKE A VEHICLE...
Pi-Pii--
HUH... ?!
WAAA!!!
NNNN

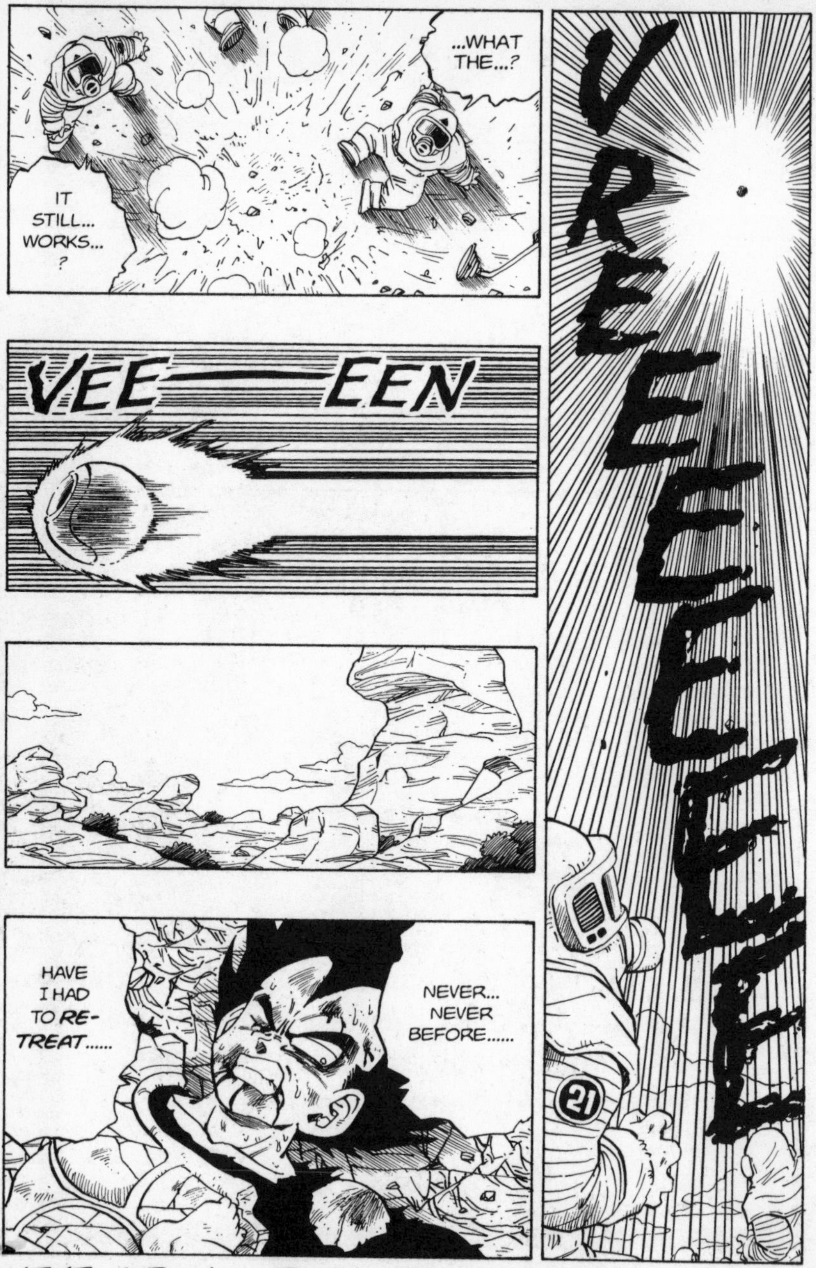
VREEEEEEEEEEE
21
...WHAT THE...?
IT STILL... WORKS... ?
VEE——EEN
NEVER... NEVER BEFORE......
HAVE I HAD TO RE-TREAT......

NEXT: A Battle to Tear the Heavens Asunder!

TITLE PAGE GALLERY

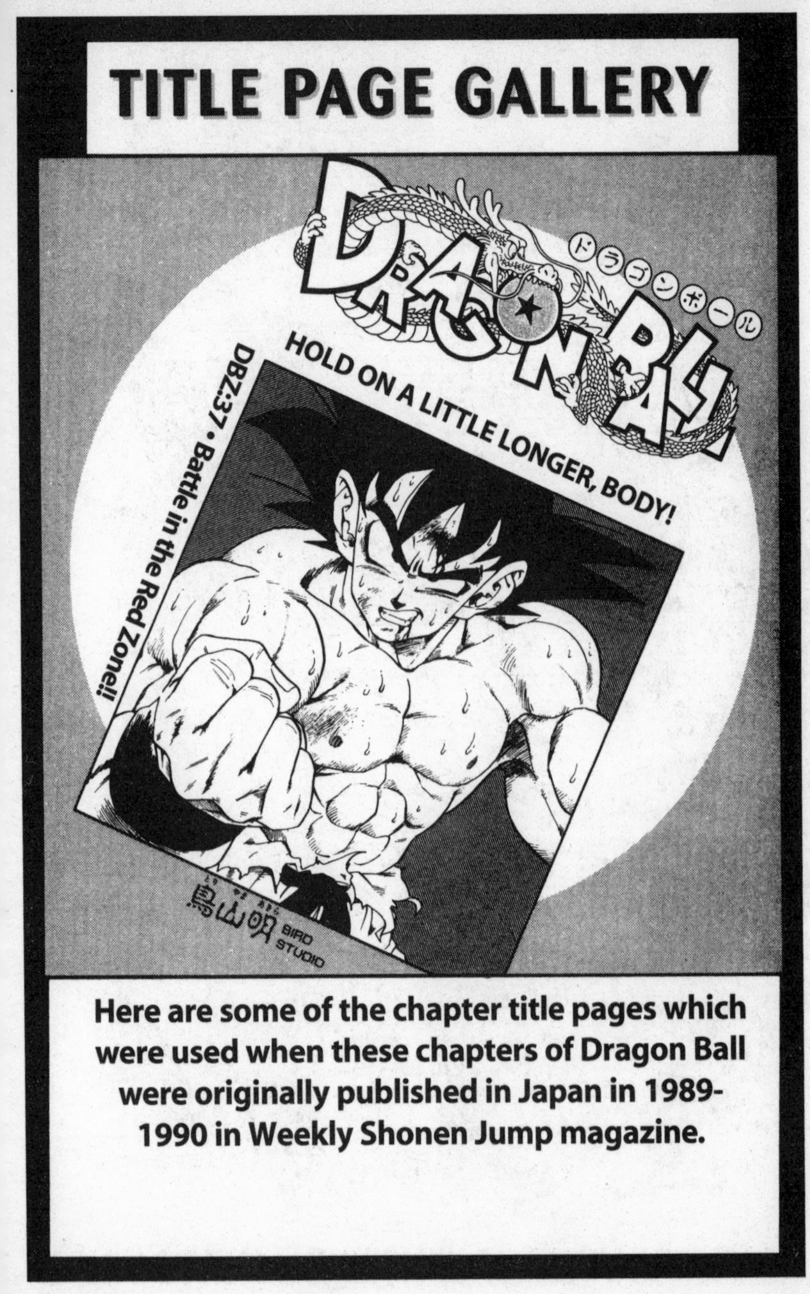
DRAGON BALL
ドラゴンボール
HOLD ON A LITTLE LONGER, BODY!
DBZ:37 • Battle in the Red Zone!!
鳥山明
BIRD STUDIO

Here are some of the chapter title pages which were used when these chapters of Dragon Ball were originally published in Japan in 1989-1990 in Weekly Shonen Jump magazine.

ドラゴンボール

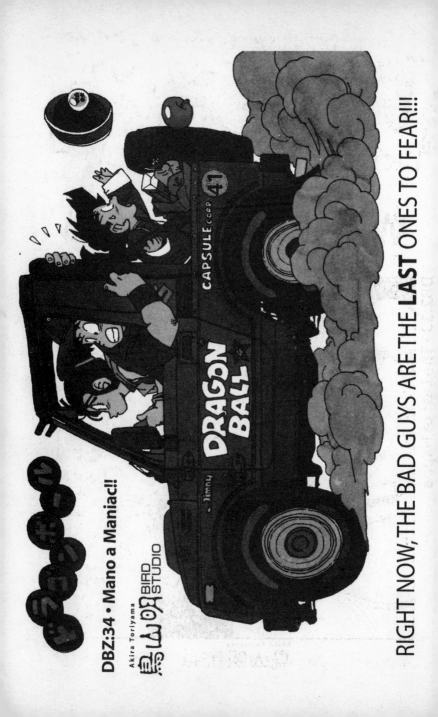

DBZ:34 • Mano a Maniac!!

Akira Toriyama
鳥山明 BIRD STUDIO

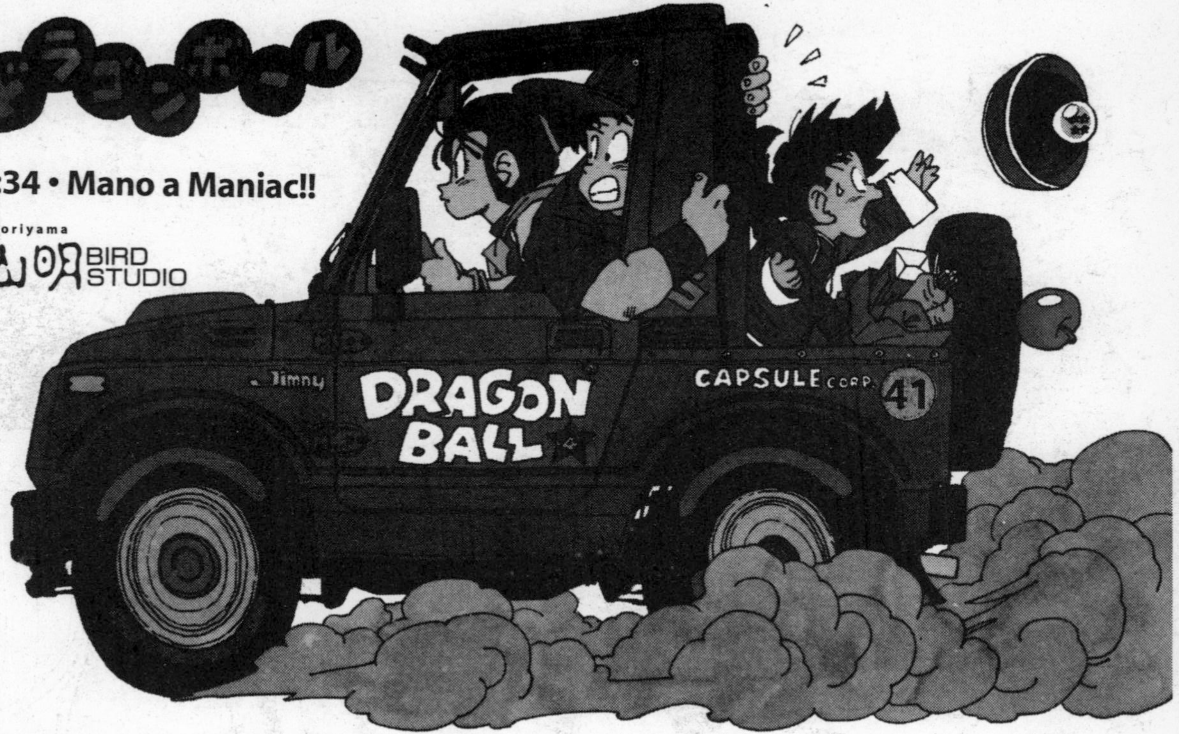

Jimny
DRAGON BALL
CAPSULE CORP.
41

RIGHT NOW, THE BAD GUYS ARE THE **LAST** ONES TO FEAR!!!

DRAGON BALL

DIE, GOKU!!! JUST DIE!!!

Akira Toriyama
鳥山明
BIRD STUDIO

DBZ:38 • The Moon

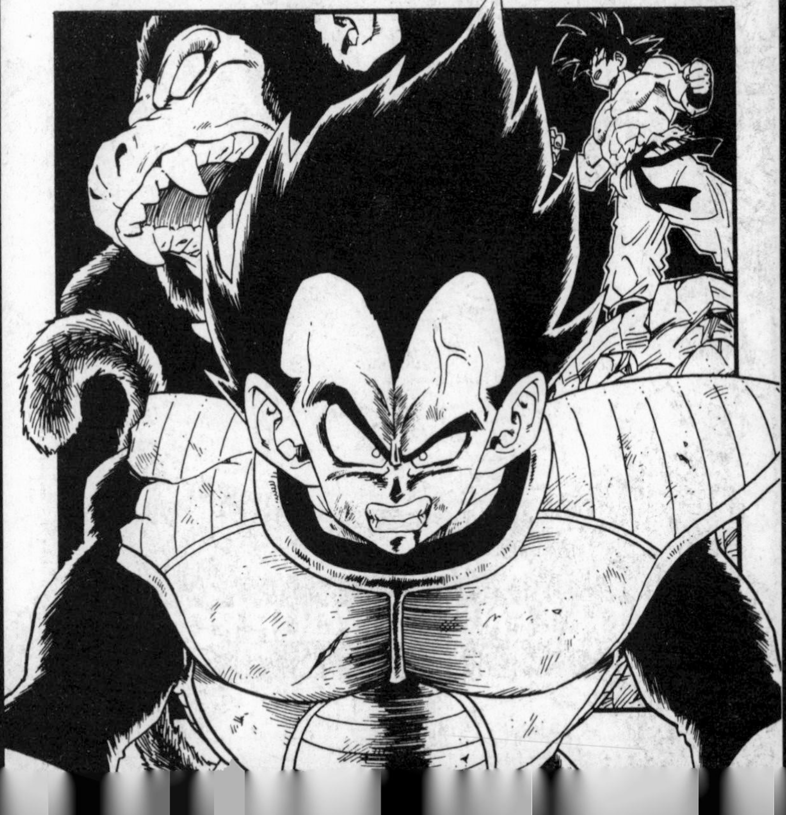

ドラゴンボール

DRAGON BALL

Akira Toriyama
鳥山明
BIRD STUDIO

DBZ:39 • The Energy Sphere

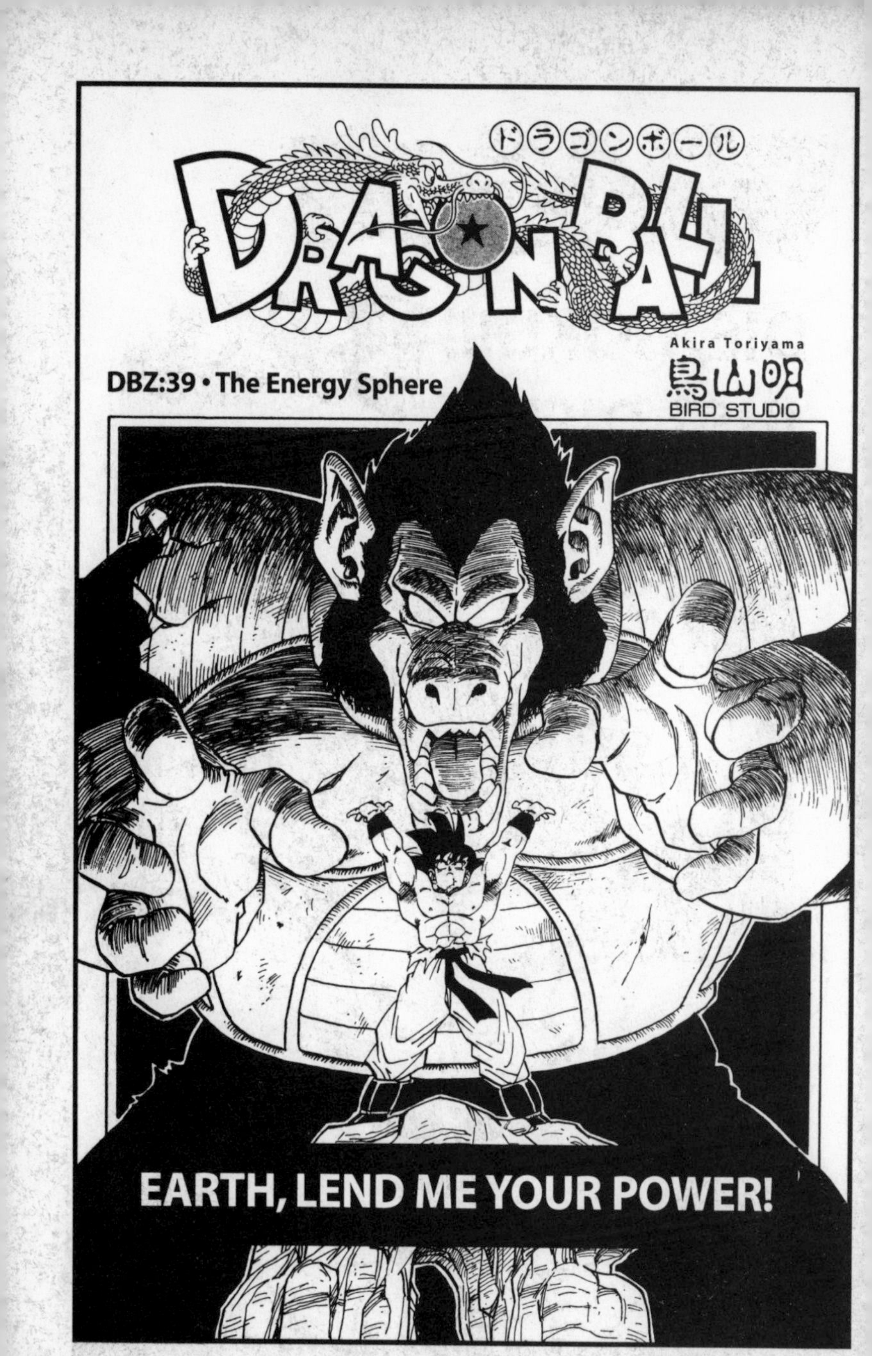
EARTH, LEND ME YOUR POWER!

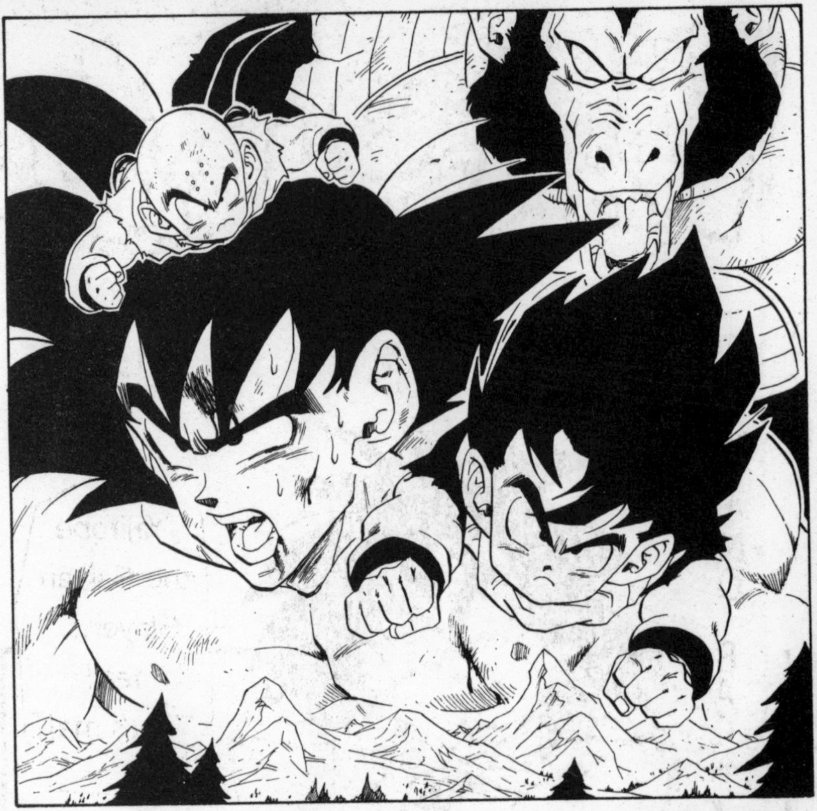

WIN!!! DRAGON BALL

DBZ:40 • All That Power...

Akira Toriyama 鳥山明 BIRD STUDIO

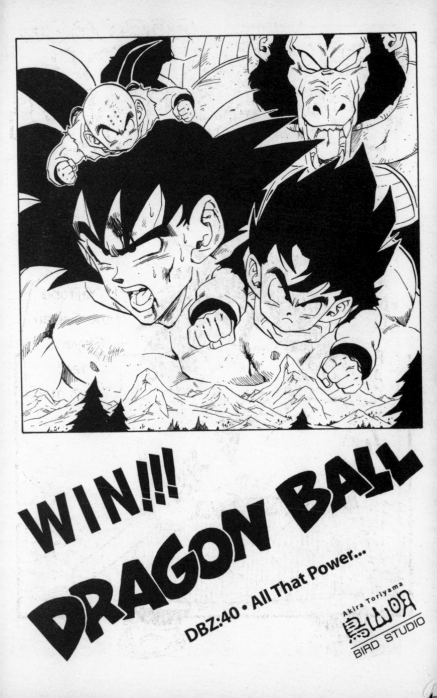

ドラゴンボール

DRAGON BALL

DBZ:41 • The Last Heartbeat

Akira Toriyama
鳥山明
BIRD STUDIO

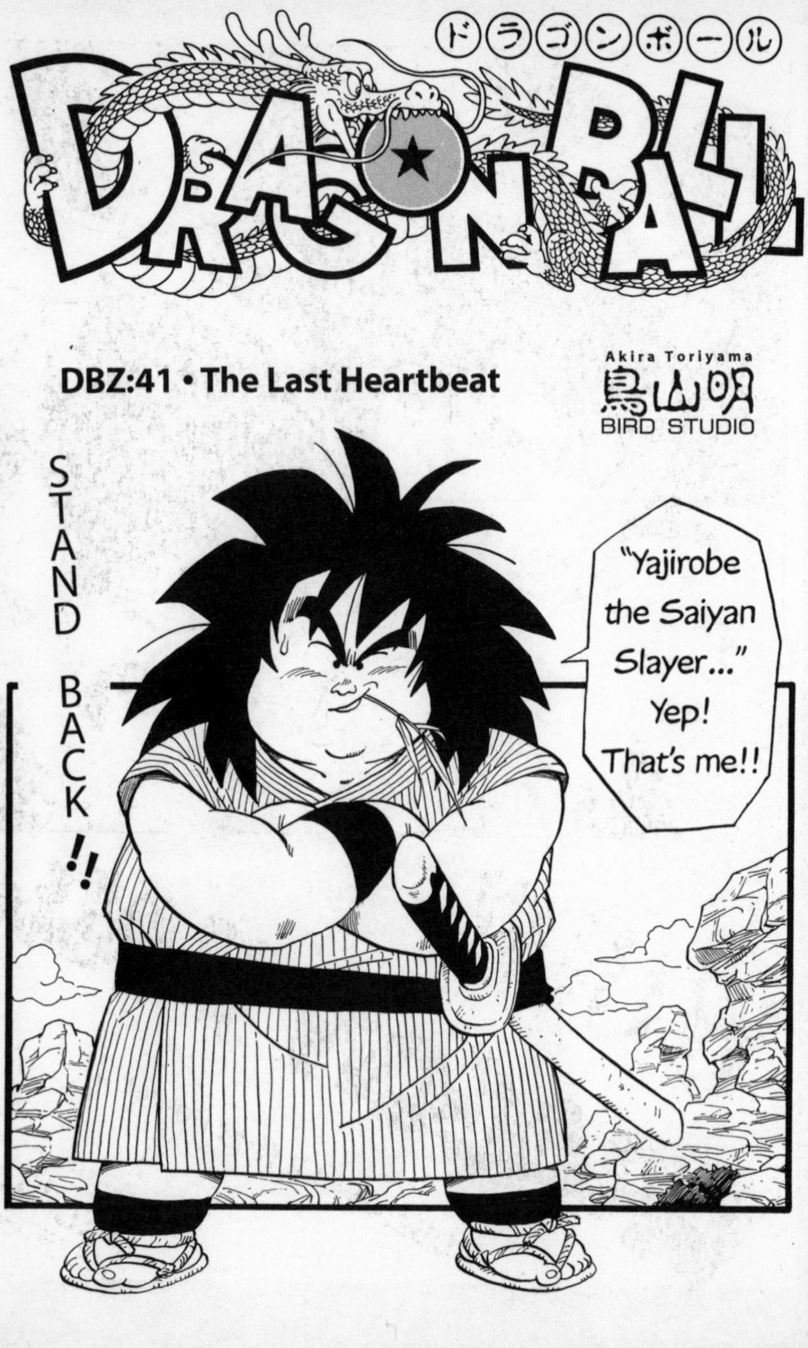
"Yajirobe the Saiyan Slayer..." Yep! That's me!!
STAND BACK!!

WE WON'T GIVE UP UNTIL IT'S ALL OVER!!!

DBZ:42 • Least Resistance

Akira Toriyama
鳥山明 BIRD STUDIO

ドラゴンボール

DBZ:43 • One More... the Sphere!

Akira Toriyama
鳥山明
BIRD STUDIO

THREE AGAINST ONE!

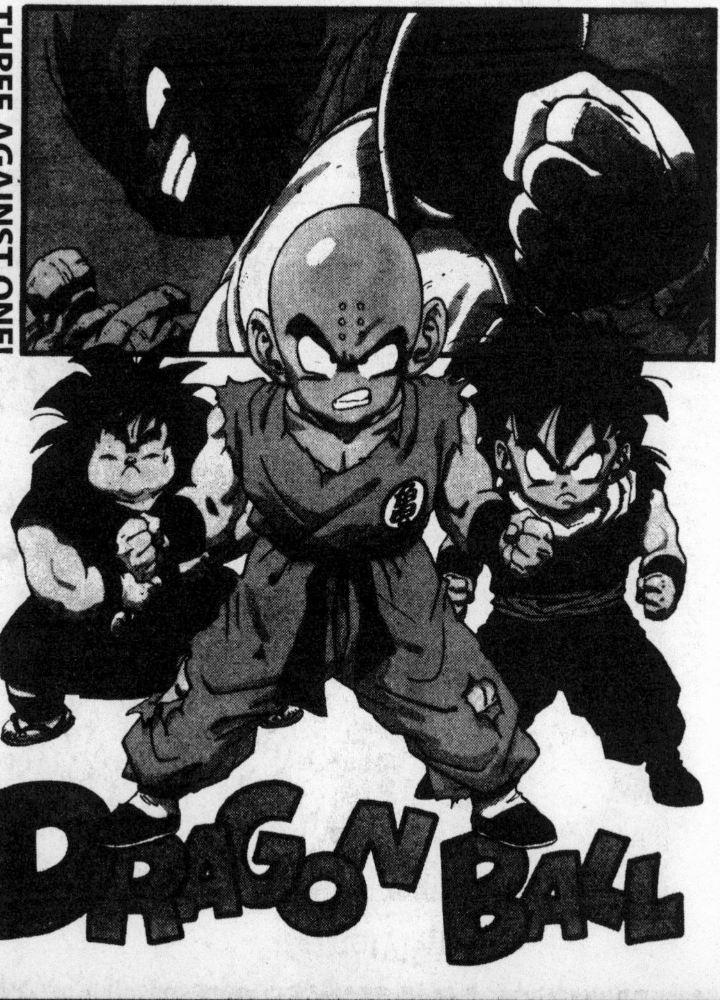
DRAGON BALL

DRAGON BALL

THAT'S IT!

WE'RE DOOMED!

Look for an exciting new manga in this spot next week due to the deaths of all the Dragon Ball characters!

DBZ:44 • The Hopes of a Planet

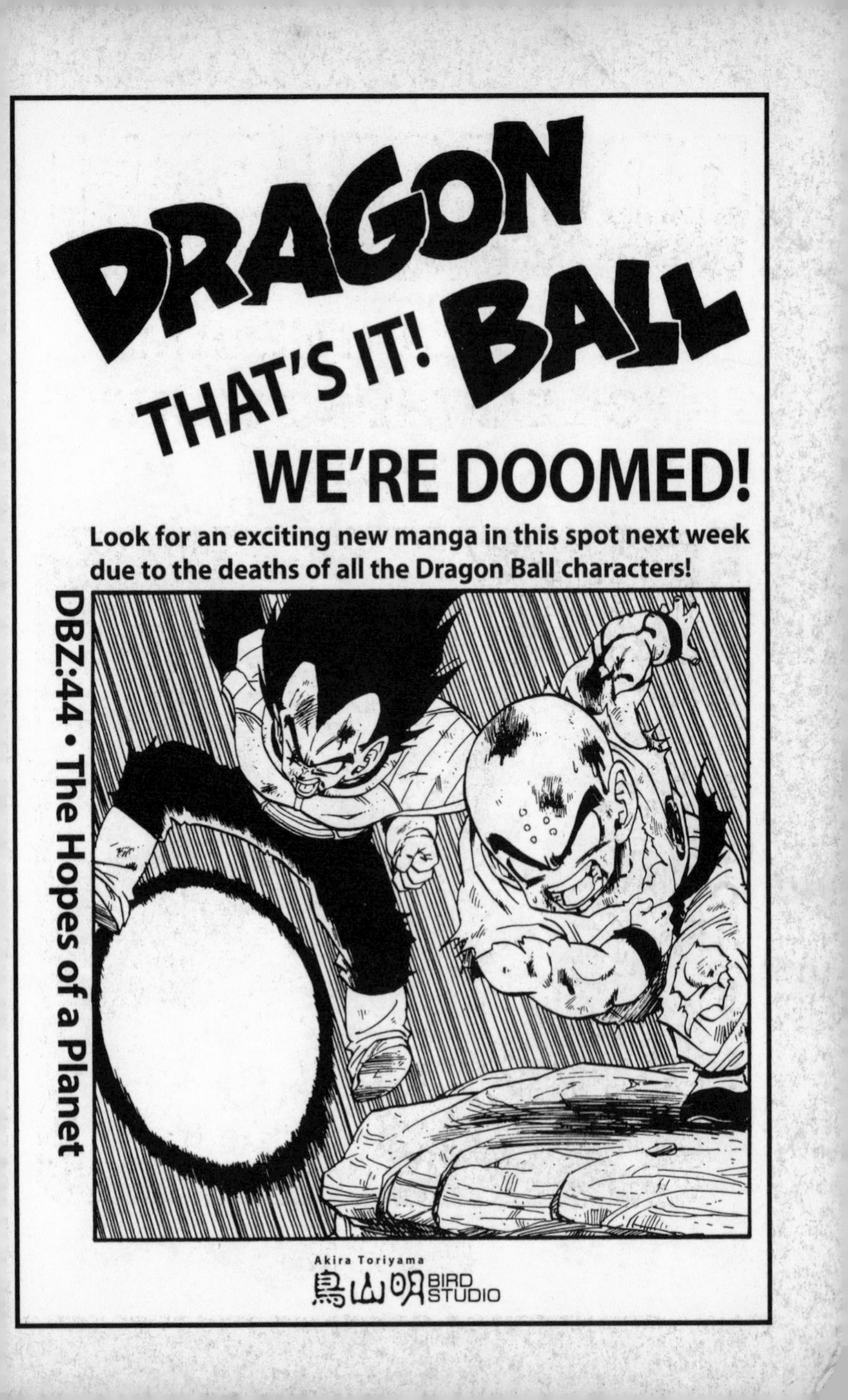

Akira Toriyama

鳥山明 BIRD STUDIO

DRAGON BALL

I WIN! DO YOU HEAR ME, YOU EARTHLING SCUM? I WIN!!!

DBZ:45 • The Worn-Out Warriors

Akira Toriyama
鳥山明 BIRD STUDIO

DRAGON BALL

Akira Toriyama
鳥山明
BIRD STUDIO

GOHAN TRANSFORMS!!!

DBZ:46 • Monkey in the Moon

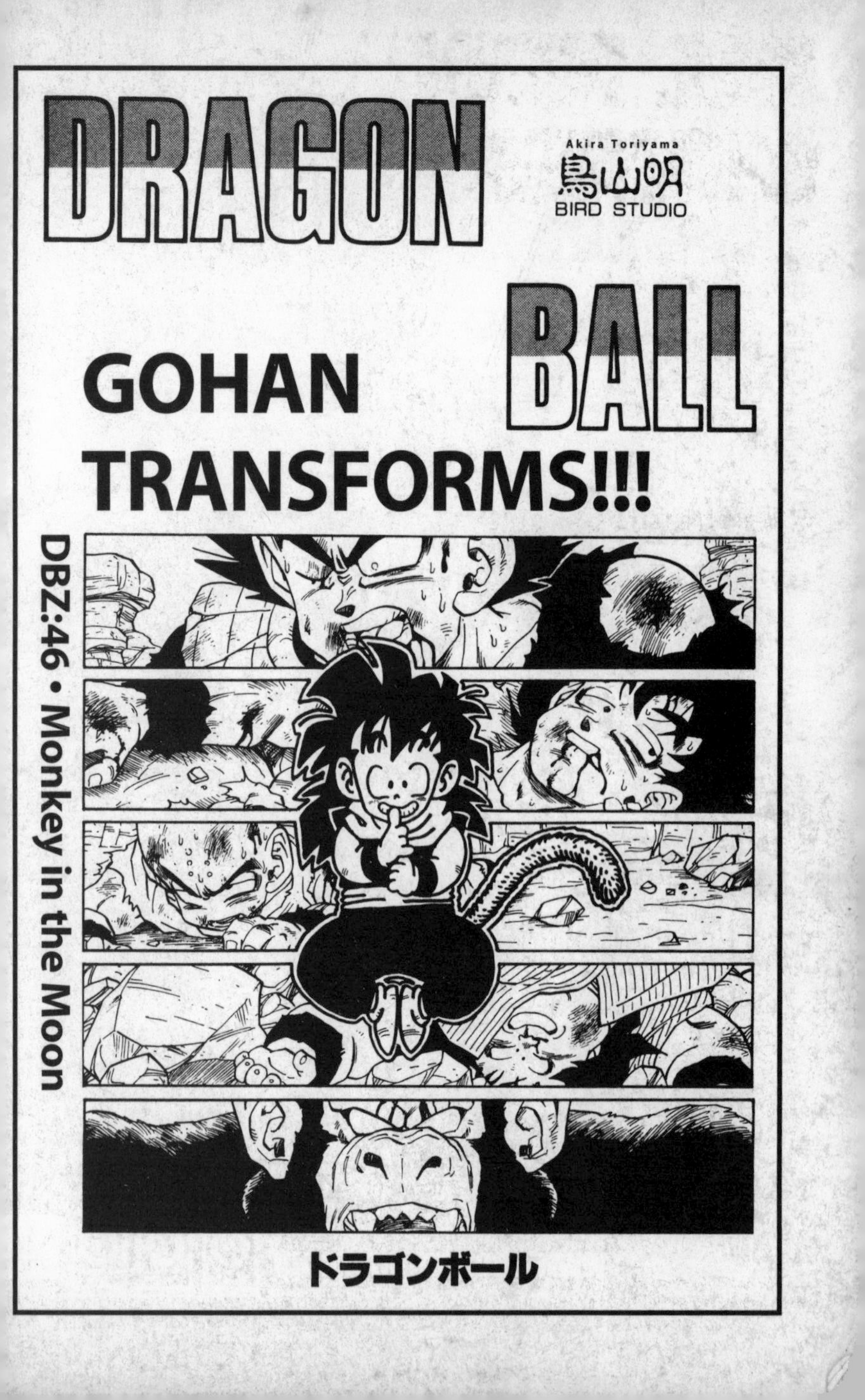

ドラゴンボール

Tell us what you think about SHONEN JUMP manga!

Our survey is now available online.

Go to: **www.SHONENJUMP.com/mangasurvey**

Help us make our product offering better!